W9-AYY-184

Our Moral Life in Christ

A Complete Course

The Didache Series

The Didache

[DID-uh-kay]

The *Didache* is the first known Christian catechesis. Written in the first century, the *Didache* is the earliest known Christian writing outside of Scripture. The name of the work, *"Didache,"* is indeed appropriate for such a catechesis because it comes from the Greek word for "teaching," and indicates that this writing contains the teaching of the Apostles.

The *Didache* is a catechetical summary of Christian sacraments, practices, and morality. Though written in the first century, its teaching is timeless. The *Didache* was probably written by the disciples of the Twelve Apostles, and it presents the Apostolic Faith as taught by those closest to Jesus Christ. This series of books takes the name of this early catechesis because it shares in the Church's mission of passing on that same Faith, in its rich entirety, to new generations.

Below is an excerpt from the *Didache* in which we see a clear example of its lasting message, a message that speaks to Christians of today as much as it did to the first generations of the Church. The world is different, but the struggle for holiness is the same. In the *Didache,* we are instructed to embrace virtue, to avoid sin, and to live the Beatitudes of our Lord.

My child, flee from everything that is evil and everything that is like it. Do not be wrathful, for wrath leads to murder, nor jealous nor contentious nor quarrelsome, for from all these murder ensues.

My child, do not be lustful, for lust leads to fornication, nor a filthy-talker nor a lewd-looker, for from all these adulteries ensue.

My child, do not be an interpreter of omens, since it leads to idolatry, nor an enchanter nor an astrologer nor a magical purifier, nor wish to see them, for from all these idolatry arises.

My child, do not be a liar, for lying leads to theft, nor avaricious nor conceited, for from all these thefts are produced.

My child, do not be a complainer, since it leads to blasphemy, nor self-willed nor evil-minded, for from all these blasphemies are produced.

Be meek, for the meek will inherit the earth.

Be long-suffering and merciful and guileless and peaceable and good, and revere always the words you have heard.[1]

The *Didache* is the teaching of the Apostles and, as such, it is the teaching of the Church. Accordingly, this book series makes extensive use of the most recent comprehensive catechesis provided to us, *The Catechism of the Catholic Church.* The *Didache* series also relies heavily on Sacred Scripture, the lives of the saints, the Fathers of the Church, and the teaching of Vatican II as witnessed by the pontificate of John Paul II.

1. Swett, Ben H. "The Didache (The Teaching)." © January 30, 1998. http://bswett.com/1998-01Didache.html

Our Moral Life in Christ

A Complete Course

General Editor: Rev. James Socias

MIDWEST THEOLOGICAL FORUM
Woodridge, Illinois

Published in the United States of America by

Midwest Theological Forum
1420 Davey Road, Woodridge, IL 60517
www.theologicalforum.org

ISBN 978-1-890177-29-4
Library of Congress Control Number: 2003109396
Revised Second Edition

Nihil obstat
Reverend Patrick J. Boyle, S.J.
Censor Deputatus
December 9, 2002

Imprimatur
Most Reverend Raymond E. Goedert, M.A., S.T.L., J.C.L.
Vicar General
Archdiocese of Chicago
January 23, 2003

The Nihil obstat and Imprimatur are official declarations that a book is free of doctrinal and moral error. No implication is contained therein that those who have granted the Nihil obstat and Imprimatur agree with the content, opinions, or statements expressed. Nor do they assume any legal responsibility associated with the publication.

General and Managing Editor: Rev. James Socias

Editorial Board: Rev. James Socias, Rev. Peter Armenio, Kimberly Kirk Hahn, Dr. Scott Hahn, Mike Aquilina

Design and Production: Marlene Burrell, Jane Heineman of April Graphics, Highland Park, Illinois

Staff Photographer: Julie Koenig

The editors would like to thank Rev. Aurelio Fernandez, whose work inspired much of the content and focus of this book.

Acknowledgements

Excerpts from the English translation of the *Catechism of the Catholic Church* for the United States of America copyright ©1994, United States Catholic Conference, Inc.–Libreria Editrice Vaticana. Used by permission.

Excerpts from the English translation of the *Catechism of the Catholic Church: Modifications from the Editio Typica* copyright ©1997, United States Catholic Conference, Inc.–Libreria Editrice Vaticana. Used by permission.

Scripture quotations contained herein are adapted from the Catholic Edition of the Revised Standard Version of the Bible, copyright ©1946, 1952, 1971, and the New Revised Standard Version of the Bible, copyright ©1989, by the Division of Christian Education of the National Council of the Churches of Christ in the United States of America, and are used by permission. All rights reserved.

Excerpts from the Code of Canon Law, Latin/English Edition, are used with permission, copyright ©1983 Canon Law Society of America, Washington, D.C.

Citations of official Church documents from Neuner, Josef, SJ, and Dupuis, Jacques, SJ, eds., The Christian Faith: Doctrinal Documents of the Catholic Church, 5th ed. (New York: Alba House, 1992). Used with permission.

Excerpts from Vatican Council II: The Conciliar and Post Conciliar Documents, New Revised Edition edited by Austin Flannery, O.P., copyright ©1992, Costello Publishing Company, Inc., Northport, NY are used by permission of the publisher, all rights reserved. No part of these excerpts may be reproduced, stored in a retrieval system, or transmitted in any form or by any means—electronic, mechanical, photocopying, recording or otherwise, without express permission of Costello Publishing Company.

Disclaimer: The editor of this book has attempted to give proper credit to all sources used in the text and illustrations. Any miscredit or lack of credit is unintended and will be corrected in the next edition.

The Midwest Theological Forum *Our Moral Life in Christ* student text, copyright ©2003, has been judged to be in conformity with the *Catechism of the Catholic Church* by the Ad Hoc Committee to Oversee the Use of the Catechism, United States Conference of Catholic Bishops.

Printed in Canada

Contents

Contents

Contents

Contents

ABBREVIATIONS USED FOR THE BOOKS OF THE BIBLE

Old Testament

Genesis	Gen	Tobit	Tb	Hosea	Hos
Exodus	Ex	Judith	Jdt	Joel	Jl
Leviticus	Lv	Esther	Est	Amos	Am
Numbers	Nm	Job	Jb	Obadiah	Ob
Deuteronomy	Dt	Psalms	Ps(s)	Jonah	Jon
Joshua	Jos	Proverbs	Prv	Micah	Mi
Judges	Jgs	Ecclesiastes	Eccl	Nahum	Na
Ruth	Ru	Song of Songs	Sg	Habakkuk	Hab
1 Samuel	1 Sm	Wisdom	Wis	Zephaniah	Zep
2 Samuel	2 Sm	Sirach	Sir	Haggai	Hg
1 Kings	1 Kgs	Isaiah	Is	Zechariah	Zec
2 Kings	2 Kgs	Jeremiah	Jer	Malachi	Mal
1 Chronicles	1 Chr	Lamentations	Lam	1 Maccabees	1 Mc
2 Chronicles	2 Chr	Baruch	Bar	2 Maccabees	2 Mc
Ezra	Ezr	Ezekiel	Ez		
Nehemiah	Neh	Daniel	Dn		

New Testament

Matthew	Mt	Ephesians	Eph	Hebrews	Heb
Mark	Mk	Philippians	Phil	James	Jas
Luke	Lk	Colossians	Col	1 Peter	1 Pt
John	Jn	1 Thessalonians	1 Thes	2 Peter	2 Pt
Acts of the Apostles	Acts	2 Thessalonians	2 Thes	1 John	1 Jn
Romans	Rom	1 Timothy	1 Tm	2 John	2 Jn
1 Corinthians	1 Cor	2 Timothy	2 Tm	3 John	3 Jn
2 Corinthians	2 Cor	Titus	Ti	Jude	Jud
Galatians	Gal	Philemon	Phlm	Revelation	Rv

ABBREVIATIONS USED FOR DOCUMENTS OF THE MAGISTERIUM

AA	*Apostolicam actuositatem*
AAS	*Acta Apostolica Sedis*
AG	*Ad gentes*
CA	*Centesimus annus*
CCC	*The Catechism of the Catholic Church*
CCEO	*Corpus Canonum Ecclesiarum Orientalium*
CDF	Congregation for the Doctrine of the Faith
CHCW	Charter for Health Care Workers
CIC	*Codex iuris canonici* (The Code of Canon Law)
CL	Christifidelis laici
CPG	*Solemn Profession of Faith:* Credo of the People of God
DD	*Dies Domini*
DRF	*Declaration on Religious Freedom*
DH	*Dignitatis humanae*
DIM	Decree *Inter mirifici*
DM	*Dives in misericordia*
DoV	*Donum vitae*
DPA	Declaration on Procured Abortion
DS	Denzinger-Schönmetzer, *Enchiridion Symbolorum, definitionum et declarationum de rebus fidei et morum* (1965)
DV	*Dei verbum*
DVt	*Donum veritas*
EN	*Evangeli nuntiadi*
EV	*Evangelium vitae*
FC	*Familiaris consortio*
GCD	*General Catechetical Directory*
GS	*Gaudium et spes*
HV	*Humanae vitae*
IM	*Inter mirifica*
IOE	Instruction on Euthanasia
LE	*Laborem exercens*
LG	*Lumen gentium*
LH	*Liturgy of the Hours*
MD	*Mulieris dignitatem*
MF	*Mysterium Fidei*
MM	*Mater et magistra*
ND	Neuner-Dupuis, *The Christian Faith in the Doctrinal Documents of the Catholic Church*
OC	*Ordo confirmationis*
OCM	*Ordo celebrandi Matrimonium*
OP	*Ordo paenitentiae*
PG	J.P. Migne, ed., *Patrologia Graeca* (Paris, 1857-1866)
PH	*Persona humanae*
PL	J. P. Migne, ed., *Patrologia Latina* (Paris, 1841-1855)
PP	*Populorum progressio*
PT	*Pacem in terris*
RH	*Redemptor hominis*
RP	*Reconciliatio et paenitentia*
SC	*Sacrosanctum concilium*
SD	*Salvifici doloris*
SRS	*Solicitudo rei socialis*
STh	*Summa Theologiae*
VS	*Veritatis splendor*

Introduction

*"**The Lord Jesus,** divine teacher and model of all perfection, preached holiness of life (of which he is the author and maker) to each and every one of his disciples without distinction: 'You, therefore, must be perfect, as your heavenly Father is perfect' (Mt 5:48). For he sent the Holy Spirit to all to move them interiorly to love God with their whole heart, with their whole soul, with their whole understanding, and with their whole strength (cf. Mk 12:30), and to love one another as Christ loved them (cf. Jn 13:34; 15:12)."* (Dogmatic Constitution on the Church, Section 40 – ed. by Rev. Austin Flannery, O.P.)

The common shared vocation for all Christian believers is holiness. The heroes and heroines of our faith are celebrated for their faithfulness to Christ and his Church. We call them saints. We should all be saints in the making. But saints in the making need the example and knowledge of those entrusted with passing on the understanding of our faith.

Our Moral Life in Christ focuses the intellectual, moral, and formational development in living a life joined to the Mystery of our Lord. This foundation affords the Christian with the only true alternative to a world which often rejects the spiritual and substitutes its own brand of convenience for that which is "right" and "true." The foundation of course is Christ and his Church.

The "culture of life" needs champions in today's society. *Our Moral Life in Christ* offers to the student those reasons which direct us to live for the good of all our brothers and sisters. Grounded in the Ten Commandments, these corner stones tie our humanity together in actions that call us to understand our human nature. The mystery of Christ illumines those right actions so that we might live fully the life gifted to us.

I have had the privilege of using this text in class and found it to be thoughtful, concise and timely. Students enjoyed the examples, and the moral content always reflected a fidelity to the Magisterium of the Church. As a teacher one hopes to have material which speaks to and challenges the student to go beyond —to take the next step. In the moral life, this commitment is necessary to be a living reflection of Christ in the world. The authors of *Our Moral Life in Christ* have given an instrument to the teacher to fulfill that task—to call us to holiness through our Lord Jesus Christ.

Most Rev. Jerome E. Listecki
Bishop of LaCrosse

OUR MORAL LIFE IN CHRIST

Part 1

Principles of Moral Theology

Living a moral life as Jesus lived in word and action.

Chapter 1

Preliminary Notions

There are so many people who can recall the stats of their favorite sports teams or the lyrics from their favorite songs. Football, basketball, baseball — you name the sport — they will give you the team's current ranking off the top of their heads. Getting a won-loss record is no problem. Mention a chart-topping musician and the words of their songs come to mind immediately. The name of their latest album? No challenge here either. Ask who the current Super Bowl champions or the latest Grammy winners are and the answers come right back.

Try asking the same people to recite the Ten Commandments. It's a different story here. The first thing you will probably hear is, "Do I have to recite them in order?" Try the Beatitudes, but don't hold your breath for the answer. "What's a beatitude?" might just be the response.

Why are sports or music more important than Jesus to so many people? Jesus Christ died to enable us to have the freedom to make correct moral choices so we could share his divine life forever. Only a few people are called to be professional athletes or famous musicians, but all of us are called to be Christ-like.

Let us ask ourselves the following questions:

- What does it mean to be "Christ-like"?
- Did Jesus Christ establish a morality for his followers?
- Is personal freedom compatible with Christian morality?

INTRODUCTION

The word *morality* refers to the standards by which we judge our actions to be good or evil, and *moral law* is the phrase used to describe the objective standards authored by God and taught by Church authority. For the last several decades, there has been heated discussion on the role of morality in the personal, political, and legal framework of society. Today, there is lively debate between the different political and philosophical traditions on this issue, and many distinct and contradictory ideas are proposed.

This chapter outlines Christian morality—a morality that aims to help the individual grow in the knowledge and love of God in order to be as Christ-like as possible. To do so, it is first necessary to outline what makes Christian morality distinctive, and how the adoption of the moral lifestyle set forth by Jesus transforms the individual at the deepest level of the soul, so that he or she truly becomes a new creation in Christ (cf. 1 Cor 5:17).

Christianity is a life based on love and directed toward the achievement of sainthood.

The acknowledgment and worship of a Triune God aides us in discovering the correct moral approach.

1. CHRISTIANITY IS NOT MERELY A MORALITY.

In order to clarify the meaning of Christian morality, one must first define its scope within the general meaning of Christianity, for Christianity is not merely a program presenting a particular moral outlook. *Christianity* is the name given to a life lived as Jesus Christ—the Son of God—lived in word and action. It is a life based on love and directed toward the achievement of sainthood, while following the moral rules set down by Jesus. Christianity answers man's question: "What is the purpose of life?" The answer is: "The purpose of life is to know, love, and serve God in order to go to heaven."

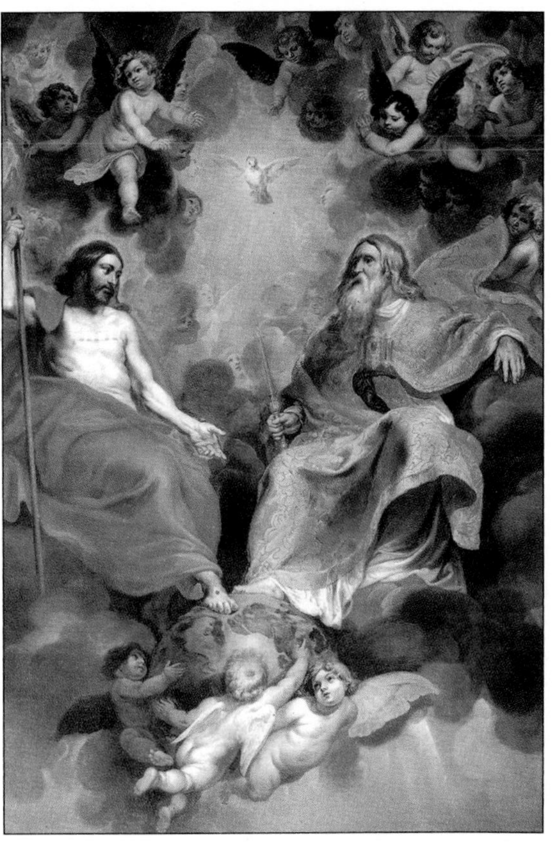

Christian morality distinguishes itself from ethical systems based on natural morality as well as non-Christian beliefs. For example, *humanism* is a moral system that denies belief in God and views humanity as the highest form of existence. Its end is to provide man with a way of life that will help him reach happiness on earth, but it denies or ignores the question of the existence of an afterlife.

Christianity, on the other hand, is the unveiling of the mystery of God as Father, Son, and Holy Spirit by Jesus Christ, who is the Son.

> **The mystery of the Most Holy Trinity is the central mystery of the Christian faith and of Christian life. God alone can make it known to us by revealing himself as Father, Son, and Holy Spirit. (CCC 261)**

God is a mystery beyond words, but Christianity is the communication of divine life and knowledge to man. Consequently, the acknowledgment and worship of a Triune God aides us in discovering the correct moral approach.

The risk of reducing Christianity to a set of rules (a kind of "don't do this and don't do that") is always present. It is as

easy for us to fall victim to this mentality as it was for many people in Jesus' time. In fact, the Old Testament revelation, which had presented to the Jewish people God's moral plan for them, was often reduced to a narrow, legalistic, and hypocritical model of morality. This explains Jesus' critical attitude toward many ideas of the Pharisees (cf. Mt 12:1-14, 22-30; 23:1-33).

Jesus did not come as a moralist, but as the incarnate love of God. He did not come to replace one set of rules with another, but to promote a new way of living. Jesus came to teach us how to identify so entirely with himself that we could demonstrate to others the saving life of God. Christianity, then, is not merely a morality, but a revelation that unveils the being of God as Father and his relation to human beings, who are his children. It is an invitation to share the love that can be experienced only by sharing in God's own life.

Together with sanctifying grace, the Holy Spirit also gives us infused moral virtues, especially the chief moral virtues of prudence, justice, fortitude, and temperance.

2. CHRISTIANITY INCLUDES A MORALITY.

Christianity is no stranger to a moral life. Jesus' saving message includes a moral system united to it in such a way that Christianity necessarily includes morality. The morality of Jesus protects the life of our relationship with him.

Together with sanctifying grace, the Holy Spirit also gives us infused moral virtues, especially the chief moral virtues of prudence, justice, fortitude, and temperance. These principal moral virtues are called *cardinal virtues* because they are the foundation of all the other moral virtues. The cardinal virtues remove the obstacles to our union with God and make us lead good Christian lives.

- ***Prudence*** makes us see what we should do and what we should avoid in order to save our souls, as well as choose the best means to reach heaven.
- ***Justice*** makes us render to each one his due.
- ***Fortitude*** gives us strength to do God's will in the midst of trials and difficulties.
- ***Temperance*** helps control evil desires and use rightly the things that please our senses.

> **The human virtues are stable dispositions of the intellect and the will that govern our acts, order our passions, and guide our conduct in accordance with reason and faith. They can be grouped around the four cardinal virtues: prudence, justice, fortitude, and temperance. (CCC 1834)**

The theological virtues (faith, hope, and charity) dispose the Christian to live in a relationship with the Father, the Son, and the Holy Spirit. They also inform the cardinal virtues and give life to them. These virtues are called *theological virtues* because they enable us to share in the divine life of God. They are given to us at Baptism.

- ***Faith*** is the virtue by which we firmly believe—on the word of God—all of the truths he has revealed.
- ***Hope*** is the virtue by which we firmly trust that God will give us eternal happiness in heaven and the means to obtain it.
- ***Charity*** is the virtue by which we love God above all things for his own sake, and our neighbors as ourselves for the love of God.

God revealed his ethical program when he created Adam and Eve.

No truly Christian life can be found that does not include the specific morality of Jesus Christ. Let's use this analogy: A person is not a brain, but is composed of different members that make up his body. In addition, the whole body is animated by the soul. But a person *also* has a brain. Furthermore, without the brain, a person ceases to be a person. Such is the relationship between Christianity and morality: They are not identical; although Christianity involves other realities, a Christian life cannot exist without morality.

This morality finds its perfection in the moral message taught by Jesus of Nazareth.

In the Acts of the Apostles, Peter announces the Christian message to the world on the day of Pentecost. He speaks of the salvific plan of God accomplished by Jesus' death and Resurrection. Upon hearing him, about three thousand are converted, and they immediately ask, "Brethren, what shall we do?" (Acts 2:37). They are baptized and believe in Jesus as God and Savior. This passage illustrates that Christian morality comes after discovering the salvific message and believing in God the Father, his Son Jesus Christ, and the Holy Spirit.[1]

3. CHRISTIANITY IS A RELIGIOUS MORALITY.

Morality is not a man-made ethical system based on one's own determination of right or wrong. *It has its origin* in the Father's gradual self-revelation of his own mystery in words and deeds through his Son. God revealed his ethical program when he created Adam and Eve. He reaffirmed it with the Ten Commandments. This morality finds its perfection in the moral message taught by Jesus of Nazareth and in the unique and perfect fashion in which he lived it.

The fact that Christian morality is a revealed religious morality gives it two characteristics that set it apart from all other religious beliefs.

a. THE CONCEPTS OF GOOD AND EVIL ARE DETERMINED BY GOD.

The sin committed by Adam and Eve is called *original sin*. Before Adam and Eve sinned, their human nature was graced by God with complete control over their moral choices. Prior to their sin, both body and soul functioned in cooperation with each other. After they sinned, their human nature was wounded, and the balance between the body and the soul was lost.

When a person is conceived, this weakness is inherited. As a direct result of Adam and Eve's sin, every person is born with an inclination to sin. As a result, human nature is flawed, making it difficult for people to understand the nature of good and evil. Though we have been taught the difference between good and evil, we often find that evil has a greater attraction than good. We find, like St. Paul, that we can say, "I do not do the good I want, but the evil I do not want is what I do" (Rom 7:19). It is easier for us to accomplish the good when we remind ourselves that we have been created in God's image. Since God has created everyone to share in his loving presence, we must do good and avoid evil in order to enter his presence. To make salvation possible, God has determined the concepts of good and evil for us. He dictates what is good for all creation, particularly for social life.

Therefore, the requirements for human conduct are derived not from what we think is reasonable, just, or coherent, but from what God indicates to be so. Divine wisdom establishes the morality that contributes to complete human fulfillment in relation to human nature. The mere fact that we find it reasonable does not make an act morally right, but if reason is used properly, we will come to know about human nature as created by God.

The requirements for human conduct are derived not from what we think is reasonable, just, or coherent, but from what God indicates to be so.

This reality gives Christian morality both its divine origin and the conviction that what is prescribed as good and evil is precisely what is *good and evil for us.* It is not a morality that changes with each new day, nor is it a self-serving one. Rather, Christian morality fulfills the human desire for happiness in this life and leads to the highest personal realization—life in and with Christ.

6. THE ETHICAL REQUIREMENTS OF THE GOSPEL REQUIRE THE AID OF GOD'S GRACE.

Grace is a supernatural gift of God bestowed on us through the merits of Jesus Christ for our salvation. We can never deserve grace through our own actions (cf. Rom 11:6).

> **Grace is the help God gives us to respond to our vocation of becoming his adopted sons. It introduces us into the intimacy of the Trinitarian life. (CCC 2021)**

There are two kinds of grace: sanctifying grace and actual grace.

Sanctifying grace is the grace that confers on our souls a new life, that is, a sharing in the life of God himself. We receive this grace in Baptism, nourish it in the Eucharist, and have it restored by the sacrament of Penance if we lose it by committing mortal sin. It is the gift of divine life whereby God the Father, God the Son, and God the Holy Spirit live in us. As sanctification is the work of God's love (charity), this gift is attributed to the Holy Spirit, but it is the three divine Persons who let us partake of the divine nature. Sanctifying grace makes us holy and pleasing to God, adopted children of the Father, brothers and sisters of Christ, temples of the Holy Spirit.

The divine life in us gives an entirely new value to our actions, prayers, works, joys, sufferings, and relations. Through sanctifying grace, our actions are truly acts of children of God, deserving an everlasting reward. Sanctifying grace—the divine life—is for us the beginning of heaven. We possess God already but in a mysterious way. In heaven, we will possess God, seeing him face to face as he is. That is why we call sanctifying grace "the seed of eternal life."

> **Sanctifying grace makes us "pleasing to God." Charisms, special graces of the Holy Spirit, are oriented to sanctifying grace and are intended for the common good of the Church. God also acts through many actual graces, to be distinguished from habitual grace which is permanent in us. (CCC 2024)**

Actual grace is a supernatural help of God that enlightens our mind and strengthens our will to do good and avoid evil. Through actual grace, God helps us to obtain and preserve sanctifying grace, which is the divine life in us. He gives light to our minds, love to our hearts and strength to our wills in order to see, desire, and carry out what is good. Actual grace is necessary for all who have attained the use of reason. Without it, we cannot carry out acts that merit a reward in heaven nor continuously resist the power of temptation. Without actual grace, we cannot keep ourselves for long in the state of sanctifying grace.

Through actual grace, God gives light to our minds, love to our hearts and strength to our wills.

The baptized person will fulfill the precepts of Christian morality to the degree that he cooperates with the grace of God, which is always present within him. When Christians are not faithful to their beliefs and practices, it becomes impossible for them to live the style of life proposed by Jesus Christ.

Since Christian ethics deals with a life lived on the level of God, it can be realized only with the aid of grace. Therefore, the fulfillment of the ethical requirements of the Gospel require the aid of God's grace, since they are above human strength and beyond natural human accomplishment.

> **What is the ultimate source of this inner division of man? His history of sin begins when he no longer acknowledges the Lord as his Creator and himself wishes to be the one who determines, with complete independence, what is good and what is evil. "You will be like God, knowing good and evil" (Gn 3:5): this was the first temptation, and it is echoed in all the other temptations to which man is more easily inclined to yield as a result of the original Fall.**
>
> **But temptations can be overcome, sins can be avoided, because together with the commandments the Lord gives us the possibility of keeping them: "His eyes are on those who fear him, and he knows every deed of man. He has not commanded anyone to be ungodly, and he has not given anyone permission to sin" (Sir 15:19-20). Keeping God's law in particular situations can be difficult, extremely difficult, but it is never impossible.[2]**

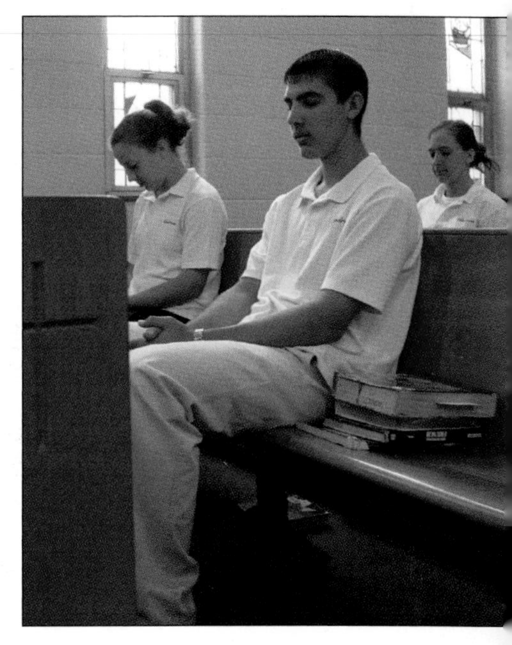

It is nearly impossible to forgive one's enemies, to be just, or to be truly chaste if one places his trust in human strength alone. But it becomes possible—often easy—if the believer cooperates with grace, is faithful to the love of God, and is united to his will.

God's grace has the power to keep us united to his will. *In short, to be Christ-like is to be a person who fully understands and lives Christian morality.*

4. CHRISTIAN MORALITY IS A MORALITY OF FOLLOWING AND IMITATING CHRIST.

Christian morality is more than a set of rules determined by social agreement. Since it is based on the principles taught by Jesus, the Son of God, it is a morality for perfection. Living a life in cooperation with Christ requires the following elements, which were experienced by the first disciples and, according to the encyclical *Veritatis splendor* of John Paul II, can be deduced from the dialogue between Jesus and the rich young man (cf. Mt 19:16-22).

a. THE CALL OR VOCATION

The Christian life stems from a call from God. Hence, the Christian life is seen as a vocation, or calling to a particular type of life. In public life, Jesus goes out and occasionally calls individually ("Follow me," [Lk 9:59]), and other times collectively ("If any man would come after me..." [Mk 8:34; cf. Mt 19:16]).

Faith is like a conversation: God initiates the dialogue, but, if there is no response, then there can be no faith.

b. THE RESPONSE

The Christian must respond affirmatively to this call from God. This response is essential since faith (which begins with God's call) cannot flourish without this affirmative answer. Faith is like a conversation: God initiates the dialogue, but, if there is no response, then there can be no faith (cf. Lk 18:18-27).[3]

c. THE FOLLOWING

The call of Jesus is a call to live life as he did, to the extent that it is humanly possible. This is why the understanding of morality as the following of Jesus is often found in Christian writings. This call respects one's freedom, as expressed by Jesus in a conditional fashion: "If any man would come after me..." (Lk 9:23).[4]

d. DISCIPLESHIP

The call of Jesus is ordered toward being his disciple since he is the teacher (cf. Mt 23:7-8). The relationship between teacher and disciple describes the relationship between Christ and those who believe in him.[5] The word *disciple* (or "follower") indicates adopting another person's way of life, taking on his particular type of discipline.

e. THE IMITATION

As is the case in the different human disciplines in which the disciple learns to follow the teacher by imitating him, the Christian also has to learn by imitating the life of Jesus. However, since Jesus is God and the only begotten

Son of God, it is clear that the historical life of Jesus cannot be emulated totally. For example:

- Jesus was crucified for all people. No human being is capable of accomplishing what Jesus accomplished when he died on the cross and was buried for us.
- Jesus himself did not assume all the circumstances that characterize human life. For example, Jesus was celibate, and this does not present an immediate model for married people.

The imitation of Jesus is not to take the form of a literal copy of his life, but of a moral approach.

Because of this, the imitation of Jesus is not to take the form of a literal copy of his life, but of a moral approach. That is, the Christian should assume the same attitudes—reflected in concrete acts—that Christ assumed. The goal is to act, in every situation of human existence, with the same disposition that Christ displayed. This imitation is possible if we cooperate with his grace. Jesus affirmed: "For I have given you an example, that you also should do as I have done to you" (Jn 13:15).[6]

The goal is to act, in every situation of human existence, with the same disposition that Christ displayed.

That was the disposition that the close followers of Christ and the baptized embraced after Pentecost. This is why Jesus says, "he who believes in me will also do the works that I do" (Jn 14:12). The apostles advise the baptized to imitate Jesus "because Christ also suffered for you, leaving you an example, that you should follow in his steps" (1 Pt 2:21). Furthermore, Jesus showed us the way in his earthly life: "Jesus began to do and teach" (Acts 1:1). As *Veritatis splendor* points out:

> **Following Christ is not an outward imitation, since it touches man at the very depths of his being. Being a follower of Christ means becoming conformed to him who became a servant even to giving himself on the Cross (cf. Phil 2:5-8). Christ dwells by faith in the heart of the believer (cf. Eph 3:17) and thus the disciple is conformed to the Lord. This is the effect of grace, of the active presence of the Holy Spirit in us.[7]**

5. IDENTIFICATION WITH CHRIST: NEW LIFE IN THE HOLY SPIRIT

The morality taught by Christ in the New Testament corresponds to the new being to be acquired by us as a result of Baptism. The Gospel of St. John and the writings of St. Paul understand Christian existence as more than just an imitation of the life of Christ; rather, they describe it as a way of identifying with Christ.

By Baptism, the Christian participates in the same life of Jesus, so much so that "the life of Christ is in him." The letter to the Philippians alone uses the phrase "in Christ" nine times, and six other times, it uses a similar phrase, "in the Lord." "I in Christ and Christ in me" is an expression repeated in the writings of St. John and St. Paul.

The life in Christ is defined in graphic literary expressions by St. Paul. For example, he uses the phrase "*put on* the Lord Jesus

Only those who are chaste, humble, just, prudent, and charitable can demonstrate for others how to act in like manner.

Christ" (Rom 13:14). These expressions are mentioned thirteen times in the sense of *putting on Christ interiorly*, not exteriorly.

In Baptism, Jesus is united to us, and the transforming force of grace causes the Christian to turn to Christ and, consequently, to act like him. This is why it can be said that every Christian is another Christ.

Also, the expression "to be formed in Christ" is used regularly in the epistles (e.g., Gal 4:19). St. Paul explains this by means of Hellenistic art: The hollow space inside the mold shapes the molten metal into the statue. Similarly, Jesus is the mold into which the baptized are placed. The result is the reception of the *form* of the Son. To be formed in the Son is to determine to think and act in every situation as Christ would.

Consequently, the Christian moral life is by definition the imitation of Christ, to the degree of identifying with him. And since the life of a person is most properly from the operation of his soul—knowledge, thought, will, freedom—the Christian ought to imitate Christ's thought, love, and actions.[8]

St. Paul gives the following ideal as a motto for the Christian life: "Have this mind among yourselves, which was in Christ Jesus…" (Phil 2:5). St. Paul gives the end of identifying with Christ in his letter to the Galatians: "It is no longer I who live, but Christ who lives in me" (Gal 2:20). This formula represents the highest prize to which human existence is called: a life lived in God's presence.

However, this goal cannot be reached by human strength alone. Christian life and morality are not merely exercises; the goal is reached only by the aid of the Holy Spirit. Prayer and the transforming grace of the sacraments (particularly the Eucharist and Confession) are the normal ways through which Jesus and the Holy Spirit act, so there is no way to live a Christian morality that excludes them.

Morally good lives make sense to others, and are seen as worthy of imitation.

> **He who believes in Christ has new life in the Holy Spirit. The moral life, increased and brought to maturity in grace, is to reach its fulfillment in the glory of heaven. (CCC 1715)**

6. CHARACTERISTICS OF CHRISTIAN MORALITY

a. CHRISTIAN MORALITY FIRST AFFECTS THE *PERSON* AND THEN THE *ACTION*.

It is important to stress that Christian morality encompasses the totality of man. Human existence includes grace, by which the Christian becomes a new creature. Consequently, grace aids the Christian to be a good Christian so that he may act accordingly.

This truth corresponds to the philosophical principle that "action follows being." This truth demonstrates that people cannot give to others what they themselves do not have. Only those who are chaste, humble, just, prudent, and charitable can demonstrate for others how to act in like manner. To show others how to be a child of God, it is first necessary to become a child of God. Morally good lives make sense to others, and are seen as worthy of imitation.

Jesus expressed this with the image of a tree and its fruits:

> **For no good tree bears bad fruit, nor again does a bad tree bear good fruit; for each tree is known by its own fruit. For figs are not gathered from thorns, nor are grapes picked from a bramble bush. The good man out of the good treasure of his heart produces good, and the evil man out of his evil treasure produces evil; for out of the abundance of the heart his mouth speaks. (Lk 6:43-45)**

Therefore, the Beatitudes, which express the heart of Christian morality, speak to the interior attitude of the person. The Christian must first accept the idea of being merciful, pure of heart, a peacemaker, and then the actions will follow.[9]

It is self-evident that it is in the interior of a person, the heart, that the moral life is forged.

6. CHRISTIAN MORALITY TRANSFORMS FIRST THE SOUL AND THEN THE MORAL APPEARANCE.

This characteristic is a result of the previous one, and is derived from it. When a morality addresses every aspect of a person's existence (particularly when that person is touched by grace) it will then influence the deepest thoughts and desires of the person. Furthermore, it is self-evident that it is in the *interior of a person*—the heart—that the moral life is forged.

Jesus expressed this in a striking manner:

> **And he called the people to him and said to them, "Hear and understand: not what goes into the mouth defiles a man, but what comes out of the mouth, this defiles a man." Then the disciples came and said to him, "Do you know that the Pharisees were offended when they heard this saying?" He answered, "Every plant which my heavenly Father has not planted will be rooted up. Let them alone; they are blind guides. And if a blind man leads a blind man, both will fall into a pit." But Peter said to him, "Explain the parable to us." And he said, "Are you also still without understanding? Do you not see that whatever goes into the mouth passes into the stomach, and so passes on? But what comes out of the mouth proceeds from the heart, and this defiles a man. For out of the heart come evil thoughts, murder, adultery, fornication, theft, false witness, slander. These are what defile a man; but to eat with unwashed hands does not defile a man." (Mt 15:10-20)**

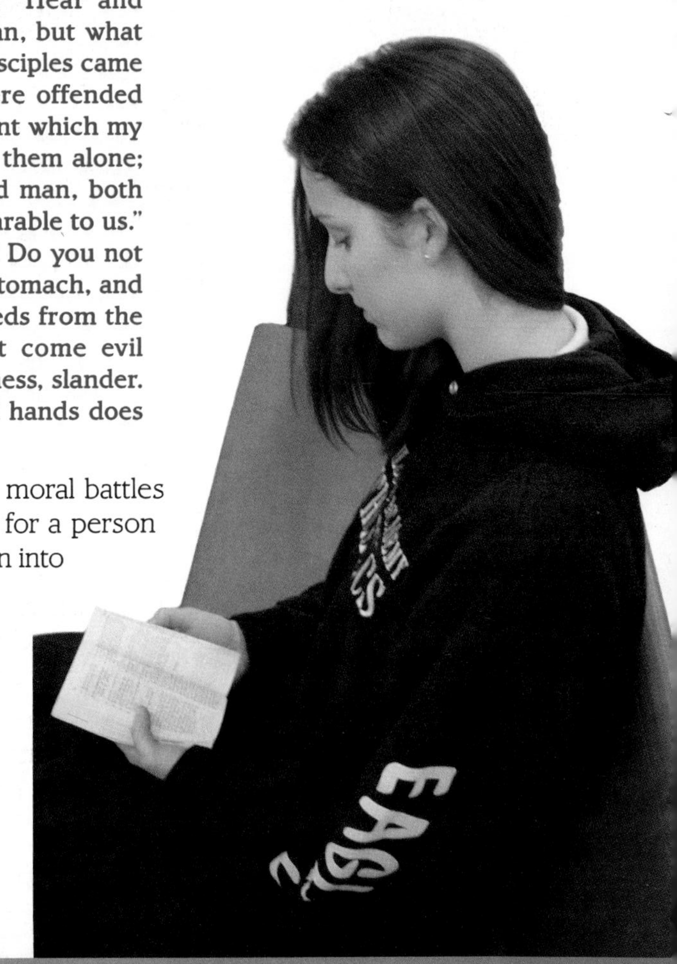

It is in the interior—in thought, will, and emotions—where moral battles are fought. One must guard against having a simple dislike for a person turn into a gesture of hate, or a temptation against purity turn into lust. This principle requires two continuous inclinations:

- The heart must be kept free from evil thoughts, desires, affections, for they can cause grave sins and lead to bad actions.
- The senses must be kept under control, since sin begins as a desire, even if sinful desires do not ultimately lead to sin.

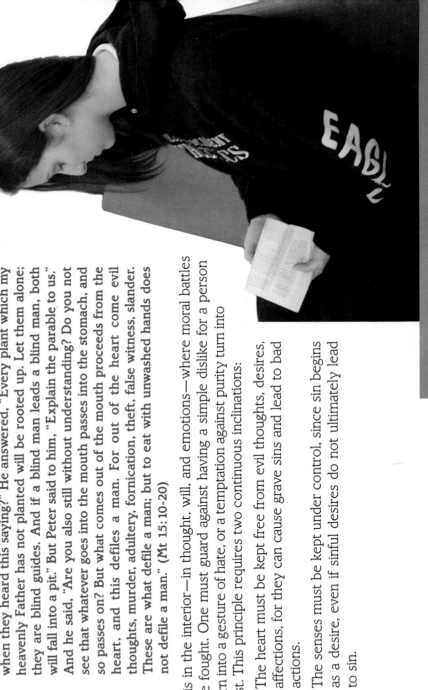

Love of neighbor springs from a loving heart which, precisely because it loves, is ready to live out the loftiest challenges.

Jesus brings God's commandments to fulfillment, particularly the commandment of love of neighbor, by interiorizing their demands and by bringing out their fullest meaning. Love of neighbor springs from a loving heart which, precisely because it loves, is ready to live out the loftiest challenges.[10]

C. CHRISTIAN MORALITY ENCOMPASSES THE ATTITUDES OF THE PERSON.

A person commits single acts, but such acts are the result of previous *habits* and *attitudes.* The first step to being a morally good person is to form good natural habits. Those who have the habit of doing what they are supposed to do will have an easier time making correct moral choices. Dispositions to do good or evil repeat themselves as a direct result of habits already formed. Those who habitually take the easy way will find it more difficult to resist sin as a result of having habitually avoided making correct choices. The best way to begin making correct choices is through frequent reception of the Sacrament of Penance where our sins are forgiven and we renew our resolution to avoid sin. In Penance, we receive sacramental graces to begin to live a new life in the Holy Spirit.

It is a fact of life that each person needs to form habits of good conduct. Good habits promote an awareness of the value of personal integrity. Good moral habits are founded on good personal habits. Those who habitually try to do the good find making correct choices easier.

Good moral habits are founded on good personal habits.

If a person tries to acquire Christian virtues, it will be easier to express these convictions in good acts. As Jesus said, "If any man would come after me, let him deny himself" (Mk 8:34). In fact, that firm and definitive decision *to be as Christ-like as possible* predisposes the believer so that all of his actions are oriented toward Christ.[11]

This command to acquire Christian attitudes does not lessen the moral value of individual acts; on the contrary, each of those actions demonstrates the results of the individual's interior attitudes. A man who abandons his wife because he "needs to enjoy life before it is too late" is acting as a result of malformed attitudes developed over time. His action is the result of habitually choosing what appeals to him over what he knows is required.

d. CHRISTIAN MORALITY ACCOUNTS FOR WHAT IS FORBIDDEN, BUT STRESSES MORE WHAT OUGHT TO BE DONE.

Christian morality is a *positive morality* that prescribes what a person, motivated by the love of God, ought to do. It can never be reduced to a merely *negative morality*, motivated by a fear of punishment, that says, "you can't do this and you can't do that." The choice to serve Jesus is the choice to return love for love. Jesus tells us the parable of the two sons who were commanded by their father to do work (cf. Mt 21:28-32). The answer to the question "Who is the son who loved his father?" is the son who did as his father asked. A person demonstrates his love for the Father by doing as Jesus asks.

It is true that the moral message preached by Jesus Christ includes many prohibitions—such as all those found in the Ten Commandments. In short, all that goes against the love of God and neighbor is *forbidden*, and Jesus does warn that those who refuse to turn away from what is evil will be punished; nevertheless, the whole of Jesus' moral preaching stresses doing good more than avoiding evil. It is about the type of person one *should be* rather than a list of *dos* and *don'ts*.

In Chapter 25 of the Gospel of Matthew, the Evangelist summarizes the judgment that Christ will impose upon the conduct of each person. The condemnations of Jesus are toward those who have abandoned the good, and not to those who are doing evil deeds. In Jesus' parable, it is not just that the foolish virgins acted wrongly, but that they did not act wisely (cf. Mt 25:1-13). In the parable of the talents, the men who received ten and five talents are rewarded because they increased them. The one who received only one talent is condemned because he refused to make use of the talent (cf. Mt 25:14-30).

Hunger, misery, and war are often falsely attributed to God when they are the product of human sin. People have the moral obligation to avoid and, if possible, prevent these evils.

The parable of the rich man stresses the need to do the good, since the rich man is apparently condemned not for his evil acts, but because he failed to care for his neighbor's needs (cf. Mt 25:31-46). The Israelites, symbolized by the rich but sterile fig tree, are rejected because they failed to provide God with the fruits that were required of them (cf. Mk 11:12-14, 20-21).

At the particular judgment, Jesus demands an accounting of the good that has been lived and the evil done: Were the hungry fed? Was shelter given to the homeless? Were the sick visited? When we fail to do the required good, we are guilty of sins of omission. Against our good actions, he will weigh the good left undone (cf. Mt 25:31-46). Thus, in the Last Judgment, those who did the good will be saved, and those who did evil and failed to do good will be condemned.

We can draw two conclusions here:

- The cause of the physical evils faced by humanity (hunger, misery, war) is often falsely attributed to God when they are the product of human sin, but people have the moral obligation to avoid and, if possible, prevent these evils.

This life of holiness is made possible through the grace received in Baptism, which unites us to Christ's roles as priest, prophet, and king.

- Many people tend to disregard the harm caused by sins of omission, but these sins should be regarded seriously, as the apostle James teaches: "Whoever knows what is right to do and fails to do it, for him it is a sin" (Jas 4:17).

e. CHRISTIAN MORALITY REQUIRES NOT ONLY JUST ACTIONS, BUT ALSO HOLINESS.

In the New Testament, Jesus and the apostles require Christians to live up to a high level of morality. The morality of the Christian requires not only a decent or honorable existence, but a saintly life. The Vatican II document *Lumen gentium* elaborates on this call to sainthood, stating that all Christians are called to the fullness of holiness. This life of holiness is made possible through the grace received in Baptism, which unites us to Christ's roles as priest, prophet, and king. It is strengthened in Confirmation to enable us to show forth sanctity in every environment.

> **In particular, the life of holiness which is resplendent in so many members of the People of God, humble and often unseen, constitutes the simplest and most attractive way to perceive at once the beauty of truth, the liberating force of God's love, and the value of unconditional fidelity to all the demands of the Lord's law, even in the most difficult situations.**[12]

To emphasize the ethical content of the Beatitudes (Mt 5:1-12; Lk 6:20-26), Jesus places his morality side by side with the Old Law, which, in God's plan, was a preparation for the New Law. In fact, he repeats the juxtaposition six times: "You have heard that…but I say to you…" (Mt 5:21-48). By doing this, Jesus fulfills the commandments of the Father, enriching their ethical content and urging that they be put into practice, with the help of the Holy Spirit.

> **Thus it is evident to everyone that all the faithful of Christ of whatever rank and status, are called to the fullness of the Christian life and to the perfection of charity; by this holiness as such, a more human manner of living is promoted in this earthly society.…They must follow in his footsteps and conform themselves to his image seeking the will of the Father in all things. (*VS*, 16)**

"You, therefore, must be perfect, as your heavenly Father is perfect" (Mt 5:48). Reflecting this call of Jesus, Vatican II declares that every baptized person is called to seek holiness.[13]

St. Cecilia

Martyred c.117; One of the most venerated martyrs of Christian antiquity, cultivated young Christian woman whose ancestors loomed large in Rome's history. Many legends are attached to the life and death of Cecilia. One account is that she was ordered to make sacrifices to the false Roman gods. She refused and, instead, converted her persecutors – 400 people were baptized in her home by Pope St. Urban. Cecilia was ultimately sentenced to a torturous death for her unwavering determination to practice and evangelize her Christian faith.

f. JESUS PROCLAIMS A SERIES OF MORAL LAWS, BUT CHRISTIAN MORALITY IS NOT A RIGID MORALITY MARKED BY A MULTIPLICITY OF PRECEPTS.

This characteristic may seem inconsistent, but it is because Christianity is more a message of salvation than of morality; but the saving message is not without laws. In Jesus' preaching, there are concrete prohibitions, such as adultery (cf. Mt 5:27), avarice (cf. Mt 6:19-24), rash judgments (cf. Mt 7:1-6), divorce (cf. Mk 10:2-10), blasphemy against the Holy Spirit (cf. Mk 3:28-30; Mt 12:31-37), scandal to the innocent (cf. Mt 18:1-5), etc.

Jesus himself fulfills the precepts of the law: He observes the Sabbath (cf. Mk 1:21; 6:2; Lk 4:16), fasting (cf. Lk 4:2; Mt 4:1-2), the purification laws (cf. Lk 2:21-39; 2:40-52; 3:21-22), and he goes to Jerusalem to celebrate the feasts (cf. Mk 11:1; Lk 2:41; Jn 5:1; 7:10; 11:55).

But Jesus' morality is not a morality of rules, but rather a morality that includes laws. These laws exist in order to guide people to the good life. Moral laws differentiate between good and evil; they show us the path we need to follow if we want to please God and save ourselves.[14]

The New Testament leaves no doubt that good behavior is rewarded, and evil ways punished.

g. THE MORALITY PREACHED BY JESUS IS A MORALITY THAT INCLUDES BOTH REWARD AND PUNISHMENT.

Lately, it has become a conviction among some segments of society that a morality that emphasizes both reward and punishment should be rejected. This false idea attempts to establish families, schools, and a society in which these two realities have no part. This leads people away from God.

Nevertheless, the New Testament leaves no doubt that good behavior is rewarded, and evil ways punished. While Jesus' preaching reflects God's habitual disposition of forgiveness and love, it is also a fact that punishment is often mentioned in the New Testament.

There are nearly ninety passages in the New Testament appealing to God's punishment for evil deeds, of which forty discuss eternal punishment. The rewards of heaven and the punishments of hell affect both the interior and exterior of a human being. Consequently, in Catholic theology, heaven and hell are real ends of human existence that correspond to the good or bad conduct of each person during his life. Every person will have a particular judgment by Christ at death. By his actions, one chooses either permanent separation from God in hell or the joyous reward of heaven.

God respects human freedom so much so that he will not force a person to do something contrary to his will.

h. CHRISTIAN MORALITY IS MORALITY FOR FREEDOM.

One of God's greatest gifts to mankind is freedom. Freedom is the power rooted in the will to act or not to act, to do this or that, and so to perform deliberate actions on one's own responsibility. The term *free will* is often used as a synonym for freedom, but there is a distinction. God gave this gift to the human person to make possible the free choice to love God, but a person has freedom only to the extent he makes correct moral choices. Also, God respects human freedom so much so that he will not force a person to do something contrary to his will. This implies that we have to use our free will for the good.

For people to make correct moral choices, freedom must be used properly. All choices to commit sin reduce or limit freedom and lead to slavery to sin. For this reason, the Christian moral message endeavors to convince everyone that it is necessary to cultivate true freedom to enable everyone to do the will of God. The message preached by Christ is a call to freedom: "For you were called to freedom, brethren" (Gal 5:13). When the baptized misunderstood the freedom for which "Christ has set us free" (Gal 5:1), St. Paul warned them not to use their freedom as an "opportunity for the flesh" (Gal 5:13), but for the good (cf. Gal 6:18). When the Christian practices the message preached by Christ, he acquires the highest degree of freedom. This is confirmed by the lives of the saints, who are models of living in freedom.[15]

Christian morality includes this warning of St. Paul to the Galatians: "For freedom Christ has set us free; stand fast therefore, and do not submit again to a yoke of slavery" (Gal 5:1). And again: "You who were once slaves of sin have become obedient from the heart to the standard of teaching to which you were committed and having been set free from sin, have become slaves of righteousness" (Rom 6:17).

i. CHRISTIAN MORALITY IS FULFILLED ON EARTH, BUT IT PERTAINS TO THE NEXT LIFE.

The Christian moral message states that "a close connection is made between eternal life and obedience to God's commandments."[16] This characteristic of Christian morality avoids two extremes: the ethical program based solely on the need for a more just world, and the other, which desires a moral life only for the salvation of one's own soul.

The former is espoused by those who hope to establish a perfectly just and peaceful society in this world. The latter can fall into the temptation of disregarding social duties and simply attending to personal struggles. A person is at the same time a citizen of this world and the next. Christian morality attends to both: It cannot ignore the grave task of making a better world, according to God's will, and it directs people to make the correct moral choices, which lead ultimately to eternal life in the future.

It is a mistake to think that, because we have here no lasting city, but seek the city which is to come, we are entitled to shirk our earthly responsibilities.

Vatican II summarizes this doctrine in the following statement:

> **This Council exhorts Christians, as citizens of both cities, to perform their duties faithfully and in the spirit of the Gospel. It is a mistake to think that, because we have here no lasting city, but seek the city which is to come, we are entitled to shirk our earthly responsibilities; this is to forget that by our faith we are bound all the more to fulfill these responsibilities according to the vocation of each one.**[17]

j. CHRISTIAN MORALITY FINDS ITS BEGINNING AND END IN LOVE.

This characteristic coming at the end of the list does not diminish its importance; on the contrary, it is the crown of all. The Christian moral message begins with love and culminates with the new commandment of love.[18] Christ calls his followers to return the Father's love for them as Jesus returns his love for the Father in the Holy Spirit.

The command to love is not only proclaimed by Jesus, who calls it "my commandment" (Jn 15:12) and "new" (Jn 13:34), but it is also stressed by the apostles in addressing the first Christians. St. Paul praises love in the so-called "hymn of love," that concludes: "So faith, hope, love abide, these three; but the greatest of these is love" (1 Cor 13:13). And St. John, who relates the love of God with the love of neighbor, teaches:

> **Beloved, let us love one another; for love is of God, and he who loves is born of God and knows God. He who does not love does not know God; for God is love. In this the love of God was made manifest among us, that God sent his only Son into the world, so**

> that we might live through him. In this is love, not that we loved God but that he loved us and sent his Son to be the expiation for our sins. Beloved, if God so loved us, we also ought to love one another. (1 Jn 4:7-11)

The love of God guarantees the authenticity of the love of neighbor, and the love of neighbor demonstrates that the love of God is real. The good of the moral life is the practice of love and not the fear of punishment, as St. John points out in his conclusion: "There is no fear in love, but perfect love casts out fear. For fear has to do with punishment, and he who fears is not perfected in love" (1 Jn 4:18).

In this fashion, the acts of the believer, conforming to the moral message preached by Christ Jesus, lead to trust and hope in life. This attitude is full of expectation and is void of any pessimism.

The Holy Eucharist occupies a unique place to which all of the other sacraments are ordained.

"It is the greatest treasure of the Church."
–John Paul II

k. THE CHRISTIAN MORAL LIFE FINDS ITS NOURISHMENT IN MASS AND THE SACRAMENTS.

> Christ is always present in his Church, especially in "liturgical celebrations." Communion with Jesus Christ leads to the celebration of his salvific presence in the sacraments, especially in the Eucharist. The Church ardently desires that all the Christian faithful be brought to that full, conscious and active participation which is required by the very nature of the liturgy and the dignity of the baptismal priesthood. For this reason, catechesis, along with promoting a knowledge of the meaning of the liturgy and the sacraments, must also educate the disciples of Jesus Christ "for prayer, for thanksgiving, for repentance, for praying with confidence, for community spirit, for understanding correctly the meaning of the creeds..." as all of this is necessary for a true liturgical life.[19]

The sacraments, which, like regenerating forces, spring from the paschal mystery of Jesus Christ, are also a whole. They form "an organic whole in which each particular sacrament has its own vital place." In this whole, the Holy Eucharist occupies a unique place to which all of the other sacraments are ordained. The Eucharist is to be presented as the "sacrament of sacraments" (GCD, 115).

> The Eucharistic Sacrifice is the "source and summit of all Christian life." It is a single sacrifice that embraces everything. It is the greatest treasure of the Church. It is her *life*. (John Paul II, Prayer on Holy Thursday, 1982)

CONCLUSION

If we examine the world around us, we can see how many people, including political and social leaders, are distant from Christian morality when speaking of "ethics" or "morality." At one time, this country operated on a Christian moral basis in its public life, but this has been replaced with a morality of individualism, which is merely an excuse to act according to feelings. Is this not due to a lack of ethical principles?

Would it not be advantageous to embrace the principles of Christian morality to guide public life? Could not the world use a great outpouring of the love of Christ that is manifested in and through his followers?

VOCABULARY

ACTUAL GRACE
The supernatural help from God to do good and avoid evil to enable us to save our souls.

CHRISTIAN MORALITY
The part of theology that specifies the moral norms derived from the new being that the Christian—because of his incorporation into Christ in Baptism—needs to follow, with the hope of imitating Jesus' life to the point of identifying with him.

CHRISTIAN VOCATION
God's call to the human being by which he is incorporated into Christ through grace and becomes a member of the Mystical Body of Christ. As one of God's people, he partakes in the life of the Church.

CHRISTIANITY
The way of life lived as Jesus Christ the Son of God lived in word and action.

DISCIPLE
A follower who adopts another person's way of life, taking on his particular type of discipline.

FREE WILL
A gift from God to make possible the free choice to love God.

FREEDOM
The power rooted in reason and the will, to act or not to act, to do this or that, and so to perform deliberate actions on one's own responsibility.

HOLINESS
The free dedication of oneself to the will of God, and the participation in the life of grace offered to the Christian. This dedication to God affects a moral transformation in the life of the individual.

HUMANISM
A moral system that denies belief in God and views humanity as the highest form of existence.

LAW OF CHRIST
An interior law that stems from grace—in connection with life in Jesus—and becomes a norm or impulse for imitating Christ and acting like him.

LOVE (charity)
The theological virtue by which we love God above all things for his own sake, and our neighbor as ourselves for the love of God.

MORAL LAW
The objective standards authored by God and taught by Church authority.

MORALITY
The standards by which we judge our actions to be good or evil. Morality looks to those human acts that impact the totality of our "personness" and which affect our final end.

NEW BEING IN CHRIST
The supernatural condition of the baptized by which they participate in the life of Jesus.

ORIGINAL SIN
The sin committed by Adam and Eve.

POSITIVE MORALITY
A moral code that prescribes what ought to be done.

SANCTIFYING GRACE
The share in the divine life of God infused into us at Baptism.

SINS OF OMISSION
Failure to do what is known to be right, good, or required.

VIRTUE
A habitual and firm disposition to do good.

SUPPLEMENTARY READINGS

1. In your life, there are two things that do not fit together: your head and your heart.

Your intelligence—enlightened by faith—shows you the way clearly. It can also point out the difference between following that way heroically or stupidly. Above all, it places before you the divine greatness and beauty of the undertakings the Trinity leaves in our hands.

Your feelings, on the other hand, become attached to everything you despise, even while you consider it despicable. It seems as if a thousand trifles were awaiting the least opportunity, and as soon as your poor will is weakened, through physical tiredness or lack of supernatural outlook, those little things flock together and pile up in your imagination, until they form a mountain that oppresses and discourages you. Things such as the rough edges of your work; your resistance to obedience; the lack of proper means; the false attractions of an easy life; greater or smaller but repugnant temptations; bouts of sensuality; tiredness; the bitter taste of spiritual mediocrity.... And sometimes also fear; fear because you know God wants you to be a saint, and you are not a saint.

Allow me to talk to you bluntly. You have more than enough "reasons" to turn back, and you lack the resolution to correspond to the grace that he grants you, since he has called you to be another Christ—*ipse Christus!*—Christ himself. You have forgotten the Lord's admonition to the Apostle: "My grace is enough for you," which is confirmation that, if you want to, you can.

— Saint Josemaría Escrivá, *Furrow*, 166

2. The Church's Magisterium intervenes not only in the sphere of faith, but also, and inseparably so, in the sphere of morals. It has the task of "discerning, by means of judgments normative for the consciences of believers, those acts which in themselves conform to the demands of faith and foster their expression in life and those which, on the contrary, because intrinsically evil, are incompatible with such demands." In proclaiming the commandments of God and the charity of Christ, the Church's Magisterium also teaches the faithful specific particular precepts and requires that they consider them in conscience as morally binding. In addition, the Magisterium carries out an important work of vigilance, warning the faithful of the presence of possible errors, even merely implicit ones, when their consciences fail to acknowledge the correctness and the truth of the moral norms, which the Magisterium teaches.

— *VS*, 110

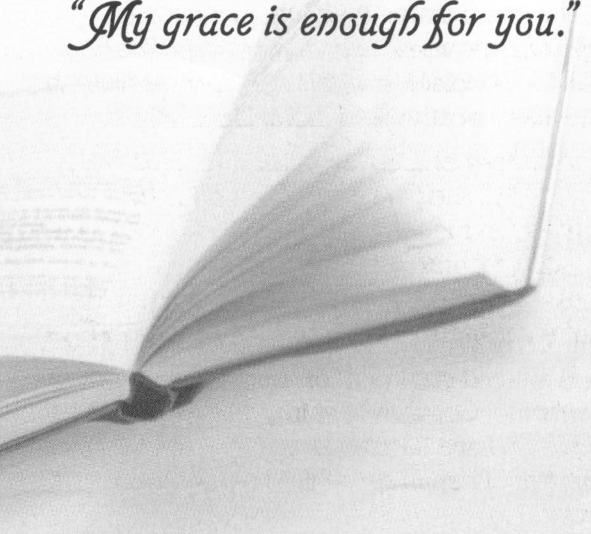
"My grace is enough for you."

QUESTIONS

1. What is the purpose of life?

2. What is the effect of living the moral lifestyle of Jesus?

3. What is Christian morality?

4. What is Christianity?

5. Why are faith, hope, and charity called the theological virtues?

6. How do Christian ethics differ from secular ethics?

7. What happens to Christianity when it is reduced to merely following a moral program?

8. What are some characteristics of a "legalistic" approach to Christianity?

9. What do we mean when we say that Christianity is a religious morality?

10. What is the origin and goal of Christian morality?

11. What two characteristics set Christian morality apart from all other religious beliefs?

12. What is grace? Sanctifying grace? Actual grace?

13. What five elements make up the morality of following and imitating Jesus?

14. What does it mean to be Christ-like?

15. What characteristics set Christianity apart from all other religious beliefs?

16. What are the characteristics of Christian morality?

17. What is the distinction between the gifts of free will and freedom?

18. What is the final lesson of Christian morality?

19. Where is Christian moral life forged?

20. How would you describe holiness?

21. How is the life of holiness made possible and how is it strengthened?

22. Why is it that Christian life surpasses that of people who follow only natural ethics?

PRACTICAL EXERCISES

1. Vatican II states that "a man is more precious for what he is than for what he has" (*GS*, 35). Explain how this sentence defines the Christian vocation and moral life in Christ.

2. *Gaudium et spes* also states, "only in the mystery of the Incarnate Word does the mystery of man take on light." How does the Person of Christ make clear the truths of human existence (for example, the meaning of human existence, the nature of good and evil)?

3. Read and comment on Chapter 25 of St. Matthew's Gospel. What importance do sins of omission have in relation to the understanding that the Christian moral life is a "following of Christ"?

4. Explain the ramifications of Christ's words in Matthew 15:10-20.

5. Read Chapter 5 of *Lumen gentium* about the "universal call to holiness." What are the practical consequences that might arise from the principles laid out in this document?

6. According to the *Catechism of the Catholic Church* (1033-1037) what does the existence of hell reveal about humanity's destiny and proper end?

7. Is it possible to accept the challenge to be holy in your life today? Explain your answer in two paragraphs.

FROM THE CATECHISM

418 As a result of original sin, human nature is weakened in its powers; subject to ignorance, suffering, and the domination of death; and inclined to sin. This inclination is called "concupiscence."

520 In all of his life Jesus presents himself as *our model.* He is "the perfect man" (*GS,* 38; cf. Rom 15:5; Phil 2:5), who invites us to become his disciples and follow him. In humbling himself, he has given us an example to imitate, through his prayer he draws us to pray, and by his poverty he calls us to accept freely the privation and persecutions that may come our way (cf. Jn 13:15; Lk 11:1; Mt 5:11-12).

1823 Jesus makes charity the *new commandment* (cf. Jn 13:34). By loving his own "to the end" (Jn 13:1), he makes manifest the Father's love which he receives. By loving one another, the disciples imitate the love of Jesus which they themselves receive. Whence Jesus says: "As the Father has loved me, so have I loved you; abide in my love." And again: "This is my commandment, that you love one another as I have loved you" (Jn 15:9, 12).

1833 Virtue is a habitual and firm disposition to do good.

1840 The theological virtues dispose Christians to live in a relationship with the Holy Trinity. They have God for their origin, their motive, and their object—God known by faith, God hoped in and loved for his own sake.

1975 According to Scripture the Law is a fatherly instruction by God which prescribes for man the ways that lead to the promised beatitude, and proscribes the ways of evil.

ENDNOTES

1. Cf. *VS,* 110.
2. Cf. *VS,* 102.
3. Cf. Ibid., 10.
4. Cf. Ibid., 11 and 19.
5. Cf. Ibid., 19-21.
6. Cf. Ibid., 10, 20.
7. Ibid., 21.
8. Cf. Ibid., 19-21.
9. Cf. *VS,* 15, 21.
10. Ibid., 15.
11. Cf. Ibid., 16.
12. Cf. Ibid., 107.
13. Cf. *LG,* 39-41.
14. Cf. *VS,* 12-13; 95-97.
15. Cf. Ibid., 17.
16. Ibid., 12.
17. *GS,* 43.
18. Cf. *VS,* 13-14.
19. *GCD,* 85.

Chapter 2

Moral Theology

God said, "Let us make man in our image, after our likeness; and let them have dominion over the fish of the sea, and over the birds of the air, and over the cattle, and over all the earth, and over every creeping thing that creeps upon the earth."

So God created man in his own image, in the image of God he created him; male and female he created them. And God blessed them, and God said to them, "Be fruitful and multiply, and fill the earth and subdue it; and have dominion over the fish of the sea and over the birds of the air and over every living thing that moves upon the earth." And God said, "Behold, I have given you every plant yielding seed which is upon the face of all the earth, and every tree with seed in its fruit; you shall have them for food. And to every beast of the earth, and to every bird of the air, and to everything that creeps on the earth, everything that has the breath of life, I have given every green plant for food." And it was so. And God saw everything that he had made, and behold, it was very good....

The Lord God took the man and put him in the garden of Eden to till it and keep it. And the Lord God commanded the man, saying, "You may freely eat of every tree of the garden; but of the tree of the knowledge of good and evil you shall not eat, for in the day that you eat of it you shall die."

Then the Lord God said, "It is not good that the man should be alone; I will make him a helper fit for him." So out of the ground the Lord God formed every beast of the field and every bird of the air, and brought them to the man to see what he would call them; and whatever the man called every living creature, that was its name. The man gave names to all cattle, and to the birds of the air, and to every beast of the field; but for the man there was not found a helper fit for him. So the Lord God caused a deep sleep to fall upon the man, and while he slept took one of his ribs and closed up its place with flesh; and the rib which the Lord God had taken from the man he made into a woman and brought her to the man.

Then the man said, "This at last is bone of my bones and flesh of my flesh; she shall be called Woman, because she was taken out of Man." Therefore a man leaves his father and his mother and cleaves to his wife, and they become one flesh. And the man and his wife were both naked, and were not ashamed. (Gn 1: 26-31; 2: 15-25)

Let us reflect on this passage of Scripture by considering these questions:

- What does it mean that God created man in his image and likeness?
- What is the Christian concept of the human being?
- Are we social beings with rights and duties because of human solidarity?

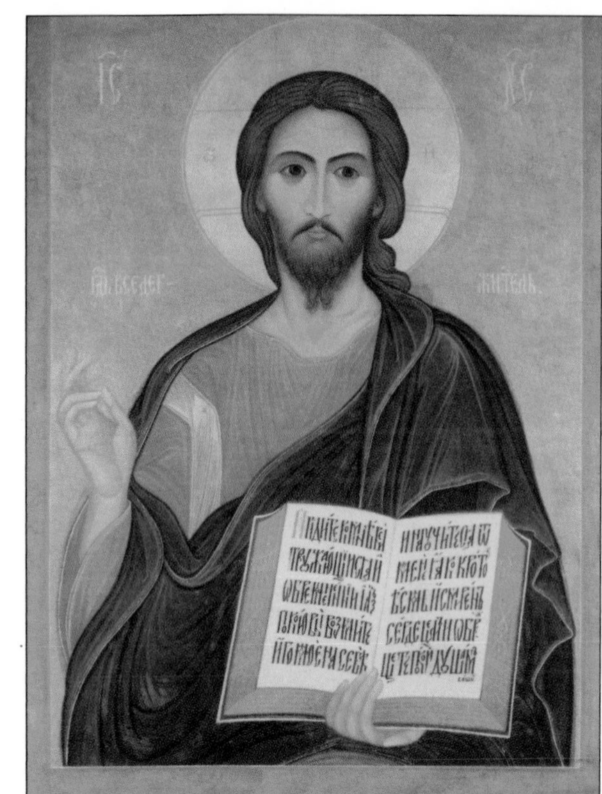

INTRODUCTION

Before moral theology can be covered as a subject, it is necessary to explain the meaning of basic concepts and principles to ensure that there is an understanding of the subject by the reader.

In order to understand Catholic moral theology, it is necessary to be familiar with ideas such as its definition, the determination of its aim or purpose, the differences between its related parts, and the sources from which its principles are deduced.

1. MORAL THEOLOGY

> The Church's moral reflection, always conducted in the light of Christ, the "Good Teacher," has also developed in the specific form of the theological science called "moral theology," a science which accepts and examines divine revelation while at the same time responding to the demands of human reason. Moral theology is a reflection concerned with "morality," with the good and the evil of human acts and of the person who performs them; in this sense it is accessible to all people. But it is also "theology," inasmuch as it acknowledges that the origin and end of moral action are found in the One who "alone is good" and who, by giving himself to man in Christ, offers him the happiness of divine life.[1]

Catholic moral theology is a science that enables the human mind to make correct moral choices guided by principles set forth by the Magisterium.

Catholic moral theology is a science that enables the human mind to make correct moral choices guided by principles set forth by the Magisterium. Catholic moral theology guides us to live the new life in Christ that is received in Baptism, and enables us to secure our reward of eternal life. It directs people in their quest for holiness that leads ultimately to sainthood. Its ethical principles are discovered in revelation and the life of Jesus, and it is aided by human sciences where appropriate.

For example, Catholic moral theology will use insights from psychology to explain how a person is motivated to make moral choices. The answers determined by moral theology are guaranteed to be sufficient and free from error as long as they are grounded in revelation and human knowledge and are in accordance with the teaching of the Church. Ethical systems based on reason alone are prone to error, because they lack the insights found in revelation and are not directed by the Magisterium.

The failure to take God's revelation into account can explain why so many ethical systems offered by different ideologies fall short of their goals. This failure is related directly to the desire to set up a system apart from God's vision that is the only true understanding of human dignity. Atheistic communism and socialism are examples of failed ideologies that ignored the truths found in revelation.

2. OUR MORAL CONDUCT DEPENDS ON THE VERY CONCEPT OF MAN.

Each person has a standard of behavior by which he lives. If a person believes that he is nothing more than a highly-evolved animal, then the moral standards by which he tries to live will be no more than biological rules; he will live as an animal because animals are not capable of making moral choices. Our morality in such cases is reduced to a morality of instinct.[2]

Buddhism emphasizes the illusory nature of our physical existence.

For example, sociobiology theorizes that man is an animal who is genetically determined. Those who support this system claim that our choices are genetically fixed, so they have no moral component. Therefore, no moral demands can be made on people.

Secular humanism is an ethical view of life that questions or does not accept the existence of God, an immortal soul, or an afterlife. While there are some common aspects shared by humanism and Christianity, the Christian view of mankind is radically different.

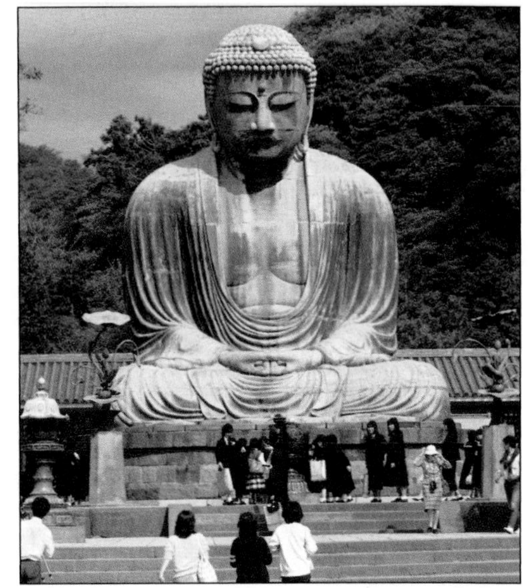

Christian humanism embraces humanity as a wonderful gift from God through which we can know, love and serve him. It recognizes the true merit of human nature in the context of its divinely ordained purpose and origin. It insists that human intellectual endeavors can and should be complementary to the belief in God and the practice of the Christian Faith. This is eminently clear when considering that Jesus Christ, God the Son himself, without change became true man.

At the other extreme is the view that humans are purely spiritual. The logical conclusion arising from this view will be to defend ethical principles that favor a spiritual life with no consideration of the body. This idea leads to an angelic morality that disregards the human being's physical side, for it denies the role of the body in relation to human perfection.

An example of this viewpoint is Buddhism. It emphasizes the illusory nature of our physical existence:

> The "enlightenment" experienced by Buddha comes down to the conviction that the world is bad, that it is the source of evil and of suffering for man. To liberate oneself from this evil, one must free oneself from this world, necessitating a break with the ties that join us to external reality—ties existing in our human nature, in our psyche, in our bodies. The more we are liberated from these ties, the more we become indifferent to what is in the world, and the more we are freed from suffering, from the evil that has its source in the world.[3]

3. THE CHRISTIAN CONCEPT OF MANKIND

a. CHRISTIANITY SEPARATES ITSELF FROM THEORIES THAT DO NOT BELIEVE IN THE EXISTENCE OF AN IMMORTAL SOUL IN EACH PERSON.

The existence of an immortal soul in each person differentiates us radically from animals. The term *soul* is applied to describe the human being's capability to think and choose in imitation of his Creator. It is fundamentally a

Western idea, though it is an undeniable reality in Eastern thought as well. Christianity, however, has been the force that confirmed and fully developed the Western understanding of an immortal soul. The inordinate stress in this century on the scientific method and materialism has led to the denial that the human has an immortal soul. Many have fallen for the claim that "if it can't be measured or observed, it doesn't exist." But this argument ignores the fact that we can conceive of abstract ideas. If we can grasp ideas that have no material basis, then there is something about us that is not material. Some would use the word *mind* to describe this phenomenon, while others would use the word *soul.* Nonetheless, there is a widespread agreement that there is an additional element in the human being that is superior to the brain, an element that is neither reducible to the brain nor identical to the mind. This facet of each of us is a profound and essential differentiating element that separates us from the animals.

The Church teaches that every spiritual soul is created immediately by God—it is not "produced" by the parents—and also that it is immortal.

b. THE HUMAN SOUL IS CREATED DIRECTLY BY GOD.

The Church teaches that every spiritual soul is created immediately by God—it is not "produced" by the parents—and also that it is immortal; it does not perish when it separates from the body at death, and it will be reunited with the body at the final resurrection.

The soul is a spiritual reality, free and immortal, that is born ordered to God from conception and is destined for heaven. Through the soul, each person is the image of God; since God is spirit, the soul is non-material. Like God, the human being has the ability to think and choose. In other words, he has an intellect and a will.

> "God created man in his own image, in the image of God he created him, male and female he created them" (Gn 1:27). Man occupies a unique place in creation: (I) he is "in the image of God"; (II) in his own nature he unites the spiritual and material worlds; (III) he is created "male and female"; (IV) God established him in his friendship. (CCC 355)

c. BOTH THE BODY AND THE SOUL BELONG TO THE BEING OF MAN.

A person, properly speaking, does not have a soul, but rather, he integrates the soul into his own being (he "is" a soul), and similarly, a person does not have a body; he *is* a body. Each person is one in body and soul.

> The human person, created in the image of God, is a being at once corporeal and spiritual. The biblical account expresses this reality in symbolic language when it affirms that "then the Lord God formed man of dust from the ground, and breathed into his nostrils the breath of life; and man became a living being" (Gn 2:7). Man, whole and entire, is therefore *willed* by God. (CCC 362)

d. BOTH BODY AND SOUL CONSTITUTE ONE UNITY.

Since the soul is created in the image of God and is united to the human body, it is a special unity. Consequently, this unity of body and soul negates any interpretation of man as two separate entities. We are a unity where both body and soul come together:

> **The unity of soul and body is so profound that one has to consider the soul to be the "form" of the body:[4] i.e., it is because of its spiritual soul that the body made of matter becomes a living, human body; spirit and matter, in man, are not two natures united, but rather their union forms a single nature. (CCC 365)**

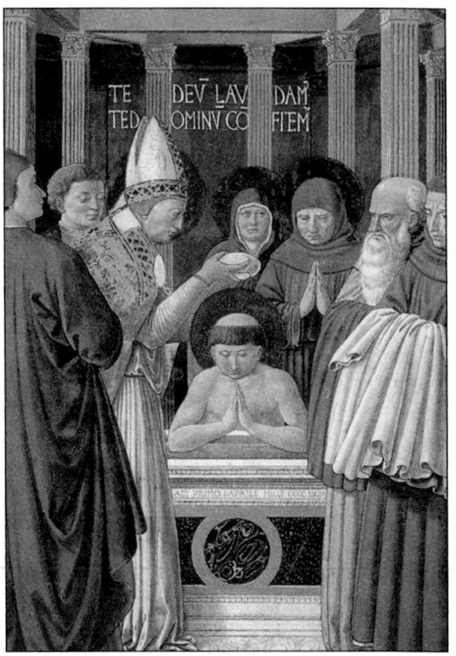

Baptism of St. Augustine

The explanation for the profound unity of the human being, as in all created things, is found under the ideas of matter and form. Just as a statue is made up of matter (for example, bronze) and a shape that gives it its particular characteristics, so are the body and soul the matter and form of a person. To separate the body and the soul is to destroy the person. And that is precisely death—the separation of body and soul. As St. Thomas Aquinas teaches, "the soul alone is not man." And a dead body is not, properly speaking, a "human body," but a corpse.[5]

Since the human is a spiritual and corporeal reality, then morality affects both the body and the spirit, for, "in fact, body and soul are inseparable: in the person, in the willing agent and in the deliberate act they stand or fall together."[6] For example, consider the runner who exercises for his physical health—to become fit, build muscle and lose extra pounds. While accomplishing these goals, he simultaneously improves his mental health—he relieves stress, clears his mind, and lifts his spirits. As a healthy, energetic, and motivated individual, the runner is more willing and able to fulfill his duty to love God and neighbor. The sacraments address this unity of body and soul: the oil in Confirmation, Holy Orders and Anointing of the Sick; the appearances of bread and wine in Holy Eucharist; the water in Baptism; the absolution in Penance; the consent of the couple in Matrimony. In instituting the sacraments, Christ acknowledged the whole person, body and soul.

In Baptism, a permanent spiritual sign is imprinted on the soul that consecrates the person to Christ.

"Man is divinized."

The truths determined by Christian anthropology are:

- the creation of man by God in his own image and likeness,
- the existence of original sin, and
- the redemption accomplished by Jesus Christ, which makes possible the life of grace given to us in Baptism.

It is through Baptism that one acquires a higher level of participation in God's life through grace. In Baptism, a permanent spiritual sign is imprinted on the soul that consecrates the person to Christ. Theology teaches that in the baptized person, the life of Christ is found, so much so that one becomes a new being, a person in Christ:

> **Incorporated into *Christ* by Baptism, Christians are "dead to sin and alive to God in Christ Jesus" and so participate in the life of the Risen Lord (Rom 6:11 and cf. 6:5; cf. Col 2:12). (CCC 1694)**

This great reality elevates the baptized person to a higher state than the unbaptized person. St. Peter teaches that the baptized "become partakers of the divine nature" (2 Pt 1:4). Just as a child participates in the physical nature of his parents through his genetic structure, so does—in a real, but spiritual

fashion—the Christian participate, by Baptism, in the nature of God. Hence the familiar quote of the Fathers: "Man is divinized." And this elevated condition requires a new type of conduct:

> **Christian, recognize your dignity. For now you partake of divine nature; do not degenerate by turning back to your past state. Remember what Head you belong to and to what Body you are a member of. Remember that you have been snatched away from the power of darkness to be transported to the light of the kingdom of God.[7]**

4. THE SPECIFICITY OF CATHOLIC MORALITY

We find in the New Testament superior values and precepts that are not found in any other philosophical or religious system.

Does the Christian, who is a new person, have the obligation to behave differently from the non-baptized? In other words, is there a specifically Christian morality superior to natural ethics and distinct from other religious confessions?

Yes. In fact, it is clear that the believer in Christ has a new way of acting since he has supernatural motives—that is, motives directly from God. Nevertheless, it is not just a new reason for doing good that Christianity offers. We find in the New Testament superior values and precepts that are not found in any other philosophical or religious system, nor are they found explicitly in the Old Testament.

An example is Christ's statement: "A new commandment I give you, that you love one another; even as I have loved you, that you also love one another" (Jn 13:34). This statement, apart from its richness, points to the measure of divine love and is a call to love even one's enemies. Jesus ended the law of retaliation *(lex talionis)*—to return an evil for an evil—when he condemned vengeance. He also said that it is not enough to forgive the enemy. He wants us to love the enemy as he loves.

The Sermon on the Mount begins with the Beatitudes. They call us to live a higher life, to seek perfection. Those who would be perfect must strive to live the Beatitudes.

All who are baptized are required to live the theological virtues of faith, hope, and charity, which have been infused at Baptism and enable us to share in the divine nature of the Father, Son, and Holy Spirit. They allow us to believe where belief does not seem possible, to hope where there is no hope, and to love even those who hate us. The grace of Baptism works a conversion that enables us to turn toward God and away from sin. The new level of ethical duties set forth in the Beatitudes directs man to live the high moral program. In fact, the morality presented by Jesus in the Sermon on the Mount supersedes any known morality.[8]

To indicate this, Jesus places the ancient rule of law "You have heard that it was said..."next to the new commandments given by him: "But I say to you..."

(Mt 5:38-48). This explains Jesus' exhortation to us regarding the commandments: "If you keep my commandments, you will abide in my love, just as I have kept my Father's commandments and abide in his love. These things I have spoken to you, so that my joy may be in you, and that your joy may be full" (Jn 15:10-11). The apostles echo this plea to the newly baptized: "And by this we may be sure that we know him, if we keep his commandments. He who says 'I know him' but disobeys his commandments is a liar, and the truth is not in him" (1 Jn 2:3-4).

"...we do not know how to pray as we ought, but the Spirit himself intercedes for us with sighs too deep for words."

As a result of Christ's death and Resurrection, the entire natural order has a new aid: the grace of God, which makes human life meritorious. Human actions become meritorious because grace transforms them as a result of God's power. The Christian accepts forgiveness and righteousness from on high, so he is enabled to rise above the purely human, not by an exterior change, but by healing and perfecting the proper order in his soul.

The Holy Spirit dwells in the Church as the source of her life and sanctifies human souls through the gift of his grace.

> He who believes in Christ has new life in the Holy Spirit. The moral life, increased and brought to maturity in grace, is to reach its fulfillment in the glory of heaven. (CCC 1715)

When a person accepts the Spirit of Christ, he establishes a way of life that is totally new and gratuitous.

> The Holy Spirit, present in the soul of the Christian, makes him a partaker of the divine nature and intimately unites him to the Father and Christ in a communion of life which not even death can break (cf. Jn 14:23). The Holy Spirit heals man of his spiritual weaknesses and infirmities, frees him from the slavery of his passions and of immoderate self-love, by giving him power to keep the divine law, strengthens him with hope and fortitude, enlightens him in the pursuit of the good, and infuses in him the fruits of charity, joy, peace, patience, kindness, goodness, longanimity, humility, fidelity, modesty, continence, and chastity (cf. Gal 5:22-23). This is why the Holy Spirit is invoked as the guest of the soul.[9]

> For all who are led by the Spirit of God are sons of God....When we cry, "Abba! Father!" it is the Spirit himself bearing witness with our spirit that we are children of God....Likewise the Spirit helps us in our weakness; for we do not know how to pray as we ought, but the Spirit himself intercedes for us with sighs too deep for words.... the Spirit intercedes for the saints according to the will of God. (Rom 8:14-16; 26-27)

5. MAN IS A SOCIAL BEING: MORAL REQUIREMENTS OF HUMAN SOLIDARITY

The natural condition of being a person makes a human both an individual and a social being. The reason for this is derived from the very structure of the human person. Each of us was made in the image of the perfect Community which is the Father, Son, and Holy Spirit. So also, a person is born into the community of the family and lives out his life in the larger human community. Since the time of Aristotle, it has been said that the human being is by his very nature a social being; sociability enters into the very definition of man. This is reflected also in the celebration of the Eucharist which has both individual and communal characteristics of worship.

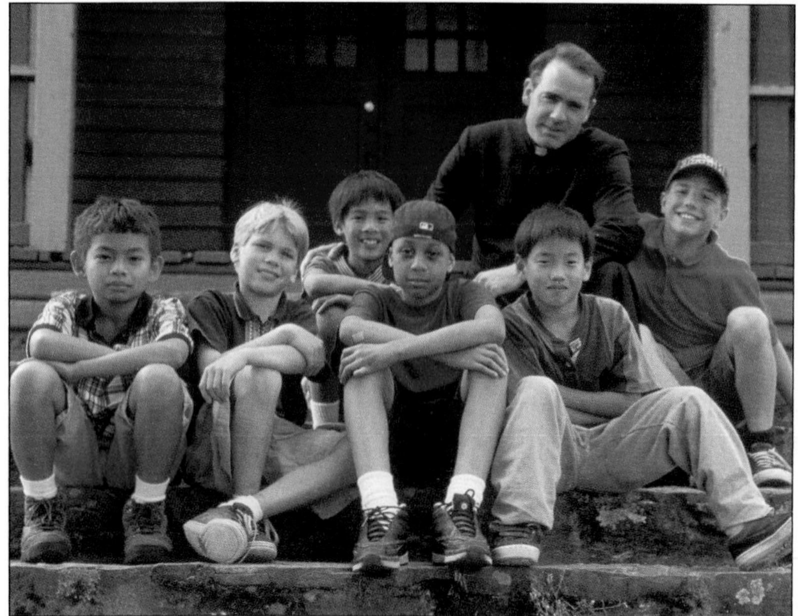

> **The human person needs to live in society. Society is not for him an extraneous addition but a requirement of his nature. Through the exchange with others, mutual service and dialogue with his brethren, man develops his potential; he thus responds to his vocation.[10]**
> **(CCC 1879)**

Man's sociability requires that certain ethical demands be accomplished as part of his relationship to others in society. For example, all have a right to own and use property for their basic needs. Coupled with this right is the obligation to respect others' rights in regards to property to ensure the common good. As a result, Christian morality has the capability to perfect both personal and social obligations.

The best way to fulfill one's obligations of justice and love is to contribute to the common good according to one's means and the needs of others...

Moreover, since man is inclined to ignore his social duties for personal gain, it is necessary to stress the importance of carrying out those duties. Vatican II states the "need to transcend an individualistic morality" (*GS*, 30).

A large portion of the *Catechism of the Catholic Church* is dedicated to the exposition of doctrine according to the requirements of life in the "human community." This is done after the presentation of the Christian idea of man (cf. CCC 1877-1948).

The teaching of the Church attempts to safeguard Christian morality from being purely individualistic in its approach, where little attention is given to social duties. This teaching is recalled and urged by Vatican II:

> **The pace of change is so far-reaching and rapid nowadays that no one can allow himself to close his eyes to the course of events or indifferently ignore them and wallow in the luxury of a merely individualistic morality. The best way to fulfill one's obligations of justice and love is to contribute to the common good according to one's means and the needs of others, even to the point of fostering and helping public and private organizations devoted to bettering the conditions of life.[11]**

6. SOURCES OF MORAL THEOLOGY

All sciences make use of ideas directly ordered to arriving at their proper knowledge. They also are aided by other sciences. For example, physics, which studies matter, uses mathematics to understand the laws governing matter.

Similarly, moral theology has its own sources, while making use of other sciences that assist it. The sources from which moral theology derives its doctrine are essentially the same as those of theology in general: Sacred Tradition and Sacred Scripture, which form one sacred deposit, a complete collection of the truths given to the Church by God. Theology is a mirror in which the Church reflects upon God, who is the source of all the riches of the Church. The Magisterium is the authority that authentically interprets this sacred deposit.

Christ entrusted his truths to the apostles, which they passed on in both preaching and writing for all generations under the protection of the Holy Spirit.

a. SACRED SCRIPTURE

Sacred Scripture was inspired by God and written down by human authors. It must be receptive to what God intended to reveal through his sacred authors regarding our salvation. Christ entrusted his truths to the apostles, which they passed on in both preaching and writing for all generations under the protection of the Holy Spirit. It is the written revelation contained in the Bible that teaches the ethical values promulgated by God.

> **These are: the subordination of man and his activity to God, the One who "alone is good"; the relationship between the moral good of human acts and eternal life; Christian discipleship, which opens up before man the perspective of divine love; and finally the gift of the Holy Spirit, source and means of the moral life of the "new creation" (cf. 2 Cor 5:17).[12]**

In the Bible, Christian morality is deduced mainly from the New Testament. In the Gospels, we find two basic principles:

- The life of Jesus is the main source from which the believer learns to live a Christian life.
- The moral doctrine that Jesus preached and taught—his words, his deeds and his precepts—constitute the "moral rule of Christian life."[13]

Besides the Gospels, other writings of the New Testament are also a principal source of moral knowledge. In fact, the apostles, besides recalling the moral teachings of Christ, expose other precepts that are derived from his doctrine, and are applied to the different circumstances of the first believers.[14]

But not all biblical teachings are meant to be binding forever. In the Old Testament, many precepts were circumstantial and

were abolished by Jesus' preaching. Among them are the ceremonial requirement that worship is to be done only in the temple in Jerusalem, and the practice of divorce, which was permitted by Moses but later prohibited by Jesus (cf. Mk 10: 2-12; Mt 5: 27-32; 19: 3-12).

Also, some New Testament teachings applied only to early Church communities because of their particular situations. An example is the abstention from certain practices as stipulated by the Council of Jerusalem (cf. Acts 15: 19-21) or the conduct of women in Corinth, as proscribed by St. Paul (cf. 1 Cor 11: 13-15).

b. SACRED TRADITION

The word *tradition* comes from the Latin *tradere*, which means "to hand on," and refers to those truths passed from generation to generation in oral rather than written form.

Tradition is the very life of the Church, preserving and guarding the teachings of Jesus Christ. The writings of the early Fathers (the second through the seventh centuries), which systematize moral doctrine and apply the New Testament teachings to different times, are an important part of Tradition. Also included is the teaching, life, and worship practices of the Church (particularly those relating to penance and the forgiveness of sins), as well as papal teachings which reflect these sources.[15]

The head of the Magisterium, the pope himself, by divine institution enjoys complete, immediate, and universal power in the care of souls.

c. THE MAGISTERIUM

Magisterium is the name given to the Church's teaching office. It is derived from the Latin *magister*, which means "teacher," and refers to the authority of the pope and the bishops united with him in teaching matters of faith and morals.

> **But the task of giving an authentic interpretation of the Word of God, whether in its written form or in the form of Tradition, has been entrusted to the living teaching office of the Church alone. Its authority in this matter is exercised in the name of Jesus Christ. Yet this Magisterium is not superior to the Word of God, but is its servant. It teaches only what has been handed on to it. At the divine command and with the help of the Holy Spirit, it listens to this devotedly, guards it with dedication and expounds it faithfully. All that it proposes for belief as being divinely revealed is drawn from this single deposit of faith.[16]**

The teaching of the hierarchy—the popes, the councils, and the bishops in their dioceses—began with the apostles. In the final analysis, the head of the Magisterium, the pope himself, by divine institution enjoys complete, immediate, and universal power in the care of souls. By right, he is guided by the Holy Spirit to authentically interpret the Christian moral message as head of the college of bishops.[17]

The Magisterium defines both the truths of faith and the Church's moral teachings and transmits them to every generation.[18] The infallibility, or immunity from error and any possibility of error, of the Magisterium extends to all elements of doctrine, including moral doctrine to preserve the truths of faith. The phrase *faith and morals* is contained in many documents of Tradition.

> The Church's Magisterium intervenes not only in the sphere of faith, but also, and inseparably so, in the sphere of morals. It has the task of "discerning...those acts which in themselves conform to the demands of faith and foster their expression in life and those which, on the contrary, because intrinsically evil, are incompatible with such demands" (*DVt*, 16). In proclaiming the commandments of God and the charity of Christ, the Church's Magisterium also teaches the faithful specific particular precepts and requires that they consider them in conscience as morally binding. In addition, the Magisterium carries out an important work of vigilance, warning the faithful of the presence of possible errors, even merely implicit ones, when their consciences fail to acknowledge the correctness and the truth of the moral norms, which the Magisterium teaches.[19]

A cultural opinion that does not admit of binding obligations in the parent-child relationship would not be considered a legitimate option.

d. ANCILLARY SCIENCES OF MORAL THEOLOGY

Some sciences are used to elaborate moral doctrine. Among them are:

- *philosophical ethics,* which aids in the understanding and posing of questions, as well as in providing a suitable language for expression,
- *law,* especially *canon law,* which systematically studies the norms of the Church, and
- other human sciences, i.e., *anthropology, psychology, medicine.*[20]

All of these sciences are only supplementary, so they neither substitute for nor diminish the authority of Scripture and Tradition—including the Magisterium—which constitute the sources of moral theology.

7. THE CHRISTIAN AND THE DEFENSE OF TRUTH

Plurality of opinion in matters of custom, politics, and other relative matters is a legitimate exercise of human freedom. For example, in family life, different ways of relating can exist between parents and their children, according to education, environment, and social customs. But it is also evident that not every opinion or cultural expression is valid. A cultural opinion that does not admit of binding obligations in the parent-child relationship would not be considered a legitimate option. A compromise in these principles could never be a Christian attitude, as it would involve renouncing the truth as revealed by God and accepting evil as compatible with Christian morality.

But while accepting a "healthy pluralism," Christians nevertheless have the obligation to acknowledge their beliefs and preach the moral message given by Jesus.

The Christian ought to defend the truth in a positive manner, respecting others and living out charity, while at the same time proclaiming the truth without fear.

Since the Church is both the means and goal of God's plan, the believer in Christ possesses a qualified certainty about the content of natural law placed in his heart by God and other truths that help guide his conduct. Consequently, he must ensure that Christian ethical principles inform human society. Pluralism must never lead anyone to refuse to accept a truth or approve its denial.

This attitude is far from any kind of fanaticism or rigid approach. The Christian cannot accept the false arguments that anyone who does not buy into a pluralism of opinions is a fanatic. On the contrary, the Christian ought to defend the truth in a positive manner, respecting others and living out charity, while at the same time proclaiming the truth without fear. The Church's defense of truth was confirmed often by John Paul II. An example is found in *Veritatis splendor:*

> The Church's teaching, and in particular her firmness in defending the universal and permanent validity of the precepts prohibiting intrinsically evil acts, is not infrequently seen as the sign of an intolerable intransigence, particularly with regard to enormously complex and conflict-filled situations present in the moral life of individuals and of society today; this intransigence is said to be in contrast to the Church's motherhood. The Church, one hears, is lacking in understanding and compassion. But the Church's motherhood can never in fact be separated from her teaching mission, which she must always carry out as the faithful Bride of Christ, who is the Truth in person. "As Teacher, she never tires of proclaiming the moral norm....The Church is in no way the author

or the arbiter of this norm. In obedience to the truth which is Christ, whose image is reflected in the nature and dignity of the human person, the Church interprets the moral norm and proposes it to all people of good will, without concealing its demands for fervor and perfection" (*FC*, 33).

In fact, genuine understanding and compassion must mean love for the person, for his true good, for his authentic freedom. And this does not result, certainly, from concealing or weakening moral truth, but rather from proposing it in its most profound meaning as an outpouring of God's eternal Wisdom, which we have received in Christ, and as a service to man, to the growth of his freedom and to the attainment of his happiness.

Still, a clear and forceful presentation of moral truth can never be separated from a profound and heartfelt respect, born of that patient and trusting love which man always needs along his moral journey, a journey frequently wearisome on account of difficulties, weakness and painful situations. The Church can never renounce "the principle of truth and consistency, whereby she does not agree to call good evil and evil good" (*RP*, 34); she must always be careful not to break the bruised reed or to quench the dimly burning wick (cf. Is 42: 3). As Paul VI wrote: "While it is an outstanding manifestation of charity towards souls to omit nothing from the saving doctrine of Christ, this must always be joined with tolerance and charity, as Christ himself showed by his conversations and dealings with men. Having come not to judge the world but to save it, he was uncompromisingly stern towards sin, but patient and rich in mercy towards sinners" (*HV*, 29).[21]

In obedience to the truth which is Christ, whose image is reflected in the nature and dignity of the human person, the Church interprets the moral norm and proposes it to all people of good will.

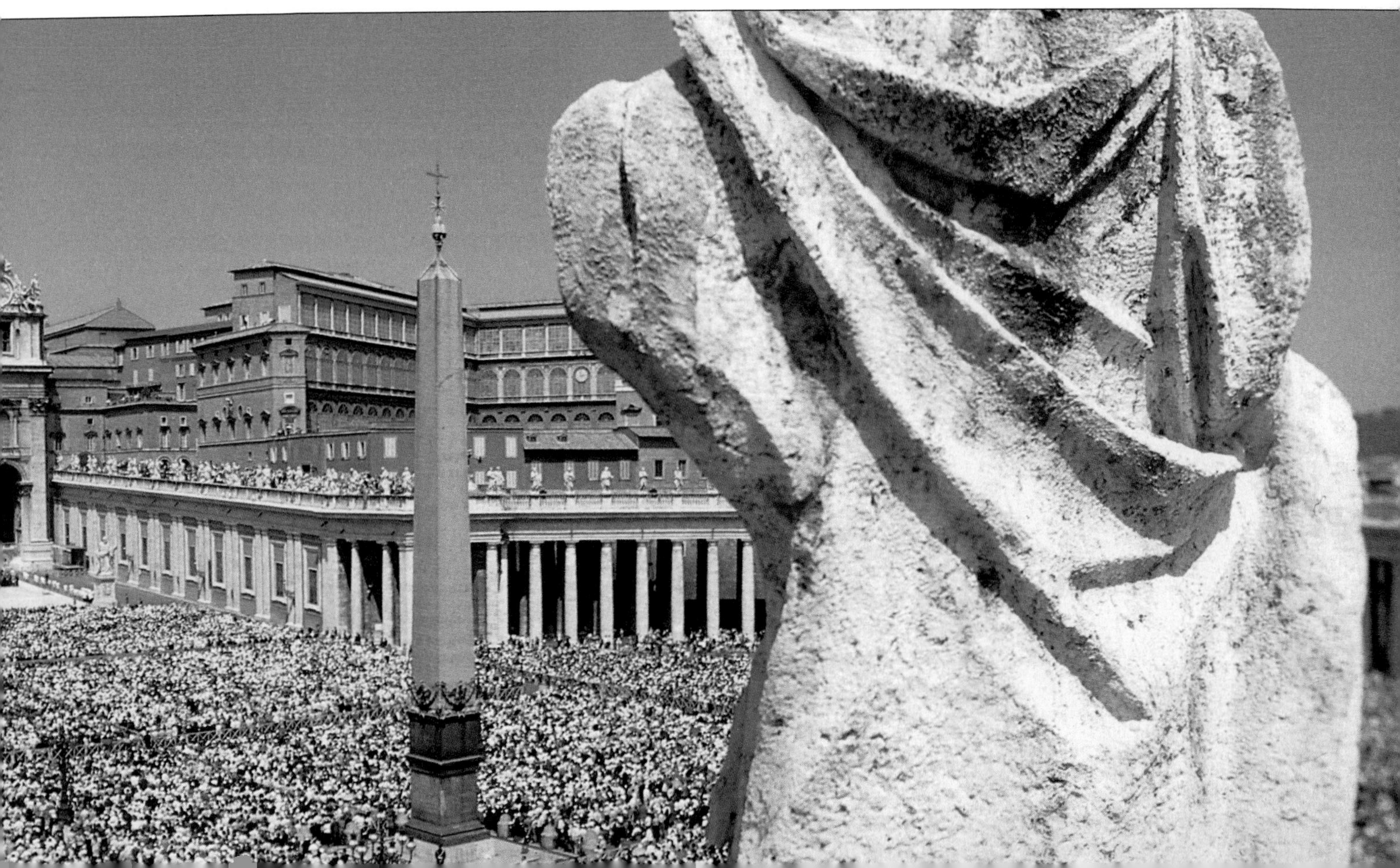

No other philosophical or moral system offers such a dignified concept of the human person.

"The Church is rich in her humanity."
–Pope Paul VI

CONCLUSION

Catholic morality offers an unmatched security. It incorporates a clear way of thinking based on sound philosophy, and a solid idea of mankind discovered from a careful reading of revelation. At the same time, it acknowledges a legitimate pluralism of opinion when it does not conflict with God's revealed truth.

No other philosophical or moral system offers such a dignified concept of the human person. Thus, Pope Paul VI stated, "The Church is rich in her humanity." The reason is obvious: Catholic anthropology is derived from God's conception of us, and the ultimate source of human dignity is our relationship to Jesus Christ—God made man. "In reality it is only in the mystery of the Word made flesh that the mystery of man truly becomes clear."[22]

In addition, Catholic morality does not elevate the human being to the point of making him faultless. Beginning with the teaching regarding original sin, the Church teaches about the precarious state in which each person finds himself:

> **When man looks into his own heart he finds that he is drawn towards what is wrong and sunk in many evils...Man therefore is divided in himself. As a result, the whole life of men, both individual and social, shows itself to be a struggle, and a dramatic one, between good and evil, between light and darkness.**[23]

This realism helps us aspire to high realms of moral life, but at the same time it acknowledges our wounded nature and inclination toward sin and therefore our need for the help of the Holy Spirit through prayer and the sacraments. These two aspects are always present in Catholic moral theology.

VOCABULARY

AMORALITY
An attitude that lacks any moral orientation, dispensing from all moral norms.

CATHOLIC MORAL THEOLOGY
A science that enables the human mind to make correct moral choices guided by principles set forth by the Magisterium.

FUNDAMENTAL MORALITY
The part of moral theology that studies the nature of the moral act and the conditions that make a concrete action moral.

GRACE
The free gift of God's own life that God makes to each person in Baptism; it is infused into the soul by the Holy Spirit to heal it of sin and to sanctify it.

IMMORALITY
Behavior that goes against moral norms.

INFALLIBILITY
Immunity from error and any possibility of error.

MAGISTERIUM
The name given to the ordinary and universal teaching authority of the pope and the bishops in communion with him, who guide the members of the Church without error in matters of faith and morals.

MATERIALISM
The belief that matter is the only reality and that everything can be explained only in terms of matter, and that comfort, pleasure, and/or wealth are the only or highest goods or values.

MORAL THEOLOGY
A science which accepts and examines divine revelation while at the same time responding to the demands of human reason.

NATURAL LAW
The participation of human beings in the plan of God in relation to human life and action insofar as the human mind can grasp that plan. The objective order established by God that determines the requirements for humans to thrive for and reach fulfillment.

ORIGINAL SIN
Adam and Eve's abuse of their human freedom in disobeying God's command. This sin separated mankind from God, darkened the human intellect, weakened the human will, and introduced into human nature an inclination toward sin.

PHILOSOPHICAL ANTHROPOLOGY
The part of philosophy that studies the specific nature of people.

PLURALISM
The existence of a variety of opinions or ideas within human society, some of which may contradict or oppose one another. A pluralism in the application of moral principles and social customs is valid insofar as it does not contradict God's revelation and sound reason.

REVELATION
The truths about God and his will which he has communicated freely to humanity by means of Sacred Scripture and Sacred Tradition.

SACRED TRADITION
The Word of God entrusted to the apostles and their successors by Christ and the Holy Spirit, and transmitted by their teaching to each generation of Christians.

SECULARISM
A system of doctrines and practices that rejects any form of religious faith and worship.

SOCIOBIOLOGY
The study of mankind as genetically determined.

THEOLOGICAL ANTHROPOLOGY
The part of theology that studies the nature of mankind according to revelation.

THEOLOGICAL VIRTUES
Virtues infused in the soul at Baptism that enable each person to share in the divine nature of God—Father, Son, and Holy Spirit. In Catholic theology, there are three: faith, hope, and charity.

TRADITION
Those truths passed from generation to generation in oral or written form.

SUPPLEMENTARY READINGS

1. There are some also who, either from zeal in attending to their own business or through some sort of aversion to their fellowmen, claim that they are occupied solely with their own affairs, without seeming to themselves to be doing anyone any injury. But while they steer clear of the one kind of injustice, they fall into the other: they are traitors to social life, for they contribute to it none of their interest, none of their effort, none of their means.

— Cicero, *De officiis*, Bk. I, 9

2. It is in accordance with their dignity that all men, because they are persons, that is, beings endowed with reason and free will and therefore bearing personal moral responsibility, are both impelled by their nature and bound by a moral obligation to seek the truth, especially religious truth. They are also bound to adhere to the truth once they have come to know it and direct their lives in accordance with the demands of truth.... In availing of any freedom man must respect the moral principle of personal and social responsibility; in exercising their rights individual men and social groups are bound by the moral law to have regard for the rights of others, their own duties to others and the common good of all. All men must be treated with justice and humanity.

— *DH*, 2 & 7

3. Hence it is evident that the state is a creation of nature, and that man is by nature a political animal. And he—who by nature and not by mere accident is without a state, is either a bad man or above humanity; he is like the "Tribeless, lawless, heartless one," whom Homer denounces—the natural outcast is forthwith a lover of war; he may be compared to an isolated player of chess.

Now, that man is more of a political animal than bees or any other gregarious animals is evident. Nature, as we often say, makes nothing in vain, and man is the only animal whom she has endowed with the gift of speech. And whereas mere voice is but an indication of pleasure or pain, and is therefore found in other animals (for their nature attains to the perception of pleasure and pain and the intimation of them to one another, and no further) the power of speech is intended to set forth the expedient and inexpedient, and therefore likewise the just and the unjust.

— Aristotle, *Politics*, Bk. 1, Ch. 2, 1253a 1-15)

4. A time will come when people will give up in practical existence those values about which they no longer have any intellectual conviction. Hence, we realize how necessary the function of a sound moral philosophy is in human society. It has to give, or to give back, to society intellectual faith in the value of its ideals.

— Jacques Maritain, *On the Use of Philosophy*

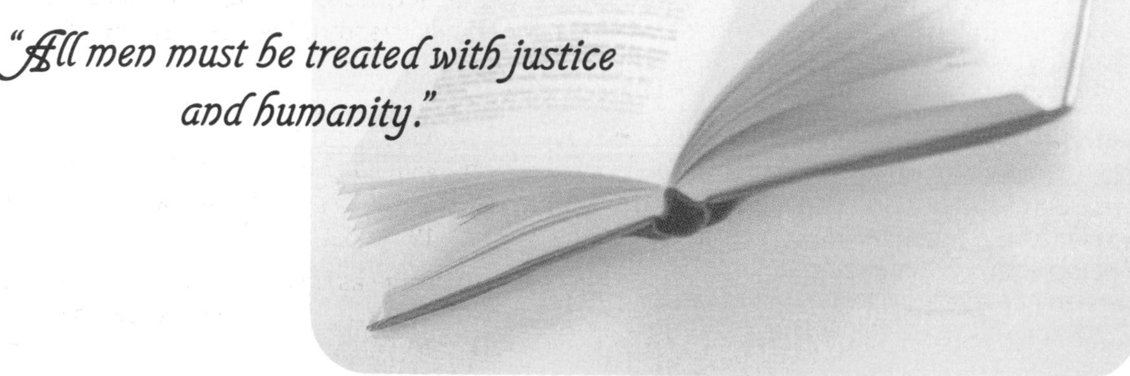

"All men must be treated with justice and humanity."

ADVANCED CONCEPTS

1. CATHOLIC MORALITY AND CIVIL ETHICS IN MODERN SOCIETY

Today's society distinguishes itself by pluralism in all fields of knowledge. Different philosophical and political systems are professed, several ways of understanding the moral life compete with one another, and diversity is found in religious beliefs.

In view of this situation, the assertion is made that it is impossible to provide a single manner of conduct for the whole of society because its citizens cannot agree on a single moral outlook. Therefore, it is necessary to come to a consensus with the hope of finding those ethical values that can be applied to each and every citizen.

Disagreement arises, however, when an attempt is made to delineate that common factor. In the first place, the advocates of secularism ask that it be free from any philosophical or religious considerations. Furthermore, many pretend to improve the concept of a morality based on natural law by substituting it with a secular morality.

These limitations, however, present some difficulties. Can we disregard some concepts, such as the spiritual understanding of man or the understanding of a universal law of good and evil? Moreover, are not those who demand complete separation of religion and law already starting with religious and political preconceptions?

In any case, it should be noted that moral demands should not be excessively reduced. The ethics that guide society ought not to be an ethics of minimums. On the contrary, it should aspire to give and demand values that favor a social order worthy of the human race. It should at least cover two levels: the defense of the individual as a person and the protection of the rights of the social order. Consequently, even the least common denominator of morality ought to demand respect for and protect by law the fundamental rights of the human being.

Hence, civil ethics cannot be a permissive ethics that favors the whim of citizens, nor can it exclusively have its foundation in a majority vote. The social agreement cannot be reached at any cost by means of fundamental concessions, or by submitting grave matter solely to a voting process.

With errors in wide sectors of the present culture,[24] the search for immediate solutions in a secular ethic, in the long run, will yield only new and greater evils in the social order.

2. THE "NEW MORALITY"

The new morality means different things to different people, but the general idea is that traditional morality placed too much emphasis on inflexible general rules, on obedience, and on abstract ideals of right and wrong; whereas the emphasis of the new morality is on the concrete situation, on love, and on the person.[25]

According to the "new morality," there is no need to categorize levels of action and types of goods, or to consider factors such as the object, intention, and circumstances that surround an action. The only important consideration is the question of love—what is the most loving response that I can make in this situation? What is the choice that increases the amount of good for my neighbor, while diminishing the amount of harm to him and anyone else?

This sort of moral philosophy is appealing to many people, especially many Christians, precisely because it appears on the surface to match exactly what Jesus spoke of as the greatest of all the commandments: "'You shall love the Lord your God with all you heart, and with all your soul, and with all your mind, and with all your strength.' The second is this, 'You shall love your neighbor as yourself'" (Mk 12:30-31).

Attractive as this philosophy is to so many, it is nevertheless flawed and bears only a superficial resemblance to Jesus' command to his followers. Why?

ADVANCED CONCEPTS CONTINUED

The first difficulty is that of defining *love* and *the good.* For many people today, love is an emotion or sentiment, while the good is equated with pleasure and happiness. The notion of self-sacrifice seldom enters into the picture when speaking of love, and any sort of action that results in unhappiness or pain for any party involved cannot possibly be good.

The idea that loving another person may occasionally involve doing or saying things that cause that person distress or hurt is rejected as unkind, judgmental, or cruel. Further, the idea that one may be required to sacrifice his good (i.e., happiness or pleasure) for the good of another is also unacceptable ("What sort of God would ask me to be unhappy?"). Finally, the idea that what is pleasurable may not necessarily be good is frequently met with scorn and derision.

The second problem is that the question of God and his will is left aside entirely, or included only insofar as asserting that he wants us to do no harm to others. But the definition of harming another is often broadened so much that it is difficult to find any way of acting that does not in some way harm another (i.e., psychological or emotional harm), and the idea that loving God could possibly involve giving assent to his will is rejected altogether. Thus, the proponents of the new morality make no room for objective moral guidelines that are binding on the consciences of every individual in all circumstances.

A final observation is that the new morality reverses the real relationship between the individual and the situation that calls for a moral response. By asserting that morality changes with each situation—so that the moral thing to do in every situation is the most loving thing to do—proponents of situation ethics believe that each situation imposes a morality on us.

But the opposite is actually true. It is our choice of actions and our intentions in response to the situation that determines the morality. If this were not true, then there would be no need for individual judgments of conscience. An individual's conscience would in fact have no role to play in discerning the morally correct response to any situation.

Situations do exist in which two people can reach different moral conclusions while acting out of a genuine desire to do what is morally right, with concern for the good of others foremost in their minds, and having access to the same information. While it is true that people can be blinded to reality by their preconceived notions of right and wrong, and can be unwilling to examine or revise these notions, it is not possible to use this as the basis for a moral philosophy that eliminates the reality of moral judgments based upon individual conscience.

Proponents of the "new morality" make no room for objective moral guidelines that are binding on the consciences of every individual in all circumstances.

QUESTIONS

1. What are the two foundations on which moral theology is built?

2. What does moral theology seek to do?

3. What is the final goal for each person, according to Catholic moral theology?

4. What is necessary to guarantee that a moral system will be correct?

5. What differentiates the Christian concept of mankind from humanistic concepts?

6. What radically differentiates man from animals?

7. What is the origin of man's soul?

8. What two realities form a radical unity for the human person?

9. What three truths does Christian anthropology add to natural anthropology?

10. What makes Jesus' call to love one's neighbor different from all other religious beliefs?

11. What is the effect of grace?

12. What makes a human both an individual and social being?

13. What are the sources of Catholic moral theology?

14. Why is the Magisterium essential to Christianity?

15. What are some of the sciences used to elaborate and supplement moral doctrine?

16. How does the Catholic idea of freedom differ from the idea that "I can do whatever I feel like doing"?

PRACTICAL EXERCISES

1. Adolf Hitler is considered by many to be one of the greatest tyrants of history. He is often referred to as the archetypal incarnation of evil. *Without reference to any moral precepts,* demonstrate why he was evil and ought to be condemned as such if he knowingly did the evil things he did. In other words, without reference to the notions of "right" and "wrong," argue that Hitler and what he did are evil. Is such an argument possible? How does this show that almost everyone (even those who deny it) believes that there are some principles of morality that exist objectively?

2. Point out the differences between philosophical ethics and Christian moral theology.

3. Outline and summarize the principal ideas expressed by Aristotle in Supplementary Reading 3.

4. Compare the ideas of Aristotle and the political and philosophical thoughts of the Roman orator Cicero in Supplementary Reading 1. What are some of the similarities and differences in their thoughts?

5. What are some of the moral principles expressed in the New Testament? Name some of the principles proposed by Christ himself in the following passages:

- Mt 5: 21-48
- Mk 9: 42-48; 10: 1-12
- Lk 17: 1-4
- Jn 13: 34-35

6. Compare and contrast the moral precepts of the Old and New Testaments. Begin with the Ten Commandments in Exodus 20, and the Beatitudes in Matthew 5: 1-12. What is the relationship between the Law of God as expressed by Moses on Mount Sinai and Jesus in the Sermon on the Mount? Are they compatible? Some people believe that Christ's teaching contradicts the Law of Moses. Are there any contradictions between the two? If so, can you reconcile these differences? What are the similarities?

7. This chapter speaks of the social obligations that one must fulfill in order to live a morally good life. What are some of these social obligations?

FROM THE CATECHISM

135 "The Sacred Scriptures contain the Word of God and, because they are inspired, they are truly the Word of God" (*DV*, 24).

382 "Man, though made of body and soul, is a unity" (*GS*, 14). The doctrine of the faith affirms that the spiritual and immortal soul is created immediately by God.

742 "Because you are sons, God has sent the Spirit of his Son into our hearts, crying, 'Abba! Father!'" (Gal 4:6).

1280 Baptism imprints on the soul an indelible spiritual sign, the character, which consecrates the baptized person for Christian worship. Because of the character Baptism cannot be repeated. (cf. DS, 1609 and DS, 1624)

ENDNOTES

1. *VS*, 29.
2. Cf. Ibid., 4, 33, 84.
3. Pope John Paul II, *Crossing the Threshold of Hope*, 14.
4. Cf. Council of Vienne (1312): DS, 902.
5. Cf. St. Thomas Aquinas, *Summa Theologiae*, III, q. 3, a. 2 ad 2.
6. *VS*, 49.
7. St. Leo the Great, *The Sermon on the Nativity*, 21, 2-3.
8. Cf. *VS*, 12.
9. *GCD*, 60.
10. Cf. *GS*, 25 § 1.
11. *GS*, 30.
12. *VS*, 28.
13. Ibid., 20.
14. Cf. Ibid., 26.
15. Cf. Ibid., 27.
16. *DV*, 10.
17. Cf. *VS*, 27, 30.
18. Cf. Ibid., 110.
19. Ibid., 110.
20. Cf. Ibid., 111.
21. Ibid., 95.
22. *GS*, 22.
23. Ibid., 13.
24. Cf. *VS*, 28-34.
25. Germain Grisez and Russell Shaw, *Beyond the New Morality*, p. xviii.

Chapter 3

Freedom And The Moral Act

In his book *The Sources of Christian Ethics*, Servais Pinckaers discusses two ideas of freedom. He speaks of a freedom of indifference, which flows from nominalism, and a freedom for excellence, found in the writings of the Church Fathers and St. Thomas Aquinas. Briefly explained, freedom of indifference is the power to choose between contraries, usually between good and evil. Freedom for excellence can be defined as the power to act freely with excellence and perfection.

Consider the example of learning music. There are two people: one is a concert pianist and the other has only a rudimentary knowledge of the piano. Who is more capable of playing the piano? The obvious answer is the concert pianist. He is able to play all types of music from the most simple to the most complex. He is also able to improvise while still playing well. The beginner is less free, only able to play the most elementary songs, and any improvisation will probably be disastrous.

At first, a child learning music may see his lessons as a reduction of his freedom. The practice and discipline may be frustrating at times and seen as an imposing burden. Yet, if he sticks with it and makes the firm decision to master the basics, the child will find himself able to play more and more difficult pieces of music. At some point, he will even be able to improvise on his own.

Banging on the piano is certainly a free act, but on the other end of the spectrum is the true master of piano, the one who has the freedom to choose between banging on the keys and playing a musical piece, but also one who is more free to play beautiful and more complicated music.

This example raises some questions; for example:

- Are we responsible for disciplining ourselves and ordering our lives in such a way that we can be truly free?
- Who has an easier, more pleasant afternoon: the child who plays outside with his friends or the child who practices the piano? Who is more truly free to make beautiful music?
- Which moral acts make us truly free?

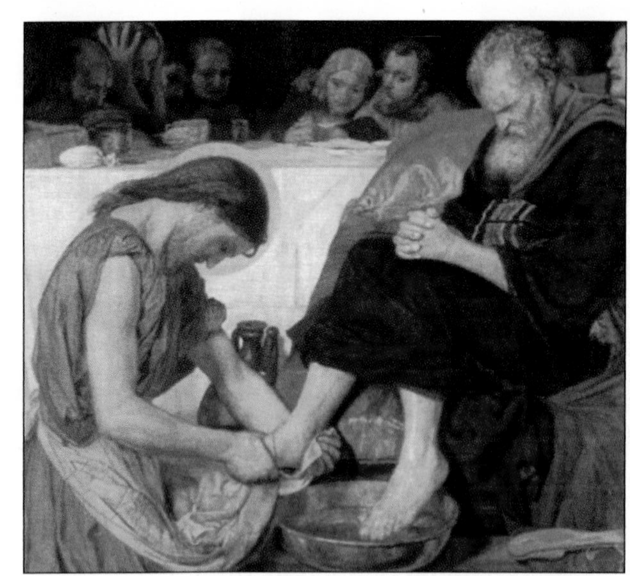

INTRODUCTION

If, indeed, morality is peculiar to human beings, when does an act become good or evil? What is the role of freedom in the moral life? When does a person take full responsibility for a particular act?

From his conduct, it is obvious that a Christian has reasons that justify his moral life that are different from those of a non-Christian. He accepts right conduct because he knows that he is created by God and has been redeemed by Christ Jesus. As a result, he rejoices in knowing that he is a son of God. If men and women are the only creatures loved by God for their own sake, then God also gives us a proper way of acting.[1]

The Christian believes that God set down what ought to be done or avoided. Since this view is not accepted by all, the believer, apart from the teaching of the Bible, needs to know the rational principles of the moral life that apply to everyone. They are:

Christian morality is the most effective means of acquiring the dignity proper to us because it is a morality of imitating Jesus Christ.

- freedom, which makes a person a moral agent,
- conscience, which gives us the capacity to discover God's will as written in our souls, and
- law, which should not limit freedom, but allow it to function properly.

Besides these three concepts, the Christian cannot ignore this radical and definitive principle: Jesus clearly set out what is good or evil for us by his words and the conduct of his life. Hence, Christian morality is the most effective means of acquiring the dignity proper to us because it is a morality of imitating Jesus Christ.

In this chapter, we propose that an authentic human existence, worthy of the person, can be reached only when one strives to live a moral life in imitation of Jesus. This entails a development of all of the person's faculties—being intelligent, free, and, consequently, responsible for his actions. It is with this end in mind that we study the conditions for true human and moral actions.

1. IMPORTANCE OF THE MORAL LIFE

Right moral conduct perfects the human being, and wrong moral conduct degrades him. Good and evil are the most interesting aspects of human life. The greatest writings about mankind have been those that confront the struggle between his good and evil choices. Other things, such as wealth, poverty, success, failure, health, illness, or any other conditions that may exist in someone's personal life are certainly important (and at times decisive), but they do not touch his life as profoundly as the effects of good and evil do.

If morality affects us deeply, then it follows that the study of ethics is of significant importance to the human being. As was stated by Socrates, "the science of good and evil" is the most important of all the forms of knowledge, since it places us on the road to true happiness. Thus, Plato also wrote, "but still I should like to examine further, for no light matter here is at stake, nothing less than the rule of human life."[2]

Moral theology is the science that teaches us how to choose good and avoid evil.

2. MAN'S ABILITY TO CHOOSE GOOD AND EVIL

Every human is a moral being, capable of doing good or evil, being just or unjust, honorable or dishonorable. Only physical good and evil are attributed to the animals, not moral good and evil. For example, a horse is said to be fast or slow in a race, a dog can have a better or worse nose for hunting, but no one would ever accuse them of sin for a poor performance. Neither the horse nor the dog can sin or practice virtue. In no way are they morally responsible for their actions.

A person, on the other hand, is morally responsible for his actions. Responsibility makes sin possible, and therefore, the sacrament of Penance necessary. He acts with thought and deliberation. The reason is that he, unlike the animals, has intellect and a will. *Intelligence* gives meaning to things and *free will* allows for the doing or omitting of actions the intellect has determined to be good or bad.

The human person, therefore, can lead an exemplary existence, striving for sanctity, or commit the most evil actions. This reality is often evident, and was noted by Aristotle:

> **For man, when perfected, is the best of animals, but, when separated from law and justice, he is the worst of all; since armed injustice is the more dangerous, and he is equipped at birth with arms, meant to be used by intelligence and virtue, which he may use for the worst ends. Wherefore, if he has not virtue, he is the most unholy and the most savage of animals, and the most full of lust and gluttony. But justice is the bond of men in states, for the administration of justice, which is the determination of what is just, is the principle of order in political society.**[3]

With these two options—the good that perfects and the evil that degrades—human existence is lived out. Moral theology is the science that teaches us how to choose good and avoid evil, so that, besides living with the dignity proper to us, we may accomplish our end: eternal salvation.

"For man, when perfected, is the best of animals, but, when separated from law and justice, he is the worst of all..."
– Aristotle

People can turn to Christ in order to receive from him the answer to their questions about what is good and what is evil. Christ is the Teacher, the risen One who has life in himself and who is always present in his Church and in the world. It is he who opens up to the faithful the book of the Scriptures and, by fully revealing his Father's will, teaches the truth about moral actions.[4]

3. THE HUMAN ACT, A MORAL ACT

While every person can make good choices, moral good and evil cannot always be attributed to every person in all circumstances. This calls for some distinctions: A moral or immoral act is truly human when someone brings it about with *knowledge* and *free will.* Consequently, those actions that lack knowledge or freedom do not fall under the realm of morality, as may be the

The first requirement for a moral act is that it be done with knowledge.

case with the insane or when a person is semi-conscious. Along with human acts, classical literature also speaks of the *acts of a human*, which are acts accomplished without knowledge or deliberation, and so are considered differently than human actions. Examples of acts of a human are breathing and blinking.

While intellect and free will are the spiritual faculties that human beings possess, they are not separate from the rest of a person's life. In other words, the human act involves the whole person, and not just the intellect and will. It is the human person—with all his virtues and vices, his character, and his interactions with others—who is moral or immoral, good or evil. "Human acts are moral acts because they express and determine the goodness or evil of the individual who performs them."[5] It is in and through choices that a person forms his character.

Sin does not come about as a surprise.

Full knowledge involves clear and deliberate knowledge of the morality of an action.

4. KNOWLEDGE AS A CONDITION FOR MORALITY

From the beginning of Western culture, man has been defined as a rational animal, and therefore reason needs to be understood as a necessary element of morality. So, the first requirement for a moral act is that it be done with knowledge.

However, there are different degrees of knowledge, and how clearly one thinks through his actions affects his culpability. Here, a distinction can be made between *full* and *partial knowledge*.

a. FULL KNOWLEDGE

Sin wounds the relationship of grace between God and the person. Sin does not come about as a surprise. It requires sufficient thought and consent to the act, so full knowledge involves clear and deliberate knowledge of the morality of an action. Full knowledge presumes two things:

- *That the agent know clearly what he is doing.* Hence, sins do not occur in the state of sleep or semi-consciousness.
- *That the agent be aware of its moral dimension.* He needs to know the act as good or evil. He does not need to know that this act "offends God." It is enough to know that it is prohibited or seriously wrong. For example, someone has full knowledge when he slanders another while knowing it is not true, but there is no sin when someone is discussing information that was shared with him by a co-worker, but is not aware that it was obtained in an unethical manner. The same can be said for good acts: there is no need to know that this pleases God; it is enough to know that it is a good act.

6. PARTIAL KNOWLEDGE

Partial knowledge is clouded by some obstacle that interferes with correct judgment, as may be the case in the use of prescribed medications or psychological alterations due to fear or depression.

Freedom is one of the central themes of moral theology since the two specific operations of our souls are found in it—intellect and will.

5. THE FREE HUMAN ACT

Freedom is our greatest quality. God created and destined us to reproduce the image of his Son, who is the visible manifestation of the invisible Father. Therefore, the proper exercise of freedom necessarily involves moral acts performed in the imitation of the Son of God.

The inorganic world is ruled by material properties, and animals are ruled by their natural instinct. The instinctive force of animals is meant to be controlled in man by his creative capacity for freedom.

> Freedom is the power, rooted in reason and will, to act or not to act, to do this or that, and so to perform deliberate actions on one's own responsibility. By free will one shapes one's own life. Human freedom is a force for growth and maturity in truth and goodness; it attains its perfection when directed toward God, our beatitude. (CCC 1731)
>
> *Imputability* and responsibility for an action can be diminished or even nullified by ignorance, inadvertence, duress, fear, habit, inordinate attachments, and other psychological or social factors. (CCC 1735)

The existence of freedom is a basic premise in Catholic morality, and its improper use leads to serious difficulties. In fact, good and evil are forged in freedom. Moreover, to the degree that a person reaches high levels of freedom, he becomes capable of high levels of morality. On the other hand, the sinful person ends up being a slave to his passions. His freedom is reduced and can be lost entirely. Thus, freedom is one of the central themes of moral theology since the two specific operations of our souls are found in it—intellect and will. In fact, free acts demand the use of the intellect and will.

In dealing with the subject of freedom, it is necessary to understand the concept of freedom:

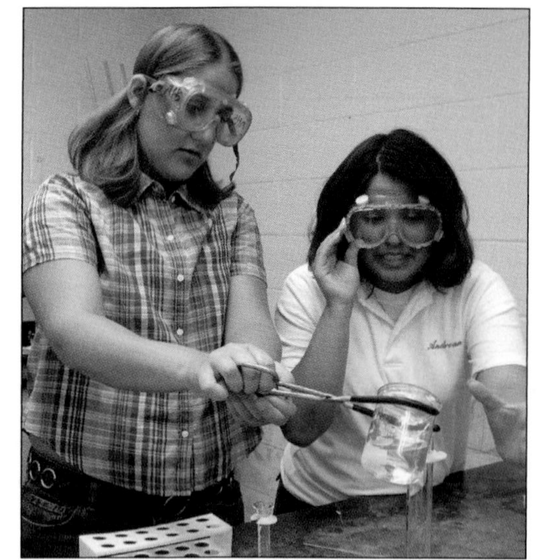

a. EXISTENCE OF FREEDOM

No other historical period has so strongly claimed the role of freedom in personal and social life as the present age.[6] The call for freedom is the loudest cry of our times. And despite all of this, there are still those who deny it. Mankind, it is said, lacks freedom, and is dominated by circumstances.

> **Side by side with its exaltation of freedom, yet oddly in contrast with it, modern culture radically questions the very existence of this freedom. A number of disciplines, grouped under the name of the "behavioral sciences," have rightly drawn attention to the many kinds of psychological and social conditioning which influence the exercise of human freedom.... But some people, going beyond the conclusions which can be legitimately drawn from these observations, have come to question or even deny the very reality of human freedom.[7]**

The reason may be found in a failure to distinguish the existence of freedom and its limitations. In fact, human freedom is limited precisely because the human is a limited being. Some human limitations are the circumstances in which a person is born and the capabilities with which he is born. While people admit that they have limited intelligence and strength, they are often unwilling to admit that they have limited freedom.

Human freedom belongs to us as creatures; it is a freedom which is given as a gift, one to be received like a seed and to be cultivated responsibly.

> **Rational reflection and daily experience demonstrate the weakness which marks man's freedom. That freedom is real but limited.... Human freedom belongs to us as creatures; it is a freedom which is given as a gift, one to be received like a seed and to be cultivated responsibly. It is an essential part of that creaturely image which is the basis of the dignity of the person. Within that freedom there is an echo of the primordial vocation whereby the Creator calls man to the true Good, and even more, through Christ's Revelation, to become his friend and to share his own divine life.... Freedom then is rooted in the truth about man, and it is ultimately directed towards communion.[8]**

In other words, one is not free to be who or what he wishes, for God has chosen each of us for himself, to share his eternal life. The freedom we have is the freedom to establish a loving relationship with Jesus Christ through the action of the Holy Spirit. When a person chooses to reject this call, he becomes a slave to his passions, which is why some people are called animals, for they have lost the freedom to choose by entangling their lives in sinful habits. They have become instinctively sinful, reducing their possibilities for repentance.

The existence of freedom can be proven by Scripture as well as by reason. In fact, the Old Testament presents the relationship between mankind and God in terms of freedom, so that, already in the beginning of humanity, people made poor use of their freedom and risked their destiny.

God gives man some precepts, but man has the ability to reject them to his detriment. As we see in the Book of Sirach:

> **It was he who created man in the beginning, and he left him in the power of his own inclination. If you will, you can keep the commandments, and to act faithfully is a matter of your own choice. He has placed before you fire and water: stretch out your hand for whichever you wish. Before a man are life and death, and whichever he chooses will be given to him. (Sir 15: 14-17)**

The history of God with his people develops in a climate of freedom. The history of salvation is the story of two wills that often disagree: that of God, and that of each person he created, constituted by the People of Israel. Many human misfortunes derive from our misuse of freedom:

> **Do not say, "It was he who led me astray"; for he has no need of a sinful man. The Lord hates all abominations, and they are not loved by those who fear him. (Sir 15: 12-13)**

Doing evil is not freedom, nor a part of freedom, but only a sign that we have the capability to choose.

b. FREEDOM AND KNOWLEDGE OF THE TRUTH

Freedom has a fundamental dependence upon truth. In fact, freedom supposes knowledge of the truth, so that ignorance is an obstacle to choosing the good.

> **According to the Christian faith and the Church's teaching, "only the freedom which submits to the Truth leads the human person to his true good. The good of the person is to be in the Truth and to do the Truth" (Pius XII, *Address to the International Congress on Moral Theology*, 970).[9]**

Furthermore, the proper use of freedom increases our capacity to love the truth and grow in the knowledge of moral virtue. When freedom is used correctly, one discovers that "the truth will make you free" (Jn 8: 32). But truth is not the same as opinion or desire. Rather, it corresponds to an objective reality. The intimate relationship between freedom and truth is broken when a person tries to determine what is right and wrong according to his likes and dislikes.

> **In this way the inescapable claims of truth disappear, yielding their place to a criterion of sincerity, authenticity and "being at peace with oneself," so much so that some have come to adopt a radically subjectivistic conception of moral judgment.[10]**

c. FREEDOM AND THE GOOD

Human freedom is ordered toward good and not evil. One never loses the capability to make choices, but the habit of making correct moral choices is necessary for freedom to function. Doing evil is not freedom, nor a part of freedom, but only a sign that we have the capability to choose. In fact, freedom is not rooted in the physical ability to do evil, but in the moral duty to do the good. A teacher, for example, has the physical ability to insult a student, but he ought not to do so. A strong student can abuse a weaker one, but he ought not to do so. We all have the physical ability to do a great number of morally objectionable things, but we have the moral duty to avoid them.

Man gains such dignity when, ridding himself of all slavery to the passions, he presses forward towards his goal by freely choosing what is good.

It is, however, only in freedom that man can turn himself towards what is good. The people of our time prize freedom very highly and strive eagerly for it. In this they are right. Yet they often cherish it improperly, as if it gave them leave to do anything they like, even when it is evil. But that which is truly freedom is an exceptional sign of the image of God in man. For God willed that man should "be left in the hand of his own counsel" so that he might of his own accord seek his creator and freely attain his full and blessed perfection by cleaving to him. Man's dignity therefore requires him to act out of conscious and free choice, as moved and drawn in a personal way from within, and not by blind impulses in himself or by mere external constraint. Man gains such dignity when, ridding himself of all slavery to the passions, he presses forward towards his goal by freely choosing what is good, and, by his diligence and skill, effectively secures for himself the means suited to this end. Since human freedom has been weakened by sin it is only by the help of God's grace that man can give his actions their full and proper relationship to God. Before the judgment seat of God an account of his own life will be rendered to each one according as he has done either good or evil.[11]

Thus, a person increases his freedom when he rejects evil and does good. On the contrary, evil enslaves. This is the meaning of St. Paul's words: "Do you not know that if you yield yourselves to any one as obedient slaves, you are slaves of the one whom you obey, either of sin, which leads to death, or of obedience, which leads to righteousness?" (Rom 6:16).

To understand freedom as the right to do evil is to set it on the wrong path of caprice, passions, and vain desires. This approach leads to the destruction of freedom and man becomes similar to animals by following his instincts.

The intimate relationship between freedom and truth is reiterated by the *Catechism:*

> The more one does what is good, the freer one becomes. There is no true freedom except in the service of what is good and just. The choice to disobey and do evil is an abuse of freedom and leads to 'the slavery of sin.' (CCC 1734)

The more one does what is good, the freer one becomes.

d. FREEDOM AND RESPONSIBILITY

Each person is responsible for his actions and their consequences, and society responds according to what those actions merit. There is no such thing as a freedom that is independent of responsibility. The way to acquire and grow in freedom is by exercising responsibility.

> Freedom makes man *responsible* for his acts to the extent that they are voluntary. Progress in virtue, knowledge of the good, and ascesis [rigorous self-discipline] enhance the mastery of the will over its acts. (CCC 1734)

> Some of you listening to me have known me for a long time. You can bear out that I have spent my whole life preaching personal freedom, with personal responsibility. I have sought freedom throughout the world and I'm still looking for it, just like Diogenes trying to find an honest man. And every day I love it more. Of all the things on earth, I love it most. It is a treasure which we do not appreciate nearly enough.[12]

We cannot blame God for the human evils that find their origins in the abuse of freedom.

e. GOD'S RESPECT OF HUMAN FREEDOM

God will not destroy the freedom of the individual, because to do so would reduce that person to the level of an animal. Therefore, we cannot blame God for the human evils that find their origins in the abuse of freedom. War, hunger, crime, drugs, AIDS—none of these are desired by God. It is obvious that the abuse of human freedom is to blame.

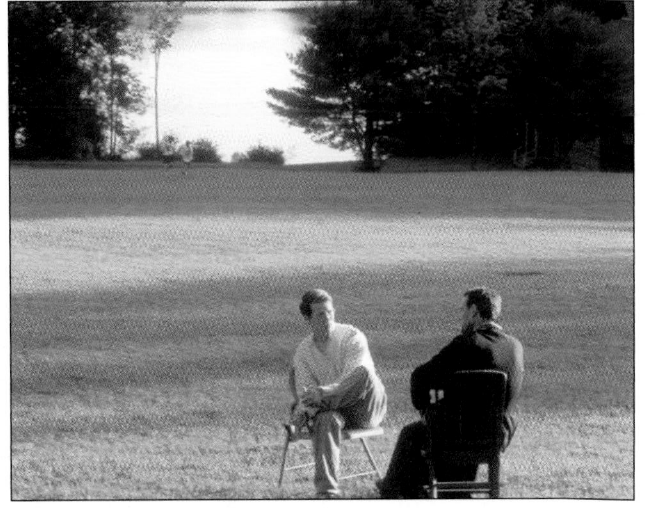

Our freedom is limited and capable of error. In fact, mankind has failed. Adam freely committed the original sin. By refusing God's love, he deceived himself and became a slave to sin. This first alienation engendered a multitude of others, first in the family and then in society. From its outset, human history attests to the wretchedness and oppression born of the human heart as a consequence of the abuse of freedom.

f. FREEDOM AND DIVINE GRACE

All of the aid that God offers to us does not diminish our freedom. Rather, it helps us to see the truth more clearly, and it gives us the required strength to conquer our passions. The proper use of freedom enables a person to gradually align his will with God's. So, the Christian who habitually makes correct moral choices—contrary to many people's opinions—is more able to make correct moral choices than the person who lives by his instincts or desires:

> The grace of Christ is not in the slightest way a rival of our freedom when this freedom accords with the sense of the true and the good that God has put in the human heart. On the contrary, as Christian experience attests especially in prayer, the more docile we are to the promptings of grace, the more we grow in inner freedom and confidence during trials, such as those we face in the pressures and constraints of the outer world. By the working of grace the Holy Spirit educates us in spiritual freedom in order to make us free collaborators in his work in the Church and in the world.
> (CCC 1742)

When conscience is correctly formed, one sees the true harmony between morally binding laws and his freedom.

g. FREEDOM AND LAW

Freedom is the power that a person has over his own acts. This power can be exercised only to the extent that correct moral choices have been made habitually. Consequently, freedom should not be used to form a neutral attitude in regard to moral choices. On the contrary, freedom ought to demand what conforms to the divine will.

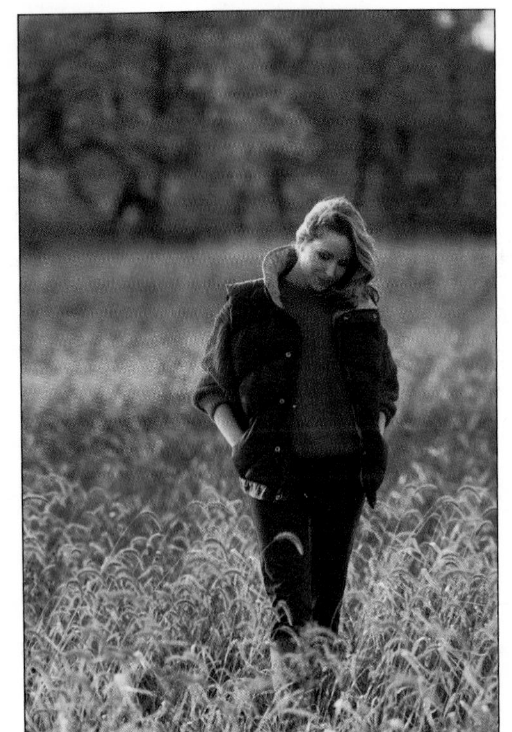

Freedom and law cannot truly oppose one another. When conscience is correctly formed, one sees the true harmony between morally binding laws and his freedom. Freedom therefore presupposes—and even demands—the law of God. As Pope John Paul II taught:

> **God's law does not reduce, much less do away with human freedom; rather, it protects and promotes that freedom. In contrast, however, some present-day cultural tendencies have given rise to several currents of thought in ethics which center upon an alleged conflict between freedom and law. These doctrines would grant to individuals or social groups the right to determine what is good or evil. Human freedom would thus be able to "create values" and would enjoy a primacy over truth, to the point that truth itself would be considered a creation of freedom. Freedom would thus lay claim to a moral autonomy which would actually amount to an absolute sovereignty.**[13]

The key to freedom is prudence, which is the ability to make and carry out correct moral decisions. To be free, we must plan to make the correct choices and carry them through. At the end of each day, one must examine his conscience to understand the results of all his moral choices and eliminate those that led to sin.

At the end of each day, one must examine his conscience to understand the results of all his moral choices and eliminate those that led to sin.

6. MAN IS RESPONSIBLE FOR THE GOOD OR EVIL OF HIS FREE ACTS

For an act to be good or evil, there needs to be knowledge and consent: Only an act that results from consent and freedom can be called a moral act. Ordinarily, this is easy to see. However, situations occur where it is difficult to determine whether true freedom is present.

CONCLUSION

Free will—which is our power to choose between different alternatives, our power to say yes or no—characterizes mankind and forms the basis of his dignity, enabling him to bear personal responsibility. The human being is free and responsible because he can choose. It is evident that to the extent to which a person has no real choice, he is not free. He is free only when he can choose this or that, when he can say yes or no. If he can only say yes, he is not free.

In addition, some of our choices aid our development, while some thwart our growth. We are not static personalities, but are changing all the time, whether we want it or not, or like it or not. In part, circumstances force us to change, but what fundamentally affects our changing personalities are our own free choices—whether we say yes when we should have said no, whether we say no when we should have said yes.

We are like people who are constantly on the road, coming to crossroads all the time and choosing. Therefore, it is important to know what sort of things one chooses, and how they affect one's own development as a person. Choices, like roads, are not indifferent. They always lead you somewhere—either toward the destination or away from it.

Is a person less free because he accepts restrictions? Not all restrictions necessarily involve a loss of freedom. Certain restrictions are in fact a safeguard of freedom. One may accept them because he is personally convinced that they help to make or keep him free, and he is also convinced that if he does not observe them, he could lose his freedom.

A road is a restriction. It has a certain paved width; it has curves and guardrails. But the person who suddenly decides he will no longer be a "slave" to these restrictions and who, instead of following the next curve, drives straight on, will probably find that his "freedom" leaves him at the bottom of a ditch or wrapped around the nearest tree.

> **The kingdom of Christ is a kingdom of freedom. In it the only slaves are those who freely bind themselves, out of love of God. What a blessed slavery of love, that sets us free! Without freedom, we cannot respond to grace. Without freedom, we cannot give ourselves freely to our Lord, for the most supernatural of reasons, because we want to.**[14]

"The kingdom of Christ is a kingdom of freedom. In it the only slaves are those who freely bind themselves, out of love of God."

— St. Josemaría Escrivá

VOCABULARY

ACTS OF A HUMAN
Acts accomplished without knowledge or deliberation.

ASCESIS
Rigorous self-discipline.

FREEDOM
The power a person has over his own acts.

FULL KNOWLEDGE
The clear and deliberate knowledge of the merit or sinfulness of an action. It is required as a condition before a person can be guilty of sin.

HUMAN ACT
An act that is performed with both *knowledge* and *free will.* Human acts, depending upon the degree of knowledge and freedom involved in their commission, are either morally good or morally evil.

IGNORANCE
The lack of required knowledge.

INDIFFERENT ACTS
Actions which have no moral value in themselves, but depend on the intention of the agent and the circumstances that surround them for their moral value.

INDIRECT RESPONSIBILITY
The attribution of the effect that secondarily follows a free act.

PARTIAL KNOWLEDGE
Knowledge that is obscured by the presence of some obstacle interfering with a moral judgment.

PRUDENCE
The ability to make and carry out correct moral decisions.

RESPONSIBILITY
The demand for an account of one's acts before oneself and before a superior authority; it includes accepting the consequences of one's actions.

VIOLENCE (external)
The coercion of an external force against a person's will.

SUPPLEMENTARY READINGS

1. I deny that freedom exists at all. I must deny it—or my program would be absurd. You can't have a science about a subject matter which hops capriciously about. Perhaps we can never prove that man isn't free; it's an assumption. But the increasing success of a science of behavior makes it more and more plausible.

— B. F. Skinner, *Walden Two*, p. 257

2. Yes. Free choice is inescapable. We are "condemned to freedom," as Sartre put it.

Why the negative language ("condemned")? Because there is something in us that fears freedom. If we are free, we are responsible. We can't pass the buck to others and blame our society, or our parents, or the government. Our problem is laziness....

...Most people love freedom when it means being able to do whatever they feel like doing. But they don't love freedom when it means the responsibility of making moral choices and living with the results. Freedom is not easy. But today we want everything to be easy. That's why our political freedom is currently in great danger. Freedom is not in danger in places like Poland today, because it is not easy there. Poles know the value of freedom. They had to struggle for it, and pay for it.

But whether or not we have political freedom, everyone has moral freedom. Every human being has the free will to choose between good and evil, and the responsibility to do so. That's essential to human nature. That's why we are all "condemned to freedom."

— Peter Kreeft, *Making Choices: Practical Wisdom for Everyday Moral Decisions*, pp. 13-14

3. A certain type of man feels, on every conceivable occasion, that his rights are threatened, or trespassed upon. He always keeps on his guard lest some impairment of his rights should escape his attention. Dominated by his fear of such an injury or encroachment, he seldom stops to consider whether a thing is valuable in itself or not, whether it glorifies God or offends him. Hence, his vision of various situations is obscured; his capacity of adequate judgment is blunted. He is incapable of a free, unwarped response to values. In his mind, the theme of his rights overshadows the question of the objective value involved; thus, instead of a disinterested love of truth and of right he is likely to develop a bitter and cantankerous attitude. Indeed, his inordinate insistence on his rights may sometimes tempt him to ride roughshod over those of others. Such people, in their cramped egoism, are as far remote from true freedom as it is possible to be.

— Dietrich von Hildebrand, *Transformation in Christ*, p. 207

"Every human being has the free will to choose between good and evil..."

QUESTIONS

1. Why is it that only human beings and not animals are able to act morally?

2. What are the rational principles of the moral life?

3. What is the rational and definitive principle of the moral life?

4. Why is man morally responsible for his acts?

5. What does moral theology teach?

6. When is an action a truly human act?

7. Why are human acts also moral acts?

8. Give three examples of "acts of a human."

9. What is the first requirement of a moral act?

10. What two things does full knowledge presume?

11. What is mankind's greatest quality?

12. Where are good and evil forged?

13. Toward what end do the highest levels of human freedom lead?

14. Is freedom limited? Give two examples.

15. What is the purpose of the freedom we have?

16. Upon what does freedom fundamentally depend?

17. What is the effect of evil?

18. Does the grace offered to us by God diminish our freedom? Explain your answer.

19. Why is prudence essential to the Catholic idea of freedom?

20. How does one acquire prudence?

PRACTICAL EXERCISES

1. Explain St. Paul's understanding of human freedom as evidenced in the following passages of Scripture:

- Rom 6:11-23; 7:2-12; 8:1-5
- Gal 4:21-23

2. Improper use of the will can lead to licentiousness—an excessive enjoyment of sense pleasures that respects no moral precepts or standards. Explain the significance of the following scriptural texts, which address this danger:

- Rom 6:15
- 1 Cor 6:12; 10:23
- Gal 5:13

3. Are you convinced by Skinner's arguments in Supplementary Reading 1 that deny human freedom? Why or why not? What arguments can be used to refute Skinner?

4. According to Supplementary Reading 3, what concerns ought to be of greater importance to someone than just "his rights"?

5. Of what kind of freedom is Saint Josemaría Escrivá speaking in the quotation contained in the conclusion to this chapter? What does he mean when he speaks of that "blessed slavery of love, that sets us free"?

6. To what degree does God respect our freedom as human beings? Are there ever instances in which he will act directly to interfere with a person's freedom? Why or why not? Do you ever wish that God would act differently? What would be the positive and negative consequences of his doing so?

FROM THE CATECHISM

1744 Freedom is the power to act or not to act, and so to perform deliberate acts of one's own. Freedom attains perfection in its acts when directed toward God, the sovereign Good.

1745 Freedom characterizes properly human acts. It makes the human being responsible for acts of which he is the voluntary agent. His deliberate acts properly belong to him.

1747 The right to the exercise of freedom, especially in religious and moral matters, is an inalienable requirement of the dignity of man. But the exercise of freedom does not entail the putative right to say or do anything.

1748 "For freedom Christ has set us free" (Gal 5:1).

1760 A morally good act requires the goodness of its object, of its end, and of its circumstances together.

2017 The grace of the Holy Spirit confers upon us the righteousness of God. Uniting us by faith and Baptism to the Passion and Resurrection of Christ, the Spirit makes us sharers in his life.

ENDNOTES

1. Cf. CCC, 1700ff.
2. Plato, *Republic,* I, 352d.
3. Aristotle, *Politics,* 1, 2.
4. Cf. *VS,* 8.
5. Ibid., 71.
6. Cf. *VS,* 32.
7. Ibid., 33.
8. Ibid., 86.
9. Ibid., 84.
10. Ibid., 32.
11. *GS,* 17.
12. St. Josemaría Escrivá, *Christ is Passing By,* 184.
13. *VS,* 35.
14. St. Josemaría Escrivá, *Christ is Passing By,* 184.

Chapter 4

The Moral Conscience

In the following passage of Scripture, the prophet Nathan confronts King David. King David had committed adultery with Bathsheba, the wife of Uriah the Hittite, who was a soldier in the King's army. In order to conceal his sin and take Bathsheba as his wife, the king had arranged for Uriah to be sent to the front line of battle on a suicide mission, thus adding murder to his sin of adultery:

And the Lord sent Nathan to David. He came to him, and said to him, "There were two men in a certain city, the one rich and the other poor. The rich man had very many flocks and herds; but the poor man had nothing but one little ewe lamb, which he had bought. And he brought it up, and it grew up with him and with his children; it used to eat of his morsel, and drink from his cup, and lie in his bosom, and it was like a daughter to him. Now there came a traveler to the rich man, and he was unwilling to take one of his own flock or herd to prepare for the wayfarer who had come to him, but he took the poor man's lamb, and prepared it for the man who had come to him." Then David's anger was greatly kindled against the man; and he said to Nathan, "As the Lord lives, the man who has done this deserves to die; and he shall restore the lamb fourfold, because he did this thing, and because he had no pity."

Nathan said to David, "You are the man. Thus says the Lord, the God of Israel, 'I anointed you king over Israel, and I delivered you out of the hand of Saul; and I gave you your master's house, and your master's wives into your bosom, and gave you the house of Israel and of Judah; and if this were too little, I would add to you as much more. Why have you despised the word of the Lord, to do what is evil in his sight? You have smitten Uriah the Hittite with the sword, and have taken his wife to be your wife, and have slain him with the sword of the Ammonites. Now therefore the sword shall never depart from your house, because you have despised me, and have taken the wife of Uriah the Hittite to be your wife.' Thus says the Lord, 'Behold, I will raise up evil against you out of your own house; and I will take your wives before your eyes, and give them to your neighbor, and he shall lie with your wives in the sight of this sun. For you did it secretly; but I will do this thing before all Israel, and before the sun.'"

David said to Nathan, "I have sinned against the Lord." And Nathan said to David, "The Lord also has put away your sin; you shall not die." (2 Sm 12:1-13)

In light of this reading, let us ask ourselves the following:

- What is conscience?
- How does conscience aid the person who seeks to live a truly Christ-like life?
- How does a person develop his conscience so that he can be confident of its judgments?

The conscience is considered sacred, for in it God speaks to us.

INTRODUCTION

"The soul of the soul is conscience."
— Origen

The concept of *conscience* is fundamental to Catholic theology because a person, in all his actions, ought to conform his conscience to the will of God. Even popular wisdom often equates one's value with his conscience. Thus, the most negative judgment passed on a person's character is "That person has no conscience," or even worse, "He has a perverted conscience." Both cases illustrate the value of conscience. The uprightness of one's conscience determines the degree of one's moral perfection.

It is also noticeable how often people appeal to their personal consciences: "I ask that my conscience be respected," "Your conscience may say this is wrong, but my conscience tells me it's all right;" "My conscience allows me to do this." We defend and protect it when someone tries to violate decisions made "in good conscience." Thus, society defends "freedom of conscience." There is a general recognition that conscience exists, but there is no agreement on what it is or how it functions.

In the Christian tradition, conscience receives the highest respect. The Fathers of the Church call it "the spark of the Holy Spirit," "the sacredness of man," and "the sanctuary of God." It is considered sacred, for in it God speaks to us. Origen affirms that conscience is the quintessence of the spirit of man ("the soul of the soul is conscience") and he assures that it can be seen as "a corrective spirit and teacher of man" (cf. Supplementary Readings).

Legal recognition of conscientious objection is necessary in modern times because civil law sometimes permits and even requires morally evil actions. A society is said to be just when its laws defend the freedom of right conscience of each of its citizens, within due limits.

1. WHAT IS CONSCIENCE?

Conscience is not a feeling, nor a theoretical judgment on whether something is good or evil, but a practical judgment: *It judges whether a particular act is right or wrong from an ethical point of view.*

> Conscience is a judgment of reason whereby the human person recognizes the moral quality of a concrete act that he is going to perform, is in the process of performing, or has already completed. (CCC 1778)

Conscience is capable of judging moral and immoral situations, so it is capable of judging *concrete acts.* Its purpose is to evaluate whether or not a particular act is good or evil, and to advise accordingly. Since it is a *judgment of reason,* it must be made with the intellect. Thus, a person is held responsible for what he does, since he knows the good and evil involved.

His conscience is man's most secret core, and his sanctuary. There he is alone with God whose voice echoes in his depths.

> According to Saint Paul, conscience in a certain sense confronts man with the law, and thus becomes a "witness" for man: a witness of his faithfulness or unfaithfulness with regard to the law, and of his essential moral rectitude or iniquity. Conscience is the only witness, since what takes place in the heart of a person is hidden from the eyes of everyone outside. Conscience makes its witness known only to the person himself. And, in turn, only the person himself knows what his own response is to the voice of conscience.[1]

The new life brought about through Baptism gives special light to the conscience. The new Christian receives special graces that help him understand and live the moral demands of Christian life. This can be seen with regard to two of these graces, as outlined in Chapter 5: the ability to interpret the natural law and, above all, the ability to know and fulfill the requirements that the "life in Christ" demands. This is the "New Law," which the Holy Spirit communicates to the baptized, with the hope that they may be able to realize their specifically Christian life.[2]

> His conscience is man's most secret core, and his sanctuary. There he is alone with God whose voice echoes in his depths. By conscience, in a wonderful way, that law is made known which is fulfilled in the love of God and of one's neighbor. Through loyalty to conscience Christians are joined to other men in the search for truth and for the right solution to so many moral problems which arise both in the life of individuals and from social relationships. Hence, the more a correct conscience prevails, the more do persons and groups turn aside from blind choice and try to be guided by the objective standards of moral conduct. Yet it often happens that conscience goes astray through ignorance which it is unable to avoid, without thereby losing its dignity. This cannot be said of the man who takes little trouble to find out what is true and good, or when conscience is by degrees almost blinded through the habit of committing sin.[3]

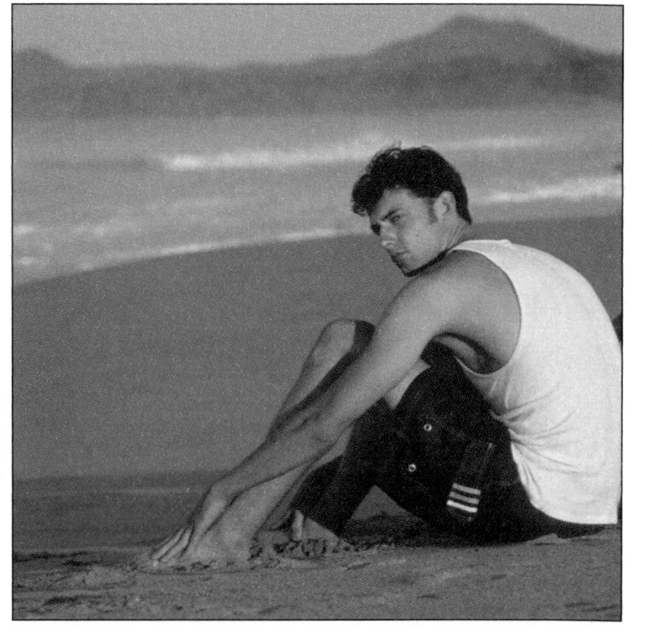

The formation of conscience is a continuing lifelong process.

2. CONSCIENCE AND TRUTH

Conscience is rooted in the truth—the truth about mankind, law, and what is good and evil. Because truth is prior to conscience, conscience must respect truth. When fundamental truths are ignored, there is error in practical judgments. That is, the conscience will make false judgments when it fails to acknowledge the truth about things. John Paul II stated that "Ethical Goodness is only another name for the truth, when it is sought by the practical intellect. One cannot obscure or harm the practical dimension of the truth without, to a large extent, injuring its theoretical aspects."[4]

Veritatis splendor shows why conscience is subordinate to truth:

> As is immediately evident, the crisis of truth is not unconnected with this development. Once the idea of a universal truth about the good, knowable by human reason, is lost, inevitably the notion of conscience also changes. Conscience is no longer considered in its primordial reality as an act of a person's intelligence, the function of which is to apply the universal knowledge of the good in a specific situation and thus to express a judgment about the right conduct to be chosen here and now. Instead, there is a tendency to grant to the individual conscience the prerogative of independently determining the criteria of good and evil and then acting accordingly. Such an outlook is quite congenial to an individualistic ethic, wherein each individual is faced with his own truth, different from the truth of others. Taken to its extreme consequences, this individualism leads to a denial of the very idea of human nature.[5]

Therefore, conscience ought to freely embrace truth since truth is a permanent light, which never fades away. Conscience shares an innate capacity to come to the truth. Insofar as a person has the use of reason, he can discern good from evil. Conscience is an inextinguishable light that is given to us by God as part of our human nature. Thus, there is an obligation to follow our judgment when truth is present.

It is a serious obligation to form one's conscience according to the teaching of the Magisterium.

3. THE FORMATION OF CONSCIENCE

Because a sound conscience is necessary in order to make correct moral judgments, every human has the obligation to correctly form his conscience. The word *conscience* is derived from the Latin *cum scientia*, which means "with knowledge."

Keep in mind that children are born without knowledge of good and evil. These concepts are acquired through education and built upon by reason, which elaborates on them by the natural law and, above all, by instruction in the truths of the faith, the grace of the Holy Spirit, and Christian reflection. In fact, just as individuals are born without knowledge but acquire it throughout life, ideas about good and evil are acquired in the same manner.

Nonetheless, just as the child who has been born without ideas has a great capacity to acquire them via reason, so too conscience is present as a capacity of the mind, an inextinguishable light that enables one to acquire moral concepts. The formation of conscience is a continuing lifelong process.

Furthermore, a child's reason takes its knowledge from different sources, such as people (parents, teachers), personal experience (he learns that fire burns by its effects), and theoretical reflection (the intellectual life).

Similarly, then, the child—with the natural law that God has planted in his heart—builds his moral criteria. This occurs because he is taught by his parents and teachers, or because good and evil resonate within himself, or by his reflection on the natural law; but above all because the Spirit assists him in finding the internal law given at Baptism.

Personal prayer, on a daily basis, brings us closer to God and develops a relationship with Jesus called the interior life.

4. MEANS TO THE FORMATION OF CONSCIENCE

There are specific means to forming a right conscience that are similar to those used in the education of the intellect.[6]

a. ACCEPTANCE OF MORAL TEACHING

A child needs to be docile to the moral lessons being communicated to him by his parents and teachers, and a Catholic adult needs to be attentive to the moral teaching being offered by the Magisterium. It is a serious obligation to form one's conscience according to the teaching of the Magisterium. The Church possesses the fullness of truth, and one is guilty of sin if he ignores or refuses to accept the truth.

b. KNOWLEDGE OF THE CHRISTIAN LIFE AND DOCTRINE

Every Catholic has an obligation to seek the truth in moral matters from the teaching of the Church. To form a right conscience, one must configure his moral criteria to the Christian moral life, which is transmitted by the teaching of the Bible and Tradition as defined by the Magisterium. This obligation does not end with the conclusion of formal education.

> [T]he highest norm of human life is the divine law itself—eternal, objective and universal, by which God orders, directs and governs the whole world and the ways of the human community according to a plan conceived in his wisdom and love. God has enabled man to participate in this law of his so that, under the gentle disposition of divine providence, many may be able to arrive at a deeper and deeper knowledge of unchangeable truth. For this reason everybody has the duty and consequently the right to seek the truth in religious matters so that, through the use of appropriate means, he may prudently form judgments of conscience which are sincere and true.[7]

c. PRAYER AND MEDITATION

It is important to attend to the dictates of one's conscience, and to carefully consider particular moral choices in our prayer. Prayer, in all its forms (worship, petition, thanksgiving), consists of a conversation with God in which he communicates his will, which should be the basis of our practical

judgments. Personal prayer, on a daily basis, brings us closer to God and develops a relationship with Jesus called the interior life. Through interior life, in concert with direction by our confessor, we can be assured that our consciences will remain well formed and in conformity with the truth.

Faced with a moral choice, conscience can make either a right judgment in accordance with reason and the divine law or, on the contrary, an erroneous judgment that departs from them. (CCC 1799)

d. PERSONAL EXAMINATION

The best means of *internalizing* one's actions is an examination of conscience. Just as intellectual objectivity is reached by critical intellectual evaluation (examination), so can moral rightness be accomplished by a serious examination of conscience. An essential result of the *examen* is the practice of *sacramental confession.* In the academic world, there is a preference for comprehensive examinations over simple tests; the same would hold true for the moral life (conscience), where Confession and the *examen* are seen as a more complete form of moral examination than mere contemplation.

e. SPIRITUAL DIRECTION

Moral rightness can be accomplished by a serious examination of conscience.

Finally, a person's conscience can acquire a more objective moral judgment when he enters into dialogue with another person who helps him overcome subjectivism or impulse. Just as the student gains deeper insight by consulting with his professor, the person who sees a spiritual director can reach a higher degree of moral rectitude. This is most easily done by speaking with our confessor during the sacrament of Penance.

5. DIVISIONS OF CONSCIENCE

A judgment of conscience can be:

- *antecedent,* which precedes action. Before acting, one deliberates and concludes that an action is good or evil;
- *concomitant,* which accompanies the action as it takes place. If a person concomitantly judges an act to be sinful, he is required to cease the action to the extent possible; and
- *consequent,* which follows the act.

Conscience is understood in relation to the law that it seeks to fulfill. Therefore, one can distinguish between:

- *true (correct) conscience,* which deduces correctly from true principles that some act is lawful. For example, the eighth commandment forbids lies, and one's conscience judges truly when he is convinced that it is never permissible to tell falsehoods to someone who deserves to know the truth.

- *erroneous conscience*, which decides from false principles *considered as true* that something is lawful which in fact is unlawful. When a person does not know what the moral law requires, his ignorance is either *vincible* or *invincible*.
    - *Vincible ignorance* is ignorance of the truth that can be overcome by ordinary diligence. It results from a person's failure to find out what is required of him. It is important to note that if the ignorance is the result of neglect (a failure to discover the truth because of laziness or disinterest), there is a risk of committing a sin.
    - *Invincible ignorance* is ignorance that cannot be overcome by ordinary diligence. It is ignorance of the moral law that is not the fault of the person acting, because he has no reasonable way to know the truth. One who acts with invincible ignorance does not sin if he has taken the necessary and reasonable steps to learn what is permitted and prohibited.

Remember that conscience is not an infallible guide; there is always the possibility of error in one's judgments.

Conscience can also be adversely affected by the will:

- A *scrupulous conscience* is one that, for little or no reason, judges an action to be morally evil when in fact it is not. The direction of a confessor is required to overcome this difficulty.
- A *lax conscience* formulates moral judgments on insufficient grounds. It judges mortal sins as venial and venial sins as no sins at all. Frequent use of the Sacrament of Reconciliation is a protection against this type of conscience.

Remember that conscience is not an infallible guide; there is always the possibility of error in one's judgments. Therefore, in order to act "in good conscience," one must first seek to know what is truly good. The person who has become blind to the truth through habitual sin, or who refuses to seek what is good, is culpable for the evil of his actions, because his ignorance is vincible.

6. ACTING ALWAYS WITH RIGHT CONSCIENCE

One is obligated to follow his conscience. When he is in error, his personal freedom to choose must be acknowledged. Vatican Council II speaks thus, regarding an erroneous conscience:

> **It is through his conscience that man sees and recognizes the demands of the divine law. He is bound to follow this conscience faithfully in all his activity so that he may come to God, who is his last end. Therefore he must not be forced to act contrary to his conscience. Nor must he be prevented from acting according to his conscience, especially in religious matters.**[8]

Since conscience is the instrument with which one must judge his actions, such judgment should always be made with a true or correct conscience. This requires knowledge of the general principles of morality and their application, by conscience, to concrete acts.

It is wrong to make judgments without knowledge of the law or its precepts.

> The dignity of the human person implies and requires *uprightness of moral conscience.* Conscience includes the perception of the principles of morality (synderesis); their application in the given circumstances by practical discernment of reasons and goods; and finally judgment about concrete acts yet to be performed or already performed. (CCC 1780)

Conduct that is modeled on right principles, then, is needed to overcome ignorance, since it is wrong to make judgments without knowledge of the law or its precepts.[9] A person may never act when his conscience is in doubt. In a case of doubtful conscience, one is required to determine the good or evil of a particular choice before acting.

Nevertheless, in rare cases, a person is obligated to act immediately. In this circumstance, since he is unable to secure an informed moral judgment, he may do what he believes would correspond with God's will. To act rightly in this circumstance, he needs to be conscious of the following:

- Evil means never justify good ends.
- Love for God and neighbor overrides any other consideration.
- We should act toward others as we would like them to act toward us.[10]

Conscience always obliges in the name of God. God wants us to follow his law, so conscience is obliged to follow the divine will. Even an invincible erroneous conscience does not give us an exception: In this case, conscience desires an evil, because it judges it to be a good and hopes to fulfill God's will. This capacity to err is one more reason to form our consciences correctly.

In the New Testament, the term conscience is mentioned 30 times in reference to the need for proper behavior.

7. THE BIBLE'S APPEAL TO OUR CONSCIENCE

The existence of conscience, besides having rational proofs, is also found in revelation. In fact, the Old Testament states that God seeks our conscience: "He searches out the abyss, and the hearts of men" (Sir 42:18). It teaches that the wicked person, "distressed by conscience...has always exaggerated the difficulties" (Wis 17:11). Moreover, according to Eastern perceptiveness, the Old Testament stresses the intimacy of conscience to the point of identifying it with the *heart*. So it counsels: "Let not loyalty and faithfulness forsake you; bind them about your neck, write them on the tablet of your heart" (Prv 3:3).

In the New Testament, the term *conscience* is mentioned thirty times in reference to the need for proper behavior. St. Paul blames the pagans for all their corruption, as "their conscience also bears witness" (Rom 2:15), and encourages the Christians to carry out good conduct, "not only to avoid God's wrath but also for the sake of conscience" (Rom 13:5), for they will have to give an account to God for their conscience (cf. 2 Cor 4:2).

8. ARGUMENTS FOR THE EXISTENCE OF CONSCIENCE

The specific nature of the rational animal (man) includes conscience. In fact, an essential characteristic of the person is his capacity of reflection—that is, being conscious of his life and actions. This capacity is reflected in three ways:

Conscience does not keep silent, for it praises and reprimands; it exhorts and corrects; it incites and represses.

a. SENSE EXPERIENCE

A person is conscious of his own sensations of pleasure, pain, cold, heat, and so forth. Even at this primary level, there is a difference between people and animals. As the Spanish philosopher Zubiri writes: "The animal senses, but it does not sense itself." Only a human being has self-awareness.

In fact, self-reflection is exclusive and proper to the human being. Animals sense heat, cold, pleasure, pain, and even the care or rejection of their master, but they do not experience it reflectively, but only instinctively. Thus, the animal acts automatically and always avoids the unpleasant, mechanically acting out what it desires at the moment.

b. RATIONAL DISCERNMENT

One's capacity to reflect and inform his conscience is not exhausted by his sensations; rather, it exists on a higher intellectual level. Thus, when people are tempted to act hastily, they are warned of the need to reflect so that they can be conscious of what they should know or do. The term *intellectual conscience* is often used to describe this faculty.

c. MORAL REFLECTION

A person's reflection does not end in sensation or thought. Rather, it accompanies him in all his actions, so that before acting, he reflects on what he ought to do. Moreover, he is conscious at the very moment of his actions and, once he has acted, later reflects on the good or evil of his actions. That is, he realizes or becomes conscious of the good or evil involved in his acts.

Consequently, moral reflection in ethical behavior is as real as sense experience or rational discernment. If an attempt is made to deny its existence, the other two will also have to be denied. Thus, the denial of moral reflection is impossible, absurd and dehumanizing, for it would destroy that which makes a person human.

Conscience is the only witness, since what takes place in the heart of the person is hidden from the eyes of everyone outside.

In fact, anyone can experience for himself that his actions are not indifferent but are always valued. In this regard, it is confirmed that conscience does not keep silent, for it praises and reprimands; it exhorts and corrects; it incites and represses.

According to Saint Paul, conscience in a certain sense confronts each of us with the law, and thus becomes a "witness" for us: a witness of our own faithfulness and unfaithfulness with regard to the law, of our essential moral rectitude or iniquity. Conscience is the only witness, since what takes place in the heart of the person is hidden from the eyes of everyone outside.

Conscience makes its witness known only to the person himself. And, in turn, only the person himself knows what his own response is to the voice of conscience.

The importance of this interior dialog of man with himself can never be adequately appreciated. But it is also a dialog of man with God, the author of the law, the primordial image and final end of man.... "Moral conscience does not close man within an insurmountable and impenetrable solitude, but opens him to the call, to the voice of God. In this, and not in anything else, lies the entire mystery and the dignity of the moral conscience: in being the place, the sacred place where God speaks to man" (General Audience, August 17, 1983).[11]

This fact shows that conscience exists, and that it is never a mute witness. Rather, it is present in all of our actions. Occasionally (particularly before grave acts), it presents itself in a strong fashion, for it is said to "bite back," almost as if the evil conduct would turn back aggressively on the agent.

Conscience does not create law; rather, it finds law and takes it as a guide.

9. CONSCIENCE AND LAW

Both in theory and in reality, there can be confrontations between conscience and law. They can occur because both elements are involved in morality, and a synthesis is needed. In our own time, there is noticeable conflict because the previous age was characterized by a sometimes excessive stress on law, while the current age overemphasizes personal conscience, which is often confused with "feelings." When these two positions are taken to their respective extremes, they give rise to two opposing positions that are not easy to harmonize.[12]

If moral value is found solely in strict adherence to law, then what we have is a normative ethics, an excessive rule of laws and imperatives, where little room is left for conscience to judge. On the other hand, if conscience is overemphasized without regard for the law, then there is the risk of falling into moral subjectivism, where the conscience of the individual becomes the only moral judge.

In certain circumstances, this contrast of opinions reaches its extreme, creating two moral paths: an *autonomous* morality and a *heteronomous* morality. The first treats conscience as the only moral authority, and professes an autonomy of mankind before any law. The latter enslaves conscience to an absolute dependence on norms. In fact, conscience and norm ought to assist one another in a *participatory theonomy,* which means that all decisions are made with a sense of God's presence.

Conscience serves as an *immediate norm of moral action,* so that the judgment of conscience is the immediate criterion for moral actions. But, at the same time, conscience does not create law; rather, it finds law and takes it as a guide. Conscience is neither autonomous nor exclusive in determining good and evil; on the contrary, in conscience, there is a deeply inscribed *principle of obedience*. Thus, conscience has traditionally been called a *normed norm*, that is, the rule for acting whose measure is prescribed by the law.[13]

The value of right conscience prevails over an unjust law.

Consequently, a continual confrontation between conscience and law is not the best way to understand the morality of our actions. Furthermore, divine natural laws are so intimately united to the proper being of each person that they have a very direct influence on the conscience. Positive law is made by those who have authority. A conflict may arise in relation to certain unjust laws made by civil authority, especially civil laws (such as those permitting abortion, euthanasia, etc.), but in such cases, the value of right conscience prevails over an unjust law.

The ultimate reason for this conflict is frequently rooted in a change in the law in modern society. Instead of defining law as an ordinance of reason—which is never in conflict with conscience—law is often seen as the arbitrary will of government or authority. Obedience to the law then becomes slavery.

Freedom of conscience is never freedom "from" the truth but always and only freedom "in" the truth.

10. DISTORTION AND DEGRADATION OF PERSONAL CONSCIENCE

"Conscience, as the judgment of an act, is not exempt from the possibility of error."[14] A person can also corrupt and distort his conscience in many ways and for many reasons. Although a substantial portion of errors stem from bad formation early in life, a right conscience can still corrupt itself at a later stage by many other causes. The most common causes are those mentioned in the *Catechism:*

> **Ignorance of Christ and his Gospel, bad example given by others, enslavement to one's passions, assertion of a mistaken notion of autonomy of conscience, rejection of the Church's authority and her teaching, lack of conversion and of charity: these can be at the source of errors of judgment in moral conduct. (CCC 1792)**

The risk of distortion of conscience—along with the degradation of personal conduct—demands from each person (especially the Christian) a concern for individual conduct. At the same time, it stresses the need to properly form one's conscience. In practice, a decisive way for the Christian to form his conscience is to follow the moral teachings of the Magisterium:

> **Christians have a great help for the formation of conscience in the Church and her Magisterium. As the Council affirms: "In forming their consciences the Christian faithful must give careful attention to the sacred and certain teaching of the Church [...]" (*DH*, 14). It follows that the authority of the Church, when she pronounces on moral questions, in no way undermines the freedom of conscience of Christians. This is so not only because freedom of conscience is never freedom**

The Church puts herself always and only at the service of conscience.

> "from" the truth but always and only freedom "in" the truth, but also because the Magisterium does not bring to the Christian conscience truths which are extraneous to it; rather it brings to light the truths which it ought already to possess, developing them from the starting point of the primordial act of faith. The Church puts herself always and only at the service of conscience, helping it to avoid being tossed to and fro by every wind of doctrine proposed by human deceit (cf. Eph 4:14), and helping it not to swerve from the truth about the good of man, but rather, especially in more difficult questions, to attain the truth with certainty and to abide in it.[15]

CONCLUSION

Conscience is the practical judgment of reason regarding the morality of an action that leads a person to perform the action or refrain from performing it. As a faculty of reason, conscience must humbly seek the truth, which is prior to it. Every person has the obligation to form his conscience according to the objective standards of good and evil that have been determined by God.

A properly formed conscience protects a person's dignity and the means necessary to reach happiness.

The highest ideal is to be faithful to right conscience, since this equals being faithful to God and to himself. A properly formed conscience protects a person's dignity and the means necessary to reach happiness. The pagan author and poet Horace states, "Our inviolable rule ought to be never to do anything that wounds our conscience or that makes us ashamed of ourselves." The Magisterium of the Church is the most certain guide to the will of God, and must be consulted in educating one's conscience.

As a way of life, the words of St. Paul are worth noting: "Brethren, I have lived before God in all good conscience up to this day" (Acts 23:1). The greatest happiness, according to classical thought, is to have a "clear conscience."

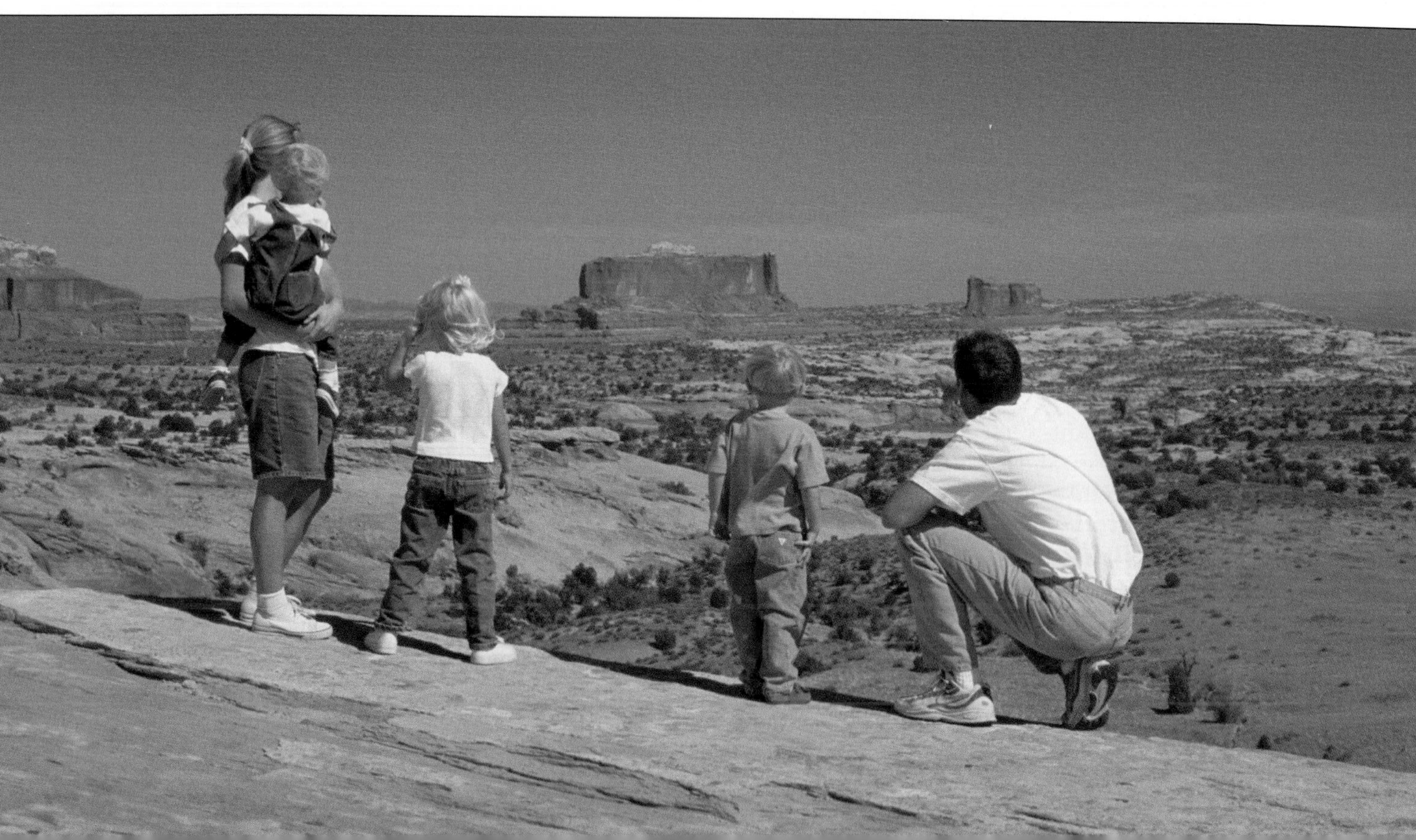

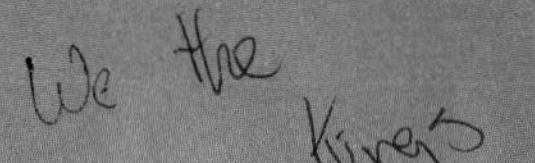

VOCABULARY

ANTECEDENT JUDGMENT OF CONSCIENCE
Judgment that precedes an action.

AUTONOMOUS MORALITY
The belief that conscience is the only moral authority.

CERTAIN CONSCIENCE
Conscience that issues a judgment in certainty that may or may not be correct.

CONCOMITANT JUDGMENT OF CONSCIENCE
Judgment that accompanies an action as it is taking place.

CONSCIENCE
Conscience is a judgment of reason whereby the human person recognizes the moral quality of a concrete act that he is going to perform, is in the process of performing, or has already completed.

CONSEQUENT JUDGMENT OF CONSCIENCE
Moral judgment made after the act.

DOUBTFUL CONSCIENCE
Judgment of conscience that occurs when there is doubt about the good or evil of an act done or omitted. Unless one is required to act immediately, man is required to determine the moral rectitude of an act before acting on a doubtful conscience (cf. CCC 1787-1789).

ERRONEOUS CONSCIENCE
A judgment of conscience that does not correspond with what the law or norm requires. The ignorance may be *vincible* or *invincible* when the content of the law is unknown. He who acts with *invincible ignorance* does not sin if he has taken the necessary steps to learn what is permitted and prohibited.

HETERONOMOUS MORALITY
Absolute dependence of conscience on laws.

INVINCIBLE IGNORANCE
Ignorance that cannot be overcome by ordinary diligence.

LAX CONSCIENCE
A conscience that formulates moral judgments on insufficient grounds. It judges mortal sins as venial and venial sins as no sins at all.

MORAL RECTITUDE
Correctness of method of judgment.

SCRUPULOUS CONSCIENCE
A conscience that judges an action to be morally evil when in fact it is not.

TRUE CONSCIENCE
Objectively coincides with the application of the moral law.

VINCIBLE IGNORANCE
Ignorance that can be overcome by ordinary diligence.

SUPPLEMENTARY READINGS

1. Conscience must be informed and moral judgment enlightened. A well-formed conscience is upright and truthful. It formulates its judgments according to reason, in conformity with the true good willed by the wisdom of the Creator. The education of conscience is indispensable for human beings who are subjected to negative influences and tempted by sin to prefer their own judgment and to reject authoritative teachings.

— CCC 1783

2. Conscience is a precious but delicate guide. Its voice is easily distorted or obscured. To dictate to conscience is to silence and, eventually, to destroy it. Conscience must be listened to and listened to sensitively. It needs to be interrogated, even to be cross-examined. And only those who habitually interrogate their conscience and are ready to pay heed even to its awkward answers, will not cheat their conscience or be cheated by it.

— Cormac Burke, *Conscience and Freedom*, 25

3. First of all, an indispensable condition is the rectitude and clarity of the penitent's conscience. People cannot come to true and genuine repentance until they recognize that sin is contrary to the ethical norm written in their innermost being; until they admit that they have a personal and responsible experience of this contrast; until they say not only that "sin exists" but also "I have sinned," until they admit that sin has introduced a division into their conscience which then pervades their whole being and separates them from God and from their brothers and sisters. The sacramental sign of this clarity of conscience is the act traditionally called the examination of conscience, an act that must never be one of anxious psychological introspection, but a sincere and calm comparison with the interior moral law, with the evangelical moral norms proposed by the Church, with Jesus Christ himself who is our Teacher and Model of life, and with the heavenly Father, who calls us to goodness and perfection.

— *RP*, 31

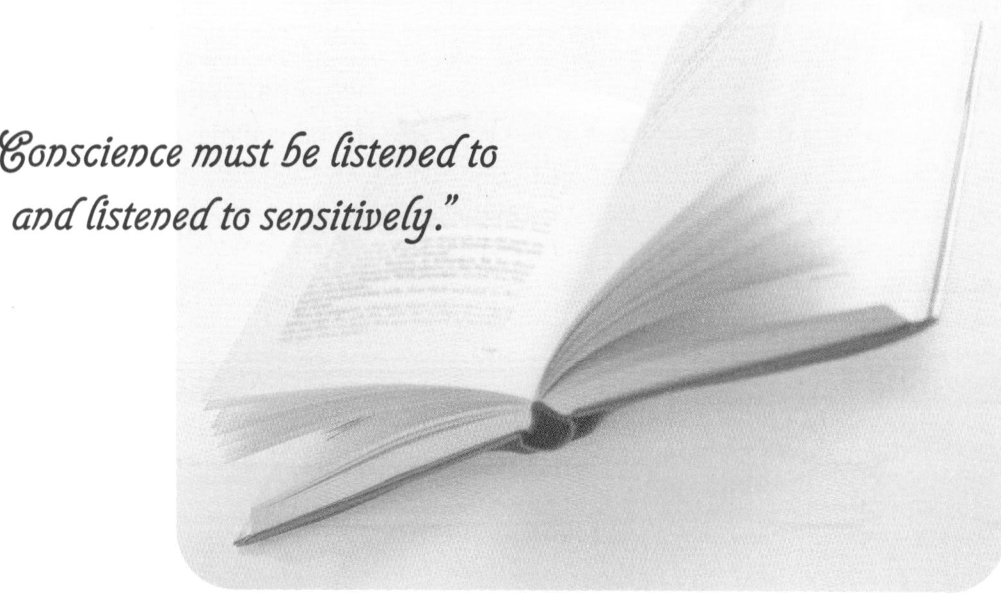

"Conscience must be listened to and listened to sensitively."

ADVANCED CONCEPTS

ADDITIONAL ARGUMENTS FOR THE EXISTENCE OF CONSCIENCE

Besides the arguments in this chapter, there are other ways to show that the human being is gifted with a moral conscience:

1. PROFOUND PERSONAL EXPERIENCE

Each person, in himself, experiences the voice of his conscience: conscience is the only witness. What occurs in the interior of the soul is hidden to those outside. Conscience directs its testimony toward only its owner. At the same time, only the person knows the proper response to the voice of conscience. Is anyone not aware of this invisible witness accompanying him? This fact, so intimately known, shows that conscience exists as a never-silent witness present in all our activity.

2. UNIVERSAL TESTIMONY

The universal agreement of all times, cultures, and religious expressions is that conscience is the precondition needed to judge human acts as good or evil.

The most diverse ethical trends speak of conscience as a type of radar that detects good and evil—what a person should do and avoid.

Present culture reflects the conviction noted above. The juridical acknowledgment of conscientious objection shows that conscience holds a high place in the modern notion of man's essence. It is seen as a fundamental right. In the end, those who pretend to deny conscience or imply that it is only a cultural prejudice of religion expose their own hypocrisy and a true lack of sincerity.

Jesus Christ is our Teacher and Model of life.

QUESTIONS

1. Why is our conscience sacred?

2. How does our conscience relate to the Catholic idea of freedom?

3. What are the means to forming a right conscience?

4. Why must conscience submit to the truth and the natural law?

5. When does conscience function?

6. What is a lax conscience?

7. What is a true or correct conscience?

8. What is an erroneous conscience?

9. What is a scrupulous conscience?

10. Contrast antecedent, concomitant and consequent judgments of conscience.

11. Contrast vincible and invincible ignorance.

12. What must a person do when his conscience is in doubt?

13. In cases where one is obliged to act immediately, what are three rules that must be applied?

14. Why does one have a serious obligation to form one's conscience according to the teachings of the Magisterium of the Catholic Church?

15. List three arguments for the existence of conscience.

16. How does St. Paul ascertain that conscience becomes a "witness" for man?

17. What happens if conscience is overemphasized without regard for the law?

18. What is the relationship between conscience and law?

PRACTICAL EXERCISES

1. The word *conscience* appears 30 times in the New Testament. Explain the exact meaning St. Paul intends when he speaks of conscience in three or four of the following instances:

- Rom 2:15; 13:5
- 1 Cor 8:12; 10:27-29
- 2 Cor 1:12; 5:11
- 1 Tm 1:19
- Heb 10:22

2. What are some situations that occur in daily life that might create problems for one's conscience?

3. Some of the causes of the moral crisis facing Christians in the world today are *materialism, hedonism, pornography,* the *"culture of death,"* and *sexual promiscuity.* Give specific examples to explain how Christians can act as a counter-force to these false cultural icons.

4. Review Practical Exercise 1 from Chapter 2. If one does not take care to form one's conscience according to true moral principles, is there not a danger that one will become like Adolf Hitler? Since conscience has the final word in moral judgments, couldn't one commit horrible crimes if he had not properly informed his conscience?

5. Reflect on instances in your own life in which conscience played a role in determining your response to a particular situation or problem, and describe how you responded in each situation.

FROM THE CATECHISM

1795 "Conscience is man's most secret core, and his sanctuary. There he is alone with God whose voice echoes in his depths" (*GS*, 16).

1796 Conscience is a judgment of reason by which the human person recognizes the moral quality of a concrete act.

1798 A well-formed conscience is upright and truthful. It formulates its judgments according to reason, in conformity with the true good willed by the wisdom of the Creator. Everyone must avail himself of the means to form his conscience.

1800 A human being must always obey the certain judgment of his conscience.

1802 The Word of God is a light for our path. We must assimilate it in faith and prayer and put it into practice. This is how moral conscience is formed.

ENDNOTES

1. *VS*, 57.
2. Cf. CCC, 1777.
3. *GS*, 16.
4. Pope John Paul II, *Discourse to Scientists*, May 8, 1993.
5. *VS*, 32.
6. Cf. CCC, 1783-1785.
7. *DH*, 3.
8. Ibid., 3.
9. Cf. *VS*, 63.
10. Cf. CCC, 1789.
11. *VS*, 58.
12. Cf. Ibid., 55.
13. Cf. CCC, 1786; VS, 60.
14. *VS*, 62.
15. *VS*, 64.

Chapter 5

Ethical Norms And Law

When in the course of human events, it becomes necessary for one people to dissolve the political bands which have connected them with another, and to assume among the powers of the earth, the separate and equal station to which the Laws of Nature and of Nature's God entitle them, a decent respect to the opinions of mankind requires that they should declare the causes which impel them to the separation.

We hold these truths to be self-evident, that all men are created equal, that they are endowed by their Creator with certain unalienable Rights, that among these are Life, Liberty and the pursuit of Happiness;

That to secure these rights, Governments are instituted among Men, deriving their just powers from the consent of the governed;

That whenever any Form of Government becomes destructive of these ends, it is the Right of the People to alter or to abolish it, and to institute new Government, laying its foundation on such principles and organizing its powers in such form, as to them shall seem most likely to effect their Safety and Happiness. (The Declaration of Independence)

Regarding our understanding of law, let us ask ourselves:

- What is the definition of law?
- What is the purpose of human laws in relation to the moral law as set forth by God?
- Are there different kinds of law, and do they make conflicting demands upon human behavior?
- How are conflicts between conscience and law to be resolved?

INTRODUCTION

A common complaint today is that there are too many laws. Those who argue for more laws claim that the government is simply attempting to protect those who have no protection of law. On the other hand, those who argue for fewer laws claim they are protecting the citizenry from too many laws that are taking away fundamental rights.

The purpose of law in general is to allow the people in society a proper measure of freedom to protect their rights, and to remind them of their responsibilities to others. When the general populace is morally upright, there is no need to increase the number of laws, but when there is a tendency toward vice, there is an inclination to enact many laws.

Without laws, personal and social life would be reduced to mob rule.

If society is to function properly, there must be laws to regulate social and personal conduct. Without laws, personal and social life would be reduced to mob rule.

1. DEFINITION OF LAW

Law is an ordinance of reason for the common good, made and promulgated by those who are in charge of the community. This definition illustrates the following properties of law:

a. LAW IS AN ORDINANCE OF REASON.

Laws must always require something reasonable; they are supposed to protect objective values, and are not something capricious stemming from the arbitrary will of authority. Laws seek to end any inconsistency on the part of either the legislator or subject.

b. LAWS EXIST FOR THE COMMON GOOD.

Laws seek a just society for all citizens, so they should secure those conditions that promote the common good.

c. LAWS ARE MADE BY THOSE WHO ARE RESPONSIBLE FOR THE CARE OF THE COMMUNITY.

The one who has power to do so executes laws—that is, by legitimate authority. Only legitimate authority can make, pass, and enforce laws.

d. LAWS MUST BE OFFICIALLY PROMULGATED.

Laws need to be promulgated or communicated in an official manner to all subjects. Before they are publicly known, they hold no legitimate power.

2. DIVISION AND KINDS OF LAW

There are different expressions of the moral law, all of them interrelated:[1]

a. ETERNAL LAW

Eternal law "is nothing other than the plan of divine wisdom as directing all acts and movements."[2] Briefly, eternal law is the cosmic order established by God. It is easy to recognize the existence of this law. The Greeks differentiated between *chaos* or confusion and *cosmos* or order. They called the universe *cosmos*, that is, an ordered thing.

In fact, all can acknowledge the harmony found in the world. Both the great planets and the minuscule atoms of matter reflect an admirable order. As the scientist calls that harmony a law of nature, so the believer acknowledges its origin in God. The believer calls it eternal law; that is, he recognizes such order is not a product of chance or contingency, but was established by God.

> **The supreme rule of life is the divine law, itself, the eternal objective and universal law by which God out of his wisdom and love, arranges, directs and governs the whole world and the paths of the human community. God has enabled man to share in this divine law, and hence man is able under the gentle guidance of God's providence increasingly to recognize the unchanging truth.[3]**

Society should see the order and harmony of the universe as a model of reference to God himself.

Eternal law has certain properties: It is the *primordial* law, and it ought to be the starting point for all laws. It is the *foundation* of all law. It is *intrinsic*, since it orders the universe internally by means of God's providence. It is *universal*, for it applies to every creature. Its purpose is to facilitate order and to establish harmony in the universe and in the social order. Society, therefore, should see the order and harmony of the universe as a model of reference to God himself:

> **The moral law presupposes the rational order, established among creatures for their good and to serve their final end, by the power, wisdom, and goodness of the Creator. All law finds its first and ultimate truth in the eternal law. Law is declared and established by reason as a participation in the providence of the living God, Creator and Redeemer of all. (CCC 1951)**

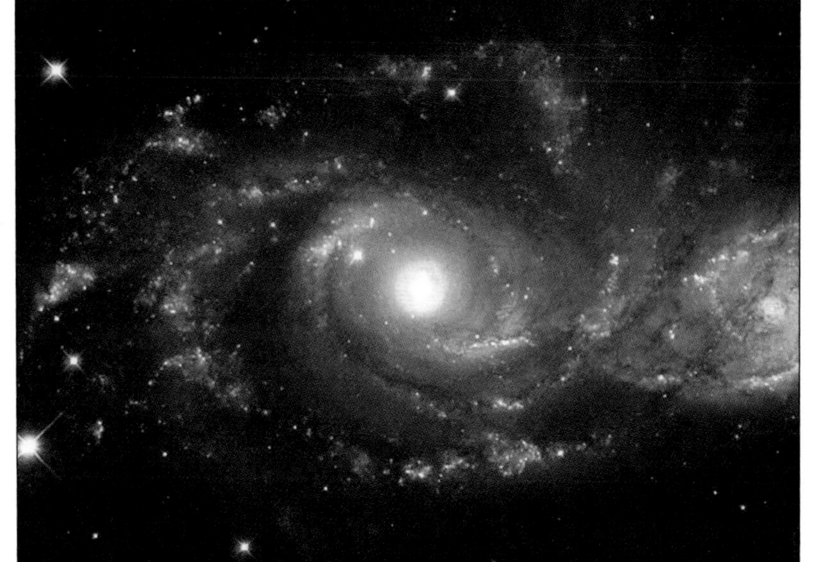

b. NATURAL LAW

The natural law "is nothing other than the rational creature's participation in the eternal law."[4] The natural law is the eternal law, written in the heart of every human being, as it applies to human life. Since we are unique in our human nature (i.e., our character, intelligence, and freedom) it is convenient

The human being surpasses both the cosmic world and the animal realm in his unique existence.

to call this law the natural law. This helps to emphasize that the human being surpasses both the cosmic world and the animal realm in his unique existence.

> **But God provides for man differently from the way in which he provides for beings which are not persons. He cares for man not "from without," through the laws of physical nature, but "from within," through reason, which, by its natural knowledge of God's eternal law, is consequently able to show man the right direction to take in his free actions....The natural law enters here as the human expression of God's eternal law.[5]**

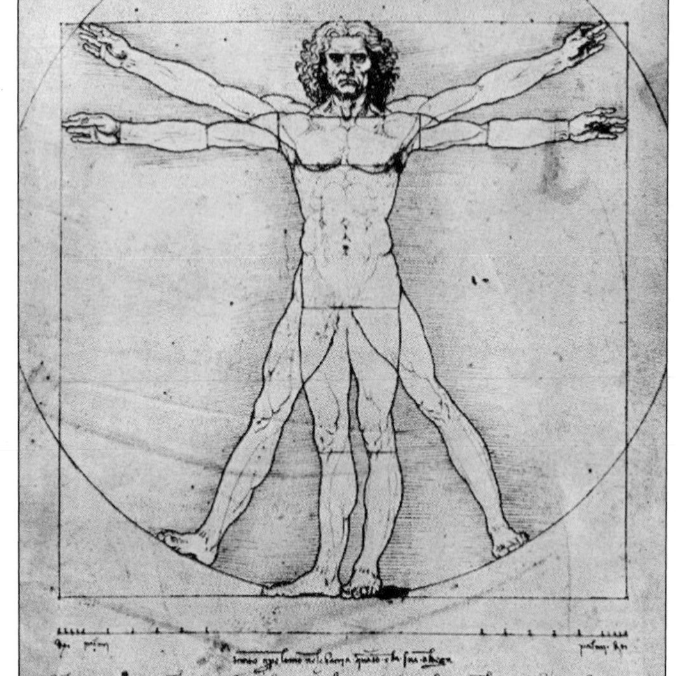

In fact, no one is a chaotic being, but rather harmony is reflected throughout our nature. Our bodily reality rests on the functioning order of all of our organs and physical elements that constitute our body, so that if some disorder appears, illness will result. Thus, health means organic order, and death the rupture of that order.

Also, there is a rich harmony reflected in spiritual life. Intelligence and will contribute to a person's spiritual character. But if there be any imbalance in the soul, then psychological abnormalities result. Sanity is harmony, while madness reflects inner disorder found in the soul of the person.

The human, besides being a living reality, is also an acting being: He not only exists, but also acts. The person who lives according to his nature cannot be chaotic in his activity, but should be ruled by an order proper to his actions. The good person follows the norms governing his existence, while the evil person follows a morally disordered path.[6]

While our body and soul are ruled by laws that are higher than us, our conduct depends on our free will.

Consequently, the existence of the natural law becomes self-evident; knowledge of theology is not necessary to understand that murder, theft, and adultery are wrong. Everyone naturally recognizes that it would be contradictory to praise cosmic order but not recognize the internal order of the human being. Also, it does not make sense to argue that we are ordered toward life and growth, but free to live a disordered life.

While our body and soul are ruled by laws that are higher than us, our conduct depends on our free will. And this is precisely what ethics demands: since we can direct our future, it is extremely important that we not act chaotically; rather, we ought to submit ourselves to those norms that will direct us to harmony and order, that is, to freedom.

> **We will never fully understand Jesus' freedom. It is immense, infinite, as is his love....Thus, we come to appreciate that freedom is used properly when it is directed toward the good....**
>
> **Reject the deception of those who appease themselves with the pathetic cry of "Freedom! Freedom!" Their cry often masks a tragic**

> **enslavement, because choices that prefer error do not liberate. Christ alone sets us free, for he alone is the Way, the Truth, and the Life....**
>
> **Throughout my years as a priest, whenever I have spoken, or rather shouted, about my love for personal freedom, I have noticed some people reacting with distrust, as if they suspected that my defense of freedom could endanger the faith. Such faint-hearted people can rest assured. The only freedom that can assail the faith is a misinterpreted freedom, an aimless freedom, one without objective principles, one that is lawless and irresponsible. In a word, license.[7]**

The natural law has two basic characteristics:

- *Universality,* which means that it applies to everyone;
- *Immutability,* which means that it does not change. Its interpreter is the Magisterium—the pope and the bishops in communion with him.

Laws of nature are not laws in the most precise meaning of the term; rather they are descriptions of the behavior of the material universe.

To act against the natural law is to oppose happiness, since such action damages human nature. On the other hand, to abide by the natural law constitutes a foundation for a personal morality, and offers a channel to order social life, since it reveals the dignity of man. At the same time, the natural law offers governments a base on which to formulate just laws that can regulate the common good of society:

> **The natural law, the Creator's very good work, provides the solid foundation on which man can build the structure of moral rules to guide his choices. It also provides the indispensable moral foundation for building the human community. Finally, it provides the necessary basis for the civil law with which it is connected, whether by a reflection that draws conclusions from its principles, or by additions of a positive and juridical nature. (CCC 1959)**

With all this in mind, it is important to state that there is no opposition between freedom and the natural law:

> **The natural law thus understood does not allow for any division between freedom and nature. Indeed, these two realities are harmoniously bound together, and each is intimately linked to the other.[8]**

It is important to distinguish between the natural law and so-called *laws of nature,* such as the law of gravity. Laws of nature are not laws in the most precise meaning of the term; rather they are descriptions of the behavior of the material universe. A law is an ordinance of reason. A rock has no intellect and cannot know if to fall is according to its nature or not. A rock simply falls. Every human person, on the other hand, can come to know what is or is not in accord with human nature. The natural law, then, is the command that human reason gives regarding what actions should be done (because they are in accord with human nature), and what actions should be avoided (because they are contrary to human nature).

c. POSITIVE LAW

Positive law is promulgated by those who have authority to communicate it to society. In moral theology, that proper authority can be either God or the hierarchy of the Church. Legitimate civil authorities can also enact positive laws. There are three kinds of positive law:

- *Divine positive law* is legislated by God. One example is the precept of charity established by Jesus Christ. The Ten Commandments are another example of divine positive law, but they are also expressions of the natural law.
- *Ecclesiastical positive law* emanates from the legislative power of the Church. Fasting in Lent and the laws that regulate a canonical marriage are two examples. The principal laws of the Church are found in her *Code of Canon Law.*
- *Civil positive law* is legislated by a legitimate government. For example, traffic laws or tax laws. They can be found in the laws of each locality.

d. EVANGELICAL OR NEW LAW

This law is specifically Christian. As was stated in Chapter 1, supernatural anthropology notes that the baptized person is a "new creature," since by Baptism, a person acquires a special likeness to God. St. Peter says, "[We] become partakers of the divine nature" (2 Pt 1:4).

The New Law:
A law of love;
A law of grace;
A law of freedom.

> **The New Law is called a *law of love* because it makes us act out of the love infused by the Holy Spirit, rather than from fear; a *law of grace,* because it confers the strength of grace to act, by means of faith and the sacraments; a *law of freedom,* because it sets us free from the ritual and juridical observances of the Old Law, inclines us to act spontaneously by the prompting of charity and, finally, lets us pass from the condition of a servant who "does not know what his master is doing" to that of a friend of Christ—"For all that I have heard from my Father I have made known to you"—or even to the status of son and heir (Jn 15:15; cf. Jas 1:25; 2:12; Gal 4:1-7, 21-31; Rom 8:15). (CCC 1972)**

It seems logical for the Christian to have a new law since the new person also needs to maintain an order and harmony in his actions, based on the new way. So the Christian, in keeping with this way of looking at life, should live a life ordered according to what he really is. The harmony between a person's actions and his being can be reached only in this way.

This goal can be reached because the New Law is an interior law—a law of the Spirit—and also an exterior one since it is found in the Sermon on the Mount.[9] This law guides the believer to his duty, and also gives him the strength through grace to do it. Similarly, this "law of grace" confirms the ethical foundations of the natural law and adds new precepts and teachings, as Jesus Christ explained in the Beatitudes (Mt 5:17-48; 6:1-24). Lastly, the New Law is the law of love, which perfects freedom and culminates in eternal glorification, where love culminates.

The content of this new law responds to the obligation of the Christian to shape his life according to Jesus Christ's. In order to do this, the Christian, with the aid of the Holy Spirit and the sacraments, needs to develop his life in grace, communicated in Baptism. Hence the different names: Law of grace or Law of the Spirit. And, since it attempts to dictate a life lived according to the Gospel, it is also called "evangelical law."

Human laws should correspond to God's will, since he creates and knows all that aids our human life.

3. MEANING AND PURPOSE OF LAW

Moral good and evil proceed from the nature of things and the effects of original sin in our human nature. Things do not become good or evil because we would like them to be or because society says that something is acceptable or unacceptable. Understanding this will help us respect the rights and duties of each person.

> **In the final analysis, human laws should correspond to God's will, since he creates and knows all that aids our human life. God is not arbitrary, but knows what aids or harms us. The supreme rule of life is the divine law itself, the eternal, objective and universal law by which God out of his wisdom and love arranges, directs and governs the whole world and the paths of the human community. God has enabled man to share in this divine law, and hence man is able under the gentle guidance of God's providence increasingly to recognize the unchanging truth.[10]**

God knows what is good or evil and he warns us by a precept or law.

Consequently, good and evil have a foundation based on the truth. It is evil to kill an innocent person not just because law prohibits it but because every person has the right to life. Similarly, it is evil to blaspheme against God because it offends the divine goodness and power, not just because it is prohibited by the first commandment. It is also evil to slander because a person's reputation belongs to him and not because society prohibits such actions.

The same could be said of the good. For example, to help rehabilitate a criminal is good because it respects human dignity, not because society seeks to include marginal people. To give alms to one who needs them is a good, not because some organization requires it but because by it charity is practiced. To demand the fulfillment of a penalty is a good because it brings about justice, not because society seeks revenge on criminals.

Law is a reasonable requirement of the legitimate authority to protect human dignity and social order. In the case of divine precepts, its origin is in the fact that God knows what is good or evil and he warns us by a precept or law.

It should be clear from this chapter that a just law is a great good. It is a support that humans use to protect their own existence, for it offers an extraordinary means to protect their personal and social being. Similarly, Christian moral life represents a light that points to the ethical values of the New Testament, so that the Christian is able to live a life worthy of a true follower of Jesus Christ.

St. Thomas Aquinas

A just law must seek the good of all members of a society, not just some of them.

4. JUST LAW

St. Thomas Aquinas teaches that a law is just if it corresponds to the natural law. If it does, then it has the power to bind us in conscience, and to disobey such a law would be a sin. St. Thomas outlines the following conditions that must be met for a law to be just:

a. IT MUST PROMOTE THE COMMON GOOD.

The common good consists of three essential elements: respect for and promotion of the fundamental rights of the person; prosperity, or the development of the spiritual and temporal goods of society; the peace and security of the group and of its members. (CCC 1925)

A just law must seek the good of all members of a society, not just some of them. By contrast, a law that seeks only the good of a certain segment of society while neglecting others would be unjust, as in the case of a law that required military service only of the poorer members of society while exempting the wealthy. A just law must also defend rights and promote the fulfillment of social duties without demanding what is impossible or extremely difficult to do.

b. THE BURDENS THAT THE LAW IMPOSES ON SOCIETY MUST REFLECT AN "EQUALITY OF PROPORTION."

This means that the burden of the law's fulfillment must be shared by all of the members of society and not just some. A law that taxes the citizens of a society for a common defense is just, but all members of that society must be taxed, and they should bear the burden of the tax in proportion to their ability to pay. To demand payment from someone who is incapable of paying is unjust.

c. ALL USE OF AUTHORITY IS A SHARE IN GOD'S AUTHORITY.

No human authority can declare what is morally evil to be morally good. For this reason, laws permitting slavery, abortion, euthanasia, divorce, and "marriages" between persons of the same gender are immoral, and therefore unjust.[11]

If any of these conditions are violated, the law is unjust, in which case it is not a law but a perversion of law.

St. Augustine said that "every just law is transcribed and transferred to the heart of the man who works justice, not by wandering but by being, as it were, impressed upon it, just as the image from the ring passes over to the wax, and yet does not leave the ring."[12]

5. CONFLICTS BETWEEN CONSCIENCE AND LAW

Although conscience can be seen as a light to moral values, it does not fabricate such values, but takes them from objective reality. Thus, law offers conscience an extraordinary means to detect moral good and evil. Hence, the natural law, divine positive law, the norms of the Church, and civil legislation offer to the conscience avenues of light as to what is good and evil, just or unjust. Conscience gratefully accepts all that it is offered by just law, and, if sincere, it listens to those teachers who instruct on what is to be done.

Obedience to law does not enslave conscience nor take away from its autonomy, since truth never enslaves, but liberates.

Obedience to law does not enslave conscience nor take away from its autonomy, since truth never enslaves, but liberates: "The truth will make you free" (Jn 8:32). Nor does just law reduce conscience's freedom, since it is part of a person's essential self. St. Paul sees the precepts of the natural law as "written on their hearts" (Rom 2:15). The New Law, by which Christians are to govern themselves, is also called the Law of the Spirit, insofar as it is found in the very soul of the baptized, and elevates each of us by virtue of the Holy Spirit; that is, the "new law is the same grace of the Holy Spirit that gives itself to the faithful of Christ."[13]

Dr. Martin Luther King, Jr., 1929-1968, recipient of the Nobel Peace Prize, dedicated his life to overturning unjust laws through nonviolent methods.

It is ordinary for an informed conscience to find with clarity what it ought to do and not do, so that there should be no need for conflicts between conscience and the law. Unfortunately, unjust laws exist. How is the Christian to respond to such laws? Given that Christians have an obligation to bear witness to the truth, one is not bound in conscience to cooperate with an unjust law. In fact, there may be times when he is called upon by his conscience to actively oppose such a law.

Such actions should never be undertaken easily. Even among unjust laws, not all bear the same degree of moral evil (laws condoning slavery and unfair parking regulations do not mandate equally evil acts). At times, it may be necessary to permit a lesser evil or to yield one's rights for the sake of a greater good, namely, the avoidance of scandal or the prevention of public disturbances (cf. Mt 5:38-41).[14] The question that should be asked in such a case is: "In what would the greater evil consist, submission to the law or the scandal and disturbance that would follow resistance to it?"

However, laws that contravene the natural law and inflict serious injury upon the members of a society cannot be cooperated with. They must be opposed and lawful means to overturn them must be sought. It is always important that a concern for justice and resistance to evil must be balanced by Christian love for all people and a genuine respect for the authority of civil government.

"The truth will make you free"
— John 8:32

It is also true that, at times, a conflict arises over the difficulty of accepting and fulfilling what the law commands. According to St. Thomas Aquinas, those who find constant conflicts in fulfilling various laws need to ask themselves if they are not lacking in consistency in their faith and Christian practice, for there can be no real conflict between just laws and a properly formed conscience. Responsibility and the desire to come to God for assistance are required, so that the person will acquiesce his unruly desires to the law of God. God provides his assistance most readily in the Sacrament of Penance.

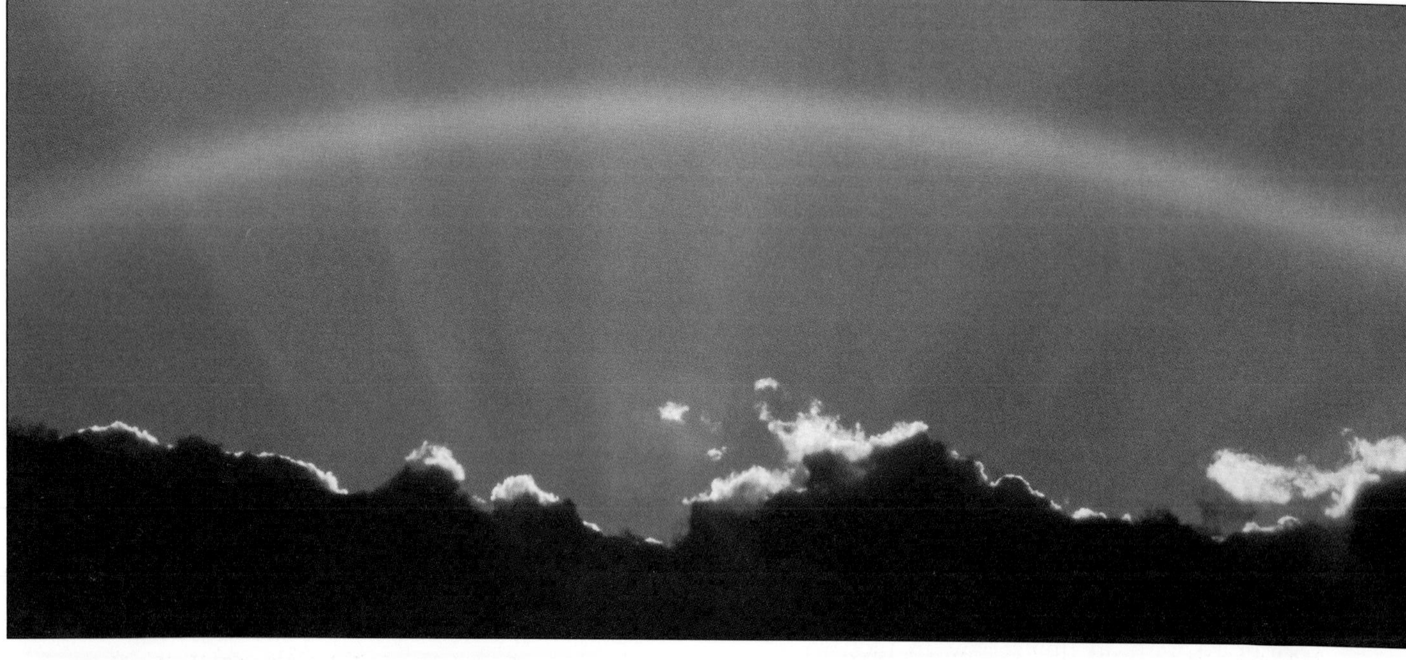

"Little children, let us not love in word or speech but in deed and in truth."

— St. John

CONCLUSION

A person ought to be always open to what has been given by just law, since it is given in good faith and it will help him act rightly in life. The prudent person always acts in this way:

> The truth about the moral good, stated in the law of reason, is recognized practically and concretely by the *prudent judgment* of conscience. We call that man prudent who chooses in conformity with this judgment. (CCC 1780)

And, in regard to Christian precepts, the Christian is guided by St. John's words:

> Little children, let us not love in word or speech but in deed and in truth. By this we shall know that we are of the truth, and reassure our hearts before him whenever our hearts condemn us; for God is greater than our hearts, and he knows everything. Beloved, if our hearts do not condemn us, we have confidence before God; and we receive from him whatever we ask, because we keep his commandments and do what pleases him. (1 Jn 3:18-22)

On the other hand, it is never permitted to follow a law that is contrary to morality as defined by reason. We are bound by conscience to resist any law that forces us to violate the natural law, and prudence dictates whether or not we should resist any law that permits such violation.

VOCABULARY

CIVIL LAW
The law promulgated by civil authority.

ECCLESIASTICAL LAW
The law that directs the life and worship of the Church.

ETERNAL LAW
God's wisdom as manifested in all acts and movements.

HUMAN LAW
Law promulgated by human authority, either civil or ecclesiastical. In order to be legitimate, human law must be consistent with laws of God, conform to the natural law and promote the good of society.

IMMUTABILITY
Not changing.

LAW (JUST LAW)
An ordinance of reason for the common good, corresponding to divine law and promulgated by one who has care of the community.

LAWS OF NATURE
Descriptions of the behavior of the material universe.

MORAL LAW
The ethical norm revealed by God, that imposes obligations on the conscience of each person.

NATURAL LAW
The part of the eternal law that applies to the rational creature.

POSITIVE LAW
Laws created by the proper authority that enjoin specific obligations upon individuals (i.e., the ecclesiastical law requiring abstinence from meat on Fridays during Lent, or a civil law mandating the payment of taxes) and bind in conscience insofar as they conform to the dictates of the divine and natural laws.

UNIVERSALITY
The ability to be applied to everyone.

UNJUST LAW
Human laws that contradict or fail to conform to divine or natural law. Such laws are never binding on a person's conscience, and must be prudentially opposed by conscientious objection.

SUPPLEMENTARY READINGS

1. Nor did I think your orders were so strong that you, a mortal man, could overrun the gods' unwritten and unfailing laws. Not now, nor yesterday's, they always live, and no one knows their origin in time. So not through fear of any man's proud spirit would I be likely to neglect these laws,draw on myself the gods' sure punishment.

— Sophocles, *Antigone*, ln. 452-460

2. True law is right reason in agreement with nature; it is of universal application, unchanging and everlasting....It is a sin to try to alter this law, nor is it allowable to attempt to repeal any part of it, and it is impossible to abolish it entirely. We cannot be freed from its obligations by senate or people, and we need not look outside ourselves for an expounder or interpreter of it.

And there will not be different laws at Rome and at Athens, or different laws now and in the future, but one eternal and unchangeable law will be valid for all nations and at all times, and there will be one master and ruler, that is, God, over us all, for he is the author of his law, its promulgator, and its enforcing judge. Whoever is disobedient is fleeing from himself and denying his human nature, and by reason of this very fact he will suffer the worst penalties, even if he escapes what is commonly considered punishment.

— Cicero, *De Republica*, III, 22

3. Two things fill the mind with ever new and increasing admiration and awe, the more often and the more steadily we reflect on them: the starry heavens above and the moral law within. I have not to search for them and conjecture them....I see them before me and connect them directly with the consciousness of my existence. The former begins from the place I occupy in the external world of sense.... The second begins from my invisible self, my personality, and exhibits me in a world which has true infinity, but which is traceable only by the understanding.

— Immanuel Kant, *Critique of Practical Reason*, Part II, Conclusion (312-313) p. 260

4. ...Rather was it intended that man alone might have something to glory of, in that he alone had been worthy to receive from God a law: and that, as a rational animal, capable of understanding and knowledge, he might be held in restraint by that rational liberty besides, being subject to God who had to him made all things subject.

— Tertullian, *Against Marcion*, II, 4

5. Deep within his conscience man discovers a law which he has not laid upon himself but which he must obey. Its voice, ever calling him to love and to do what is good and to avoid evil, tells him inwardly at the right moment: do this, shun that. For man has in his heart a law inscribed by God. His dignity lies in observing this law, and by it he will be judged.

— *GS*, 16

SUPPLEMENTARY READINGS CONTINUED

6. This becomes even clearer if one considers that the highest norm of human life is the divine law itself—eternal, objective and universal, by which God orders, directs and governs the whole world and the ways of the human community according to a plan conceived in his wisdom and love. God has enabled man to participate in this law of his so that, under the gentle disposition of divine providence, many may be able to arrive at a deeper and deeper knowledge of unchangeable truth....

It is through his conscience that man sees and recognizes the demands of the divine law.

— *DH*, 3

7. No believer will wish to deny that the teaching authority of the Church is competent to interpret even the natural moral law. It is, in fact, indisputable, as our predecessors have many times declared, that Jesus Christ, when communicating to Peter and to the apostles his divine authority and sending them to teach all nations his commandments, constituted them as guardians and authentic interpreters of all the moral law, not only, that is, of the law of the Gospel, but also of the natural law, which is also an expression of the will of God, the faithful fulfillment of which is equally necessary for salvation.

— *HV*, 4

8. Man, as the living image of God, is willed by his Creator to be ruler and lord. Saint Gregory of Nyssa writes that "God made man capable of carrying out his role as king of the earth.... Man was created in the image of the One who governs the universe. Everything demonstrates that from the beginning man's nature was marked by royalty.... Man is a king. Created to exercise dominion over the world, he was given a likeness to the king of the universe; he is the living image who participates by his dignity in the perfection of the divine archetype."

Called to be fruitful and multiply, to subdue the earth and to exercise dominion over other lesser creatures (cf. Gn 1:28), man is ruler and lord not only over things but especially over himself, and in a certain sense, over the life which he has received and which he is able to transmit through procreation, carried out with love and respect for God's plan. Man's *lordship* however is not absolute, but *ministerial:* it is a real reflection of the unique and infinite lordship of God. Hence man must exercise it with *wisdom and love*, sharing in the boundless wisdom and love of God. And this comes about through obedience to God's holy law: a free and joyful obedience (cf. Ps 119) born of and fostered by an awareness that the precepts of the LORD are a gift of grace entrusted to man always and solely for his good, for the preservation of his personal dignity and the pursuit of his happiness.

— *EV*, 52.3

"Deep within his conscience man discovers a law which he has not laid upon himself but which he must obey."

SUPPLEMENTARY READINGS CONTINUED

9. Consequently, there is a need to recover the *basic elements of a vision of the relationship between civil law and moral law,* which are put forward by the Church, but which are also part of the patrimony of the great juridical traditions of humanity.

Certainly *the purpose of civil law* is different and more limited in scope than that of the moral law. But "in no sphere of life can the civil law take the place of conscience or dictate norms concerning things which are outside its competence." Rather, the civil law is responsible for ensuring the common good of people through the recognition and defense of their fundamental rights, and the promotion of peace and of public morality. The real purpose of civil law is to guarantee an ordered social coexistence in true justice, so that all may "lead a quiet and peaceable life, godly and respectful in every way" (1 Tm 2:2).

Precisely for this reason, civil law must ensure that all members of society enjoy respect for certain fundamental rights which innately belong to the person, rights which every positive law must recognize and guarantee. First and fundamental among these is the inviolable right to life of every innocent human being. While public authority can sometimes choose not to put a stop to something which—were it prohibited—would cause more serious harm, it can never presume to legitimize as a right of individuals—even if they are the majority of the members of society—an offense against other persons caused by the disregard of so fundamental a right as the right to life.

The legal toleration of abortion or of euthanasia can in no way claim to be based on respect for the conscience of others, precisely because society has the right and the duty to protect itself against the abuses which can occur in the name of conscience and under the pretext of freedom.

— *EV,* 71

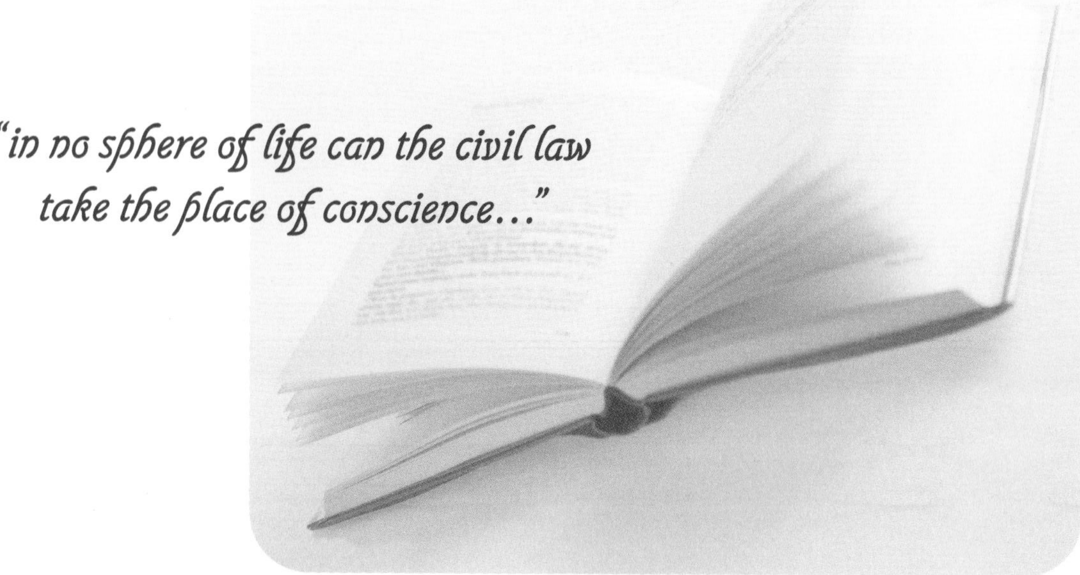
"in no sphere of life can the civil law
take the place of conscience..."

ADVANCED CONCEPTS

LEGAL POSITIVISM

Legal (or juridical) positivism is a concept of law that looks exclusively to existing laws or to those that have existed previously for evaluating a situation. Within the concept is an explicit desire to exclude any supernatural or metaphysical basis for law, replacing it with the study of laws already enacted in a particular time and place. The authority of law, therefore, exists within the power of the existing state that promulgates them.

The question that positivism raises is whether these laws or norms are legitimate by the mere fact that they have been issued by a secular authority. Christianity (and more exactly, Catholicism) says no, because all law must reflect the law of God. Since the state has the power to command according to reason, the obligatory source of law must emanate from the natural order, which has God as its source and ultimate end.[15]

Positivists deify the state by reducing moral compulsion to the will of the lawmaker. This theory attributes a gross majesty to purely human laws, eventually separating law from morality. Without a guiding natural law, the will of the legislator must find its principles in the collective will of the majority. As such, positive law may deviate from right reason and end up doing violence to the natural order, because it has placed moral compulsion in the hands of legislators, who may or may not be virtuous.[16]

Catholicism responds by affirming that all legitimate human authority derives from the natural law. The natural law originates from God and guides humanity to right action. How do we know this law? St. Paul tells us that it is the law "written in our hearts" (cf. Rom 2:15) and discernible by the use of reason. Human beings, created in the image and likeness of God, have this knowledge as part of their nature. We are, so to speak, "wired for the truth." Enactments by the state, then, must pattern their legal commands upon the natural order.

If one recognizes that God is the author of all life and the only one with true authority to ordain how it should be lived, then this will indeed influence one's views on abortion, euthanasia, capital punishment, homosexuality, *in vitro* fertilization, and many other issues. The Church is a sure guide in resolving these issues through its divine mandate as teacher and in its reflection on God's "positive" law found in the Bible. As such, one must critique human law in light of what is known of the law of God.

"The natural law originates from God and guides humanity to right action."

QUESTIONS

1. What is the purpose of law?

2. What are the four properties of law?

3. What is the foundation of all law?

4. What is the basis of eternal law? What are the properties of the eternal law?

5. What is the basis of natural law? What are the two basic characteristics of the natural law?

6. What three things does natural law (from the Creator) provide?

7. What is the difference between the natural law and laws of nature?

8. What are the three kinds of positive law? Give an example of each kind.

9. What is the new law and why is it called the evangelical law?

10. How does an unjust "law" differ from a just law?

11. What are the three requirements for a law to be just?

12. What are some instances in which we are not bound to obey a particular law? Before resisting an unjust law, what question must be answered?

13. What is legal positivism? What is its failing?

14. Do any of God's laws seem unjust? Would the world be a better place if *everyone* were allowed to disobey this law?

PRACTICAL EXERCISES

1. Upon what does Antigone base her argument to disobey the king (whom she is addressing) in Supplementary Reading 1? Now compare Supplementary Readings 1 and 6. What truth, identified in this chapter, are both Antigone and the Second Vatican Council defending in their statements?

2. Summarize and explain the characteristics of the natural law, according to Cicero.

3. List the characteristics of the natural law as described by the Catechism of the Catholic Church (CCC 1954-1960).

4. What are some civil and ecclesiastical laws that oblige one in conscience? Why are they obligatory?

5. Why does the Magisterium have the authority and duty to interpret the natural law?

6. Some people claim that law and freedom are mutually exclusive. How would you persuade them that law and freedom complement each other?

7. In 1854, the U.S. Supreme Court decided that Dred Scott, a slave, was not a human being, but the property of his "owner." What arguments would you use to refute this decision? Would you appeal to a positivist understanding of law? Would you appeal to the natural law? What other decisions of the Supreme Court neglect to consider the natural law?

FROM THE CATECHISM

1976 "Law is an ordinance of reason for the common good, promulgated by the one who is in charge of the community" (St. Thomas Aquinas, *Summa Theologiae*, I-II, 90, 4).

1977 Christ is the end of the law (cf. Rom 10: 4); only he teaches and bestows the justice of God.

1978 The natural law is a participation in God's wisdom and goodness by man formed in the image of his Creator. It expresses the dignity of the human person and forms the basis of his fundamental rights and duties.

1979 The natural law is immutable, permanent throughout history. The rules that express it remain substantially valid. It is a necessary foundation for the erection of moral rules and civil law.

1985 The New Law is a law of love, a law of grace, a law of freedom.

ENDNOTES

1. Cf. CCC, 1952.
2. St. Thomas Aquinas, *Summa Theologiae,* I-II, q. 93, a. 1.
3. *VS,* 43.
4. St. Thomas Aquinas, *Summa Theologiae,* I-II, q. 91 a. 2.
5. *VS,* 43.
6. Cf. Ibid., 50.
7. St. Josemaría Escrivá, *Friends of God,* 26, 32.
8. *VS,* 50.
9. Cf. CCC, 1716-1717.
10. *DH,* 3.
11. Cf. St. Thomas Aquinas, *Summa Theologiae,* I-II, q. 96, a. 5.
12. *De Trinitate,* XIV, 15, 21: CCL 50/A, 451.
13. St. Thomas Aquinas, *Summa Theologiae,* I-II, q. 106, a. 1.
14. Ibid., I-II, q. 96, a. 5.
15. Cf. *PT,* n. 47.
16. Cf. St. Thomas Aquinas, *Summa Theologiae,* I-II, q. 93, a. 3.

Chapter 6

Morality And Action

And they heard the sound of the Lord God walking in the garden in the cool of the day, and the man and his wife hid themselves from the presence of the Lord God among the trees of the garden. But the Lord God called to the man, and said to him, "Where are you?" And he said, "I heard the sound of thee in the garden, and I was afraid, because I was naked; and I hid myself." He said, "Who told you that you were naked? Have you eaten of the tree of which I commanded you not to eat?" The man said, "The woman whom thou gavest to be with me, she gave me fruit of the tree, and I ate." Then the Lord God said to the woman, "What is this that you have done?" The woman said, "The serpent beguiled me, and I ate." The Lord God said to the serpent, "Because you have done this, cursed are you above all cattle, and above all wild animals; upon your belly you shall go, and dust you shall eat all the days of your life. I will put enmity between you and the woman, and between your seed and her seed; he shall bruise your head, and you shall bruise his heel." To the woman he said, "I will greatly multiply your pain in childbearing; in pain you shall bring forth children, yet your desire shall be for your husband, and he shall rule over you." And to Adam he said, "Because you listened to the voice of your wife, and have eaten of the tree of which I commanded you, 'You shall not eat of it,' cursed is the ground because of you; in toil you shall eat of it all the days of your life; thorns and thistles it shall bring forth to you; and you shall eat the plants of the field. In the sweat of your face you shall eat bread till you return to the ground, for out of it you were taken; you are dust, and to dust you shall return." (Gn 3: 8-19)

The sin of Adam and Eve is one of the most decisive human acts in the history of mankind. Its consequences are so far-reaching that they have yet to be fully understood. Adam and Eve's sin will affect the lives of all people until the end of time.

Let us ask the following questions:

- How often in a lifetime does one make decisive human acts?
- Should the responsibility for leading another into a sinful act fall on both parties equally?
- What factors must be taken into account when determining the morality of an action?

INTRODUCTION

In a sense, human lives can be compared to a canvas on which a picture is to be painted. On the day a person is born, he is like a blank canvas on which parents and relatives will paint for the first year or so. Sometime during the second year of life, the person begins to add some paint himself. From ages two to six, more or less, he adds the paint of personal responses to different situations. For the most part, the colors are bright ones, indicating the joys of growing up. Around age six, there is a definite change, for the child begins to make choices between good and evil. With the beginning of school, he becomes more formally aware of the rules of right and wrong that guide life. From this point forward, the painting will be mainly the work of the individual person. At the end of life, each person has a painting that reflects his choices—both good and bad—that have been made during life. Since the colors of the paint represent his choices, it can be said that the choices he made to a large extent determined the moral portrait he has painted. This portrait will be presented to God at the moment of judgment.

On the day a person is born, he is like a blank canvas on which parents and relatives will paint for the first year or so.

1. HUMAN ACTS

A human act is one done with intellect and will, knowledge and consent. Those acts that do not involve the intellect and will can be called *acts of humans* or *non-human actions:* breathing, sneezing, and the like. A human act is one that is preceded by knowledge, for to be able to choose, one must have a choice between two alternatives. A human act may be good or evil.

2. COMPONENTS OF THE MORAL CHOICE

A moral choice involves three elements: the act, the surrounding circumstances, and the intention of the person who performs the act. This truth is captured in the *Catechism of the Catholic Church* in the following words:

> **A *morally good* act requires the goodness of the object, of the end, and of the circumstances together....the object, the intention, and the circumstances make up the three "sources" of the morality of human acts. (CCC 1755, 1757)**

The sources or principles of a moral act are the object, the end or intention, and the circumstances. All three elements need to be considered in order to determine whether an act is morally good or evil.

To evaluate the goodness or malice of an act, it is necessary to consider the act being done (object), the intention in mind (end), and the different conditions surrounding the act (circumstances). But these three elements do not have the same level of importance. The object and the end are the primary moral elements, while the circumstances only shape the other elements in a lesser manner. Remember that Christian morality is directed toward enabling a person to make the correct choice in all situations. For a Christian, doing the moral minimum is never enough. A key element in doing good and avoiding evil, therefore, is being disposed to do the best that can be done in all situations.

Remember that Christian morality is directed toward enabling a person to make the correct choice in all situations.

> **Will any one of you, who has a servant plowing or keeping sheep, say to him when he has come in from the field, "Come at once and sit down at table"? Will he not rather say to him, "Prepare supper for me, and gird yourself and serve me, till I eat and drink; and afterward you shall eat and drink"? Does he thank the servant because he did what was commanded? So you also, when you have done all that is commanded you, say, "We are unworthy servants; we have only done what was our duty." (Lk 17:7-10)**

a. THE OBJECT

The *object* is the matter of a human act or the action itself. The object determines the morality of an act. Evil actions are immoral. Thus, it is immoral to steal, lie, or blaspheme. On the contrary, good actions are moral. It is good to be just, tell the truth, and respect God's name. The human act receives its goodness or malice primarily from the morality of the act itself. For example, adultery is always evil by its object, independently of the purpose of the one who does it. So, when the moral object is in itself an absolute evil, the action in question is an intrinsically evil act.

For a Christian, doing the moral minimum is never enough.

By their objects, acts can be either good or evil. As the encyclical *Veritatis splendor* teaches:

> **The morality of the human act depends primarily and fundamentally on the "object" rationally chosen by the deliberate will, as is borne out by the insightful analysis, still valid today, made by Saint Thomas.[1]**

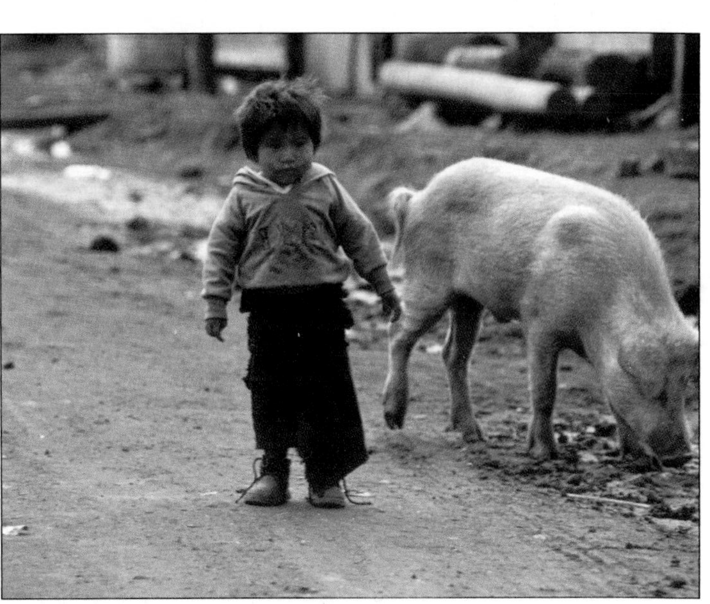

b. THE INTENTION OR END

The *end* refers to the subject or person: the end is the motive or intention for which a person commits a good or evil act.

It is common to find different results of an action: one can be the determining factor while the others concur, without being decisive. The end of an action is not to be confused with the result. A person can perform an act with a certain intention in mind, with the act resulting in something else. Such would be the case of a gift by a rich person to a poor person. This gift reduces the poor person's suffering, and at the same time raises the status of the donor in the eyes of society (cf. Mt 6:2-4). The giver can wish to aid the poor, while merely

Stealing is intrinsically evil, even if it is done for the purpose of doing good.

accepting the honor. On the other hand, he can also give the gift out of vanity in order to secure praise, while not being concerned about the poor person's plight. In this case, the gift is an evil act because of its evil end, which is vainglory.

If an act has both an evil object and an evil end, then the malice of the act increases. For instance, if someone slanders another in order to deny him a significant post, the slanderer is also guilty of injustice, and so his guilt is increased.

On the other hand, a good intention can reduce the guilt of a morally bad act, but it cannot make an intrinsically evil act a good act. For example, stealing is intrinsically evil, even if it is done for the purpose of doing good. The fact that the stealer has a good intention does not make it morally acceptable for him to steal. "And why not do evil that good may come?—as some people slanderously charge us with saying" (Rom 3:8). The Magisterium also addresses this issue:

The primary and decisive element for moral judgment is the object of the human act, which establishes whether it is capable of being ordered to the good and to the ultimate end, which is God.[2]

C. CIRCUMSTANCES

The word *circumstance* comes from the Latin *circum-stare,* that is, to stand around. They are, in other words, those factors that occur with the act and that contribute to the morality of the act. Six circumstances have traditionally been cited:

Who?

The person acting: A lie said by a child and one said by a president carry different moral weight.

What?

The thing done: It is more serious to steal a sacred object than it is to steal an ordinary one, although they may have the same monetary value.

Where?

The place where the act occurs: A sin in public is different from a sin in private.

But no circumstance can make an intrinsic evil a good action.

Why?

Either the immediate situation of a particular action (e.g., "I stole the film because my boss was out of town"), or some additional reason that a sinner may have for committing a sin (e.g., "I lied because she had previously hurt me in some other way"). This should not be confused with the *intention.* For example, if a son steals money from his father's wallet, the son's intention is to obtain the money, but a situation would be that his father was not in the room when the money was stolen. An additional reason may be that his father withheld his allowance. These influence the boy's decision to steal the money, but are not the intention.

How?

The manner in which the act is done.

When?

The timing of an act: For example, it is not serious to miss Mass on a weekday, but it is serious to miss Mass on a Sunday or holy day of obligation.

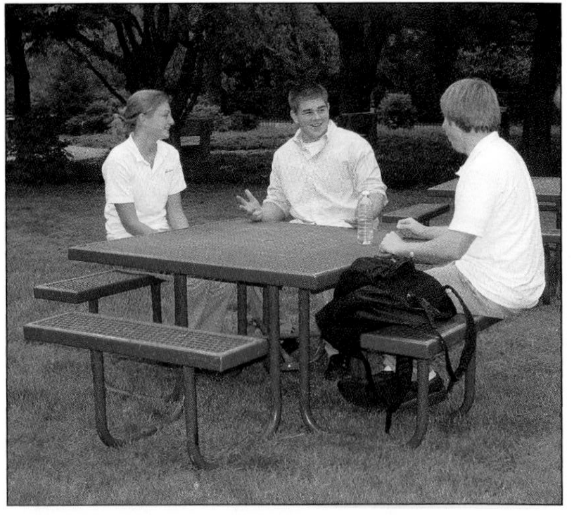

Although the repeated commission of venial sins in itself does not make mortal sin, venial sin does weaken a person's resistance to mortal sin. For example, the habit of pilfering small items from the workplace diminishes the person's love of justice, and readies the pilferer to commit more serious injustices. Or, stealing items that are dedicated for Church use, such as a chalice or other sacred vessel, is a circumstance that aggravates the theft by adding the sin of sacrilege, or the profanation of something dedicated to the service of God. Sometimes, the circumstances of a venial sin produce the more serious sin of scandal, as when a person who holds authority commits a transgression in a circumstance that leads others to imitate his bad example.

The best way to approach moral choices is to always do the best that can possibly be done in a given situation.

Not all circumstances influence the morality of an act in the same manner. Some circumstances actually lessen the gravity of a sin. To steal a bottle of water from a well-stocked canteen is not the same as to steal the last supply of water from a person stranded in the desert. But *no circumstance can make an intrinsic evil a good action,* and so every intrinsically evil act is impermissible, regardless of the circumstances. As the *Catechism* states:

> **Circumstances of themselves cannot change the moral quality of acts themselves; they can make neither good nor right an action that is in itself evil. (CCC 1754)**

Or, as *Veritatis splendor* teaches, "particular circumstances can diminish their evil, but they cannot remove it."[3] For an act to be morally good, the object of the act, the intention behind it, and the circumstances surrounding it must all be good.

> **A morally good act requires the goodness of its object, of its end, and of its circumstances together. (CCC 1760)**

Again, Christian morality teaches that we should not do only the moral minimum in a given situation. For instance, a discussion on how to help the poor should not lead to determining the least a person should give. The best way to approach moral choices is to always do the best that can possibly be done in a given situation.

These sources must always be on our minds when we confront an action. We must analyze every act in all the points: the act itself *(object)*, the ends sought *(intention)*, and the different conditions surrounding the act *(circumstances)*. In this regard, the teachings of the encyclical *Veritatis splendor* are very clear.[4]

3. THE PRINCIPLE OF DOUBLE EFFECT

Not every human action has only good effects or bad effects. Some bring about evil results even though the agent intends to do good. Moral theologians have offered the Principle of Double Effect to determine whether or not actions that have a good and an evil effect are permissible.

The decision to carry out this kind of action may be made when the good effect cannot be reasonably brought about in any other way and with the following conditions:

a. THE ACTION MUST BE GOOD IN ITSELF OR AT LEAST INDIFFERENT.

An intrinsically evil action like abortion is never permissible, even if it has a good effect, because abortion is always evil in itself.

b. THE AGENT MUST HAVE THE RIGHT INTENTION.

The good effect must be directly intended, and the evil effect, although foreseen, must not be intended but only permitted or tolerated. One may never directly intend an evil; rather one allows the evil to occur because it cannot be separated from the good intended.

One cannot commit an action in which the good effect comes about as a direct result of the evil effect.

c. THE EVIL EFFECT CANNOT BE THE MEANS TO THE GOOD EFFECT.

The good effect must be the direct result of the action taken, since the end does not justify the means. One cannot commit an action in which the good effect comes about as a direct result of the evil effect.

d. THE GOOD EFFECT MUST BALANCE THE EVIL EFFECT.

The good effect of the action taken must be equal to or outweigh the evil effect. In other words, when there is a foreseeable evil effect of an action, there must be a proportionately grave reason for acting.

An action that meets all four of these conditions may be permissible. Now let us apply this principle to a specific situation:

A young woman is expecting her third child when she is diagnosed with uterine cancer. The cancer is advanced, and without an immediate hysterectomy (removal of the uterus), the expectant mother will die. Her unborn child, however, is unable to survive outside the womb at this point, and to await the viability of the child would, in the doctor's best judgment, likely cause the death of both the mother and the child. However, the proposed operation will also certainly cause the child's death, though it will save the mother's life.

Is the surgeon morally permitted to perform the operation?

Applying the first condition to this case, we can first ask whether the action is good or indifferent. The removal of a diseased organ that threatens the life of a young woman is surely a good action. Therefore the action is good in itself.

The second condition would be met if the physician intends to save the mother's life, and, although he foresees the risk of the death of the unborn child, he only permits or tolerates it as an undesired and inseparable side effect of his actions.

Modern secular ethics has undergone a denial of the reality of the morally good and evil.

The third condition is whether the good effect comes about as a result of the evil effect. In this case, the good effect (saving the life of the mother) is not a result of the death of the child. The mother's life is saved by the removal of the diseased uterus. Whether an unborn child is in that uterus or not does not change the fact that removing the organ saves the mother's life. The good effect (saving the life of the mother) does not come about as a result of the bad effect (the death of the child).

The fourth condition must also be applied. The good effect must be equal to or outweigh the bad effect. In this situation, the life of the mother and the life of the child are both important. The good of saving the mother's life is commensurate with the evil of causing the child's death.

In conclusion, this action meets all four conditions of the Principle of Double Effect. The doctor is therefore permitted to remove the cancerous uterus, despite the fact that the death of the unborn child will result.

4. THE OBJECTIVITY OF GOOD AND EVIL

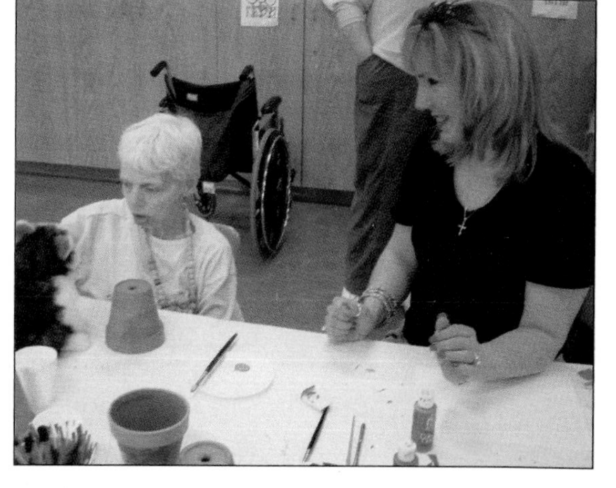

Modern secular ethics has undergone a denial of the reality of the morally good and evil. Many acknowledge the existence of good and evil, but few see these divisions as objective. They see them instead as corresponding to the different circumstances of an individual, and thus susceptible to change.

It is said that an action is good or evil in a particular circumstance and for a particular person. So it is said, "What is evil for you may be good for me," or "What is good today can be evil tomorrow," and vice versa. With this attitude, the moral categories of good and evil lose their objectivity and are turned into variables.

> **This train of thought leads to a moral relativism (morality changes with each new situation) that destroys any correct ethical system, since it denies any moral divisions of acts into good and evil. This ethics is called *moral relativism*, where good and evil are relative terms.[5]**

Charity done out of supernatural motives is more praiseworthy than one that is done for purely human reasons.

The causes behind this ethical relativism are many and complex. They relate to cultural influences and to different philosophical ideas.

5. THE HISTORICAL ARGUMENT FOR MORAL OBJECTIVITY

A basketball is a basketball. It cannot be changed into a baseball by giving it to a pitcher and telling him to throw it. Similarly, blasphemy is always blasphemy, and it cannot be changed into something else by calling it something else. Blasphemy done by an unbeliever or a believer is still blasphemy, though the degree of guilt is different. The same is true with charity. Whether it is done

by a Christian or by an unbeliever, it is always charity, though an action which is done out of supernatural motives is more praiseworthy than one that is done for purely human reasons.

There are acts that have transcended time and are seen as heroic by all, such as the love of enemy exemplified by the saints. Also, there are acts that have been considered evil from the beginning of time. Who could deny that injustice, slander, and homicide are not morally objective evils, independent of any personal opinion or historical circumstance?

As has been shown, circumstances can be a significant factor in judging the goodness or malice of an act, but never does the morally good or evil depend solely on the circumstances.

6. SOME ERRORS DERIVED FROM ETHICAL RELATIVISM

This error in moral thought has given rise to different erroneous and deficient theories. The most common are situation ethics, consequentialism, and proportionalism.

a. SITUATION ETHICS

Situation ethics maintains that moral good and evil result from the situation in which the person finds himself. Hence, it is said that the act cannot be judged alone, but only in its circumstances. It is also called *circumstantial ethics.* For example: John decided not to get drunk on Friday night since he was driving, but on Saturday he got drunk because he was home and no one would be hurt by his action. Thinking that he acted morally in not driving drunk, he has ignored the question of the morality of drunkenness itself.

Ethical relativism has given rise to erroneous theories such as situation ethics, consequentialism, and proportionalism.

Situation ethics claims that moral conduct cannot be guided by universal principles, but must be guided by the concrete circumstances in which each person finds himself. This doctrine, in its origins, was described by Pope Pius XII:

> The characteristic of this morality is that it is not based, in any way, in universal moral laws—as are, for example, the Ten Commandments—but in the conditions or circumstances, real and concrete, in which the action takes place and according to which each individual conscience judges and chooses. A particular state of things is unique and valid for each human action. The particular decision of the conscience—state the defenders of this ethic—cannot be directed by universal ideas, principles and laws.[6]

The pope also explains the objection that had motivated the error: How is it possible to apply a universal law to each person when they are all in different circumstances?

> It will be asked in what way can the moral law, which is universal, apply to and even be obligatory for a particular case, which in its concrete situation is always unique and happens only once. It can and it does because, precisely as a result of its universality, the

> **moral law comprehends necessarily and intentionally all of the particular cases in which its concepts are verified. And in these innumerable cases it acts with such conclusive logic that even the conscience of simple faith perceives immediately and with full certainty the decision that must be made.[7]**

6. CONSEQUENTIALISM

Situation ethics practically disappeared from Catholic morality after the condemnation by Pius XII. But a new theory followed, which is also held by some moral theologians. Those theologians derive the moral concepts of good and evil from the consequences that follow an act, and not from the objectivity of the law that determines them. For consequentialists, an act is good if goodness results from the act, and if evil results from the action, then the act is evil.

This theory was originally applied in the social realm when Max Weber, its inventor, distinguished between ethics of responsibility and social ethics. The former, Weber said, ought to be followed by one who keeps the consequences of his actions in mind, while the latter is exercised by a person who is guided by conscience. Weber's error was to argue there were situations in which consequences could justify acts that are evil in themselves. He saw these two ethics as incompatible. This is not so. We do act responsibly when we follow a correct conscience. Weber's argument that there are situations in which consequences could justify acts that are evil in themselves can find merit only if we have a shallow concept of love and put no value on suffering.

For example, suppose that a young man pressured his girlfriend into having an abortion because they are both young and have very little money with which to support a child, and have discovered through prenatal tests that the child will be born severely handicapped. Weber argues that it is better to abort the child because, in this way, the child will not suffer a life of pain, their families will not be burdened by the child's handicap, and they will not have to face the huge financial burden of caring for a handicapped child. For the consequentialist, this action is morally justified because he judges the consequences that will result from his actions to be good.

Never do evil to bring about a good.
— St. Paul, cf. Rom 3: 8

This doctrine slowly spread to other levels until it reached all of the dimensions of human activity. According to its advocates, the purpose is to create a moral responsibility so that one always keeps in mind the consequences of his actions. If the consequences will be solely evil, then the action ought to be avoided; but if there are good effects, the act can be done even if the act itself is evil.

There are at least three errors in consequentialism:

- The effects of an action are overvalued, so that it ignores the principle set by St. Paul: Never do evil to bring about a good (cf. Rom 3: 8).
- It justifies the morality of means, regardless of their nature, and violates the basic moral principle that "the end does not justify the means."

Morality based on proportionalism would destroy the moral concepts of good and evil, rendering them meaningless.

- It could happen that the advocate of consequentialism may consider those consequences that are good for him, but not good for another person or for society. Thus, the advocates of this ethical system can use immoral means, or seek immediate personal gain, and, in the end, become egotistical. The fact that consequentialism is also known as "ethics of intention" makes even clearer its fundamental flaw since good intentions cannot justify immoral acts.

c. PROPORTIONALISM

Proportionalism is a variation of consequentialism. It seeks to justify the morality of an act by the proportion of the effects that follow it. If the evil that follows is less in proportion to the good, then the act is good. And if the evils are greater in proportion to the goods, then the act is evil and, therefore, is to be avoided.

Returning to the earlier example of abortion, suppose that the young man pressured his girlfriend into having an abortion with the argument that the scandal of unmarried pregnancy would be avoided, their reputations would not be destroyed, and she would not be forced to give up her future plans. Pope John Paul II addressed this proportionalist approach to the morality of abortion in the following words:

> **It is often claimed that the life of an unborn child or a seriously disabled person is only a relative good: According to a proportionalist approach or one of sheer calculation, this good should be compared with and balanced against other goods. It is even maintained that only someone present and personally involved in a concrete situation can correctly judge the goods at stake: Consequently, only that person would be able to decide on the morality of his choice. The state, therefore, in the interest of civil coexistence and social harmony, should respect this choice, even to the point of permitting abortion and euthanasia.**[8]

This method trivializes the importance of morality, and many rights can be undermined as a result. For example: Edward burned down his business to get insurance money to buy better, faster equipment, arguing that insurance companies are not persons so no one was hurt, and the fire had saved his employees' jobs. According to consequentialism, this action would be justified.

Each person has the opportunity to serve God or serve himself.

Neither the circumstances nor the results are the criteria for judging human actions. If this were the case, there would always be a circumstance not to forgive, or an end that would justify stealing, or an innumerable list of goods that follow an unjust act. A morality based on such criteria would destroy the moral concepts of good and evil, rendering them meaningless.

These risks, in themselves, show that the ethical criteria defended by these systems are not valid. Thus, these errors are rejected by the *Catechism of the Catholic Church:*

> **It is therefore an error to judge the morality of human acts by considering only the intention that inspires them or the circum-**

> **stances (environment, social pressure, duress or emergency, etc.) which supply their context. There are acts which, in and of themselves, independently of circumstances and intentions, are always gravely illicit by reason of their object; such as blasphemy and perjury, murder and adultery. One may not do evil so that good may result from it. (CCC 1756)**

This same teaching is stressed by *Veritatis splendor:*

> **One must therefore reject the thesis, characteristic of teleological and proportionalist theories, which holds that it is impossible to qualify as morally evil according to its species—its "object"—the deliberate choice of certain kinds of behavior or specific acts, apart from a consideration of the intention for which the choice is made or the totality of the foreseeable consequences of that act for all persons concerned.[9]**

The rule to keep in mind is that no good, however great, may be sought by committing an evil act.

CONCLUSION

The errors discussed in this chapter are attractive to some people because they contain an element of truth. It is true that circumstances are important, but the crucial belief that must be remembered is that *each person* has a final end, which is eternal life with the Father, Son, and Holy Spirit. If every choice were made with this end in mind, moral choices would be easier. Likewise, one cannot reduce morality to a kind of mathematical formula in which actions are justified because "the proportion of good outweighs the amount of evil."

Each person has the opportunity to serve God or serve himself. It is in the specific moral choices that we make that we direct ourselves to our final end: happiness with God. The rule to keep in mind is that no good, however great, may be sought by committing an evil act.

VOCABULARY

ACTS OF HUMANS
Acts that do not involve the intellect and will (e.g., breathing, sneezing).

CONSEQUENTIALISM
An ethical system that determines good and evil from the consequences that follow an act.

CIRCUMSTANCES
The moral conditions that are added to and modify the moral nature of an action. Circumstances can increase or lessen the seriousness of morally evil actions, but they cannot make them morally good.

END (of an action)
The first goal of the intention and the purpose pursued in the action.

FUNDAMENTAL OPTION
The free and responsible choice a person makes to orient, in a radical manner, his whole existence in a moral direction toward good or evil.

HUMAN ACTS
Actions that are performed with deliberation and free choice. Actions that are performed unknowingly or unwillingly are not imputable to the subject who is doing the act. Only properly human actions can be morally good or evil.

INTENTION (of an action)
A movement of the will toward the end, the goal of the activity.

MORAL RELATIVISM
The belief that there are no absolute truths, and that morality changes with each new situation.

OBJECT (of an action)
A good toward which the will directs itself. The object of an action should not be confused with the *intention* that a person has when performing the act.

PROPORTIONALISM
An ethical system that deduces the moral value of an act from the proportion of good and evil effects.

RATIONALISM
The doctrine that rejects supernatural revelation and makes reason the sole source of knowledge.

SITUATION ETHICS
An ethical theory that derives good and evil from the circumstances that accompany the acting agent.

SUPPLEMENTARY READINGS

1. The problem of truth to which I have briefly alluded is only a single example. The same situation arises in the case of the moral and juristic standard, which is supposed to regulate our wills, as truth regulates our thought. Goodness and justice, if they are what they claim to be, must necessarily be unique. Justice which is only just for a certain time, or for a certain race, cancels its own meaning. In ethics and law, then, too, the principles of relativism and rationalism arise, as they do also in art and religion. This is as much as to say that the problem of truth is dispersed throughout all the spiritual orders which we imply when we use the word, *culture*.

— Jose Ortega y Gasset, *The Modern Theme*, 37

2. Reason attests that there are objects of the human act which are by their nature "incapable of being ordered" to God, because they radically contradict the good of the person made in his image. These are the acts which, in the Church's moral tradition, have been termed "intrinsically evil" *(intrinsece malum):* they are such always and per se, in other words, on account of their very object, and quite apart from the ulterior intentions of the one acting and the circumstances. Consequently, without in the least denying the influence on morality exercised by circumstances and especially by intentions, the Church teaches that "there exist acts which per se and in themselves, independently of circumstances, are always seriously wrong by reason of their object...."

In teaching the existence of intrinsically evil acts, the Church accepts the teaching of Sacred Scripture. The Apostle Paul emphatically states: "Do not be deceived: neither the immoral, nor idolaters, nor adulterers, nor sexual perverts, nor thieves, nor the greedy, nor drunkards, nor revilers, nor robbers will inherit the Kingdom of God" (1 Cor 6: 9-10).

— *VS*, 80-81

3. In reality, it is precisely the fundamental option which in the last resort defines a person's moral disposition. But it can be completely changed by particular acts, especially when, as often happens, these have been prepared for by previous more superficial acts. Whatever the case, it is wrong to say that particular acts are not enough to constitute mortal sin.

— *PH*, 10

"Goodness and justice, if they are what they claim to be, must necessarily be unique."

SUPPLEMENTARY READINGS CONTINUED

4. In any case, in the democratic culture of our time it is commonly held that the legal system of any society should limit itself to taking account of and accepting the convictions of the majority. It should therefore be based solely upon what the majority itself considers moral and actually practices. Furthermore, if it is believed that an objective truth shared by all is *de facto* unattainable, then respect for the freedom of the citizens—who in a democratic system are considered the true rulers—would require that on the legislative level the autonomy of individual consciences be acknowledged. Consequently, when establishing those norms which are absolutely necessary for social coexistence, the only determining factor should be the will of the majority, whatever this may be. Hence every politician, in his or her activity, should clearly separate the realm of private conscience from that of public conduct.

As a result we have what appear to be two diametrically opposed tendencies. On the one hand, individuals claim for themselves in the moral sphere the most complete freedom of choice and demand that the State should not adopt or impose any ethical position but limit itself to guaranteeing maximum space for the freedom of each individual, with the sole limitation of not infringing on the freedom and rights of any other citizen. On the other hand, it is held that, in the exercise of public and professional duties, respect for other people's freedom of choice requires that each one should set aside his or her own convictions in order to satisfy every demand of the citizens which is recognized and guaranteed by law; in carrying out one's duties, the only moral criterion should be what is laid down by the law itself. Individual responsibility is thus turned over to the civil law, with a renouncing of personal conscience, at least in the public sphere.

— *EV*, 69

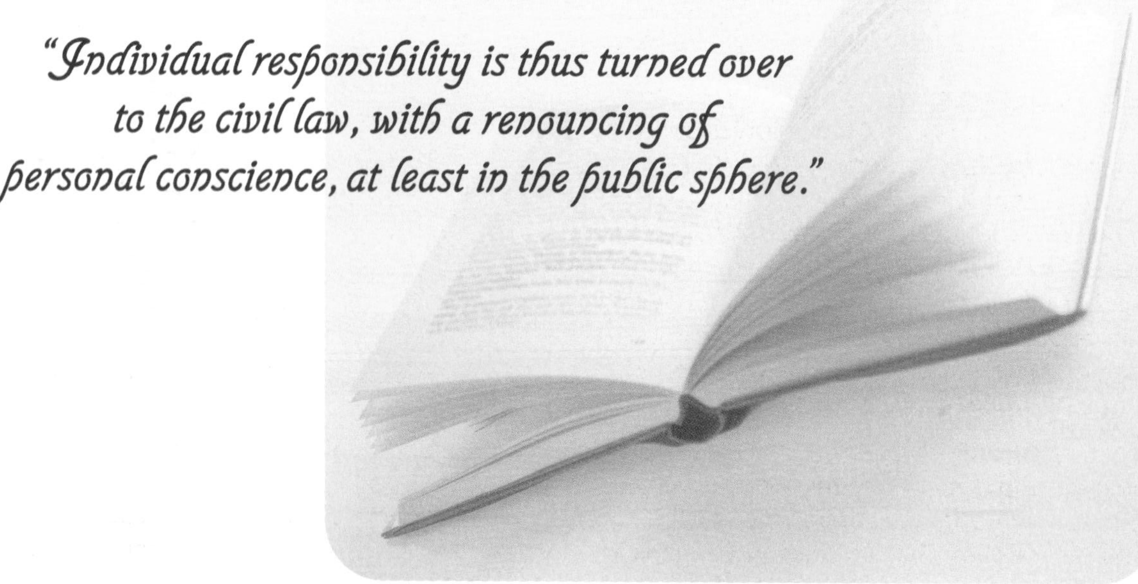

"Individual responsibility is thus turned over to the civil law, with a renouncing of personal conscience, at least in the public sphere."

ADVANCED CONCEPTS

THE "FUNDAMENTAL OPTION"

The basic commitment for or against God made by a human person—the basic orientation of his life in relation to God, either toward obedience and fidelity or to selfishness and disobedience of God—could be called the "fundamental option." This basic commitment gives unity to the moral and spiritual life of a person and, as St. Thomas Aquinas noted, is "not easily lost."[10]

There is no doubt that Christian moral teaching, even in its biblical roots, acknowledges the specific importance of a fundamental choice which qualifies the moral life and engages freedom on a radical level before God.[11]

Nevertheless, some contemporary theologians use the term *fundamental option* in a way that is contrary to revelation as presented by the Church's Magisterium. According to them, the fundamental option is "brought about by that fundamental freedom whereby the person makes an overall self-determination, not through a specific and conscious decision on the level of reflection, but in a 'transcendental' and 'athematic' way."[12] But for them, particular moral acts that flow from this option only partially express a person's basic stance. The fundamental option itself remains untouched by specific moral choices.

They assert that mortal sin, which separates one from God, is that which involves a direct and formal refusal to respond to the call of God, or is found in an egoism by which one completely and deliberately closes himself to love of God and neighbor. Only then, they say, will there be a change in the fundamental option, that is to say, one of those decisions that completely commits the person and will be necessary in order to constitute mortal sin.

At the same time, according to these authors, a change in the *fundamental option* is very difficult, especially in the area of sexual activity. They say that a person generally does not destroy the moral order in a way that is entirely deliberate and responsible when he acts under the influence of passion, weakness, or immaturity, at those moments when he wants to demonstrate his love for another person. Besides, such actions are frequently the result of pressures in the social environment in which he lives.

They reduce serious sin to an act of *fundamental option* against God, which consists either in an explicit and formal rejection of God (as in the case of apostasy) or in an implicit and unconscious repudiation of charity (as in the case of lifelong debauchery).

As we have just seen, reflection on the fundamental option has also led some theologians to undertake a basic revision of the traditional distinction between mortal sins and venial sins. They insist that the opposition to God's law which causes the loss of sanctifying grace—and eternal damnation, when one dies in such a state of sin—could only be the result of an act which engages the person in his totality: in other words, an act of fundamental option. According to these theologians, mortal sin, which separates man from God, only exists in the rejection of God, carried out at a level of freedom which is neither to be identified with an act of choice nor capable of becoming the object of conscious awareness. Consequently, they go on to say, it is difficult, at least psychologically, to accept the fact that a Christian, who wishes to remain united to Jesus Christ and to his Church, could so easily and repeatedly commit mortal sins, as the "matter" itself of his actions would sometimes indicate. Likewise, it would be hard to accept that man is able, in a brief lapse of time, to sever radically the bond of communion with God and afterwards be converted to him by sincere repentance. The gravity of sin, they maintain, ought to be measured by the degree of engagement of the freedom of the person performing an act, rather than by the matter of that act.[13]

These contemporary theologians, rather than attend to the morality of particular actions,

ADVANCED CONCEPTS CONTINUED

fix their attention on the habitual disposition of the person who has decided to do good or evil.

The conclusion to which this eventually leads is that the properly moral assessment of the person is reserved to his fundamental option, prescinding in whole or in part from his choice of particular actions, of concrete kinds of behavior.[14]

In one sense, it is true that a person possesses a profound inclination toward or away from God, but this disposition is formed, confirmed, or altered by each particular action. A person's *fundamental option* can be radically changed by particular acts.[15] The object chosen by the will in any individual action is either properly ordered toward our true end or misdirected toward some other object. The moral determination of an action lies in the rectitude of the object chosen.

Therefore, mortal sin does not consist only in a formal rejection of Christian charity—it also consists in that opposition to authentic love that is part of every deliberate transgression, in grave matters, of the moral law.

For mortal sin exists also when a person knowingly and willingly, for whatever reason, chooses something gravely disordered. In fact, such a choice already includes contempt for the divine law, a rejection of God's love for humanity and the whole of creation: the person turns away from God and loses charity. Thus the fundamental orientation can be radically changed by individual acts. Clearly there can occur situations which are very complex and obscure from a psychological viewpoint, and which have an influence on the sinner's subjective culpability. But from a consideration of the psychological sphere one cannot proceed to the construction of a theological category, which is what the "fundamental option" precisely is, understanding it in such a way that it objectively changes or casts doubt upon the traditional concept of mortal sin.[16]

In short, the ideal moral person is not only one who chooses a definitive and radical mode of conduct befitting a follower of Christ, but one who also believes that he ought to be careful of each and every one of his actions, because they manifest the coherency of his faith and his commitment to God.

"mortal sin does not consist only in a formal rejection of Christian charity —it also consists in that opposition to authentic love..."

QUESTIONS

1. What is a human act? What distinguishes a *human act* from an *action performed by a human being* (i.e., breathing)?

2. List the three components of moral choice.

3. What is the aim of Christian morality?

4. What is the key element in doing good?

5. What does the object determine?

6. What effect does the intention have on the morality of an act?

7. Can a bad intention make an action with a morally good object immoral? Give an example.

8. Define the six circumstances of an act.

9. Can a good intention make an action with a morally bad object a good action?

10. What effect does the object (the act itself) have on whether a particular action is moral or not?

11. Explain: The moral categories of good and evil are objective.

12. What is an intrinsically evil act?

13. What are some errors derived from ethical relativism?

14. What is wrong with situation ethics?

15. Can you come up with any actions that would show the ridiculousness of situation ethics?

16. List three errors of consequentialism.

17. Do the ends ever justify the means: Does a good intention ever justify an action whose object is immoral?

PRACTICAL EXERCISES

1. In the story of Adam and Eve's sin, determine the object, the end, and the circumstances that surround the case.

2. Explain behavior occurring today that is excused by some because "the ends justify the means."

3. Determine the object, the end, and the circumstances of the actions in Luke 21:1-4.

4. Write a brief essay discussing the similarities, differences and connections between situation ethics, proportionalism, and consequentialism.

5. Read the appendix about the fundamental option, and explain the errors in this theory.

FROM THE CATECHISM

417 Adam and Eve transmitted to their descendants human nature wounded by their own first sin and hence deprived of original holiness and justice; this deprivation is called "original sin."

1750 The morality of human acts depends on:

- the object chosen;
- the end in view or the intention;
- the circumstances of the action.

The object, the intention, and the circumstances make up the "sources," or constitutive elements, of the morality of human acts.

1761 There are concrete acts that it is always wrong to choose, because their choice entails a disorder of the will, i.e., a moral evil. One may not do evil so that good may result from it.

1873 The root of all sins lies in man's heart. The kinds and the gravity of sins are determined principally by their objects.

ENDNOTES

1. *VS*, 78.
2. Ibid., 79.
3. Cf. Ibid., 74-78.
4. Ibid., 81.
5. Cf. *VS*, 33.
6. Pope Pius XII, Discourse, June 18, 1952, n. 4.
7. Ibid., n. 9.
8. *EV*, 68.
9. *VS*, 79.
10. St. Thomas Aquinas, *De Veritate*, 27, 1 and 9.
11. *VS*, 66.
12. Ibid., 65.
13. Ibid., 69.
14. Ibid., 65.
15. Cf. Ibid., 67.
16. *RP*, 17.

Chapter 7

Sin And Conversion

The following is the true story of Bernard Nathanson, M.D. Dr. Nathanson was a leading abortionist who came to realize the sanctity of unborn human life. His belief in the pro-life cause led him to the recognition of his own need and desire for God. This story was taken with permission from Dr. Bernard Nathanson's book entitled *The Hand of God,* published by Regnery Publishing, Inc.

It was not supposed to work this way. The whole unimaginable sequence has moved in reverse, like water flowing uphill. The usual and customary progression is: belief in God and his splendid gift of life leads the believer to defend it, and to become pro-life. With me, it was just the opposite. Perversely, I journeyed from being anti-life to belief in God. I was not seeking anything spiritual; my desires have always been, for the most part, earthly and of the flesh, my goals concrete and tangible—and readily liquefiable into cash. To make matters worse, I was openly contemptuous of all this, as a stiff-backed Jewish atheist, or as Richard Gilman would have taxonomized, "a perfunctory Jew."

Getting from there to here wasn't easy. I went through a ten year "transitional time"—perhaps 1978-1988—when I felt the burden of sin growing heavier and more insistent. It was as if the contents of the baggage of my life were mysteriously absorbed in some metaphysical moisture, making them bulkier, heavier, more weighty and more impossible to bear. I found myself longing for a magical phlogiston, a substance that would contribute a negative weight to my heavy burden.

During this decade, it was the hour of the wolf that was the most trying time. I would awaken each morning at four or five o'clock, staring into the darkness and hoping (but not praying, yet) for a message to flare forth acquitting me before some invisible jury. After a suitable period of thwarted anticipation, I would once again turn on my bedside lamp, pick up the literature of sin (by this time I had accumulated a substantial store of it), and reread passages from St. Augustine's Confessions (a staple), Dostoyevski, Paul Tillich, Kierkegaard, Niebuhr, and even Lewis Mumford and Waldo Frank. St. Augustine spoke most starkly of my existential torment but, with no St. Monica to show me the way, I was seized by an unremitting black despair....

Like the diagnostician I was trained to be, I commenced to analyze the patient's humors, the patient being myself. I determined that I was suffering from an affliction of the spirit; the disorder had arisen, at least in part, from an excess of existential freedom, and this had created penumbral despair. I had been cast adrift in a limitless sea of sensual freedom—no sextant, no compass, no charts, simply the dimly apprehended stars of the prevailing penal code, an imitative grasp of the manners and mores of society (a chimpanzee could be trained to do so well), a minimalist concept of justice, and a stultified sense of decency. I required not a cure but healing.

I had performed many thousands of abortions on innocent children, and I had failed those whom I loved...

continued on next page

Excerpt from "The Hand of God" continued

The keenest of human tortures is to be judged without law, and mine had been a lawless universe. Santayana once wrote that the only true dignity of man is his capacity to despise himself. I despised myself. Perhaps I had at least arrived at the beginning of the quest for human dignity. I had begun a serious self-examination (the unexamined life is barely worth living) and had begun to face the twisted moral homunculus reflected in the mirror of self-examination.

I knew now that the primary illness is the severing of the links between sin and fault, between ethically corrupt action and cost. There had been no concrete cost to my corrupt actions, only behavioral exegesis, and that would not do. I needed to be disciplined and educated. I had become as Hannah Arendt had described Eichmann: a collection of functions rather than an accountable human being.

Now I had not been immune to the religious fervor of the pro-life movement. I had been aware in the early and mid-1980s that a great many of the Catholics and Protestants in the ranks had prayed for me—were praying for me—and I was not unmoved as time wore on. But it was not until I saw the spirit put to the test on those bitterly cold demonstration mornings, with pro-choicers hurling the most fulsome epithets at them, the police surrounding them, the media openly unsympathetic to their cause, the federal judiciary fining and jailing them, and the municipal officers threatening them—through it all they sat smiling, quietly praying, singing, confident and righteous of their cause, and ineradicably persuaded of their ultimate triumph—that I began seriously to question what indescribable Force led them to this activity. Why, too, was I there? What had led me to this time and place? Was it the same Force that allowed them to sit serene and unafraid at the epicenter of legal, physical, ethical, and moral chaos?

And for the first time in my entire adult life, I began to entertain seriously the notion of God—a god who problematically had led me through the proverbial circles of hell, only to show me the way to redemption and mercy through his grace. The thought violated every eighteenth century certainty I had cherished; it instantly converted my past into a vile bog of sin and evil; it indicted me and convicted me of high crimes against those who had loved me, and against those whom I did not even know; and simultaneously—miraculously—it held out a shimmering sliver of hope to me, in the growing belief that Someone had died for my sins and my evil two millennia ago.

This dramatic story of Dr. Nathanson's personal moral conversion can help us to reflect on the following questions about the nature of sin and conversion:

- What is sin?
- Where did sin originate, and in what does it consist?
- What personal responsibility do we each bear for sin?
- What are the means to conversion and the forgiveness of sin?

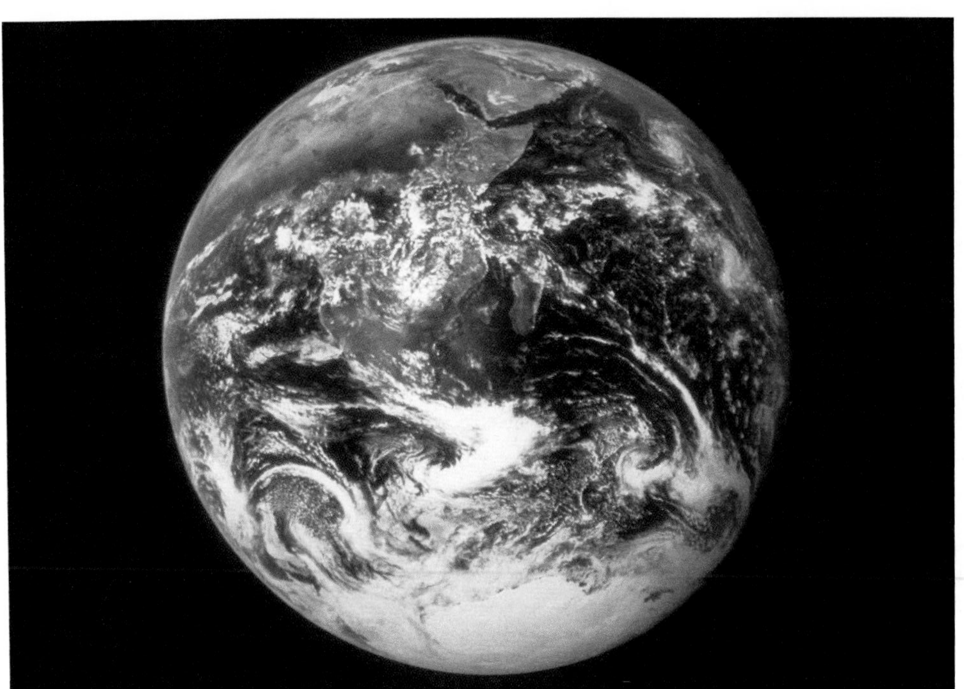

Before the original sin, there was no evil in the world, moral or physical.

INTRODUCTION

Revelation states that man and woman were created in a state of original holiness and justice as friends of God. Before the original sin, there was no evil in the world, moral or physical. Original sin changed this situation. Perhaps God's permission of moral and physical evil is the greatest mystery of human life, but this mystery has been illumined by Jesus, who died and rose from the dead to destroy evil of every type.

Once Adam and Eve had sinned, their intellect and will were affected adversely, so physical and moral evils became ever-present facts in the lives of every living person. Their original sin affected the faculties of human nature and was passed on to all their descendants by propagation.

Unfortunately, people tend to focus on physical evils to the exclusion of moral evils.

Unfortunately, people tend to focus on physical evils to the exclusion of moral evils. Physical evils often cause scandal, for the premature death of an infant, floods, earthquakes, and wars obviously have the power to touch all of us negatively. Yet besides physical evils, many moral evils—sins—are committed, such as slander, infidelity, murder of unborn children, abandonment of the elderly, and blasphemy, which do not appear to touch us in the same way.

There is a noticeable difference in the reaction to physical evil and moral evil. In the former case, there is much sadness and sympathy, and the cry is often heard, "Why did God let this happen?" Some even wish to place the blame on God directly, with the false assumption that God creates evil. In the case of moral evil, there is much indifference—sometimes even happiness—over a sinful life. Today, people who are guilty of acts that once were recognized as sins are now treated as celebrities. Watching people on talk shows who brag about their sinful lives has become common. Some of them will admit to having made mistakes, and say they are sorry, but there is rarely a

Physical Evil: If there are famines, it is because hunger in the world has its origin in the sin of Adam.

recognition or admission of guilt for sin. This difference in reaction ought to be seriously evaluated. If the culture celebrates sin, how is one to determine what sin is?

To understand the problem better, distinctions should be made:

a. ALL PHYSICAL EVILS ARE THE RESULT OF ADAM'S SIN.

If there are famines, it is because hunger in the world has its origin in the sin of Adam. "Because you have listened to the voice of your wife, and have eaten of the tree of which I commanded you, 'You shall not eat of it,' cursed is the ground because of you" (Gn 3:17). There are physical evils, such as disease, that are not dependent on the will of the one who suffers them, and that are unavoidable.

b. MORAL EVIL, ON THE OTHER HAND, IS ALWAYS FREELY COMMITTED AND CAN ALWAYS BE AVOIDED. A PERSON IS THEREFORE GUILTY OF SIN IF HE CHOOSES MORAL EVIL.

Moral evil hurts both the agent and recipient, but it engenders worse consequences in the agent than in the victim. Every sin causes an immeasurable evil for the sinner. Human passions may have an initially pleasant effect, but they leave an emptiness and a restlessness. For example, lustful sexual satisfaction degrades the person, and the result is an internal battle between the physical and spiritual sides in the sinner, who is enslaved by appetites.

Socrates constantly repeated this maxim, which applies to all evil: "The one who commits an injustice merits more compassion than the one receiving the injustice, even if the one receiving it is myself." This is so because moral evil denigrates the person and it ends up leading him to disgrace and unhappiness.

Sin is not unique to Catholic morality; rather, all religions have a list of sins that are condemned as offenses against God and injure human dignity. But sin is not a human evil only because it carries with it disgrace and restlessness, but also because it is an offense against God. Thus, it is the only persistent evil, and it is the cause of many other evils.

1. DEFINITION OF SIN

Sin has many definitions. The following three are the classical definitions of two of the Church's greatest theologians, St. Augustine and St. Thomas Aquinas:

a. SIN IS ANY DEED, WORD, OR DESIRE AGAINST ETERNAL LAW. (St. Augustine)

Eternal law is the divine wisdom directing creatures to their proper end. Thus, to act against eternal law is to transgress moral law, which is part of eternal law, offending God.

This Augustinian definition considers both eternal law, which refers to the cosmos, and *natural law,* which is the application of eternal law to human creatures. With respect to natural law, all that violates human nature is considered sinful. This definition takes into consideration the fact that sin can occur in thought, word, or deed.

b. SIN IS THE VOLUNTARY TRANSGRESSION OF THE DIVINE MORAL LAW. (St. Thomas Aquinas)

According to this definition, a sin occurs when God's law is broken. Thus, acts that break the Ten Commandments are sinful. And, since the hierarchy of the Church has the power to impose positive laws on Christians, one sins by ignoring ecclesiastical laws, for example, the precepts of the Church, one of which is the requirement to attend Mass on Sundays and holy days. It is also sinful to disobey just civil laws.

A person sins when he chooses out of his own egotism and out of disdain for God's will.

c. SIN IS A TURNING AWAY FROM GOD, TO CREATURES, IN A DISORDERED WAY. (St. Thomas Aquinas)

This definition graphically expresses the actual makeup of sin. In fact, the human being, in his freedom, is constantly choosing. For example, he can fulfill his will by doing as he pleases, or by doing God's will, which calls for the love of neighbor. He can say the truth or simply lie; he can follow God's directives for sexuality or act sexually according to his own ideas. In summary, a person sins when he chooses out of his own egotism and out of disdain for God's will.[1]

In fact, consciously or unconsciously, people at times prefer themselves before God. When choosing between his will or God's will, a person will often favor his own desire, and so he sins.

These three definitions are implicitly stated in the *Catechism of the Catholic Church:*

> Sin is an offense against reason, truth, and right conscience; it is failure in genuine love for God and neighbor caused by a perverse attachment to certain goods. It wounds the nature of man and injures human solidarity....
>
> Sin is an offense against God....Sin sets itself against God's love for us and turns our hearts away from it. Like the first sin, it is disobedience, a revolt against God through the will to become "like gods" (Gn 3:5) knowing and determining good and evil....In this proud self-exaltation, sin is diametrically opposed to the obedience of Jesus, which achieves our salvation. (CCC 1849-1850)

2. THE REAL MEANING OF SIN IN THE BIBLE

The sacred writers, by divine inspiration, tried to convey the evil of sin through different terms. In the original Hebrew of the Old Testament, sin is signified as a *deviance* or *fall.* Another term used is *rebelliousness.* Other terms are *error, disgrace, madness, crime, impiety, evil act, treachery, malice* and *foolishness.* The New Testament writers also used a number of terms to designate the reality of sin. The most frequent are *deviance* or *"to lose the path," iniquity, injustice* and *impiety.*

The Bible—God's revelation of himself and his will for mankind—gives us a history of the evil effects of sin. There is no lower form of existence than to be permanently in the state of serious sin.

3. SIN AS A PERSONAL ACT

Since sin is an act of human freedom, which proceeds from our knowledge, a person is always responsible for his sins.

> Sin, in the proper sense, is always a *personal act*, since it is an act of freedom on the part of an individual person, and not properly of a group or community. This individual may be conditioned, incited and influenced by numerous and powerful external factors. He may also be subjected to tendencies, defects and habits linked with his personal condition. In not a few cases such external and internal factors may attenuate, to a greater or lesser degree, the person's freedom, and therefore his responsibility and guilt. But it is a truth of faith, also confirmed by our experience and reason, that the human person is free. This truth cannot be disregarded in order to place the blame for individuals' sins on external factors such as structures, systems or other people. Above all, this would be to deny the person's dignity and freedom, which are manifested—even though in a negative and disastrous way—also in this responsibility for sin committed. Hence there is nothing so personal and untransferable in each individual as merit for virtue or responsibility for sin.
>
> As a personal act, sin has its first and most important consequences in the *sinner himself:* that is, in his relationship with God, who is the very foundation of human life; and also in his spirit, weakening his will and clouding his intellect.[2]

"The sin of the century is the loss of the meaning of sin."

— Pius XII

4. THE LOSS OF THE MEANING OF SIN

The judgment of sin found in the Bible contrasts radically with the view of sin today. In fact, some societies that were once Christian have lost the understanding of what sin is. For example, assisted suicide is gaining increasing acceptance in many of the countries of Western Europe and the United States, and societies that previously did not permit civil divorce, contraception, or pornography now accept them.

Pope Pius XII made the first warning in 1946 when he stated that "the sin of the century is the loss of the meaning of sin."[3] This warning is repeated in later documents of the Magisterium. The most recent and solemn of these is the following of Pope John Paul II:

> Nevertheless, it happens not infrequently in history, for more or less lengthy periods and under the influence of many different factors, that the moral conscience of many people becomes seriously clouded....Too many signs indicate that such an eclipse exists in our time. This is all the more disturbing in that conscience, defined by the Council as "the most secret core and sanctuary of a man"

> (*GS*, 16) is "strictly related to human freedom.... For this reason conscience, to a great extent, constitutes the basis of man's interior dignity, and, at the same time, of his relationship to God" (Pope John Paul II, *Angelus* of 14 March, 1982). It is inevitable therefore that in this situation there is an obscuring also of the sense of sin, which is closely connected with the moral conscience, the search for truth and the desire to make a responsible use of freedom.[4]

The loss of the meaning of sin represents a great evil for the whole of humanity, not just for the Christian. In fact, humanity is already suffering greatly because, to a certain extent, the notion of sin is being lost, and with it the notion of what is good and evil. A culture that becomes insensitive to such issues becomes impoverished and ignorant, since good and evil exist regardless of any denial or acceptance on the part of society. Here, we recall St. John: "If we say we have no sin, we deceive ourselves, and the truth is not in us" (1 Jn 1:8).

Examples of this relativism abound on radio and television today, where both music and conversation are used to promote all kinds of vices.

The moral evil of sin cannot disappear; what can diminish is the awareness of sin and the hate for it. Some factors that contribute to the loss of the sense of sin are the following:

a. CULTURAL AND ETHICAL RELATIVISM

The denial of sin as something real and permanent will increase if society professes a cultural and ethical relativism that permits the individual person to decide what is good for himself.[5]

Examples of this relativism abound on radio and television today, where both music and conversation are used to promote all kinds of vices.

b. INCORRECT STATEMENTS OF MODERN PSYCHOLOGY

Some psychologists today deny the existence of sin, based on the idea that it shocks the conscience. They propose a morality without sin that liberates people from a morose feeling of shame. They refuse to see that sin can permanently harm people only when shame and pardon are lacking. According to the Christian conception, an awareness of sin—far from harming—helps liberate, since in Christianity, every sin has the possibility of forgiveness, in which God's love is seen.[6]

c. THE CONFUSION BETWEEN MORALITY AND LEGALITY

It is clear that a society that is ruled by laws will naturally judge those things permitted by the law as good, and will condemn those things prohibited by law as evil. Divorce and abortion are two sins that have come to be accepted as moral because they are legal.

d. SECULARISM

Secularism is a philosophy that rejects any reference to God or religion and seeks the improvement of human society through purely human means, i.e., science, social organization, and human reason.

Secularism sees the world as having no place for God or permanent ideas of good and evil. A religious view of existence will facilitate the acceptance of sin as a reality, and a lack of religious sense will diminish that acceptance. Perhaps this is the reason today for the loss of the meaning of sin. After all, where the sense of God is obscured, so will the sense of sin be blurred.

Where the sense of God is obscured, so will the sense of sin be blurred.

As Pope John Paul II noted:

> The attempt to set freedom in opposition to truth, and indeed to separate them radically, is the consequence, manifestation and consummation of another more serious and destructive dichotomy, that which separates faith from morality.
>
> This separation represents one of the most acute pastoral concerns of the church amid today's growing secularism, wherein many, indeed too many, people think and live "as if God did not exist."[7]

The very life of the Church is affected by this trend. John Paul II stated this fact in the following words:

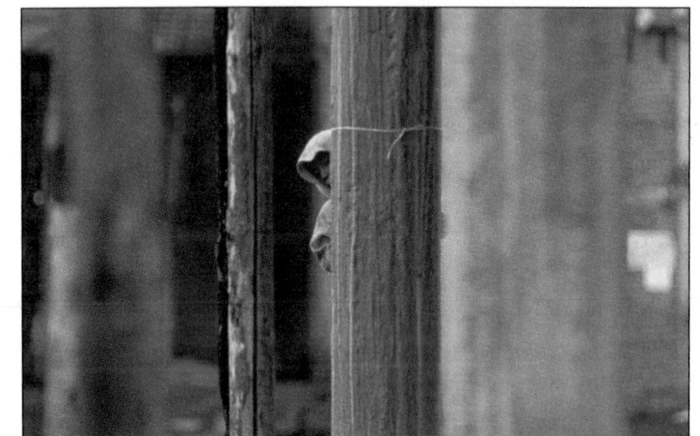

> Even in the field of the thought and life of the Church certain trends inevitably favor the decline of the sense of sin. For example, some are inclined to replace exaggerated attitudes of the past with other exaggerations: from seeing sin everywhere they pass to not recognizing it anywhere; from too much emphasis on the fear of eternal punishment they pass to preaching a love of God that excludes any punishment deserved by sin; from severity in trying to correct erroneous consciences they pass to a kind of respect for conscience which excludes the duty of telling the truth.[8]

Briefly, then, we could say that the shift has been from a misconception of seeing sin everywhere to not seeing sin anywhere—a clear case of going from one extreme to the other.

We could say that the shift has been from a misconception of seeing sin everywhere to not seeing sin anywhere.

Thus, there is a need for a rediscovery of the existence of sin, that is, of the meaning of good and evil as an offense against God. But we must first return to living out our faith before this can truly happen, for "faith is a decision involving one's whole existence."[9]

5. DIVISIONS OF SIN

The reading of Sacred Scripture shows that sins are not all of the same kind, nor are all immoral acts equally sinful. There are five classifications of sin:

a. BY ITS ORIGIN: ORIGINAL OR ACTUAL

Original sin is the sin of disobedience committed by the first parents at the beginning of human history, and every person is born with its effect on his soul, which inclines him toward sin. *Actual sin* is the sin committed by each one of us.

b. BY ITS GRAVITY: MORTAL OR VENIAL

Mortal sin is a grave offense against God that destroys our relationship with him by severing us from his divine love. Mortal sin is "something grave and disordered."[10] This relationship can be restored through reconciliation.

Moral theology lists three conditions for mortal sin:

- *Grave matter* "is specified by the Ten Commandments," that is, it must be a serious violation of the natural law; (CCC 1858)
- *Full knowledge* "presupposes knowledge of the sinful character of the act, of its opposition to God's law"; (CCC 1859)
- *Complete consent* "implies a consent sufficiently deliberate to be a personal choice." It is enough that one has done a prohibited thing deliberately for him to have complete consent. (CCC 1859)

If these three conditions are not met, no mortal sin is committed.[11] Consequently, there is no such thing as committing a sin "by surprise." However, one can commit sin even though he does not desire to offend God.

Venial sins should be confessed in order to avoid mortal sin.

Venial sin is a less serious offense that offends the love of God. While it does not separate us from God, it weakens our relationship with him. Venial sins should be confessed in order to avoid mortal sin.

> One commits *venial sin* when, in a less serious matter, he does not observe the standard prescribed by the moral law, or when he disobeys the moral law in a grave matter, but without full knowledge or without complete consent. (CCC 1862)

The repetition of sins—even venial sins—can lead to commission of mortal sins and a life of vice.

c. BY ITS INTENT: FORMAL OR MATERIAL

A *formal sin* is a voluntary and freely chosen action contrary to the law of God; a *material sin* is an involuntary transgression committed without either required knowledge or full deliberation. In the case of formal sin, there is culpability. A material sin, however, is not a culpable transgression, since the perpetrator is not aware that it is a sin.

d. BY ITS MANNER: COMMISSION OR OMISSION

A *sin of commission* is the choice to do an evil act. Stealing would be an example.

A *sin of omission* occurs when a required act is omitted, such as choosing to miss Mass on Sunday.

In Jesus' preaching, all sins are condemned, but in the Gospel of Matthew, the punishment for sins of omission is stressed (cf. Mt 25:1-46). The reason may be that it is easier to be sorry for those sins committed than it is for those omitted, since it requires more sensitivity to see sin of omission.

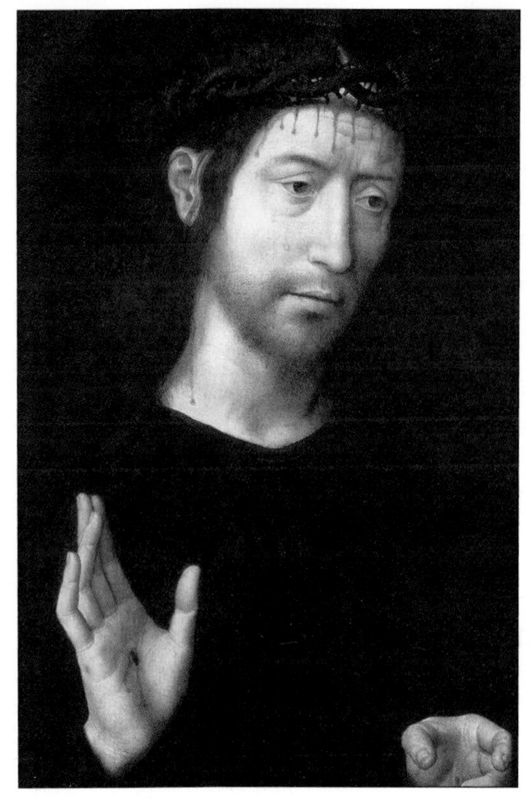

Both sins of commission and omission create a corrupt atmosphere in which evil is sought. This state can lead to *social* or *institutional sins.*

> To speak of *social sin* means in the first place to recognize that, by virtue of a human solidarity which is as mysterious and intangible as it is real and concrete, each individual's sin in some way affects others. This is the other aspect of that solidarity which on the religious level is developed in the profound and magnificent mystery of the Communion of Saints....
>
> To this law of ascent there unfortunately corresponds the law of descent. Consequently one can speak of a communion of sin, whereby a soul that lowers itself through sin drags down with itself the Church and, in some way, the whole world. In other words, there is no sin, not even the most intimate and secret one, the most strictly individual one, that exclusively concerns the person committing it. With greater or lesser violence, with greater or lesser harm, every sin has repercussions on the entire ecclesial body and the whole human family. According to this first meaning of the term, every sin can undoubtedly be considered as social sin.[12]

These two realities are often mentioned in recent Church documents and in the *Catechism:*

A soul that lowers itself through sin drags down with itself the Church and, in some way, the whole world.

> Sins give rise to social situations and institutions that are contrary to the divine goodness. "Structures of sin" are the expression and effect of personal sins. They lead their victims to do evil in their turn. In an analogous sense, they constitute a "social sin." (CCC 1869)

e. BY ITS MANIFESTATION: EXTERNAL OR INTERNAL

External sin is committed with words or actions. *Internal sin* is found in thought or desire. Hence, evil thoughts, evil daydreaming, and evil desires are sins that need to be confessed.

Some find it hard to admit that one can sin in thought or desire, without sinning in action. However, internal sins are clearly condemned by Jesus (cf. Mt 15:10-20; Mk 7:14-23).

Concomitant with the prohibition against sinning is the requirement to avoid all occasions of sin. An occasion of sin is any person, place, or thing that will likely lead to sin. In effect, it is sinful to deliberately place oneself in a situation where there is certainty that one can be tempted.

6. COOPERATION IN EVIL

One may never explicitly or implicitly cooperate in the sin of another. Cooperation in the sin of another is the help afforded to another in the execution of his sinful purpose. Cooperation may be *formal* or *material.*

Formal cooperation is cooperation in or agreement with the evil will of the person acting. Explicit formal cooperation is willing cooperation in the evil act, such as a doctor who assists another doctor in performing an abortion.

Implicit formal cooperation is not direct participation in the act itself, but occurs when the cooperator's will cannot be distinguished from the person acting, such as a secretary at an abortion mill. Both explicit and implicit formal cooperation are wrong.

Material cooperation is when the cooperator does an act that is not in itself evil, but which helps another person do an evil act. Material cooperation is divided into immediate and mediate.

One may never explicitly or implicitly cooperate in the sin of another.

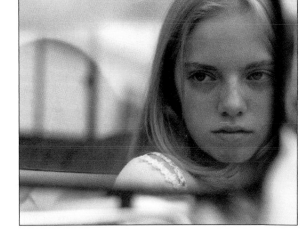

Immediate material cooperation is the concurrence in the evil act of another that, apart from the intention of the cooperator, tends to produce the evil intended by the agent. Immediate material cooperation is equivalent to implicit formal cooperation and is therefore wrong. A nurse at an abortion mill serves as an example of immediate material cooperation.

In the case of mediate material cooperation, the object or intention of the cooperator is not that of the person committing the evil act. The morality of mediate material cooperation depends on how closely connected it is to the action, i.e. whether it is proximate or remote. An example of proximate mediate material cooperation would be the person who cleans the surgical instruments in a hospital that performs abortions (as well as other surgical procedures). An example of remote mediate material cooperation would be the person who washes the windows at such a hospital.

The circumstances in which a person may cooperate in an action that has unintended evil consequences are:

- the evil must not be a direct result of the act;
- the cooperator may not intend the evil which occurs; and
- there must be no possibility of scandal.

Consider the case of a bus driver whose route passes an abortion mill. From experience, he knows that there have been occasions when he has dropped off and picked up passengers who have had abortions. He personally disapproves of abortion, and his contribution to the abortions is not a direct result of his employment as a bus driver. In this case, the bus driver is not committing a sin.

Cooperation may be formal or material.

On the other hand, consider a case where a man drives a woman to have an abortion. If he intends for the girl to have the abortion, his cooperation with the evil act is not only material, but formal as well, and therefore sinful. If he wishes she would not get the abortion, but realizes his material cooperation would produce the evil, his act is sinful.

7. EFFECTS OF SIN

The *Catechism* has this to say about the effects of mortal and venial sins:

> ***Mortal sin*** **destroys charity in the heart of man...; it turns man away from God, who is his ultimate end and his beatitude....**

> ***Venial sin*** **allows charity to subsist, even though it offends and wounds it. (CCC 1855)**

As stated before, habitual, deliberate venial sin can lead to mortal sin through a gradual weakening of the love of God.

8. CONVERSION AND FORGIVENESS

The call to conversion is the central theme of the preaching of John the Baptist, who sees repentance as the preparation for the coming of the Messiah: Only those who repent will be able to enter the Kingdom of God, which will be instituted by the Messiah (cf. Mt 3:1-12; Mk 1:2-4; Lk 3:3-18). "Prepare the way of the Lord, make his paths straight" (Mk 1:3).

The public ministry of Jesus also begins with the call to conversion: "The time is fulfilled, and the kingdom of God is at hand; repent, and believe in the gospel" (Mk 1:15). "Repent, for the kingdom of heaven is at hand" (Mt 4:17). Forgiveness is exemplified by narratives of the adulterous woman (Jn 8:1-11), the Samaritan woman (Jn 4:4-42), the public sinner who is forgiven because "she loved much" (Lk 7:36-50), and the case of the criminal who seeks forgiveness at the end of his life (Lk 23:43). There are, then, no lost cases for "the Son of man came to seek and to save the lost" (Lk 19:10).

"Let him who is without sin among you be the first to throw a stone at her."

— John 8:7

St. Luke narrates the three great parables of sin that speak of God's attitude toward the repentant sinner (cf. Lk 15). And Jesus still points out that his mission is "to seek and to save the lost" (Lk 19:10). Thus, he accomplishes the meaning of his own name, *Jesus:* "For he will save his people from their sins" (Mt 1:21).

The call to conversion is one of the objectives of moral doctrine:

> **It is the Gospel which reveals the full truth about man and his moral journey, and thus enlightens and admonishes sinners; it proclaims to them God's mercy, which is constantly at work to preserve them both from despair at their inability fully to know and keep God's law and from the presumption that they can be saved without merit. God also reminds sinners of the joy of forgiveness, which alone grants the strength to see in the moral law a liberating truth, a grace-filled source of hope, a path of life.[13]**

9. THE SACRAMENT OF RECONCILIATION

Baptism is the first and chief sacrament of forgiveness. For sins committed after Baptism, Christ instituted the Sacrament of Reconciliation in the Church, and gave the apostles authority to forgive sins. The Sacrament of Reconciliation plays a central role in forgiveness, since it gives peace to the one who receives it. Sacramental reconciliation is, by Jesus' designation, the ordinary path to forgiveness of sins for those who believe in him:

> **And when he had said this, he breathed on them, and said to them, "Receive the Holy Spirit. If you forgive the sins of any, they are forgiven; if you retain the sins of any, they are retained." (Jn 20: 22-23)**

According to St. Luke, this was Jesus' last recommendation before the Ascension:

> **Then he opened their minds to understand the scriptures, and said to them, "Thus it is written, that the Christ should suffer and on the third day rise from the dead, and that repentance and forgiveness of sins should be preached in his name to all nations, beginning from Jerusalem." (Lk 24: 45-47)**

Like Jesus, the Church is faced with a world that has lost an awareness of sin, so it responds with a call to conversion.

Like Jesus, the Church is faced with a world that has lost an awareness of sin, so it responds with a call to conversion. Such is the content of *Reconciliation and Penance*. The *Catechism of the Catholic Church* also teaches:

> **The Lord Jesus Christ, physician of our souls and bodies, who forgave the sins of the paralytic and restored him to bodily health (cf. Mk 2: 1-12), has willed that his Church continue, in the power of the Holy Spirit, his work of healing and salvation, even among her own members. This is the purpose of the two sacraments of healing: the sacrament of Penance and the sacrament of Anointing of the Sick. (CCC 1421)**

The Sacrament of Reconciliation should be received regularly (monthly confession is a good practice in keeping with sound Christian piety) to enable a program to be followed that would make overcoming sinful habits a real possibility.

10. JUSTIFICATION

Justification from sin and God's indwelling in the soul are results of grace. When we say that a sinner is justified by God, is given life by the Holy Spirit, possesses in himself Christ's life, or has grace, we are using expressions that in different words mean one and the same thing: namely, dying to sin, becoming partakers of the divinity of the Son through the spirit of adoption, and entering into an intimate communion with the Most Holy Trinity.

> **Justification is not only the remission of sins, but sanctification and renovation of the interior man through the voluntary reception of grace and gifts, whereby a man becomes just, instead of unjust, and a friend, instead of an enemy, that he may be an heir in the hope of life everlasting. The causes of this justification are the following: The final cause is the glory of God and of Christ, and life everlasting. The efficient cause is the**

merciful God, who freely washes and sanctifies, sealing and anointing with the Holy Spirit of the promise, who is the pledge of our inheritance. The meritorious cause is the beloved only-begotten Son of God, our Lord Jesus Christ, who, when we were enemies, by reason of His very great love wherewith He has loved us, merited justification for us by His own most holy Passion on the wood of the Cross, and made satisfaction for us to God the Father. The instrumental cause is the Sacrament of Baptism, which is the Sacrament of Faith; *without Faith no one has ever been justified.* Finally, the only formal cause is the justice of God, not the justice by which He is Himself just, but the justice by which He makes us just: namely, the justice which we have as *a gift from Him* and by which we are renewed in the spirit of our mind. And not only are we considered just, but we are truly said to be just, and we are just, each one of us receiving within himself his own justice, according to the measure the Holy Spirit imparts to each one as He wishes, and according to the disposition and cooperation of each one.

Justification has been merited for us by the Passion of Christ. It is granted us through Baptism. It conforms us to the righteousness of God, who justifies us. It has for its goal the glory of God and of Christ, and the gift of eternal life. It is the most excellent work of God's mercy.[14]

11. CONTRITION

Without contrition, sin cannot be forgiven, even in the Sacrament of Confession.

Contrition is sincere sorrow for having offended God, and hatred for the sins we have committed, with a firm purpose of sinning no more. Contrition is necessary for the forgiveness of sin. Without contrition, sin cannot be forgiven, even in the Sacrament of Confession.

Perfect contrition forgives mortal sin immediately, even before one goes to Confession—although naturally, perfect contrition always includes the intention to confess one's sins as soon as possible. Perfect contrition is expressed in the words: "O my God, I am heartily sorry for having offended you…most of all because you are all good and deserving of all my love." Our contrition is imperfect when we are sorry for our sins because we fear God's punishment. This is called *attrition.*

Imperfect contrition does not forgive sins immediately, but it is sufficient to obtain forgiveness when accompanied by sacramental absolution. It is not true contrition when we are merely ashamed of our dishonor or sorry only for the punishments we may incur, so that if there were no punishment, we would still sin.

12. CONVERSION

The parable of the prodigal son expresses in a simple but profound way the reality of conversion. Conversion is the most concrete expression of the working of love and of the presence of mercy in the human world....

Therefore, the Church professes and proclaims conversion. Conversion to God always consists in discovering his mercy, that is, in discovering that love which is patient and kind (cf. 1 Cor 13:4) as only the Creator and Father can be; the love to which the "God and Father of our Lord Jesus Christ" (2 Cor 1:3) is faithful to the uttermost consequences in the history of his covenant with man: even to the Cross and to the death and Resurrection of the Son. Conversion to God is always the fruit of the "rediscovery" of this Father, who is rich in mercy.[15]

Jesus Christ taught that man not only receives and experiences the mercy of God, but that he is also called "to practice mercy" towards others: "Blessed are the merciful, for they shall obtain mercy." The Church sees in these words a call to action, and she tries to practice mercy. All the beatitudes of the Sermon on the Mount indicate the way of conversion and of reform of life, but the one referring to those who are merciful is particularly eloquent in this regard. Man attains to the merciful love of God, His mercy, to the extent that he himself is interiorly transformed in the spirit of that love towards his neighbor.[16]

Sin has always existed, and Christ will always be there to forgive sinners and bring them back.

CONCLUSION

In a period of history in which the reality of sin is being denied, and there is general indifference to moral evil, the Christian is called to be Christ to others by his conduct. People will attempt to invent other theories or explanations of the way to live life, but in regard to any attempt to justify evil, the revelation of God will speak out, as it has done in the Bible. Nevertheless, the Christian cannot withdraw into seclusion, because Christians are given life to be witnesses to the truth. Sin has always existed, and Christ will always be there to forgive sinners and bring them back. The surest way to evangelize others is to strive to imitate Christ in all one's actions. Through God's grace, personal holiness is possible for all faithful members of the Church.

VOCABULARY

ACTUAL SIN
Sins against God committed by the deliberate will of the individual.

ATTRITION
Imperfect contrition resulting from being sorry for sins due to fear of God's punishment.

COMPLETE CONSENT
Consent sufficiently deliberate to be a personal choice.

CONTRITION
Sincere sorrow for having offended God and hatred for the sins we have committed, with a firm purpose of sinning no more.

EXTERNAL SIN
Sin committed by word or deed.

FORMAL SIN
A sin that is freely and deliberately committed. A formal sin always involves knowledge of the evil of the action that is being committed, and freedom to do or to avoid the action.

FULL KNOWLEDGE
The knowledge of the sinful character of the act, of its opposition to God's law.

GRAVE MATTER
A serious violation of the natural law.

HABITUAL SIN
The permanent state of culpability, caused by the frequent commission of actual sins.

INTERNAL SIN
Sin committed in thought or desire.

MATERIAL SIN
An action that is sinful but does not admit culpability because of ignorance.

MORTAL SIN
A grave offense against God that destroys our relationship with him by severing us from his divine love.

NUMERICAL DISTINCTION
The concrete number of acts that are committed contrary to a virtue or precept.

OCCASION OF SIN
A person, place, or thing that can lead to temptation.

ORIGINAL SIN
The act of disobedience committed by the first parents at the beginning of human history. Every person is born with its effect on his soul that inclines us toward sin.

SECULARISM (Secular Humanism)
A philosophy that rejects any reference to God or religion and seeks the improvement of human society through purely human means, i.e., science, social organization, and human reason.

SIN
An offense against God.

SIN OF COMMISSION
A choice to do an evil act—i.e., stealing.

SIN OF OMISSION
A failure to perform some act required by a positive precept—i.e., missing Mass on Sunday.

SPECIFIC DISTINCTION
The categorization of sins according to the specific virtues they violate.

VENIAL SIN
A less serious offense against the love of God that does not deprive the soul of sanctifying grace, but which weakens a person's love for God and neighbor.

SUPPLEMENTARY READINGS

1. It is not difficult to see how certain sins—idolatry, for example—offend God. But all immoral acts offend God. Treating one's neighbor unfairly is an offense against God. But why? How is it that every kind of immorality concerns God?

In considering this question, it is necessary to put aside anthropomorphic notions. God is not offended as we are. He does not get angry in the way we do, his feelings are not hurt, he does not suffer wounded pride. Yet our sins do offend him. How?

We begin by considering our relationship with God in the context of the covenant. God offers us the covenant for our good, for the sake of our human well-being. When we do moral evil, we act against God's love, contrary to his will. Even apart from the covenant, moreover, one who sins sets aside reason and so implicitly sets aside God, the source and meaning and value in creation. Sinners, as it were, declare their independence of anything beyond themselves, including God. In that sense, too, sin is an offense against God.

— Germain Grisez and Russell Shaw,
Fulfillment in Christ, p. 154

2. Verbally, there is very general agreement; for both the general run of men and people of superior refinement say that it is happiness, and identify living well and faring well with being happy; but with regard to what happiness is, they differ, and the many do not give the same account as the wise. For the former think it is some plain and obvious thing, like pleasure, wealth, or honor; they differ, however, from one another—and often even the same man identifies it with different things, with health when he is ill, with wealth when he is poor; but, conscious of their ignorance, they admire those who proclaim some great thing that is above their comprehension... Men of this kind are evidently quite slavish in their tastes, preferring a life suitable to beasts.... A consideration of the prominent types of life shows that... according to them, at any rate, virtue is better.

— Aristotle, *Nichomachean Ethics*, I, 4-5

3. Sin has become almost everywhere today one of those subjects that is not spoken about. Religious education of whatever kind does its best to evade it. Theater and films use the word ironically or in order to entertain. Sociology and psychology attempt to unmask it as an illusion or a complex. Even the law is trying to get by more and more without the concept of guilt. It prefers to make use of sociological language, which turns the concept of good and evil into statistics and in its place distinguishes between normative and non-normative behavior. Implicit here is the possibility that the statistical proportions will themselves change: what is presently non-normative could one day become the rule; indeed, perhaps one should even strive to make the non-normative normal.

In such an atmosphere of quantification, the whole idea of the moral has accordingly been generally abandoned. This is a logical development if it is true that there is no standard for human beings to use as a model—something not discovered by us but coming from the inner goodness of creation.

— Joseph Cardinal Ratzinger,
In The Beginning, pp. 78-79

SUPPLEMENTARY READINGS CONTINUED

4. In any case, in the democratic culture of our time, it is commonly held that the legal system of any society should limit itself to taking account of and accepting the convictions of the majority. It should therefore be based solely upon what the majority itself considers moral and actually practices. Furthermore, if it is believed that an objective truth shared by all is *de facto* unattainable, then respect for the freedom of the citizens—who in a democratic system are considered the true rulers—would require that on the legislative level the autonomy of individual consciences be acknowledged. Consequently, when establishing those norms that are absolutely necessary for social coexistence, the only determining factor should be the will of the majority, whatever this may be. Hence every politician, in his or her activity, should clearly separate the realm of private conscience from that of public conduct.

As a result, we have what appear to be two diametrically opposed tendencies. On the one hand, individuals claim for themselves in the moral sphere the most complete freedom of choice and demand that the State should not adopt or impose any ethical position but limit itself to guaranteeing maximum space for the freedom of each individual, with the sole limitation of not infringing on the freedom and rights of any other citizen. On the other hand, it is held that, in the exercise of public and professional duties, respect for other people's freedom of choice requires that each one should set aside his or her own convictions in order to satisfy every demand of the citizens which is recognized and guaranteed by law; in carrying out one's duties, the only moral criterion should be what is laid down by the law itself. Individual responsibility is thus turned over to the civil law, with a renouncing of personal conscience, at least in the public sphere.

At the basis of all these tendencies lies the *ethical relativism* which characterizes much of present-day culture. There are those who consider such relativism an essential condition of democracy, inasmuch as it alone is held to guarantee tolerance, mutual respect between people and acceptance of the decisions of the majority, whereas moral norms considered to be objective and binding are held to lead to authoritarianism and intolerance.

But it is precisely the issue of respect for life which shows what misunderstandings and contradictions, accompanied by terrible practical consequences, are concealed in this position.

It is true that history has known cases where crimes have been committed in the name of "truth." But equally grave crimes and radical denials of freedom have also been committed and are still being committed in the name of "ethical relativism." When a parliamentary or social majority decrees that it is legal, at least under certain conditions, to kill unborn human life, is it not really making a "tyrannical" decision with regard to the weakest and most defenseless of human beings? Everyone's conscience rightly rejects those crimes against humanity of which our century has had such sad experience. But would these crimes cease to be crimes if, instead of being committed by unscrupulous tyrants, they were legitimated by popular consensus?

Democracy cannot be idolized to the point of making it a substitute for morality or a panacea for immorality. Fundamentally, democracy is a "system" and as such is a means and not an end. Its "moral" value is not automatic, but depends on conformity to the moral law to which it, like every other form of human behavior, must be subject: in other words, its morality depends on the morality of the ends which it pursues and of the means which it

SUPPLEMENTARY READINGS CONTINUED

employs. If today we see an almost universal consensus with regard to the value of democracy, this is to be considered a positive "sign of the times," as the Church's Magisterium has frequently noted. But the value of democracy stands or falls with the values which it embodies and promotes. Of course, values such as the dignity of every human person, respect for inviolable and inalienable human rights, and the adoption of the "common good" as the end and criterion regulating political life are certainly fundamental and not to be ignored.

The basis of these values cannot be provisional and changeable "majority" opinions, but only the acknowledgment of an objective moral law which, as the "natural law" written in the human heart, is the obligatory point of reference for civil law itself. If, as a result of a tragic obscuring of the collective conscience, an attitude of skepticism were to succeed in bringing into question even the fundamental principles of the moral law, the democratic system itself would be shaken in its foundations and would be reduced to a mere mechanism for regulating different and opposing interests on a purely empirical basis.

Some might think that even this function, in the absence of anything better, should be valued for the sake of peace in society. While one acknowledges some element of truth in this point of view, it is easy to see that without an objective moral grounding not even democracy is capable of ensuring a stable peace, especially since peace which is not built upon the values of the dignity of every individual and of solidarity between all people frequently proves to be illusory. Even in participatory systems of government, the regulation of interests often occurs to the advantage of the most powerful, since they are the ones most capable of maneuvering not only the levers of power but also of shaping the formation of consensus. In such a situation, democracy easily becomes an empty word.

— *EV*, 69-70

"Democracy cannot be idolized to the point of making it a substitute for morality or a panacea for immorality."

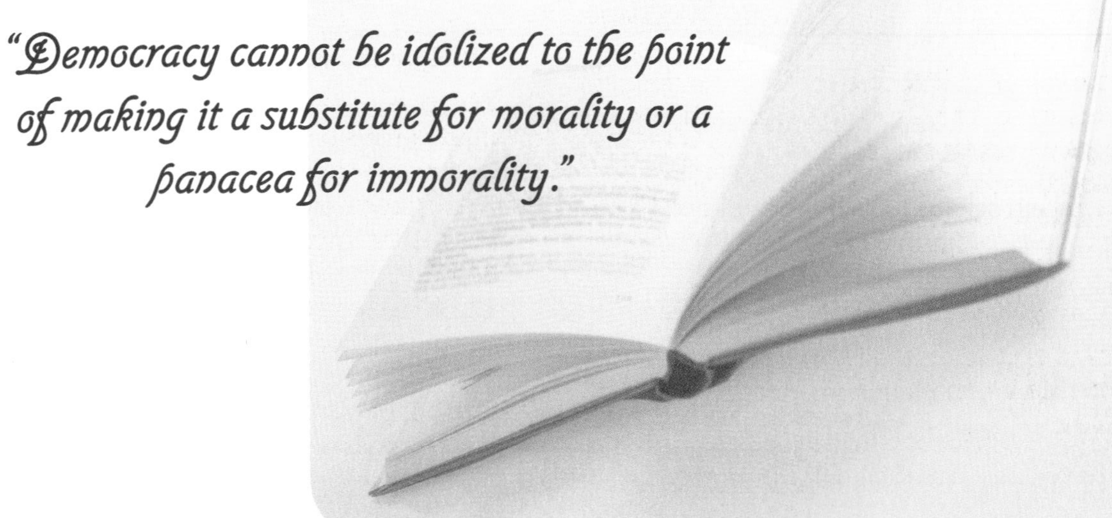

ADVANCED CONCEPTS

MORTAL, GRAVE, OR VENIAL?

Certain authors have recently introduced a threefold division of sin: *mortal, grave* and *venial.*

- *Mortal sins* are done in express and direct rebellion against God. Such sins, according to these authors, are very rare, and only these sinful actions can separate people from God.
- *Grave sins,* on the other hand, are a lesser species of serious sin, closer to venial sins, but still somewhat distinct because the matter is more serious or the subject more malicious. These sins are committed only out of weakness.
- *Venial sins,* like grave sins, are committed primarily out of weakness or habit, but involve neither a direct rebellion against God nor a matter that is serious nor a subject that is malicious.

The Magisterium of the Church has condemned this triple distinction, saying it has no foundation in Scripture, which specifies only two classes of sin. Consequently, mortal and "grave" sins are identical. Serious sins do admit of a difference in degree (for example, blasphemy against God is more serious than sins against charity toward one's neighbor); nonetheless, all separate a person from God, and are, therefore, serious sins.

This threefold distinction might illustrate the fact that there is a scale of seriousness among grave sins. But it still remains true that the essential and decisive distinction is between sin which destroys charity, and sin which does not kill the supernatural life: there is no middle way between life and death.[17]

QUESTIONS

1. Compare and contrast the three definitions of sin given in the chapter (from Augustine and Aquinas).

2. List some of the terms used by the sacred writers of the Bible to convey the evil of sin.

3. Why is sin always a personal act?

4. List some examples regarding modern society's denial of the reality of sin.

5. List and briefly explain the four factors that contribute to this loss of the sense of sin.

6. What are the five classifications of sin?

7. What led to original sin?

8. What were the consequences of original sin?

9. How does actual sin differ from original sin?

10. What are the consequences of actual sin?

11. Contrast mortal sin with venial sin.

12. List the three conditions necessary to commit a mortal sin.

13. What is the lowest form of existence?

14. Why should venial sin be avoided?

15. Are there any circumstances under which something that is a venial can become a mortal sin?

16. What is the difference between a sin of omission and a sin of commission?

17. What is meant by social sin?

18. What is the usual means of forgiveness in the Catholic Church?

19. Is it possible for sin to be forgiven without contrition, even though we go to Confession?

PRACTICAL EXERCISES

1. List the sins that can be found in the following texts of St. Paul:

- Rom 1:29-31; 13:13
- 1 Cor 5:10-11; 6:9-10
- 2 Cor 12:20-21
- Gal 5:19-21
- Eph 4:31; 5:3-5
- Col 3:5-8
- 1 Tm 1:9-10; 4:12; 6:9-11
- 2 Tm 3:2-5
- Ti 3:3

2. Compare the seriousness of sins against justice and chastity.

3. Comment on the following words of Socrates:

- "But if it were necessary for me either to do or to suffer injustice, I'd elect to suffer injustice rather than do it." (Plato, *Gorgias*, 469 c)
- "Then we ought not to retaliate or render evil for evil to any one, whatever evil we may have suffered from him." (Plato, *Crito*, 49 c-d)

4. Comment on the excerpt of Pope John Paul II's writing on the Sacrament of Reconciliation contained in the reading in "Advanced Concepts." Why does the Church reject the distinction between *mortal sin* and *grave sin?* Why is it impossible for a person to commit a sinful action, involving *grave matter,* without this action involving a concrete rebellion against God?

5. Resolve the following case: John and his friend Patrick are discussing the human sins of passion, namely the sins of lust, anger, and gluttony. John holds that actions such as blasphemy against God and grave social injustices are sins, but he denies that pre-marital sex is a sin. "How can you call it a sin if a man and a woman of mutual consent decide to have sexual relations, when children are starving in Africa and being murdered in wars all over the globe?" he asks. Patrick argues that any evil consists in an offense against God, and since extramarital relations are serious disorders of the human passions and contrary to the express purpose for which God created human sexuality, they offend the dignity of the person, who is made in the image of God (cf. Gn 1:27).

6. Explain why, according to the text, people like John tend to reduce sin to blasphemy and social crimes. According to Scripture, why are the most serious sins those that offend human dignity? What criteria can be given to determine both what is sinful and the gravity of the sin?

FROM THE CATECHISM

324 The fact that God permits physical and even moral evil is a mystery that God illuminates by his Son Jesus Christ who died and rose to vanquish evil. Faith gives us the certainty that God would not permit an evil if he did not cause a good to come from that very evil, by ways that we shall fully know only in eternal life.

1490 The movement of return to God, called conversion and repentance, entails sorrow for and abhorrence of sins committed, and the firm purpose of sinning no more in the future. Conversion touches the past and the future and is nourished by hope in God's mercy.

1492 Repentance (also called contrition) must be inspired by motives that arise from faith. If repentance arises from love of charity for God, it is called "perfect" contrition; if it is founded on other motives, it is called "imperfect."

1857 For a *sin* to be *mortal*, three conditions must together be met: "Mortal sin is sin whose object is grave matter and which is also committed with full knowledge and deliberate consent" (*RP*, 17 § 12).

1868 Sin is a personal act. Moreover, we have a responsibility for the sins committed by others when *we cooperate in them:*

- by participating directly and voluntarily in them;
- by ordering, advising, praising, or approving them;
- by not disclosing or not hindering them when we have an obligation to do so;
- by protecting evil-doers.

1873 The root of all sins lies in man's heart. The kinds and the gravity of sins are determined principally by their objects.

1874 To choose deliberately—that is, both knowing it and willing it—something gravely contrary to the divine law and to the ultimate end of man is to commit a mortal sin. This destroys in us the charity without which eternal beatitude is impossible. Unrepented, it brings eternal death.

1875 Venial sin constitutes a moral disorder that is reparable by charity, which it allows to subsist in us.

2018 Like conversion, justification has two aspects. Moved by grace, man turns toward God and away from sin, and so accepts forgiveness and righteousness from on high.

ENDNOTES

1. Cf. *VS*, 70.
2. *RP*, 16.
3. Pope Pius XII, *Radio message to the United States National Catechetical Congress*, October 26, 1946.
4. *RP*, 18.
5. Cf. *VS*, 53.
6. Cf. Ibid., 61.
7. Ibid., 88.
8. *RP*, 18.
9. *VS*, 88.
10. *RP*, 17.
11. Cf. *VS*, 70.
12. *RP*, 16.
13. *VS*, 112.
14. Council of Trent, DS, 1529.
15. *DM*, 6, 13.
16. Ibid., 14.
17. *RP*, 17.

OUR MORAL LIFE IN CHRIST

Part 2

Applications To The Moral Life

The connection between moral good and the fulfillment of man's destiny.

Chapter 8

The Ten Commandments And The Eight Beatitudes

And behold, one came up to [Jesus], saying, "Teacher, what good deed must I do, to have eternal life?" And he said to him, "Why do you ask me about what is good? One there is who is good. If you would enter life, keep the commandments." He said to him, "Which?" And Jesus said, "You shall not kill, You shall not commit adultery, You shall not steal, You shall not bear false witness, Honor your father and mother, and, You shall love your neighbor as yourself." The young man said to him, "All these I have observed; what do I still lack?" Jesus said to him, "If you would be perfect, go, sell what you possess and give to the poor, and you will have treasure in heaven; and come, follow me." (Mt 19:16-21)

The question which the rich young man puts to Jesus of Nazareth is one which rises from the depths of his heart. It is an essential and unavoidable question for the life of every man, for it is about the moral good which must be done, and about eternal life. The young man senses that there is a connection between moral good and the fulfillment of his own destiny. He is a devout Israelite, raised as it were in the shadow of the Law of the Lord.[1]

In his reply to the young man, Jesus expresses the nucleus and spirit of Christian morality. Through this dialogue Christ reveals "the essential elements of revelation in the Old and New Testament with regard to moral action" (*VS,* 28). The answer to the question about moral goodness and its connection to eternal life can be found only in God. One cannot know what is good without knowing goodness itself. For the believer, God is "the One who 'alone is good'; the One who despite man's sin remains the 'model' for moral action" (*VS,* 10). To become good is to become like God. People need to turn to Christ; they receive from him "the answer to their question about what is good and what is evil" (*VS,* 8). Essential to all morality is the recognition of God's sovereignty over the moral order: "acknowledging the Lord as God is the very core, the heart of the Law" (*VS,* 11).[2]

The specific obligations that guide the Christian life are enumerated in the Ten Commandments. It is therefore appropriate to ask the following:

- What are the Ten Commandments?
- Are these ancient codes of moral conduct still relevant guides for life in the modern world?
- How do the Ten Commandments guide us in forming and fulfilling the dictates of conscience?

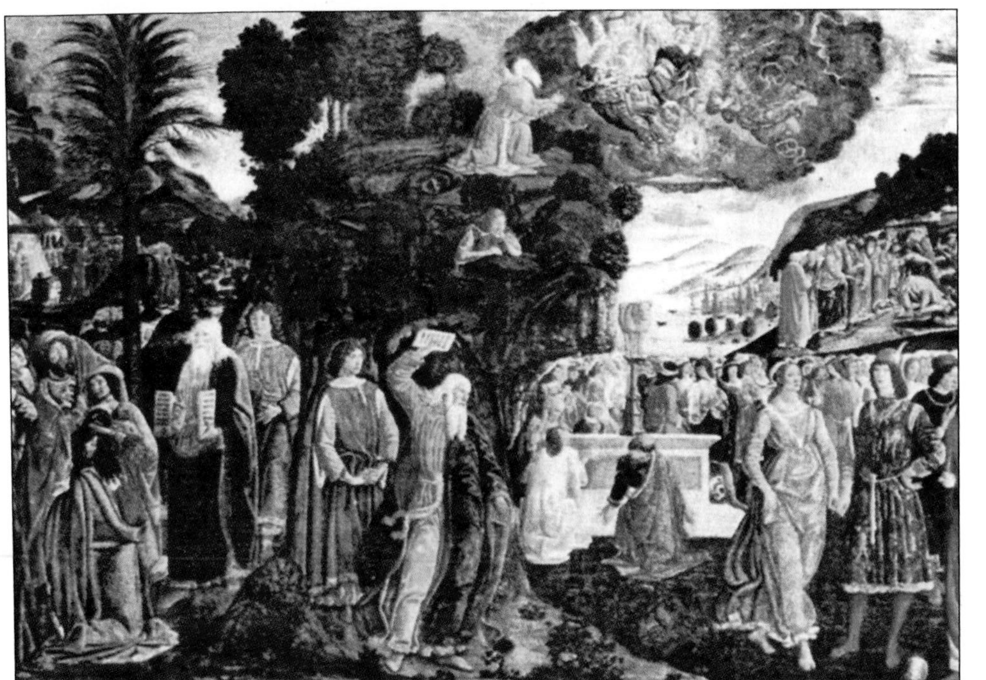

INTRODUCTION

Christian morality has new elements—*foundations* and *principles*—that are not founded on human reason alone, but are given by revelation. In fact, Christian ethics is rooted in the new condition of the baptized. Baptism communicates a singular participation in divine nature, by which the Christian is a son of God in Christ and is expected to conduct his life in a Christ-like manner. Consequently, Christian morality demands of the baptized a life appropriate to a son of God.

Christian norms of conduct: The Ten Commandments of the Old Testament and the ethical commands of the New Law, proposed by Christ.

For this end, the Father has given Christians some norms of conduct. These are the Ten Commandments of the Old Testament and the ethical commands of the New Law, proposed by Christ. By fulfilling these precepts, we discover the will of the Father.

Christian morality demands of the baptized a life appropriate to a son of God.

1. THE TEN COMMANDMENTS

The Ten Commandments were given by God to Moses on Mount Sinai. At the time of the exodus from Egypt, the Israelites were a nation of common ancestry whose sufferings had united them closely, but they were also stubborn and unorganized. Nonetheless, God had a plan for them:

> **On the third new moon after the people of Israel had gone forth out of the land of Egypt, on that day they came into the wilderness of Sinai. And when they set out from Rephidim and came into the wilderness of Sinai, they encamped in the wilderness; and there Israel encamped before the mountain. (Ex 19:1-2)**

Then Moses went up the mountain to pray, and God manifested himself and asked him to prepare his people, for he was going to make a pact, by virtue of which they would be "his people" and he would be their God. This

Also known as "the ten words," they constitute the Decalogue, or Ten Commandments, which God gave to his people.

pact is called the Covenant. In this pact, God gives Israel some norms of behavior, a code of conduct, which is the Ten Commandments. They are given in Exodus 20:

1. I am the Lord your God: You shall not have strange gods before me.
2. You shall not take the name of the Lord your God in vain.
3. Remember to keep holy the Lord's day.
4. Honor your father and your mother.
5. You shall not kill.
6. You shall not commit adultery.
7. You shall not steal.
8. You shall not bear false witness against your neighbor.
9. You shall not covet your neighbor's wife.
10. You shall not covet your neighbor's goods.

The Book of Deuteronomy later reiterates and synthesizes these commandments (Dt 5:6-21), which are also known in Judaism as "the ten words" (cf. Ex 34:28; Dt 4:13; 10:4). They constitute the Decalogue, or Ten Commandments, which God gave to his people. Fidelity to these precepts carries with it God's aid and assistance, and it was the people's duty to transmit those precepts to the future generations:

> **"When your son asks you in time to come, 'What is the meaning of the testimonies and the statutes and the ordinances which the Lord our God has commanded you?' then you shall say to your son, 'We were Pharaoh's slaves in Egypt; and the Lord brought us out of Egypt with a mighty hand; and the Lord showed signs and wonders, great and grievous, against Egypt and against Pharaoh and all his household, before our eyes; and he brought us out from there, that he might bring us in and give us the land which he swore to give to our fathers. And the Lord commanded us to do all these statutes, to fear the Lord our God, for our good always, that he might preserve us alive, as at this day. And it will be righteousness for us, if we are careful to do all this commandment before the Lord our God, as he has commanded us.'" (Dt 6:20-25)**

The Israelites knew that their destiny—for better or worse—was tied to the fulfillment of the precepts. This was their history: When the people of Israel worshipped God with fidelity, they prospered. But when they were not faithful, God permitted them to suffer.

2. THE CODE OF THE COVENANT

The Ten Commandments are part of the revelation given to Moses, and ought to be understood within the context of the Covenant of God with his people and, ultimately, humanity. The fulfillment of these general precepts represents one's fidelity to and acceptance of the plan of God in his life:

> The "ten words" are pronounced by God in the midst of a theophany ("The LORD spoke with you face to face at the mountain, out of the midst of the fire" [Dt 5:4]). They belong to God's revelation of himself and his glory. The gift of the Commandments is the gift of God himself and his holy will. In making his will known, God reveals himself to his people. (CCC 2059)

Since God is faithful, we ought to also be loyal through the grace of the Holy Spirit. The guarantee of such fidelity is the fulfillment of these precepts:

> The Commandments take on their full meaning within the covenant. According to Scripture, man's moral life has all its meaning in and through the covenant....
>
> The Commandments properly so-called come in the second place: they express the implications of belonging to God through the establishment of the covenant. Moral existence is a *response* to the Lord's loving initiative. It is the acknowledgement and homage given to God and a worship of thanksgiving. It is cooperation with the plan God pursues in history. (CCC 2061-2062)

Since God is faithful, we ought to also be loyal through the grace of the Holy Spirit.

Consequently, when a person keeps these precepts, he gives an affirmative response to the grace of the Holy Spirit. He tells God that he accepts the will of the Father in his life. The fruit of this fidelity is every person's goal—happiness.

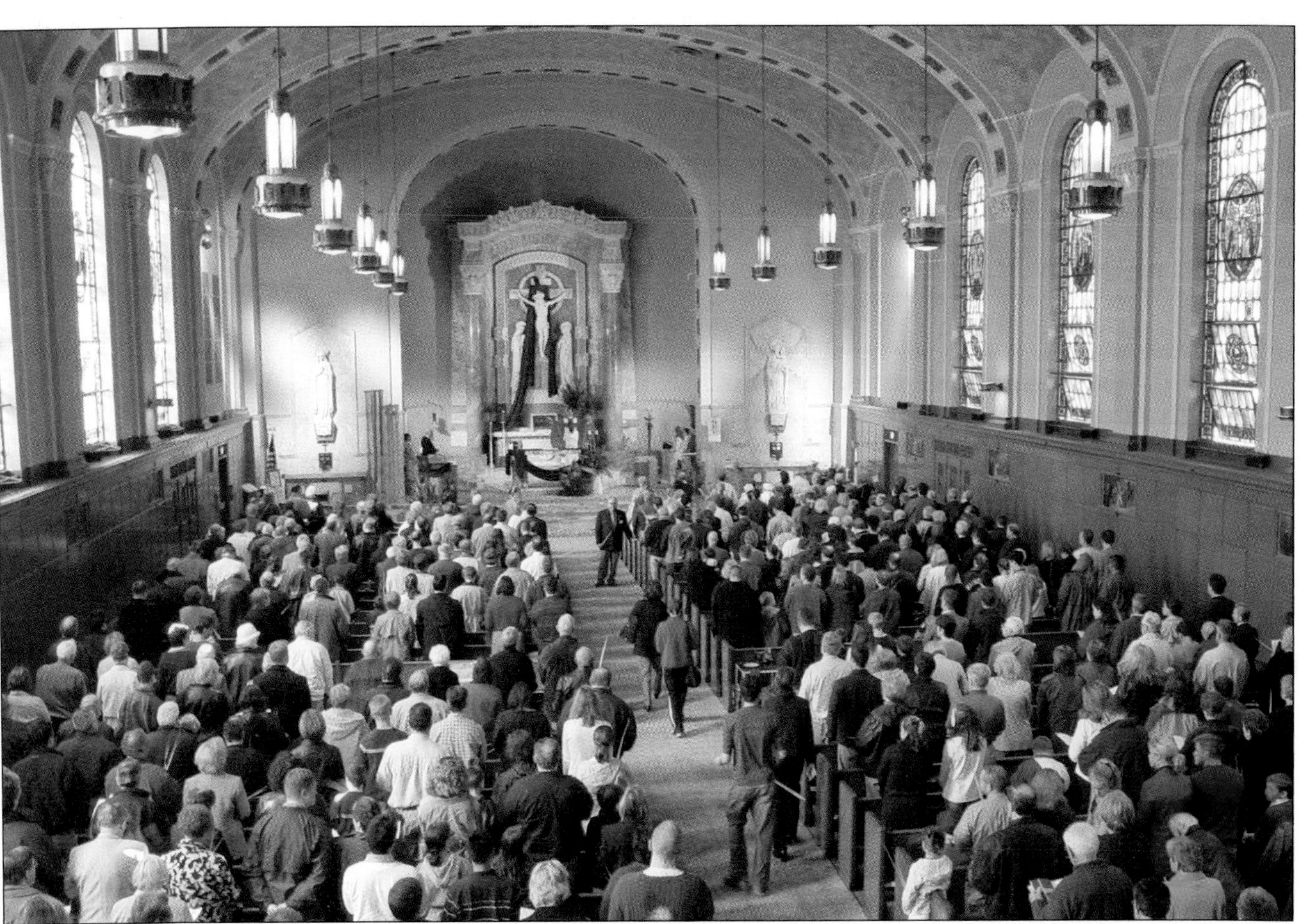

3. THE ETHICAL CONTENT OF THE TEN COMMANDMENTS

The reading of the Decalogue (Ex 20:2-17; Dt 5:6-21) confirms that we have a basic code of conduct. In fact, in the Ten Commandments, God does not offer a complete ethical program, but general and basic principles of conduct. The reason is clear: God could not demand from the Israelites great ethical requirements because Israel, at that time, was an unsophisticated culture.

4. THE TEN COMMANDMENTS AND THE NATURAL LAW

The ethical content of the Decalogue corresponds to what later is called natural law. God made us with an interior code of conduct, which, if we fulfill it, will aid us in living a life of dignity. On the other hand, if one does not keep it, he destroys himself. The Decalogue points to the fundamental nature of us all:

> **The Ten Commandments belong to God's revelation. At the same time they teach us the true humanity of man. They bring to light the essential duties, and therefore, indirectly, the fundamental rights inherent in the nature of the human person. The Decalogue contains a privileged expression of the natural law. (CCC 2070)**

God made us with an interior code of conduct, which, if we fulfill it, will aid us in living a life of dignity.

The Fathers teach constantly that the Decalogue is a primal statement of natural law. The sins of humanity had obscured it, and the Father reveals it to help us remember to fulfill it. Thus, St. Irenaeus said:

> **From the beginning of time, God had placed in the hearts of men the precepts of natural law. Firstly, he was pleased to call their attention to them.[3]**

5. DEVELOPMENT OF CHRISTIAN MORALITY IN VIEW OF THE TEN COMMANDMENTS

Despite the novel message preached by Jesus, Christians have had difficulty with the precepts found in the Decalogue. Already, in the second century, St. Irenaeus of Lyons states:

> **The Lord prescribed the love of God and taught justice towards our neighbor so that man might not be unjust, or unworthy of God. Thus, with the Decalogue, God was preparing man to be his friend and to have the same heart for his friend....The words of the Decalogue persist also among us. Far from being abolished, they have received an amplification and development in the Incarnation of the Lord.[4]**

The Ten Commandments are enriched by the life and teachings of Jesus Christ and given life by the Holy Spirit. For example, the acceptance and worship of one God is enhanced by the love of God as Father, and the transcendence of God as Triune is acknowledged. The respect for life is enriched by the new commandment to love all people, including one's enemies. Sexuality no longer just prohibits adultery, but now seeks internal chastity of thoughts and desires (cf. Mt 5:17-48). Likewise, they no longer merely forbid injuring another through malicious acts, but now seek internal charity and an active love of neighbor manifested in word and deed.

Consequently, when the Decalogue is proposed in moral theology and an attempt is made to articulate its moral content, the Ten Commandments then become the framework upon which the rich moral teachings of Jesus can be understood.

6. THE PRECEPTS OF THE CHURCH

From time to time, the Church has listed certain specific duties of Catholics. These cannot be replaced by good intentions, nor should they be practiced grudgingly or even superficially. "Never flag in zeal, be aglow with the Spirit, serve the Lord" (Rom 12:11). The purpose of the Precepts is to foster a strong relationship with God who is *Love*. There are five Precepts that bind all baptized members of the Church, according to CCC 2042-2043:

1. You shall attend Mass on Sundays and on holy days of obligation and rest from servile labor. This precept requires participation in the Eucharistic celebration on the day commemorating the Resurrection of the Lord and the principal liturgical feasts which honor the mysteries of the Lord, the Virgin Mary, and the saints. It also requires abstinence from those works and activities that impede the worship owed to God or the appropriate relaxation of mind and body.
2. You shall confess your sins at least once a year. This precept ensures preparation for the Eucharist by the reception of the Sacrament of Penance, which continues Baptism's work of conversion and forgiveness.
3. You shall receive the Sacrament of the Eucharist at least during the Easter season. This precept guarantees as a minimum the reception of the Lord's Body and Blood in connection with the Paschal feasts, the origin and center of the Christian liturgy.
4. You shall observe the days of fasting and abstinence established by the Church. This precept ensures times of penance that prepare for liturgical feasts; they help acquire freedom of heart and mastery over instincts.
5. You shall help to provide for the needs of the Church. This precept requires the faithful to contribute to the Church according to their abilities.

Lead a sacramental life: receive Holy Communion frequently and the Sacrament of Reconciliation regularly.

The Precepts acknowledge that the moral life depends on nothing so much as the grace of God given to us by the Holy Spirit in the sacraments, especially the Mass.

Those who seek the highest levels of sanctity can be said to be truly blessed.

> *The moral life is spiritual worship.* We "present [our] bodies as a living sacrifice, holy and acceptable to God,"[5] within the Body of Christ that we form and in communion with the offering of his Eucharist. In the liturgy and the celebration of the sacraments, prayer and teaching are conjoined with the grace of Christ to enlighten and nourish Christian activity. As does the whole of the Christian life, the moral life finds its source and summit in the Eucharistic sacrifice. (CCC 2031)
>
> In her motherly care, the Church grants us the mercy of God which prevails over all our sins and is especially at work in the sacrament of reconciliation. With a mother's foresight, she also lavishes on us day after day in her liturgy the nourishment of the Word and Eucharist of the Lord. (CCC 2040)

7. THE TEN COMMANDMENTS AND THE BEATITUDES

Jesus began the Sermon on the Mount with the Beatitudes to indicate that those who follow them are living the moral life at the highest level—a level that is only possible through the grace of the Holy Spirit. Those who seek the highest levels of sanctity can be said to be truly blessed. As a result of God's grace in seeking personal sanctity, they reach the highest levels of happiness in this life. The closer we come to union with the Father, Son, and Holy Spirit in this life, the happier we will be. It is a foretaste of the permanent happiness that is heaven.

The word *beatitude* comes from the Latin word meaning "blessed." Those who keep the Beatitudes will be blessed with the love of God both here and in the heavenly home. Jesus' preaching takes up the promises made to the chosen people from the time of Abraham that "They will possess the earth." Jesus leads us to see that this promise refers to the heavenly territory. Jesus gives us the Holy Spirit so that we might join him in his Kingdom.

Those who keep the Beatitudes will be blessed with the love of God both here and in the heavenly home.

In the previous chapters, we found that we are called to imitate Jesus to the point of identifying totally with him in the Holy Spirit. Total identification with Jesus means accepting a life of sacrifice for the salvation of others, just as he did. To accomplish this, we must learn to live the Beatitudes. They take us beyond the commandments and lead us to perfection.

In the Gospel of Matthew, the eight Beatitudes are listed. They are:

- Blessed are the poor in spirit, for theirs is the kingdom of heaven.
- Blessed are those who mourn, for they shall be comforted.
- Blessed are the meek, for they shall inherit the earth.
- Blessed are those who hunger and thirst for righteousness, for they shall be satisfied.
- Blessed are the merciful, for they shall obtain mercy.
- Blessed are the pure in heart, for they shall see God.

- Blessed are the peacemakers, for they shall be called sons of God.
- Blessed are those who are persecuted for righteousness' sake, for theirs is the kingdom of heaven.
- Blessed are you when men revile you and persecute you and utter all kinds of evil against you falsely on my account. Rejoice and be glad, for your reward is great in heaven (Mt 5:3-12)

The *Catechism* offers these insights into the Beatitudes:

> The Beatitudes depict the countenance of Jesus Christ and portray his charity. They express the vocation of the faithful associated with the glory of his Passion and Resurrection; they shed light on the actions and attitudes characteristic of the Christian life; they are the paradoxical promises that sustain hope in the midst of tribulations; they proclaim the blessings and rewards already secured, however dimly, for Christ's disciples; they have begun in the lives of the Virgin Mary and all the saints. (CCC 1717)

"Think not that I have come to abolish the law and the prophets; I have come not to abolish them but to fulfill them."

— Mt 5:17

8. THE MORAL VALUE OF THE DECALOGUE AND THE BEATITUDES

Since it formulates the fundamental duties of everyone, the Decalogue has a value that is not limited to a particular time; it is still valid today. In addition, the Ten Commandments are not abolished by the moral message of the New Testament.

Jesus emphatically states: "Think not that I have come to abolish the law and the prophets; I have come not to abolish them but to fulfill them" (Mt 5:17). Neither the new commandment of love nor the Sermon on the Mount diminish the value of the Decalogue.

> Since they express man's fundamental duties towards God and towards his neighbor, the Ten Commandments reveal, in their primordial content, grave obligations. They are fundamentally immutable, and they oblige always and everywhere. No one can dispense from them. The Ten Commandments are engraved by God in the human heart. (CCC 2072)

And John Paul II related the Decalogue to the Beatitudes:

> The Beatitudes are not specifically concerned with certain particular rules of behavior. Rather, they speak of basic attitudes and dispositions in life and therefore they do not coincide exactly with the commandments. On the other hand, there is no separation or opposition between the Beatitudes and the commandments: both refer to the good, to eternal life. The Sermon on the Mount begins with the proclamation of the Beatitudes, but also refers to the commandments (cf. Mt 5:20-48). At the same time, the Sermon on the Mount demonstrates the openness of the commandments and their orientation toward the horizon of the perfection proper to the Beatitudes. These latter are above all promises, from which there also indirectly flow normative indications for the moral life. In their originality and profundity they are a sort of self-portrait of Christ, and for this very reason are invitations to discipleship and communion of life with Christ.[6]

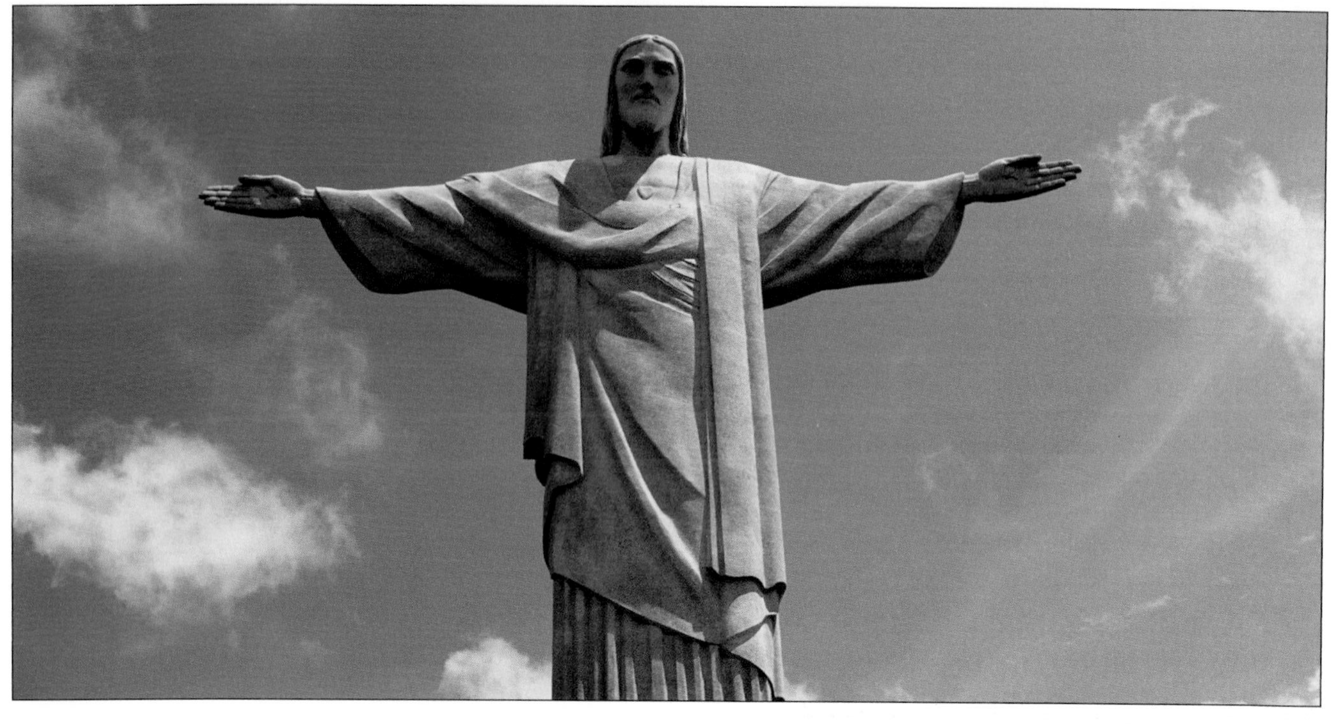

The Church, in presenting the Decalogue and the Beatitudes to every culture, performs a great service for all of humanity.

CONCLUSION

A Christian knows that when he obeys the Ten Commandments and lives according to Christ's teaching in the Beatitudes, besides fulfilling the moral content that fortifies him, he also lives in union with the Holy Spirit. And the Church, in presenting the Decalogue and the Beatitudes to every culture, performs a great service for all of humanity, since, at times, people lose their orientation in life and thus obscure fundamental elements of the moral life. According to some theologians, this was precisely the moral situation of humanity at the time of God's revelation to Moses:

> In the state of sin, a full explanation of the commandments of the Decalogue was necessary because of the obscurity of the light of reason and the deviation of the will.[7]

Additionally, there is need for the Church to remind people of every age that simply avoiding evil and satisfying our duties to our neighbors in a minimalistic way can never be acceptable if we wish to have a truly just society. This is the importance of the Beatitudes, which point the way to a truly free and human existence.

Today, as Christians, we know the ethical contents of natural law by reason and by revelation, as understood by the Magisterium of the Church.[8] We are truly only able to follow this law by the grace of the Holy Spirit.

> It is not easy for man, wounded by sin, to maintain moral balance. Christ's gift of salvation offers us the grace necessary to persevere in the pursuit of the virtues. Everyone should always ask for this grace of light and strength, frequent the sacraments, cooperate with the Holy Spirit, and follow his calls to love what is good and shun evil. (CCC 1811)

VOCABULARY

BEATITUDE
Happiness or blessedness, especially the eternal happiness of heaven, which is described as the vision of God, or entering into God's rest by those whom he makes "partakers of the divine nature."

BEATITUDES
The teachings of Jesus in the Sermon on the Mount on the meaning and way to true happiness (cf. Mt 5:1-12; Lk 6:20-23).

COMMANDMENT
A norm of moral and/or religious action; above all the Ten Commandments given by God to Moses.

COVENANT
A solemn agreement between human beings or between God and a human being involving mutual commitments and guarantees.

DECALOGUE
The Ten Commandments given by God to Moses.

ISRAEL
The Jewish people, chosen by God to be his people and named after Israel (Jacob), from whose twelve sons the tribes of Israel descend.

NEW COVENANT
The new "dispensation" or order, established by God in Jesus Christ, to succeed and perfect the Old Covenant.

SUPPLEMENTARY READINGS

1. Here one discerns how the account of the cardinal virtues (prudence, temperance, fortitude, justice) and the theological virtues (faith, hope, and charity) provides the context to understand spiritual growth. One prays and strives to develop virtue so as not to fall beneath that minimal threshold of charity indicated by the final six negative precepts of the Decalogue—but virtue is ordered far beyond this minimal threshold. One needs virtue not merely to avoid sin (and surmount obstacles), but to enable one to move powerfully and joyously toward the ends of a good life—to blossom in enacting the love of God and neighbor. The moral virtues aid the moralist and the catechist to enumerate in concrete and specific ways the right way to fulfill the commandment of love.

— Augustine DiNoia, O.P.; Gabriel O'Donnell, O.P.; Romanus Cessario, O.P.; Peter John Cameron, O.P. *The Love that Never Ends.* Huntington, IN: Our Sunday Visitor, 1996. p. 119.

2. If man, then must be a personal spirit able to exist and act on the foundation of a natural structure and reality, he must also be open to the personal invitation of God's love. He must have the capacity for the infinite; he must be a being not closed in upon himself but able to go out in knowledge and love to a personal encounter with the personal God. The natures of created beings lesser than man are not open in this way to God, for lower creatures cannot transcend themselves; they are enclosed, in a sense, in their own natural being. But by his nature, man is capable of going out of himself to meet God. He is created in such a way as to be able to enter into relationship with the divine persons. Not only is man capable of this in an absolute sense; he is so constituted that he can welcome God in virtue of his own deepest longings and desires.

— P. Gregory Stevens, OSB. *The Life of Grace.* Englewood Cliffs, NJ: Prentice-Hall, 1963. p. 69.

3. Christ ratified the Decalogue, both as a whole and in its parts (cf. Mt 19:17-19; Mk 10:17-19; Lk 18:18-20). He also ratified the Deuteronomist's summary on love of God (cf. Mt. 22:37-38), and He added a summary of the last seven commandments: "You shall love your neighbor as yourself" (Mt 22:39).

This command of love of neighbor was not new (cf. Lv 19:18), and Christ did not say it was new. But Christ did give a new commandment of love: "A new commandment I give to you, that you love one another; even as I have loved you, that you also love one another" (Jn 13:34).

What is new in Christ's commandment of love is the standard which He sets, the standard which He Himself is. Christ's love for us is not only the maximum of human love. Jesus loves us in the way the Father loves Him. "As the Father has loved Me, so have I loved you…" (Jn 15:9). The Father's love for the Son is divine; Jesus' love for us is divine; our love for one another is to be divine.

— Ronald Lawler, O.F.M. Cap., Donald W. Wuerl, Thomas Comerford Lawler. *The Teaching of Christ.* Huntington, IN: Our Sunday Visitor, 1979. p. 184.

QUESTIONS

1. In whom can the question about moral goodness be answered?

2. What is essential to all morality?

3. Where are the specific obligations that guide Christian life found?

4. In what are Christian ethics rooted?

5. What does Christian morality demand of the baptized?

6. When did Moses receive the Ten Commandments?

7. List the Ten Commandments.

8. With what was the destiny of Israel tied?

9. Why did God give the Israelites a simplified code of conduct?

10. With what does the Decalogue's ethical code of conduct correspond?

11. List the precepts of the Church.

12. Where is the highest moral code found?

13. Why is "the beatitudes" an appropriate name for Jesus' statement?

14. What do the Beatitudes reflect?

15. What is the specific concern of the Beatitudes?

16. List the eight Beatitudes.

17. Give some examples of how the Ten Commandments are enriched by the life and teachings of Jesus Christ.

PRACTICAL EXERCISES

1. Compare and contrast the Ten Commandments as they are set down in Exodus 20: 2-17 and Deuteronomy 5: 6-21.

2. Choose a different Beatitude to exemplify for each of the next six weeks. At the end of each week, note your results and the reaction of others.

3. Do you think the Beatitudes are easier to live than the Commandments? Why?

4. Write an essay regarding the practical consequences for social order if a majority of people lived the Beatitudes.

5. Write a comment on this statement from the Catechism:

The Beatitudes depict the countenance of Jesus Christ and portray his charity. They express the vocation of the faithful associated with the glory of his Passion and Resurrection; they shed light on the actions and attitudes characteristic of the Christian life; they are the paradoxical promises that sustain hope in the midst of tribulations; they proclaim the blessings and rewards already secured, however dimly, for Christ's disciples; they have begun in the lives of the Virgin Mary and all the saints. (CCC 1717)

FROM THE CATECHISM

1724 The Decalogue, the Sermon on the Mount, and the apostolic catechesis describe for us the paths that lead to the Kingdom of heaven. Sustained by the grace of the Holy Spirit, we tread them, step by step, by everyday acts. By the working of the Word of Christ, we slowly bear fruit in the Church to the glory of God (cf. Mt 13:3-23).

1726 The Beatitudes teach us the final end to which God calls us: the Kingdom, the vision of God, participation in the divine nature, eternal life, filiation, rest in God.

1728 The Beatitudes confront us with decisive choices concerning earthly goods; they purify our hearts in order to teach us to love God above all things.

2075 "What good deed must I do, to have eternal life?"—"If you would enter into life, keep the commandments" (Mt 19:16-17).

2077 The gift of the Decalogue is bestowed from within the covenant concluded by God with his people. God's commandments take on their true meaning in and through this covenant.

ENDNOTES

1. *VS,* 8.
2. J. Michael Miller, C.S.B., *The Encyclicals of Pope John Paul II,* p. 654.
3. St. Irenaeus, *Against Heretics,* IV, 15, 1.
4. Ibid., IV, 16, 3-4.
5. Rom 12:1.
6. *VS,* 16.
7. St. Bonaventure, *Commentary on the Sentences,* IV, 37, 1-3.
8. Cf. CCC, 2071; *VS,* 13-15.

Chapter 9

The Social Teaching Of The Church

But he, desiring to justify himself, said to Jesus, "And who is my neighbor?" Jesus replied, "A man was going down from Jerusalem to Jericho, and he fell among robbers, who stripped him and beat him, and departed, leaving him half dead. Now by chance a priest was going down that road; and when he saw him he passed by on the other side. So likewise a Levite, when he came to the place and saw him, passed by on the other side. But a Samaritan, as he journeyed, came to where he was; and when he saw him, he had compassion, and went to him and bound up his wounds, pouring on oil and wine; then he set him up on his own beast and brought him to an inn, and took care of him. And the next day he took out two denarii and gave them to the innkeeper, saying, 'Take care of him; and whatever more you spend, I will repay you when I come back.' Which of these three, do you think, proved neighbor to the man who fell among robbers?" He said, "The one who showed mercy on him." And Jesus said to him, "Go and do likewise." (Lk 10: 29-37)

The parable of the Good Samaritan summarizes the Christian vocation to love one's neighbor. With this in mind, let us ask the following questions:

- What are the obligations of government toward citizens, and vice versa?
- How should Jesus' call to charity influence the relations between nations?
- What does the Church have to say about racism?

The Church was founded out of God's concern for every living soul.

INTRODUCTION

Jesus' teaching regarding one's relationship with neighbors is a model for the social teaching of the Church. It is set out in simple form with the call to "love one's neighbor" and is demonstrated in the parable of the Good Samaritan. True love of neighbor is the foundation of all of the social teachings of the Church. All Christians are called to do "the good" to their neighbor.

True love of neighbor is based on the virtue of justice, which renders to each person his due:

> In order that the demands of justice may be met, and attempts to achieve this goal may succeed, what is needed is the gift of grace, a gift which comes from God. Grace, in cooperation with human freedom, constitutes that mysterious presence of God in history which is Providence.
>
> The newness which is experienced in following Christ demands to be communicated to other people in their concrete difficulties, struggles, problems and challenges, so that these can then be illuminated and made more human in the light of faith. Faith not only helps people to find solutions; it makes even situations of suffering humanly bearable, so that in these situations people will not become lost or forget their dignity and vocation.[1]

Therefore, success in resolving social problems is only possible when faith is joined to the grace offered by the Holy Spirit, allied to the proper use of human freedom.

The Church was founded out of God's concern for every living soul. Christ died to save all people, and it is the vocation of the Christian to be concerned for the spiritual, psychological, and bodily health of every person to the extent it is reasonable and possible. While the Church does not offer specific solutions to every social problem, it proposes principles, criteria, and guidelines for action based on the Gospels to be used to solve social problems.

The Church proposes two virtues to ensure equity among peoples: social justice and social charity.

The Church's social teaching is based on the concept of Christian charity, which is directed to the spiritual and social perfection of all people for the common good. There are some who would argue that the Church has no place or right to teach anything about social doctrine. In response, the Church indicated that when sin and human rights are involved, she has not only a right but an obligation to speak.[2]

> **The social doctrine of the Church developed in the nineteenth century when the Gospel encountered modern industrial society with its new structures for the production of consumer goods, its new concept of society, the state and authority, and its new forms of labor and ownership. The development of the doctrine of the Church on economic and social matters attests the permanent value of the Church's teaching at the same time as it attests the true meaning of her Tradition, always living and active.[3] (CCC 2421)**

The teaching of the Church—based on Christian revelation—aids all people to better understand the laws of social living. The Church was the first to defend the rights of workers to organize in order to obtain just rights (which include a right to work) and financial compensation commensurate with family needs.

The Church proposes two virtues to ensure equity among peoples. The first is *social justice*, which requires from each person all that is necessary for the common good. The second is *solidarity* or *social charity*, which requires active concern and love for the common good. Those who acquire these virtues will not have an excessive preoccupation with individual pleasures and material possessions. They will easily avoid the trap of a class conflict based on the false premise of seeing themselves as exploiters or as being among the exploited.

"One for all and all for one."
— Fr. Heinrich Pesch S.J.

Fr. Heinrich Pesch S.J., a German Catholic priest writing in the nineteenth century, originated the concept of solidarity among people and suggested the motto, "One for all and all for one." This is an excellent motto for those who practice social justice and solidarity.

True social justice requires:

- application of the virtues of social justice and solidarity;
- well-formed individual consciences;
- independent groups organized to secure the common good; and
- complementary state regulation based on the principle of subsidiarity.

Christian charity must be learned in the family, for it is the foundation of social justice.

1. THE FAMILY

The family is the first school of social justice. It is this domestic church in which the children receive their initial instruction in their proper places in society. The family should be inspired by Gospel teachings.

> **The family is the *original cell of social life.* It is the natural society in which husband and wife are called to give themselves in love and in the gift of life. Authority, stability, and a life of relationships within the family constitute the foundations for freedom, security, and fraternity within society. The family is the community in which, from childhood, one can learn moral values, begin to honor God, and make good use of freedom. Family life is an initiation into life in society. (CCC 2207)**

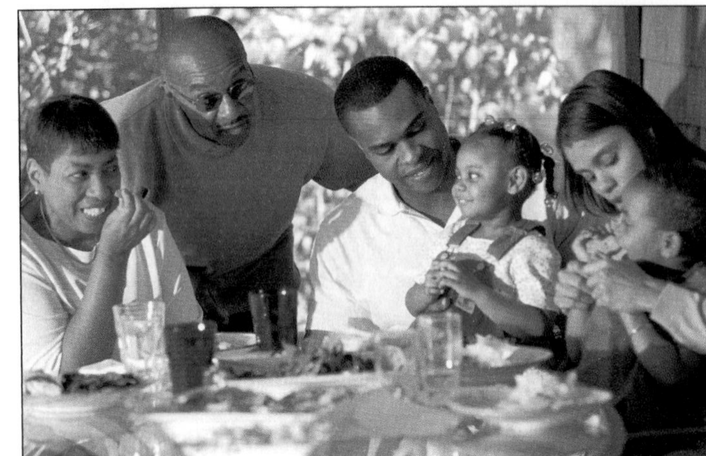

The family must be a place of piety. Piety is the virtue that gives one a sense of duty toward one's family, church, and country. It applies the virtue of charity in a special manner as an act of love to those things that deserve respect. Family life must also be inspired by the spirit of the Gospel and open to new life. The couple is also called upon to create an atmosphere in which children can be happy and lead full and worthy human lives.

As a hierarchical body with a head (the father) and a heart (the mother), the family has rules, obligations, and rewards. Both parents are equal in dignity while having different functions. In a sense, it is a miniature society. Little by little, the children should be formed in correct attitudes toward God and neighbor. The words and example of the parents are crucial, for parents are the first teachers to form the minds of the children. Families will be joyful if the parents teach each child to serve the others and share their burdens.

Christian charity must be learned in the family, for it is the foundation of social justice. If the children see the parents respecting all with whom they come in contact, the children will do likewise. Family life must be instructional in the way of true love of neighbor. Each member of the family has to become in a special way the servant of the others. Genuine concern must be shown for the lives of all.

Moreover, parents have a serious obligation to avoid scandalizing the children by word or conduct. If the home is a place of harsh language or disregard for the rights of its members, the children will see this as the norm.

Conversation must be kept on a high level. When it isn't, the dinner table can become a dangerous place for the ears and minds of children.

2. OBLIGATIONS OF NATIONAL GOVERNMENTS

Human communities are made up of persons who have rights, which governments must protect and guarantee. Every human community possesses a common good around which it is organized in its political manifestation. The conditions that make for the common good are the total of social conditions that allow persons or groups to reach their human and spiritual fulfillment more easily. The common good is for all and should be the concern of all. Prudence is the key virtue in obtaining the common good and is a requirement particularly for those in authority.

The common good has three components:

- Respect for all persons' natural freedom, conscience, and choice of vocation as members of society;
- Accessibility to each what is necessary for a truly human life to include: work, food, clothing, health, education, participation in culture, the right to establish a family, and suitable information for their spiritual and mental formation; and
- Peace and stability of a just order with those in authority using morally acceptable means to ensure the security of society.

The common good must be founded on truth, built up in justice, animated by love, and directed toward the progress of persons both spiritually and materially.

The common good must be founded on truth, built up in justice, animated by love...

The political community has a duty to honor the family, to assist it, and to ensure especially:

- the freedom to establish a family, have children, and bring them up in keeping with the family's own moral and religious convictions;
- the protection of the stability of the marriage bond and the institution of the family;
- the freedom to profess one's faith, to hand it on, and raise one's children in it, with the necessary means and institutions;
- the right to private property, to free enterprise, to obtain work and housing, and the right to emigrate;
- in keeping with the country's institutions, the right to medical care, assistance for the aged, and family benefits;
- the protection of security and health, especially with respect to dangers like drugs, pornography, alcoholism, etc.;
- the freedom to form associations with other families and so to have representation before civil authority.[4] (CCC 2211)

Steps must be taken to stop exploitation of poorer nations…

These rules, which apply to national governments, apply equally to lower levels of government, such as the state, county, and city. The judgment as to which level of government has immediate responsibility must be determined by the rule of subsidiarity. It states that a community of the higher order should not interfere in the life of the lower order to deprive the latter of its functions, but rather should support it and help to coordinate its activity with that of the rest of society, always with a view to the common good.[5]

3. INTERNATIONAL RELATIONSHIPS

Just as families and levels of government within a given country have obligations toward each other, so also do individual countries. The Church reminds everyone that these obligations can be acted upon only if there is an increase in the sense and awareness of the Triune God.

> Various causes of a religious, political, economic, and financial nature today give "the social question a worldwide dimension."[6] There must be solidarity among nations which are already politically interdependent. It is even more essential when it is a question of dismantling the "perverse mechanisms" that impede the development of the less advanced countries.[7] In place of abusive if not usurious financial systems, iniquitous commercial relations among nations, and the arms race, there must be substituted a common effort to mobilize resources toward objectives of moral, cultural, and economic development, "redefining the priorities and hierarchies of values."[8]

Catholic laymen have a distinctive role to play in accomplishing international social justice based on Catholic social teaching.

The Church first points out the interdependent nature of nation states today; then, she demands a redirection of objectives for the common good of all peoples. It is good for rich nations to ensure the development of those nations that are unable to develop on their own because they are without the means or have been exploited.

> Many other people, while not completely marginalized, live in situations in which the struggle for a bare minimum is uppermost. These are situations in which the rules of the earliest period of capitalism still flourish in conditions of "ruthlessness" in no way inferior to the darkest moments of the first phase of industrialization. In other cases the land is still the central element in the economic process, but those who cultivate it are excluded from ownership and are reduced to a state of quasi-servitude…In spite of the great changes which have taken place in the more advanced societies, the human inadequacies of capitalism and the resulting domination of things over people are far from disappearing. In fact, for the poor, to the lack of material goods has been added a lack of knowledge and training which prevents them from escaping their state of humiliating subjection.
>
> Unfortunately, the great majority of the people in the Third World still live in such conditions.[9]

Steps must be taken to stop exploitation of poorer nations, for richer nations are encouraged in charity (and as an act of fraternal solidarity) to aid the poorer nations. Countries that have benefited from resources for which they have not paid a fair price have a greater obligation as a matter of justice. In some instances, this will require the reform of international economic aid and financial institutions. This may be accomplished by direct aid, the loan of equipment, funds, and professional expertise.

The role of the Church is to set out principles for development, but it is the role of the laity to develop and carry out plans keeping the message of the Gospel and the common good in mind. Catholic laymen have a distinctive role to play in accomplishing international social justice based on Catholic social teaching.

Every nation has the moral obligation to avoid war, which must only be a last resort, for governments cannot be denied the right of lawful self-defense once all efforts to avoid war have failed.[10]

Jesus' words and works always express tender care for the women with whom he comes in contact.

4. THE ROLE OF WOMEN

When the Father created the first man and woman in his likeness, it was a clear indication that both share a special dignity. As a direct result of original sin, women have been placed in an inferior role to men who will "rule over you" (cf. Gn 3:16). Because of that sin, many women have suffered from injurious and unjust situations in marriage and social situations, which continues to this day. The Church has offered practical solutions to remedy this problem.

In its closing message, the Second Vatican Council noted that the human race was undergoing a deep transformation, which would offer women who are imbued with a deep spirit of the Gospel many opportunities to aid humanity.

At the synod of bishops in 1971, Pope Paul VI set up a special commission to study ways in which women's special dignity and responsibility might be recognized and promoted so that the potentialities of women may be accepted and honored. To encourage a better understanding of the role of women in both private and public life, John Paul II wrote the Apostolic Letter on the Dignity of Women. In the letter, he points out that the redeeming actions of Christ were directed, in part, to a recognition of the dignity and vocation of women. Christ's explanation regarding the question about whether divorce is permissible (cf. Mt 19:7) was also meant to indicate that men may no longer dominate women. In all Jesus' actions directed toward women, there is nothing that condones unjust discrimination

Every word and gesture of Christ about women must therefore be brought into the dimension of the Paschal Mystery.

against women. His words and works always express tender care for the women with whom he comes in contact. This is particularly evident in his treatment of women who had been identified as sinners.

> Jesus' attitude to the women whom he meets in the course of his Messianic service reflects the eternal plan of God, who, in creating each one of them, chooses her and loves her in Christ (cf. Eph 1:1-5). *Each woman therefore is "the only creature on earth which God willed for its own sake." Each of them from the "beginning" inherits as a woman the dignity of personhood.* Jesus of Nazareth confirms this dignity, recalls it, renews it, and makes it a part of the Gospel and of the Redemption for which he is sent into the world. Every word and gesture of Christ about women must therefore be brought into the dimension of the Paschal Mystery. In this way everything is completely explained.[11]

5. THE GOODS OF CREATION

The *Catechism* states that "the goods of creation are destined for the whole human race" (CCC 2402). It has been correctly noted that a majority of the world's goods are consumed by a minority of the world's population. Personal wealth must not be made an excuse to purchase and consume whatever one's heart desires.

> An increased sense of God and increased self-awareness are fundamental to any *full development of human society.* This development multiplies material goods and puts them at the service of the person and his freedom. It reduces dire poverty and economic exploitation. It makes for growth in respect for cultural identities and openness to the transcendent.[12] (CCC 2441)

Every Christian has a personal obligation to use the goods of the earth as God wishes according to the promptings of the Holy Spirit.

Those living in dire poverty cannot readily be open to the transcendent when their lives are consumed by the struggle to keep themselves alive. Those who merely contribute to charity without regard for the use of goods are only half-conscious of their obligations to use the goods of this world as the Father intended.

When God created Adam and Eve, he instructed them to "be fruitful and multiply, and fill the earth and subdue it" (Gn 1:28). The phrase "be fruitful and multiply" can be applied by extension to the goods of the earth as well. If mankind is to "fill the earth," he must make wise use of the fruits of this planet to support the people who will fill the earth.

> The seventh commandment enjoins respect for the integrity of creation. Animals, like plants and inanimate beings, are by nature destined for the common good of past, present, and future humanity (cf. Gn 1:28-31). Use of the mineral, vegetable, and animal resources of the universe cannot be divorced from respect for

> **moral imperatives. Man's dominion over inanimate and other living beings granted by the Creator is not absolute; it is limited by concern for the quality of life of his neighbor, including generations to come; it requires a religious respect for the integrity of creation.[13] (CCC 2415)**

The wise use of goods requires that we not only be just in our dealings with others, but that we should not be excessive in our consumption of the goods of the earth. Care must be taken to protect the "goods of the earth" through responsible regulations in a financially responsible way. Every Christian has a personal obligation to use the goods of the earth as God wishes according to the promptings of the Holy Spirit.

6. LOVE FOR THE POOR

It is by what they have done for the poor that Jesus Christ will recognize his chosen ones.

One constant of life is that whether times are good or bad, the poor rarely are given the consideration that is necessary to make possible a minimum standard of life.

> **God blesses those who come to the aid of the poor and rebukes those who turn away from them: "Give to him who begs from you, do not refuse him who would borrow from you"; "you received without pay, give without pay" (Mt 5:42; 10:8). It is by what they have done for the poor that Jesus Christ will recognize his chosen ones (cf. Mt 25:31-36). When "the poor have the good news preached to them," it is the sign of Christ's presence (Mt 11:5; cf. Lk 4:18). (CCC 2443)**

Love for the poor is incompatible with the attitude that a person has earned the right to spend wealth as they choose. Unfortunately, the American culture has projected the false concept that a person has a right to do with their possessions without regard for the needs of others.

This false concept is contrary to Christ's call to love the poor. This has been further complicated by governmental action which has gradually taken over some programs meant to give aid to the poor when there was no justification. As a result, many Christians have lost sight of the requirement incumbent on each person to assist the poor.

Jesus lived a life of poverty to indicate his concern for the poor. Since he shared in their suffering, his message had more appeal for the poor. The Church has followed the example of Christ from the beginning to reach out to the poor in order that this good example might lead them to consider Christ's message of salvation.

Everyone is encouraged to aid the poor to the extent reasonable and possible after they have taken care of personal needs. The Gospel and the call of the beatitudes infer that assistance should be given not only in cases of material poverty, but also *cultural and religious poverty.* The Church has given us the corporal and spiritual works of mercy to delineate areas to which personal social concern can be directed.

Many opportunities to aid the poor are available in areas of cultural and religious poverty. Both of these areas can be dealt with by taking on the role of catechist because it presents the opportunity to form those with whom one comes in contact as regards not only the truths of the faith but also to direct the hearers toward areas which raise their esthetic sights.

Knowledgeable Catholics must present the Catholic viewpoint on social organization as a cure to the problems facing the country.

7. RELATIONS WITH THOSE WHO ARE DIFFERENT

One problem that has persisted for a long time in the United States is "the race problem." The Church has repeatedly called for an end to racial injustice, despite cultural trends that have often gone in the opposite direction.

> Discrimination based on sex, race, ethnicity, or age... constitutes a grave injustice and an affront to human dignity. It must be aggressively resisted by every individual and rooted out of every social institution and structure....Where the effects of past discrimination persist, society has the obligation to take positive steps to overcome the legacy of injustice.[14]

Though primarily directed at blacks, prejudice also affects Hispanics, Asians, Jews, Native Americans, and even Catholics. In the early part of the nineteenth century, the predominantly Protestant American culture was responsible for discrimination against Catholics, which sometimes became violent. The opportunity to change all of this has arrived. The public morality in the United States for over two centuries was referred to as the *Protestant Ethic.* Law, morality, and cultural attitudes were based to a large extent on a Protestant outlook on life.

After the conclusion of World War II, there was a gradual breakdown culturally which has left the country without a generally accepted public morality. This has led one writer, Father Richard John Neuhaus, to proclaim this as "the Catholic moment" in American life. Knowledgeable Catholics must present the Catholic viewpoint on social organization as a cure to the problems facing the country not only in the areas of race but also marriage, the family, and public morality.

Francis Cardinal George, Archbishop of Chicago, explains the Church's position on racism in his pastoral letter *Dwell in My Love:*

> Racism, whether personal, social, institutional or structural, contradicts the purpose of the incarnation of the Word of God in the womb of the Virgin Mary. Racism contradicts God's will for our salvation. We cannot claim to love God without loving our neighbor (Mt 22:34ff). Since racism is a failure to love our neighbor, only freedom from racism will enable us to be one with God and one another.[15]

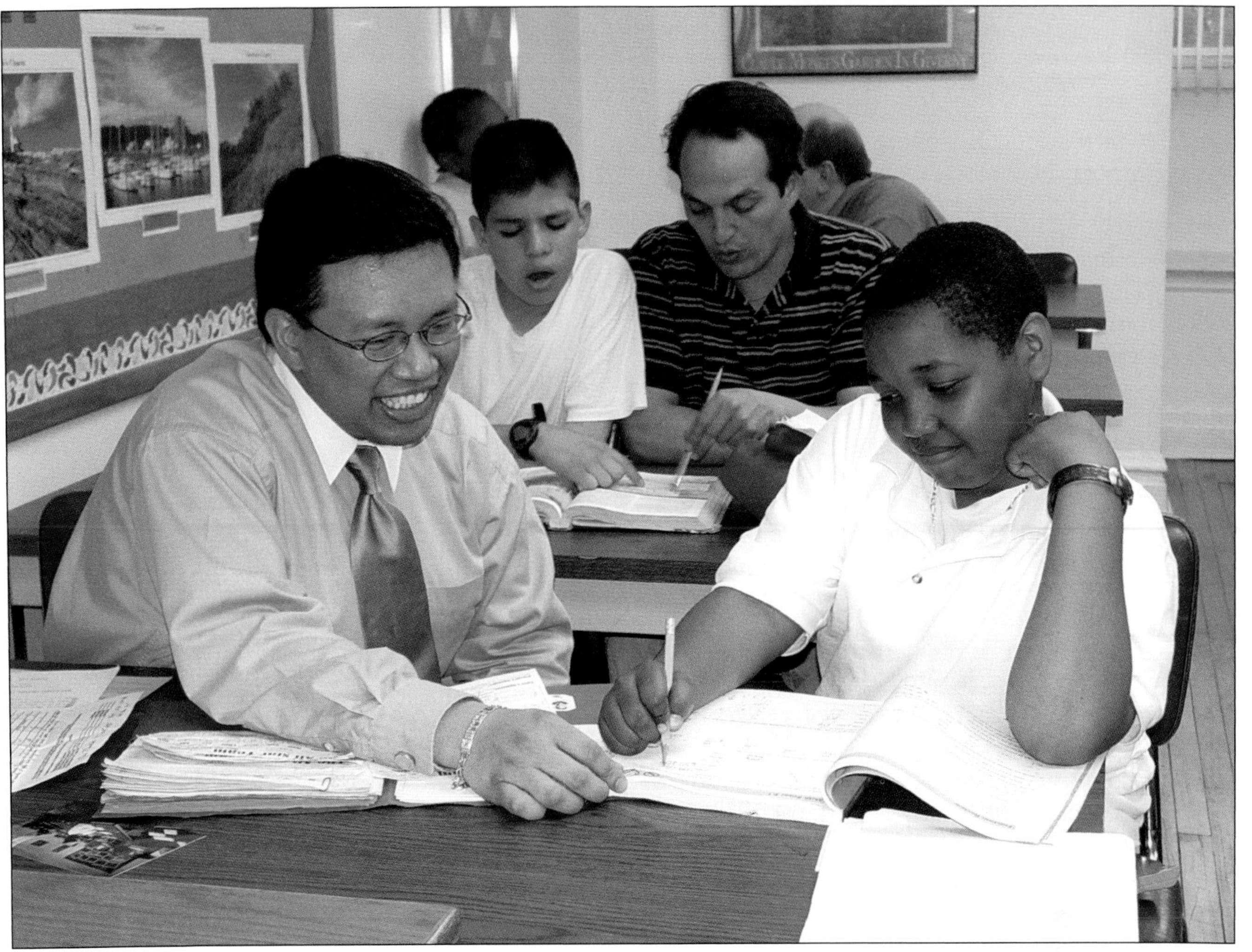

CONCLUSION

There is no social justice worthy of the name that excludes any person or group from its reach. Social justice is not directed to accomplishing the perfect society; rather, it is directed to enabling every person in society to reach the highest perfection that the Holy Spirit can bring him or her to—physically, morally, and spiritually. Every Christian is obligated to work for solidarity among all the members of society. This will come to fruition only when the truth of the Gospel is guided by the Holy Spirit to the highest sense of justice, and motivated by true love of neighbor.

Every Christian is obligated to work for solidarity among all the members of society.

VOCABULARY

CATECHIST
One who teaches about Jesus Christ—especially his Incarnation, Passion, and glorious Resurrection and Ascension.

COMMON GOOD
The total of social conditions that will allow both individuals and groups to reach their human and spiritual fulfillment more easily.

INTERDEPENDENCE
Mutual reliance for support or existence.

PIETY
The virtue that gives one a sense of duty toward one's family, church, and country.

PRINCIPLE OF SUBSIDIARITY
The principle that states that a community of a higher order should not interfere in the internal life of a community of a lower order, depriving the latter of its functions, but rather should support it in case of need and help to coordinate its activity with the activities of the rest of society, always with a view to the common good.

POVERTY
The condition of want experienced by those who are poor—whom Christ called blessed, and for whom he had a special love. *Poverty of spirit* signifies detachment from worldly things and voluntary humility.

RACISM
Unjust discrimination on the basis of a person's race. It is a violation of human dignity, and a sin against justice.

SOCIAL JUSTICE
The virtue that requires from each person all that is necessary for the common good.

SOLIDARITY
The virtue that requires active concern and love for the common good.

SUPPLEMENTARY READINGS

1. **SPIRITUAL WORKS OF MERCY**

Counseling the doubtful
Instructing the ignorant
Admonishing sinners
Comforting the afflicted
Forgiving offenses
Bearing wrongs patiently
Praying for the living and the dead

CORPORAL WORKS OF MERCY

Feeding the hungry
Giving drink to the thirsty
Clothing the naked
Sheltering the homeless
Visiting the sick
Visiting the imprisoned
Burying the dead

2. ...another name for peace is development. Just as there is a collective responsibility for avoiding war, so too there is a collective responsibility for promoting development. Just as within individual societies, it is possible and right to organize a solid economy which will direct the functioning of the market to the common good, so too there is a similar need for adequate interventions on the international level. For this to happen, a great effort must be made to enhance mutual understanding and knowledge and to increase the sensitivity of consciences. This is the culture which is hoped for, one which fosters trust in the human potential of the poor and consequently in their ability to improve their conditions through work or to make a positive contribution to economic prosperity. But to accomplish this, the poor, be they individuals or nations, need to be provided with realistic opportunities. Creating such conditions calls for a concerted worldwide effort to promote development, an effort which also involves sacrificing the positions of income and power enjoyed by the more developed countries.

Faced with the poverty of the working class, Pope Leo XIII wrote: "We approach this subject with confidence, and in the exercise of the rights which manifestly pertain to us... By keeping silence we would seem to neglect the duty incumbent on us." During the last hundred years the Church has repeatedly expressed her thinking, while closely following the continuing development of the social question. She has certainly not done this in order to recover former privileges or to impose her own vision. Her sole purpose has been care and responsibility for the human person, who has been entrusted to her by Christ himself; for this person, whom, as the Second Vatican Council recalls, is the only creature on earth which God willed for its own sake, and for which God has his plan that is, a share in eternal salvation. We are not dealing here with humanity in the "abstract," but with the real, "concrete," "historical" person. We are dealing with each individual, since each one is included in the mystery of Redemption, and through this mystery Christ has united himself with each one forever. It follows that the Church cannot abandon humanity, and that "this human person is the primary route that the Church must travel in fulfilling her mission...the way traced out by Christ himself, the way that leads invariably through the mystery of the Incarnation and the Redemption."

This, and this alone, is the principle which inspires the Church's social doctrine. The Church has gradually developed that doctrine in a systematic way, above all in the century that has followed the date we are commemorating, precisely because the horizon of the Church's whole wealth of doctrine is the human being in his concrete reality as sinful and righteous.

— *Centesimus annus* No. 52, 53

QUESTIONS

1. What parable of Jesus is a model for the Church's social teaching?

2. What is the foundation of the Church's social teaching?

3. For the demands of justice to be met, what is needed?

4. What is the relation of the virtue of faith to solutions based on social justice?

5. What are the aims of Christian charity?

6. What does true social justice require?

7. Which virtue gives one a sense of duty toward one's family, church, and country?

8. List attributes of the family inspired by Gospel teachings.

9. Where is the common good founded?

10. List three components of the common good.

11. What is necessary for the common good to flourish?

12. List the rights of the family.

13. List some inequities that the Church desires to overcome.

14. What are the obligations of richer nations?

15. Who has the obligation to make concrete plans for solutions to society's problems?

16. What is the moral obligation of every nation with regard to war? Explain.

17. What has the Church done to enhance the role of women?

18. What is Jesus' attitude toward women?

19. What is necessary for a full development of society?

20. What is the role of the catechist in aiding the poor?

21. What does the Church say regarding discrimination based on sex, race, ethnicity, or age, and what must be done about it?

PRACTICAL EXERCISES

1. Write an essay on what Catholics can do to resolve the problems of race, marriage, and public morality.

2. Help organize a charity event for the physically, spiritually, or religiously poor. This may be a food, clothing, and/or toy drive; a blood drive; an auction where the proceeds go to a local charity; or anything else you can imagine.

3. Volunteer at a homeless shelter or nursing home.

4. Debate in class the pro's and con's of government involvement in charity. Are government programs wasteful? Do they take away personal initiative? Are they the only way to ensure that the poor receive what they need to survive? Do they provide the things which are most needed?

5. Consider the Corporal and Spiritual Works of Mercy. Which are more important? Based on this hold a debate about which modern Catholic has had the largest impact on society. (Some possibilities are Josemaría Escrivá, Pius X, Leo XIII, John Paul II, Mother Teresa, Bernadette of Lourdes, and Katharine Drexel.)

FROM THE CATECHISM

1925 The common good consists of three essential elements: respect for and promotion of the fundamental rights of the person; prosperity, or the development of the spiritual and temporal goods of society; the peace and security of the group and of its members.

1927 It is the role of the state to defend and promote the common good of civil society. The common good of the whole human family calls for an organization of society on the international level.

1945 The equality of men concerns their dignity as persons and the rights that flow from it.

2451 The seventh commandment enjoins the practice of justice and charity in the administration of earthly goods and the fruits of men's labor.

2452 The goods of creation are destined for the entire human race. The right to private property does not abolish the universal destination of goods.

2463 How can we not recognize Lazarus, the hungry beggar in the parable (cf. Lk 17:19-31), in the multitude of human beings without bread, a roof or a place to stay? How can we fail to hear Jesus: "As you did it not to one of the least of these, you did it not to me" (Mt 25:45)?

ENDNOTES

1. *CA*, 59.
2. Cf. *GS*, 76.
3. Cf. *CA*, 3.
4. Cf. *FC*, 46.
5. Cf. *CA*, 25.
6. *SRS*, 9.
7. Cf. *SRS*, 17, 45.
8. *CA*, 28; cf. 35.
9. Ibid., 33.
10. Cf. CCC, 2308-09.
11. *MD*, 13.
12. Cf. *SRS*, 32; *CA*, 51.
13. Cf. *CA*, 37-38.
14. U.S. Catholic Bishops, *Brothers and Sisters to Us*, 1989.
15. Francis Cardinal George, *Dwell in My Love*, 1.

Chapter 10

The First Commandment:
To Love God Above All Else

Peter was raised a Catholic, and had attended a Catholic grade school. He received a good education in general, but never gained a meaningful understanding of his faith. When he went to college, he began to date Rebecca, a non-practicing Jewish girl. As Peter began spending more and more time with Rebecca, he became less diligent in the practice of his faith. He often neglected to attend Sunday Mass in order to go to the beach or to do other social activities with Rebecca.

After several years, Peter and Rebecca realized that they had fallen in love, and began to consider marriage seriously. Peter recalled that as a Catholic, he had to insist that the children whom he and Rebecca might have would be baptized and raised Catholics.

Rebecca was very skeptical about the Catholic faith and refused to agree to raise her future children as Catholics. As Peter tried to persuade Rebecca to accept his opinion, he began to realize how important his faith was to him. He regretted his recent laxity in religious matters. He reevaluated his relationship with God, realizing that he owed everything to his Creator. He had a serious duty to carry out his obligations as a Christian, and so he returned to the active practice of his Catholic faith.

With these realizations, Peter faced more of a dilemma than ever. He truly loved Rebecca, but he also knew his love of God prevented him from marrying a woman who would not agree to raise their children in the Faith. Although he did his utmost to persuade Rebecca, she remained adamant in her opposition to Catholicism. After much careful thought and prayer, Peter came to the conclusion that he must break up with Rebecca and pursue their relationship no further.

In light of this story, let us ask the following questions:

- Why does the Catholic Church teach that human beings have an obligation to worship God?
- How does the Christian's relationship with God differ from that of the followers of other religions?
- What is the relationship between love of God and love of neighbor?

Without an awareness of God, we are confined to an existence that lacks meaning.

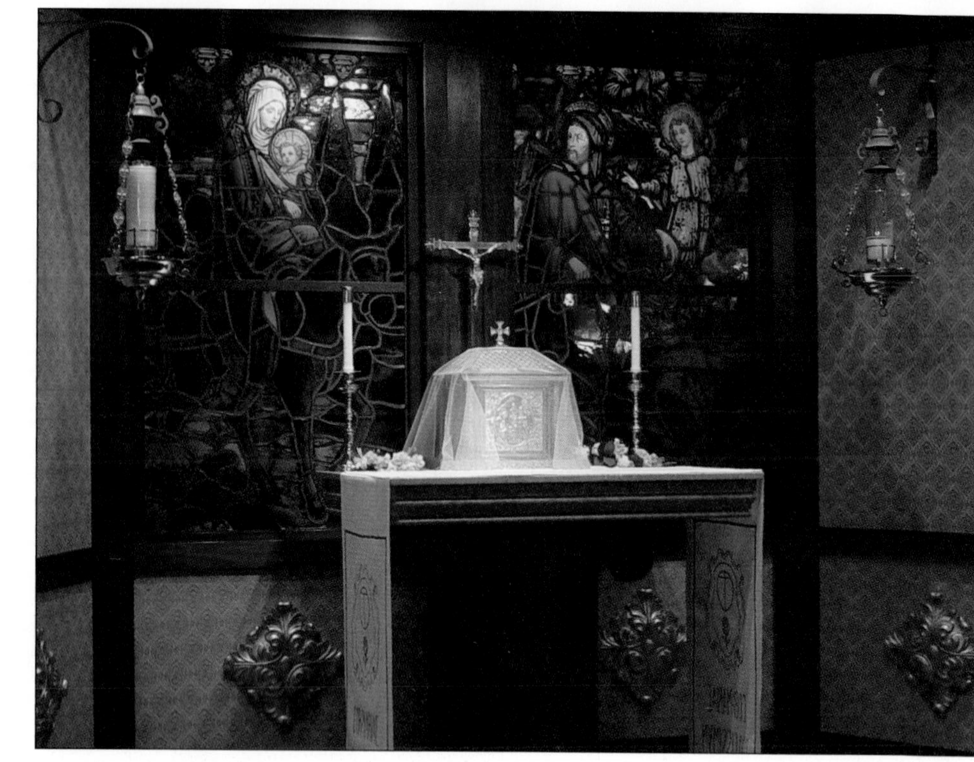

INTRODUCTION

From the start, the theologian tries to unite God to mankind by religion, for he knows that the commandment to worship God is clearly stated in the Bible and flows out of the revelation that there is but one God. The original formulation of biblical monotheism is forceful: "You shall have no other gods before me" (Ex 20: 3; Dt 5: 7). This precept demands a proper monotheism (belief in one God) in the midst of the cultural polytheism (belief in many gods), so firmly rooted in the regions surrounding Israel.

Moral theology seeks only to determine what a person must do to maintain his relationship with God.

The Book of Deuteronomy is richer and more explicit in its treatment of our obligation to love and worship God. "Hear, O Israel: The Lord our God is one Lord, and you shall love the Lord your God with all your heart, and with all your soul, and with all your might" (Dt 6: 4-5).

The love of neighbor immediately follows the love of God because God calls us to love our neighbor to secure his love. This double precept is found throughout the Jewish tradition, just as it is found in Jesus' response to the scribes:

> **And one of them, a lawyer, asked him a question, to test him. "Teacher, which is the great commandment in the law?" And he said to him, "You shall love the Lord your God with all your heart, and with all your soul, and with all your mind. This is the great and first commandment. And the second is like it. You shall love your neighbor as yourself. On these two commandments depend all the law and the prophets." (Mt 22: 35-40)**

The first great commandment summarizes the first three commandments of the Decalogue—*the first tablet*. The second one that Jesus mentions is a synopsis of the remaining seven commandments of the Decalogue—*the second tablet.* This is why Jesus presents these two precepts to be a summary of the law and the teachings of the prophets.

The Incarnation of the Son is nothing less than God's will to save the whole of humanity.

It is important to bear in mind that the commandments, above all else, reflect the Father's love for us, and we, therefore, are expected to return the love of the Father by fulfilling the commandments.

> God has loved us first. The love of the One God is recalled in the first of the "ten words." The commandments then make explicit the response of love that man is called to give to his God. (CCC 2083)

1. GOD, THE FOUNDATION OF HUMAN EXISTENCE: THE VIRTUE OF RELIGION

The first commandment states the fundamental human obligation to acknowledge the existence of God and worship him, because without God, we would not exist. Without an awareness of God, we are confined to an existence that lacks meaning.

The very name of Jesus means "God saves."

Moral theology uses practical judgments to direct human acts toward God, under the guidance of revelation. Moral theology seeks only to determine what a person must do to maintain his relationship with God. Since we owe our existence to God, we ought, in justice, to acknowledge him within the context of worship.

What distinguishes Christian revelation is not God's existence, but his relation to humanity, for the God revealed in the Bible is not a "solitary god," but one who continuously acts in favor of people, as a father for his children. Questioned by Moses, Yahweh responds: "I am who I am. . . .The God of your fathers, the God of Abraham, the God of Isaac, and the God of Jacob..." (Ex 3:14-15). Before giving the Decalogue, God speaks of himself: "I am the Lord your God, who brought you out of the land of Egypt, out of the house of bondage" (Ex 20:2).

The loving intervention of God on behalf of people is a theme of Scripture. The Incarnation of the Son is nothing less than God's will to save the whole of humanity: "For God so loved the world that he gave his only Son" (Jn 3:16). Briefly stated, Christianity is the history of salvation, God's plan concerning humanity. The Christian God is not, then, a distant and impassive god, but an intimate and active one. The very name of Jesus means "God saves" (cf. Mt 1:21).

Since God's intention is to save people from their sin, then one cannot remain passive before his Holy Spirit, but must respond appropriately. The response must be to believe in him, to trust in his aid, and to love him.[1] When that threefold intention is maintained before God, the Christian is in fact exercising the three theological virtues: faith, hope and charity.

Believing
Trusting
Loving

2. WORSHIP OF GOD AS A PRACTICAL EXERCISE OF THE THEOLOGICAL VIRTUES

Believing, trusting, and loving someone are three basic attitudes of human existence found in personal relationships. To foster and to practice them furthers personal maturity. For a Christian, that threefold attitude finds new meaning in the grace freely infused by the Holy Spirit into the soul to heal it and sanctify it, as it springs forth from the new life in Baptism. In fact, sanctifying grace makes it possible for the baptized to believe in, hope in, and love God by the Holy Spirit's infusion of the three theological virtues:

a. FAITH

Faith is the theological virtue by which we believe in God and believe all that he has said and revealed to us, and that Holy Church proposes for our belief, because he is truth itself. (CCC 1814)

Faith is a supernatural gift from the Holy Spirit that enables the recipient to accept all of the truths revealed by God, even though they cannot be proven. Believing is a free human act, consciously done in accordance with human dignity. It is the personal adherence of the heart and soul to God's self-revelation. In this sense, faith widens the capacity of human knowledge, since we will not only have a collection of truths discerned by reason, but will add those truths revealed by God and believed by his Church, which proposes them for our belief. In this sense, to believe is to accept truths that are guaranteed by the authority of God. One cannot be saved without faith.

Faith widens the capacity of human knowledge.

Faith does not contradict reason. Rather, it enables each person to turn to the Father, the Son, and the Holy Spirit as the beginning and end of all things. Therefore, once the truths that are revealed by God are accepted, human reason attempts to understand and defend these truths. Reason seeks and questions, rigorously attempting to understand these revealed truths, for it desires to understand both what God has revealed and the consequences of those truths for human life. Theology may be understood as "faith seeking understanding."[2]

A response to God's revelation involves two fundamental attitudes:

Receiving It With Humility

If, according to the Greeks, human truth manifests itself only to those who seek it humbly, then only those who are humble can accept divine revelation. Thus, the biblical passage: "God opposes the proud, but gives grace to the humble" (Jas 4:6).

Intellectually Cultivating It

Faith, by its very nature, requires that it be strengthened through efforts to understand its content more clearly. A faith that one refuses to understand (as intended by God) is no faith at all.

Once faith is known and its content understood, the Christian has two additional duties:

Safeguarding The Faith

Since faith is necessary for salvation, we have the serious obligation of protecting our faith and avoiding any risks to it. Faith can be lost, either by false theories planting doubt in the truth of revelation, or by the habit of error obscuring it.

A faith that one refuses to understand, as intended by God, is no faith at all.

Prudence needs to be exercised in the material one reads. Reading books that attack or distort the faith is to be avoided. The most profound convictions can be obscured when attacked by contradictory ideologies that are often presented in clever and appealing ways. When there is a question regarding a particular subject or book, it is imperative that the matter be discussed with one's confessor. Prudence requires that the same discretion be used when choosing what we watch and hear as well.

Communicating The Faith

To have faith is to sustain oneself in God, to trust in him.

Since the Father, Son, and Holy Spirit reveal to us certain realities, we should share them with others. From this stems the obligation to "transmit the faith which has been received." Jesus advised this with severe words:

> **So every one who acknowledges me before men, I also will acknowledge before my Father who is in heaven; but whoever denies me before men, I also will deny before my Father who is in heaven. (Mt 10: 32-33)**

This warning, while it primarily refers to acknowledging the Person of Jesus, can also be seen to include his teachings:

> **The disciple of Christ must not only keep the faith and live on it, but also profess it, confidently bear witness to it, and spread it. (CCC 1816)**

But faith is not exercised exclusively in the mind. The Aramaic word for faith is *emet*, which means "to sustain." To have faith is to sustain oneself in God, to trust in him.

The greatness of faith contrasts with the sins against this virtue:

- *Voluntary doubt* disregards or refuses to hold what God has revealed as true.
- *Involuntary doubt* hesitates in believing or overcoming difficulties connected with the faith and fails to attempt to dispel them.
- *Atheism* is the refusal to accept God's existence.
- *Heresy* is the obstinate denial by a baptized person of some truth that must be believed with divine faith.
- *Apostasy* is the total repudiation of the Christian faith.
- *Schism* is the refusal to submit to the pope or be united with the Church subject to him.[3]

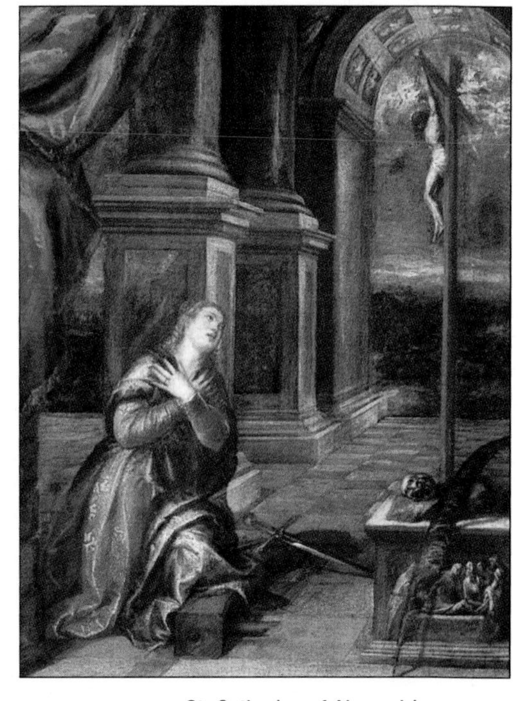

St. Catherine of Alexandria
Persecuted by Emperor Maxentius; martyred for her faith, c. 310.

b. HOPE

> Hope is the theological virtue by which we desire the kingdom of heaven and eternal life as our happiness, placing our trust in Christ's promises and relying not on our own strength, but on the help of the grace of the Holy Spirit....
>
> The virtue of hope responds to the aspiration to happiness which God has placed in the heart of every man; it takes up the hopes that inspire men's activities and purifies them so as to order them to the Kingdom of heaven; it keeps man from discouragement; it sustains him during times of abandonment; it opens up his heart in expectation of eternal beatitude. Buoyed up by hope, he is preserved from selfishness and led to the happiness that flows from charity. (CCC 1817-1818)

All of these aspirations find their fulfillment in God's will. Thus, in the Old Testament, God continually fosters the hope of his people. He sustains it while chastising their infidelity (cf. Ez 36:6-38), but he also fosters hope when they are faithful. Moreover, that hope also includes the hope of salvation for all (cf. Is 49:6). The Bible praises the hope found in Abraham: "In hope he believed against hope, that he should become the father of many nations" (Rom 4:18).

Hope relies not on our own strength, but on the help of the grace of the Holy Spirit.

The first commandment infers that the Christian should have trust in God and foster hope in eternal life. A sin against this commandment can occur either by defect or excess:

1. *Despair* is the loss of trust in God because of doubt in his fidelity or his interest in each of us.

> By *despair*, man ceases to hope for his personal salvation from God, for help in attaining it or for the forgiveness of his sins. Despair is contrary to God's goodness, to his justice—for the Lord is faithful to his promises—and to his mercy. (CCC 2091)

2. *Presumption* can occur in two ways: when one expects salvation without personal effort, or when he trusts solely in his effort without the Holy Spirit's aid.

> There are two kinds of *presumption*. Either man presumes upon his own capacities, (hoping to be able to save himself without help from on high), or he presumes upon God's almighty power or his mercy (hoping to obtain his forgiveness without conversion and glory without merit). (CCC 2092)

Close to the certainty that God is faithful to his word, hope includes fear of punishment if one should offend God: A son's trust does not negate a father's justice.

c. CHARITY (Love)

> Charity is the theological virtue by which we love God above all things for his own sake, and our neighbor as ourselves for the love of God. (CCC 1822)

Christian love has three objects: God, neighbor, and self.

Christian love has three objects: God, neighbor, and self.

Love of God

We ought to love God because he is our Creator, our Father, and our Savior. Our love for God should reflect God's love for us. As St. John states, we ought to love God "because he first loved us" (1 Jn 4:19). John notes the real motive behind the love of God for us and vice versa:

> **See what love the Father has given us, that we should be called children of God; and so we are. The reason why the world does not know us is that it did not know him. (1 Jn 3:1)**

One can sin against God's love in various ways:

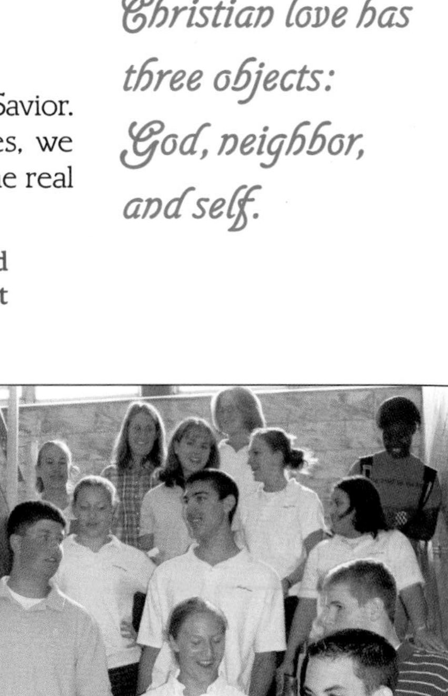

- Indifference is the refusal to reflect on the prior goodness and power of divine charity.
- Ingratitude is the refusal to acknowledge divine charity or return God's love.
- Lukewarmness is failure or hesitation in responding to divine love, and can imply refusal to obey the prompting of charity.
- Acedia is the refusal of the joy God gives, and it causes one to be repelled by divine goodness. It is a form of depression that leads to discouragement.
- Hatred of God opposes the love of God, denies his goodness, and curses him as the one who forbids sin and inflicts punishment. It is a result of pride.[4]

Love of Neighbor

All human beings are children of God and thereby brothers and sisters to one another. All human persons have a dignity bestowed by God that we should not only respect but also love. Due to our many differences as individual human beings, this calling often appears excessive and impossible to accomplish. How is a victim to love the person who robs him? What could lead the family of a murder victim to love the murderer?

All human beings are children of God and thereby brothers and sisters to one another.

Victims should expect to have painful feelings, but these feelings should not develop into hatred. Jesus said, "Love your enemies, do good to those who hate you" (Lk 6:27). With Christ's grace, even victims of horrific crimes can eventually forgive and love their enemies.

St. John encourages the love of neighbor for many reasons. Among them:

- Since "God is Love," charity flows from God; whoever does not love does not know God:

  > **Beloved, let us love one another; for love is of God, and he who loves is born of God and knows God. He who does not love does not know God; for God is love. (1 Jn 4:7-8)**

- The path of Jesus and his commandment of love continue to be stressed in the teachings of the New Testament:

Jesus makes charity the *new commandment* (cf. Jn 13:34). By loving his own "to the end" (Jn 13:1), he makes manifest the Father's love which he receives. By loving one another, the disciples imitate the love of Jesus which they themselves receive. Whence Jesus says: "As the Father has loved me, so have I loved you; abide in my love." And again: "This is my commandment, that you love one another as I have loved you" (Jn 15:9, 12). (CCC 1823)

Love of Self

The Christian is asked to love others as he loves himself because he is created in the image and likeness of God. That he is to have a genuine love for himself is presupposed by the command that he love his neighbor "as himself." Because our bodies, as well as our souls, were created for eternal glory, this commandment asks us to care for both.

3. THE RELATIONSHIP BETWEEN THE LOVE OF GOD AND OF NEIGHBOR

Because our bodies, as well as our souls, were created for eternal glory, this commandment asks us to care for both.

The question is often asked: Which of the two loves comes first and is more significant? Should the Christian love God first or his neighbor? In reality, it is impossible to separate these loves because God himself, who "is love" (1 Jn 4:8), is the source of both. There is, then, no Christian love that does not flow from God the Holy Spirit.

Which love should be given first priority? The love of God ought to be first since the Decalogue calls it the first love. At the same time, a genuine love of God necessarily leads to the love of neighbor. St. John clearly states this: "If any one says, 'I love God,' and hates his brother, he is a liar" (1 Jn 4:20). Hence, since the love of God comes first, the proof of its validity is found in the love of neighbor.

Veritatis splendor addresses the relationship between these two great commandments:

> **This certainly does not mean that Christ wishes to put the love of neighbor higher than, or even to set it apart from, the love of God. This is evident from his conversation with the teacher of the Law....**
>
> **These two commandments, on which "depend all the Law and the Prophets" (Mt 22:40), are profoundly connected and mutually related. Their inseparable unity is attested to by Christ in his words and by his very life: his mission culminates in the Cross of our Redemption (Jn 3:14-15).[5]**

4. WORSHIP OF GOD: THE VIRTUE OF RELIGION

The virtue of religion requires us to render to God the worship, devotion, honor, and service that he deserves. The first commandment mandates the acknowledgment of God and the worship due to him. In other words, the requirements of justice lead one to give God the honor and worship due him. This virtue regulates the relationship between us and God.

The fulfillment of this virtue—for Catholics—is fundamentally accomplished through prayer, and especially in the sacrifice of the Mass.[6]

A summary of the acts belonging to the virtue of religion is commonly found in the Mass: adoration, atonement, petition, and thanksgiving.

Adoration
Atonement
Petition
Thanksgiving

The progression of these four acts is self-evident. First, the Father's greatness is poured out, which then elicits acknowledgment by an act of worship (adoration). Then, a person sees his actions as not measuring up to what Jesus the Son desires of him, so he becomes aware of the need for forgiveness (atonement). At the same time, he recognizes his limits and his need for the Holy Spirit's aid, so he asks for it (petition). Finally, the greatness of God and his forgiveness create an attitude of constant thanksgiving.

The virtue of religion is essential to Christian life. Practicing this virtue sometimes requires heroic effort, for secular society has become a hindrance to religious expression, in both the personal and social spheres. As a consequence, a Christian should be ever more vigilant in the protection of his faith and the development of the virtue of religion.

The greatness of God and his forgiveness create an attitude of constant thanksgiving.

5. SINS AGAINST THE VIRTUE OF RELIGION

In worshipping God, a person often defiles the very act of worship by corrupt and false forms of religiosity. There are many reasons for this corruption, the main one being a false concept of God. These false forms of religiosity can be reduced to five:

a. IDOLATRY

Idolatry is the elevation of other realities to the state of gods, thereby making them take the place of the real God:

> **Idolatry not only refers to false pagan worship. It remains a constant temptation to faith. Idolatry consists in divinizing what is not God. Man commits idolatry whenever he honors and reveres a creature in place of God, whether this be gods or demons (for example, satanism), power, pleasure, race, ancestors, the state, money, etc.... Idolatry rejects the unique Lordship of God; it is therefore incompatible with communion with God (cf. Gal 5: 20; Eph 5: 5). (CCC 2113)**

b. SUPERSTITION

Superstition is any belief or practice that renders false worship to God, or attributes supernatural or magical powers to certain objects or ritual actions. Superstition takes many forms. Sometimes, it involves believing that objects have secret powers, or using legitimate religious devotions in a superstitious

Even religious devotions can be distorted into superstitious practices.

way (such as the use of chain prayers as a way to force God to grant requests). At other times, it involves a form of idolatry because it attributes to created things powers that belong to God alone.

Superstitious practices vary according to the times and culture of the individual or society. Consequently, it is not easy to list them, but a few examples may be provided:

- A Catholic who formally worships God in non-Christian or pagan religious ceremonies commits a sin of superstition, for the truth of Jesus' divinity is denied.
- Legitimate religious devotions such as the rosary, novenas, medals of patron saints, and the like are a manifestation of the virtue of religion. But even these can be distorted into superstitious practices. For example, a sin of superstition occurs if one insists that certain prayers be said a particular number of times for an exact number of days in order to expect God to act exactly how the believer wants him to act, or when one uses candles only of a certain color for specific prayers. These practices are wrong because they attribute the results to the external rituals involved and not to God's goodness.

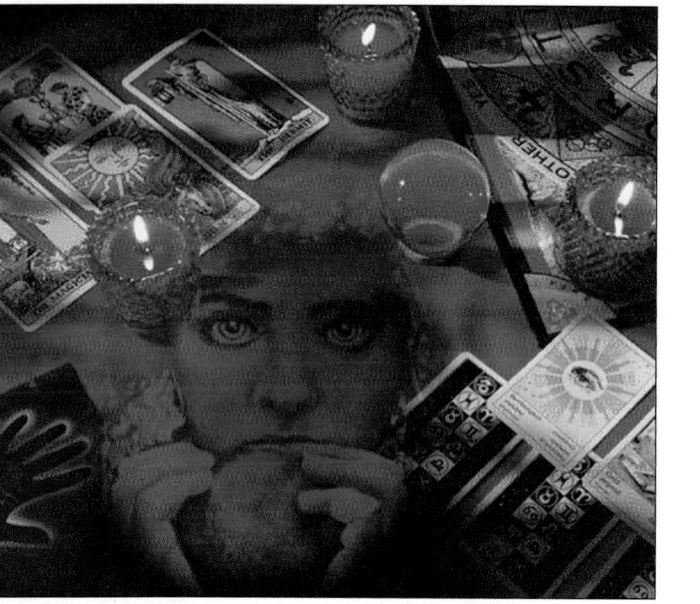

- A football player who believes that his team's loss was due to his failure to perform some pre-game ritual or wear a particular article of clothing is guilty of a sin of superstition. Such actions attribute supernatural powers to created things.
- The businessman who refuses to schedule meetings or flights on the 13th day of the month also sins by superstition, for by so doing, he denies God's providence and refuses to trust him to direct and protect his life.

Divination tries to predict the future and unveil the mystery of life without reference to God's revelation.

c. DIVINATION

Divination is the prediction of the future or the revelation of the unknown through so-called paranormal means. The desire to know the future is natural, but while the religious person trusts in God, divination tries to predict the future and unveil the mystery of life without reference to God's revelation.

The desire to predict the future by means that contradict a true religious faith cannot be seen as religious practice, and is false worship of God. The false means are many; the *Catechism of the Catholic Church* summarizes them in the following manner:

> All forms of *divination* are to be rejected: recourse to Satan or demons, conjuring up the dead or other practices falsely supposed to "unveil" the future (cf. Dt 18:10; Jer 29:8). Consulting horoscopes, astrology, palm reading, interpretation of omens and lots, the phenomena of clairvoyance, and recourse to mediums all conceal a

> desire for power over time, history, and, in the last analysis, other human beings, as well as a wish to conciliate hidden powers. They contradict the honor, respect, and loving fear that we owe to God alone. (CCC 2116)

All of these practices deny a person's freedom and ability—with God's aid—to reach his destiny.

The desire to know and control the occult forces has always been an attractive temptation for human beings.

d. MAGIC

Magic is the desire to know and control the occult forces that supposedly influence the world. This has always been an attractive temptation for human beings, and has existed in various forms in every human culture. Witchcraft is one of the most common and seriously sinful forms of this evil.

Characteristic of magic are the various practices in which an individual attempts—through rituals or formulas—to use occult forces, not only to avoid some evils, but also to bring about other evils.

> All practices of *magic* or *sorcery*, by which one attempts to tame occult powers, so as to place them at one's service and have a supernatural power over others—even if this were for the sake of restoring their health—are gravely contrary to the virtue of religion. These practices are even more to be condemned when accompanied by the intention of harming someone, or when they have recourse to the intervention of demons. Wearing charms is also reprehensible. (CCC 2117)

Magic is essentially different from the veneration of images. Images are religious representations of different Christian mysteries, and their veneration is based on the mystery of Jesus' Incarnation. They represent the Lord, the Virgin Mary and the saints. The Christian veneration of images unfolds in a sacred environment, whose form is the Eucharistic Liturgy, which is the highest form of worship.

The Christian veneration of images unfolds in a sacred environment.

e. IRRELIGION

Irreligion is also condemned by the first commandment. The following are some sins of irreligion:

- *Tempting God* is testing, in word or deed, the goodness and power of God.
- *Sacrilege* is disrespect for sacred persons, places or things.
- *Simony* is the buying or selling of spiritual powers or gifts.[7]

6. BIBLICAL CONDEMNATION OF ALL FORMS OF SUPERSTITION

The condemnation of superstitions is not just a recent stance by the Magisterium; rather, it has been constant in the history of Christianity. The first biblical testimonies recall these condemnations. The Old Testament fought against superstitions commonly present at that time:

It is a great insult when a person turns from God to creatures and pleasures of limited value.

> "When you come into the land which the Lord your God gives you, you shall not learn to follow the abominable practices of those nations. There shall not be found among you any one who burns his son or his daughter as an offering, any one who practices divination, a soothsayer, or an augur, or a sorcerer, or a charmer, or a medium, or a wizard, or a necromancer. For whoever does these things is an abomination to the Lord; and because of these abominable practices the Lord your God is driving them out before you. You shall be blameless before the Lord your God. For these nations, which you are about to dispossess, give heed to soothsayers and to diviners; but as for you, the Lord your God has not allowed you so to do." (Dt 18:9-14)

Also, the New Testament condemns all forms of superstitions, as in the case of St. Paul, who praises those who "turned to God from idols, to serve a living and true God" (1 Thes 1:9). The Apostle asks, "What agreement has the temple of God with idols?" (2 Cor 6:16). In the list of sins found in the New Testament, there is mention of idolatry and sorcery (cf. Gal 5:20; Rv 21:8), and those who have accepted the Gospel and later turn to idols are rejected (cf. 1 Cor 10:14; 2 Cor 6:14-17).

In the New Testament, however, the term *idols* refers not only to pagan gods, but also pagan values; accordingly, St. Paul speaks of the "immoral or impure man, or one who is covetous (that is, an idolater)" (Eph 5:5).

CONCLUSION

Humanly speaking, there is no way to understand God's love for humanity. At the same time, there is a return owed to God for the love he has lavishly poured forth on all of us. God is owed a certain amount of respect as a matter of justice, but the Christian is called to go beyond justice and give his life to Jesus through the Holy Spirit. It is a great insult when a person turns from God to creatures and pleasures of limited value.

The Old Testament compares sin against God to the adulterous spouse. This metaphor offers a good way to understand God's love, for the greatest tragedies are the result of the abuse of the marital relationship. How much greater is the tragedy of refusing the love of God?

VOCABULARY

ACEDIA
Spiritual sloth or indifference that can extend as far as the refusal of the joy that God gives. It causes one to be repelled by divine goodness.

ADORATION
Worship in which we acknowledge and respond to the revelation of the glory and power of God.

APOSTASY
The total repudiation of the Christian faith.

ATHEISM
The refusal to accepts God's existence.

CHARITY
The theological virtue by which we love God above all things for his own sake, and love our neighbor as ourselves for the love of God.

DESPAIR
The loss of trust in God because of doubt in his fidelity or interest in each person.

DIVINATION
The prediction of the future or revelation of the unknown through so-called paranormal means.

FAITH
The theological virtue by which we believe in all that God has said and revealed to us and that the Church proposes for our belief.

HATRED OF GOD
The sin of opposing the love of God, denying his goodness, and cursing him as the one who forbids sin and inflicts punishment.

HERESY
The obstinate denial by a baptized person of some truth that must be believed with divine faith.

HOPE
The theological virtue by which we desire the kingdom of heaven and eternal life as our happiness, placing our trust in Christ's promises and relying on the help of the grace of the Holy Spirit.

IDOLATRY
The religious worship of imaginary gods, the devil or other created things, such as forces of nature, the stars or the cosmos, animals, etc.

INDIFFERENCE
The refusal to reflect on the prior goodness and power of the divine charity.

INGRATITUDE
The refusal to acknowledge divine charity or return God's love.

INVOLUNTARY DOUBT
The sin against faith that hesitates in believing or overcoming difficulties connected with the Faith and fails to attempt to dispel them.

LUKEWARMNESS
The failure or hesitation in responding to divine love.

MAGIC
The desire to know and control the occult forces that supposedly influence human life.

VOCABULARY CONTINUED

MORAL THEOLOGY
That part of theology that makes use of practical judgments to direct human acts towards their supernatural end—God—under the guidance of revelation.

PRESUMPTION
The sin by which one expects salvation without personal effort, or when he trusts solely in his efforts without God's aid.

RELIGION
The virtue that enables us to render God the worship, honor, devotion and service he deserves.

SACRILEGE
Profaning the sacraments or other liturgical actions, or things consecrated to God in a special way, such as priests, religious women and men, churches, shrines, convents or monasteries, icons, statues, etc.

SCHISM
The refusal to submit to the pope or be united with the Church subject to him.

SIMONY
The buying or selling of spiritual powers or gifts.

SUPERSTITION
Beliefs or practices that render false worship to God, or attribute supernatural or magical powers to certain objects or ritual actions. The most common and grave sins of superstition are divination and magic.

THEOLOGICAL VIRTUES
The virtues of faith, hope, and love (charity), which enable the Christian to live in a close relationship with God. They are called *theological* because they not only originate with God, but also have God as their object. They help to lead the believer to perfect union with him by enabling him to love God for his own sake.

THEOPHANY
A word meaning "the manifestation of God." A theophany can be an actual appearance of God in his glory (as Moses witnessed on Mt. Sinai), or a manifestation of God through some medium such as a storm, fire, or angelic apparition.

VOLUNTARY DOUBT
The sin against faith that disregards or refuses to hold what God has revealed as true.

WORSHIP
The response of a person that acknowledges the greatness of God, and renders signs of submission, reverence and love to him.

SUPPLEMENTARY READINGS

1. "The first commandment embraces faith, hope, and charity. When we say 'God' we confess a constant, unchangeable being, always the same, faithful and just, without any evil. It follows that we must necessarily accept his words and have complete faith in him and acknowledge his authority. He is almighty, merciful, and infinitely beneficent....Who could not place all hope in him? Who could not love him when contemplating the treasures of goodness and love he had poured out on us? Hence the formula God employs in the Scripture at the beginning and end of his commandments: 'I am the Lord.'"[8]

— CCC 2086

2. What the Church has decided definitively on matters of faith and morals, all Catholics must accept. On what has not been decided definitively, you may follow what theologian seems most reasonable to you. On matters of policy you may disagree, or on matters of opinion. You do not have to accept everything your particular pastor says unless it is something defined by the whole Church, i.e., defined or canon law. We are all bound by Friday abstinence. This does not mean that the sin is in eating meat but that the sin is in refusing the penance; the sin is in disobedience to Christ who speaks to us through the Church; the same with missing Mass on Sunday...

— Flannery O'Connor, *Collected Works: Letter to Cecil Dawkins,* 23 December 1959, p. 1117

3. If I speak in the tongues of men and of angels, but have not love, I am a noisy gong or a clanging cymbal. And if I have prophetic powers, and understand all mysteries and all knowledge, and if I have all faith, so as to remove mountains, but have not love, I am nothing. If I give away all I have, and if I deliver my body to be burned, but have not love, I gain nothing.

Love is patient and kind; love is not jealous or boastful; it is not arrogant or rude. Love does not insist on its own way; it is not irritable or resentful; it does not rejoice at wrong, but rejoices in the right. Love bears all things, believes all things, hopes all things, endures all things.

Love never ends; as for prophecies, they will pass away; as for tongues, they will cease; as for knowledge, it will pass away....Now I know in part; then I shall understand fully, even as I have been fully understood. So faith, hope, love abide, these three; but the greatest of these is love.

— 1 Cor 13:1-13

4. Now the human mind, in order to be united to God, needs to be guided by the sensible world, since "invisible things...are clearly seen, being understood by the things that are made," as the Apostle says (Rom 1:20). Wherefore in the Divine worship it is necessary to make use of corporeal things, that man's mind may be aroused thereby, as by signs, to the spiritual acts by means of which he is united to God. Therefore the internal acts of religion take precedence of the others and belong to religion essentially, while its external acts are secondary, and subordinate to the internal acts.

— St. Thomas Aquinas, *Summa Theologiae,* II-II, q. 81, a. 7

SUPPLEMENTARY READINGS CONTINUED

5. Here we touch upon an aspect of evangelization which cannot leave us insensitive. We wish to speak about what today is often called popular religiosity.

One finds among the people particular expressions of the search for God and for faith, both in the regions where the Church has been established for centuries and where she is in the course of becoming established. These expressions were for a long time regarded as less pure and were sometimes despised, but today they are almost everywhere being rediscovered. During the last Synod the bishops studied their significance with remarkable pastoral realism and zeal.

— *EN*, 48

6. The practice of placing sacred images in churches so that they be venerated by the faithful is to be maintained. Nevertheless their number should be moderate and their relative positions should reflect right order. For otherwise the Christian people may find them incongruous and they may foster devotion of doubtful orthodoxy."

— *SC*, 125

7. I answer that, as stated above (81, 5; I-II, 101, 4), a thing is called "sacred" through being deputed to the divine worship. Now just as a thing acquires an aspect of good through being deputed to a good end, so does a thing assume a divine character through being deputed to the divine worship, and thus a certain reverence is due to it, which reverence is referred to God. Therefore whatever pertains to irreverence for sacred things is an injury to God, and comes under the head of sacrilege.

— St. Thomas Aquinas, *Summa Theologiae*, II-II, q. 99, a. 1

8. The New Age is…appropriated by its disciples and is presented to its proselytes as a salvific wisdom. In this, it approximates to the gnostic enthusiasm which have troubled the Church from her inception, and which in fact ground all heresy. Gnosticism consists, in all its varied presentations, in a reversion to paganism under pseudo-Christian auspices. This camouflaging of an absolute and comprehensive antagonism to Christianity has characterized Gnosticism from its origins, as it did in the flower children in the Age of Aquarius, and as it does in the New Age disciples today. The New Age movement is only the current Western version of this perennial perversion of the Christian faith.…

…In the end, the New Age is no more than one more pagan soteriology: it looks to the extinction of the good creation that is in Christ, the Image of God, in order that one may image Nothing.

— Archbishop Francis J. Stafford, "The 'New Age' Movement: Analysis of a New Attempt to Find Salvation Apart from Christian Faith," *Catholic Position Papers*, March 1993

ADVANCED CONCEPTS

1. RELIGIOUS LIBERTY

Since we ought to worship God, society has to not only recognize this right, but also facilitate and defend the exercise thereof. It must be treated as a fundamental right, as Vatican II proclaims:

> The Vatican Council declares that the human person has a right to religious freedom. Freedom of this kind means that all men should be immune from coercion on the part of individuals, social groups and every human power so that, within due limits, nobody is to be forced to act against his convictions in religious matters in private or in public, alone or in association with others.[9]

In virtue of this principle, civil authority has no power to limit the exercise of the right to worship God in private. The Tradition of the Church has always affirmed these truths, which were solemnly declared at Vatican II:

> But his own social nature requires that man give external expression to these internal acts of religion, that he communicate with others on religious matters, and profess his religion in community. Consequently to deny man the free exercise of religion in society, when the just requirements of public order are observed, is to do an injustice to the human person and to the very order established by God for men.[10]

Many nations have come to recognize this right by including it in their constitutions. The United Nation's *Universal Declaration on the Rights of Man* enumerates religious liberty with the rights to freedom of thought and conscience:

> Everyone has the right to freedom of thought, conscience and religion; this right includes freedom…either alone or in his community with others and in public or private, to manifest his religion or belief in teaching, practice, worship and observance.[11]

The First Amendment of the Constitution of the United States likewise formulates this fundamental right of all people: "Congress shall make no law respecting an establishment of religion, or prohibiting the free exercise thereof…"

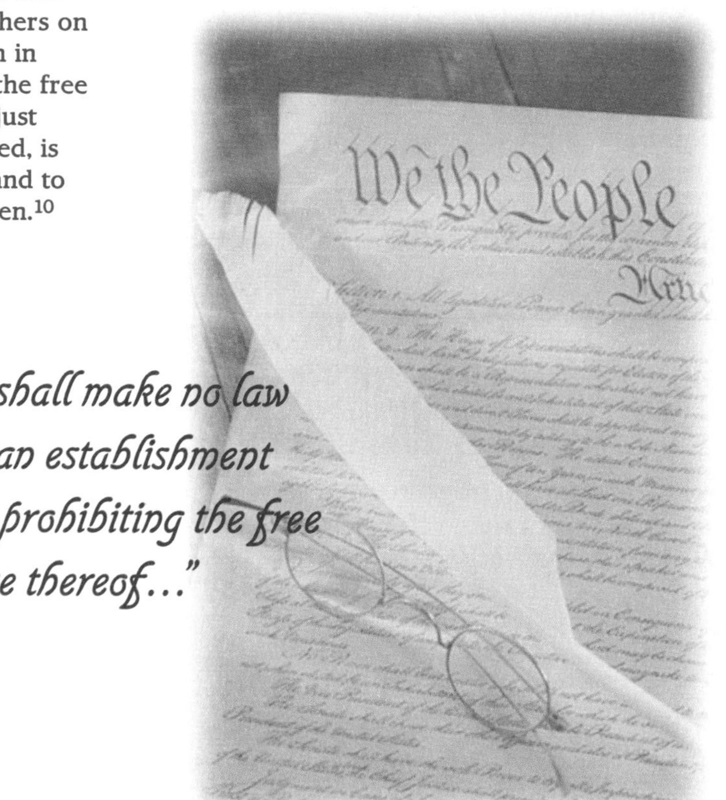

"Congress shall make no law respecting an establishment of religion, or prohibiting the free exercise thereof…"

ADVANCED CONCEPTS CONTINUED

2. THE "NEW AGE" MOVEMENT

A growing phenomenon in Western culture during the past thirty years has been the New Age movement.

The New Age movement is not really new in one sense: followers of the various groups who classify themselves as New Age incorporate ideas from numerous sources. Ancient religious systems such as gnosticism, oriental religions such as Buddhism and Hinduism, occult practices from Western history, and even modern science and psychology are all sources from which the New Age religions have drawn their beliefs and philosophies. The result is a strange blend of Eastern religion, humanistic psychology, occultism, and superstition.

However, the New Age movement appears to have its specific historical inception (or perhaps its catalyst) in the theosophist and occultist speculations of Alice Anne Bailey (1880-1949), whose copious and repetitive publications have been in print over the past 70 years. The contemporary rediscovery of and fascination with her New Age doctrine owes a great deal to those millions of unchurched people in the Western world who, once anchored in the certitudes of the Christian faith, have lost that spiritual security under the pervasive and corrosive influence of a counter-Catholic symbolism of modernity. And now, seeking another spiritual haven, they find themselves in the position of the apostate from Christianity who, instead of now believing nothing, believes anything.

In order to borrow from so many varied—and sometimes contradictory—sources, the followers of the New Age movements must dilute and transform the beliefs of these systems. (It is also important to stress here that Buddhism and Hinduism, for example, are major world religions; they are *not* part of the New Age movement. Some of their religious beliefs have been absorbed into the New Age movement, but these beliefs have often been drastically modified in order to make them acceptable to New Age believers.)

In addition, it is sometimes difficult to understand the different groups that belong to the New Age movement, because they tend to be very loosely structured. There is no central organization of these groups into a single, unified movement as such.

Stated most simply, New Age philosophies and religious practices are contrary to the First Commandment and to the revelation that God has given to humanity. They are, therefore, incompatible with the Christian faith. This can be demonstrated clearly by examining some of the errors common to all New Age groups:

a. MONISM

In general, most New Age religions are characterized by *monism*, the belief that everything that exists (human beings, the universe, God) is one. Christians, on the other hand, believe that God is unique and separate from the created universe. God is eternal, while the material universe had a beginning and will have an end. Similarly, God is infinite, while the created world is finite.

b. PANTHEISM

New Age believers also believe that the nature of this monistic universe is divine, that everything that exists is God. While New Age books tend to focus more on the divine nature

ADVANCED CONCEPTS CONTINUED

of human beings rather than of plants and animals, it is nevertheless possible to find many that equate human life with animal and plant life. After all, if everything is divine, then no part of the world can be inherently more valuable than any other part.

This is a denial of mankind's unique position in the created order, as well as the unique nature of his relationship with God. Christianity teaches that humans alone, because we are spiritual as well as physical being, are created in the image and likeness of God. We alone can acknowledge and love our Creator. Further, God clearly states in the Old Testament that there is nothing in physical creation that is like himself, and therefore the Jews are warned not to make images of God in the form of any living creature, nor to fall into the error of worshipping created things as divine (cf. Dt 4:15-19).

c. SYNCRETISM

New Age believers practice *syncretism,* a method by which one attempts to bring into harmony contrasting or conflicting ideas. In religion, syncretists try to eliminate conflicts between different religious faiths by eliminating those doctrines that contradict each other, while holding on to the doctrines that seem to agree or complement one another. Thus, a syncretistic approach to the differences between, say, Christianity and Hinduism, would be to accept Jesus' divinity by claiming that Jesus is an *avatar.* Because a number of men in the history of Hinduism claimed to be avatars, or incarnations of the divine being, a syncretist equates their claims with that of Jesus, while ignoring the fact that Jesus clearly stated that he alone is "the way, and the truth, and the life," apart from whom no one can come to salvation (cf. Jn 14:6).

d. GNOSTICISM

The word *gnosticism* comes from the Greek word *gnosis,* meaning knowledge. Gnostics are people who believe that a person can achieve enlightenment, healing, or transformation only through possession of secret knowledge given to a special few. In order to obtain this knowledge, one must turn to this select elite for "enlightenment." This contrasts sharply with the Christian message that salvation is intended for all people, and that it is our relationship with Jesus—not our knowledge—that brings salvation.

A final problem with the New Age movement is its denial of our need for salvation. For followers of the New Age movement, because all people are inherently divine, there is no need for salvation bestowed on us from the outside by a redeemer. All that is necessary is that each person become conscious of his or her own divine nature. Further, there is a denial of the reality of sin. There are no objective moral goods or evils—there is only ignorance and lack of knowledge.

Stated most simply, New Age philosophies and religious practices are contrary to the First Commandment and to the revelation that God has given to humanity.

QUESTIONS

1. What is the role of the theologian?

2. What are the two great commandments?

3. Above all else, what do the commandments reflect?

4. Why is God the basic principle of our life and being?

5. How does moral theology use practical judgments?

6. What does moral theology seek to do?

7. What distinguishes Christian revelation from all other faiths?

8. What is the theme of all of Scripture?

9. What is the obligation of each person to God's intervention?

10. What gift of God makes the practice of the theological virtues possible?

11. What two fundamental attitudes are required in response to revelation?

12. When faith is known, what two duties are expected of us?

13. What are the sins against faith?

14. What are the sins against hope?

15. What are the three objects of Christian love?

16. What does the virtue of religion require us to render to God?

17. What acts belonging to the virtue of religion are commonly found in the Mass?

PRACTICAL EXERCISES

1. Read Supplementary Reading 1 and answer this question: What treasury of goodness has God poured out upon humanity?

2. Comment on 1 Corinthians 13. Include an enumeration of the qualities of charity, and determine if any of the marks of Christian love show up in everyday life.

3. Examine and comment on point 2117 in the *Catechism of the Catholic Church.*

4. Read and take note of the principles found in the following Scriptural passages that condemn superstition:

- Lv 19:26; 19:31; 20:6; 20:27
- Dt 13:2-4

5. Read Supplementary Reading 5 and describe the pros and cons of some popular devotions with which you are familiar. Do you think that even legitimate Christian devotions can be abused and become superstitious? Support your answer with an example.

6. Discuss and enumerate several classes of superstition. Analyze and assess their plausibility. Do these superstitions describe what is real in any way? Why would anyone believe them?

7. What is the difference between wearing amulets or good-luck charms and wearing devotional medals, such as the Miraculous Medal or a patron saint medal? What is the difference between divination with the dead and prayers to saints?

FROM THE CATECHISM

1842 By faith, we believe in God and believe all that he has revealed to us and all that the Holy Church proposes for our belief.

1843 By hope we desire, and with steadfast trust await from God, eternal life and the graces to merit it.

2138 Superstition is a departure from the worship that we give to the true God. It is manifested in idolatry, as well as in various forms of divination and magic.

2139 Tempting God in words or deeds, sacrilege, and simony are sins of irreligion forbidden by the first commandment.

2140 Since it rejects or denies the existence of God, atheism is a sin against the first commandment.

ENDNOTES

1. Cf. CCC, 2086.
2. Cf. Ibid., 154-159.
3. Cf. Ibid., 2087-2089, 2123.
4. Cf. Ibid., 2094.
5. *VS*, 14.
6. Cf. CCC, 2099-2100.
7. Cf. Ibid., 2118-2132; cf. Acts 8: 9-24.
8. *Roman Catechism* 3, 2, 4.
9. *DH*, 2.
10. *DH*, 3.
11. *Universal Declaration on the Rights of Man*, 18.

Chapter 11

The Second Commandment:
You Shall Not Take The Name Of The Lord In Vain

"What's in a name? That which we call a rose by any other name would smell as sweet." These famous words of Shakespeare are only half true. A name, whether it is of a person or a thing, gathers many emotional overtones by constant use. A name ceases to be just a group of letters taken from the alphabet; a name comes to represent the person or the thing which bears the name. The emotions aroused in us by the word *"rose"* are quite different from those evoked by the name *"skunk cabbage."* A young man in love only has to hear his sweetheart's name mentioned, even casually by a stranger, to make his pulse rate rise. A man who has suffered great injury at the hands of someone named George will forever have a great distaste for the name *"George."* Men have killed—and have been killed—*"in defense of their good name."* Whole families have been grieved because some member of the family "brought disgrace on the family name." In short, a name stands for the one who bears the name—and our attitude towards a name reflects our attitude towards the person whose name it is.

All this is obvious, of course. But it serves to recall to mind why it is a sin to misuse God's name—to use it carelessly or irreverently. If we love God we shall love His name and never speak it except with reverence and respect. We shall never use it as an expletive, as an expression of anger or impatience or surprise; we shall do nothing to bring infamy upon his name. Indeed, our love for God's name will extend to those of Mary, his Mother, and to his friends the saints, and to all holy things which belong to God. Their names, too, will pass our lips only with thoughtful reverence. That we may never forget this aspect of our love for God, he has given us the second commandment.[1]

Let us ask ourselves:

- Under what circumstances may God's name be legitimately invoked?
- What are the obligations that the invocation of God's name places upon a person?
- How can sins against the second commandment be avoided?

The sense of the sacred is part of the virtue of religion.

When a person takes an oath using God's name, it is a statement saying that the personhood of God is standing behind the oath.

INTRODUCTION

The expression "He is a man of his word" indicates that the person is of high moral character. When he makes a promise or a statement, there is no need for him to sign his name, and this guarantee arises out of who he is, for his personhood guarantees that he will follow through and keep his word.

When a person takes an oath using God's name, it is a statement saying that the personhood of God is standing behind the oath, so it would be seriously wrong to use the holy name of God to guarantee a lie.

1. THE GRANDEUR OF GOD'S NAME

As the Supreme Being and Creator, God is owed such reverence and devotion that his very name is sacred. As the *Catechism* states:

> **Among all the words of Revelation, there is one which is unique: the revealed name of God. God confides his name to those who believe in him; he reveals himself to them in his personal mystery. (CCC 2143)**

In the New Testament, St. Paul emphasizes the importance and power of God's name in the person of Christ.

> Therefore God has highly exalted him and bestowed on him the name which is above every name, that at the name of Jesus every knee should bow, in heaven and on earth and under the earth, and every tongue confess that Jesus Christ is Lord, to the glory of God the Father. (Phil 2: 9-11)

It is good to avoid calling upon God's testimony in unimportant matters, for to use such words demands the greatest possible discretion.

The title "Lord" indicates divine sovereignty, the recognition of Jesus as God. It is, therefore, the duty of every Christian to avoid the irreverent use of God's name, and, furthermore, to accord the name of God devotion and praise.

> Respect for his name is an expression of the respect owed to the mystery of God himself and to the whole sacred reality it evokes. The *sense of the sacred* is part of the virtue of religion...
>
> The faithful should bear witness to the Lord's name by confessing the faith without giving way to fear (cf. Mt 10: 32; 1 Tm 6: 12). Preaching and catechizing should be permeated with adoration and respect for the name of our Lord Jesus Christ. (CCC 2144-2145)

2. OATHS

> An oath is the invocation of the divine Name as witness to the truth. It cannot be taken except in truth, judgment and justice.[2]

In order to take a true oath, one must call upon God as a witness.

To take an oath is to call upon God as a witness. Expressions like "God is my witness," "I speak before God," and "As God is my Judge" are often repeated in everyday conversation. On some occasions, they are spoken spontaneously; ordinarily such statements are not truly oaths, for the speaker has no intention to make an oath. Nevertheless, it is good to avoid calling upon God's testimony in unimportant matters, for to use such words demands the greatest possible discretion.

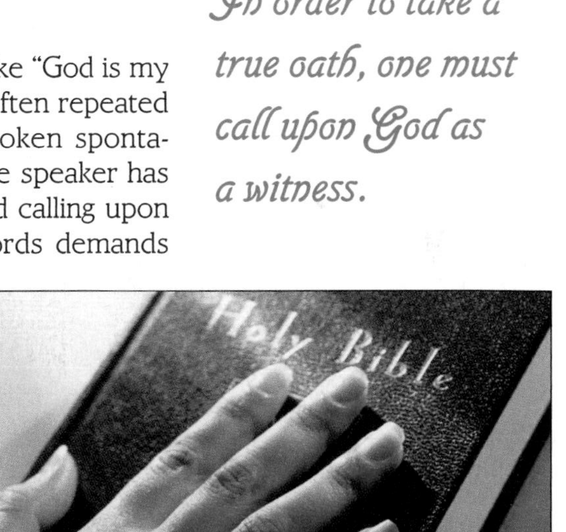

We can distinguish two kinds of oaths: *assertory* and *promissory.* In an assertory oath, God is called on as a witness to the truth of what is being said. An example would be the oath taken by witnesses in court when giving testimony in a trial. One takes a promissory oath when he calls upon God as witness to what he intends to do in the future. This oath is often taken to guarantee certain conditions will be met. An example of a promissory oath is one taken by an elected public official who solemnly swears before God to fulfill the duties of his office.

In order to take a true oath, one must call upon God as a witness. When one only mentions God, but does not call him as witness to testimony, it is not considered to be an oath. For this reason, formulas like "only God knows" do not constitute oaths. Formulas like "on my word of honor" are used to guarantee a higher grade of veracity, but should not be considered oaths.

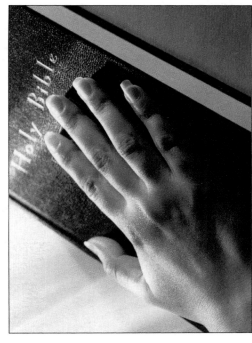

3. OLD TESTAMENT DOCTRINE CONCERNING THE CUSTOM OF TAKING OATHS

The recognition of only one God—transcendent and Creator—besides requiring from people the worship due to him, also demands that we respect God's very name. This respect may be seen in a particular way in oaths.

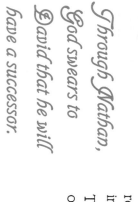

The custom of making oaths was not unknown in ancient Israel. For this reason, when Yahweh dictates the moral code to his people, he forbids them to use his name in vain. The two expressions of this commandment in the Old Testament fully agree on this point: "You shall not take the name of the Lord your God in vain; for the Lord will not hold him guiltless who takes his name in vain" (Ex 20:7; Dt 5:11).

The phrase *in vain* means "uselessly." It is worth noting that the Old Testament relates the promises of God, which are accompanied by oaths. For example, God promises his blessings with this oath:

"By myself I have sworn, says the Lord, because you have done this, and have not withheld your son, your only son, I will indeed bless you, and I will multiply your descendants as the stars of heaven and as the sand which is on the seashore. And your descendants shall possess the gate of their enemies..." (Gn 22:16-17)

This oath is remembered by Moses (cf. Dt 6:3), is recorded in the *Magnificat* (cf. Lk 1:73), and is mentioned in the Letter to the Hebrews (cf. Heb 6:13-17). Through Nathan, God swears to David that he will have a successor (cf. 2 Sm 7:11-13). The psalmist also recalls this oath (cf. Ps 132:11) and St. Peter mentions it in his first discourse, in which he acknowledges Christ as God of all humanity (cf. Acts 2:30).

Through Nathan, God swears to David that he will have a successor.

The Book of Numbers regulates the use of oaths (Nm 30:2). Later, the Book of Sirach gives this advice:

> Do not accustom your mouth to oaths, and do not habitually utter the name of the Holy One; for as a servant who is continually examined under torture will not lack bruises, so also the man who always swears and utters the Name will not be cleansed from sin. A man who swears many oaths will be filled with iniquity, and the scourge will not leave his house; if he offends, his sin remains on him, and if he disregards it, he sins doubly; if he has sworn needlessly, he will not be justified, for his house will be filled with calamities. (Sir 23:9-11)

4. NEW TESTAMENT DOCTRINE CONCERNING OATHS

The second commandment is a practical application of the virtue of religion, which guides our conversations with God, demands respect for his name and person, and promotes refinement in holy things. But the words of Jesus are restrictive:

> "Again you have heard that it was said to the men of old, 'You shall not swear falsely, but shall perform to the Lord what you have

> sworn.' But I say to you, Do not swear at all, either by heaven, for it is the throne of God, or by the earth, for it is his footstool, or by Jerusalem, for it is the city of the great King. And do not swear by your head, for you cannot make one hair white or black. Let what you say be simply 'Yes' or 'No'; anything more than this comes from evil." (Mt 5:33-37)

From a brief look at this reading, one might deduce that Jesus revises the teaching of the Old Testament and condemns every kind of oath. This is not true, however. For example, in the Gospel of Matthew, Jesus does not rebuke the high priest who demanded a response under oath (cf. Mt 26:63-64). Therefore, Jesus' words do not contain an absolute no. They intend to purify this practice, which was corrupt in his time:

> Following St. Paul (cf. 2 Cor 1:23; Gal 1:20), the tradition of the Church has understood Jesus' words as not excluding oaths made for grave and right reasons (for example, in court). (CCC 2154)

Following St. Paul, the tradition of the Church has understood Jesus' words as not excluding oaths made for grave and right reasons.

Nevertheless, the *Catechism* indicates some limitations on legitimate use of an oath:

> The holiness of the divine name demands that we neither use it for trivial matters, nor take an oath which on the basis of the circumstances could be interpreted as approval of an authority unjustly requiring it. When an oath is required by illegitimate civil authorities, it may be refused. It must be refused when it is required for purposes contrary to the dignity of persons or to ecclesial communion. (CCC 2155)

5. NECESSARY CONDITIONS FOR THE LAWFUL USE OF OATHS

Because taking an oath is an action of the most solemn and serious nature, it cannot be taken except in truth, necessity, and justice.[3] To do otherwise is a sin. Let us examine these three necessary conditions:

a. TRUTH

An oath may not be taken to support a lie. This condition is decisive—moral certainty is required in order to take an oath; probability is not sufficient. When one takes an oath and lies, he commits the very grave sin of perjury.

b. NECESSITY

An oath should be taken with discretion, out of necessity and not for superficial things when one's word would suffice. God should never be called as witness to a trivial matter.

c. JUSTICE

An oath can be taken only for something morally good. To take an oath about something illicit is unjust. For example, "I swear I'll get revenge" would have absolutely no validity, for revenge is in itself a condemnable act. One may never take an oath to do evil.

For a promissory oath to be valid, one must have the following:

- Intention of taking an oath, or committing oneself before God;
- Reflection before taking an oath;
- Full knowledge of what is being promised and the difficulties that go with its accomplishment.

6. VOWS

A vow is a deliberate and free promise made to God, concerning some good which is possible and better. The virtue of religion requires that it be fulfilled.[4]

Vows are acts of devotion in which Christians dedicate themselves to God or promise him some good work. The difference between an oath and a vow is the fact that one makes an oath to another person with God as the witness, while one makes a vow to God with another person as the witness. The validity of a vow depends on the completion of the conditions that define it:

One makes an oath to another person with God as the witness.

One makes a vow to God with another person as the witness.

a. PROMISE

Promise is the intention before God to complete the conditions of the vow. We must distinguish between a vow and a simple promise. A vow is a firm will, while a simple promise is a *wish* or *intention* of doing something.

b. DELIBERATE

A vow requires that the person who takes it has considered what he is doing and has decided on this commitment to the Father, Son, and Holy Spirit.

c. FREE

A vow cannot be imposed by anyone. It may be taken only as a condition of a determined state of life in the Church (for example, to be a member of a religious order, or to be married). It must be taken with complete consent.

The *Code of Canon Law* lists six cases where the accomplishment of vows is not binding:

> A vow ceases by lapse of the time specified for the fulfilment of the obligation, or by a substantial change in the matter promised, or by cessation of a condition upon which the vow depended or of the purpose of the vow, or by dispensation, or by commutation.[5]

On other occasions, when difficulties arise, a vow may be dispensed by proper ecclesiastical authority. The different cases are determined in the *Code of Canon Law*.[6]

But besides guiding the right use of oaths and vows, the second commandment forbids acts that violate the virtue of religion, such as the irreverent use of the name of God, and above all, blasphemy.

7. THE IRREVERENT USE OF THE NAME OF GOD AND HOLY THINGS

Jewish piety is summarized in this passage of the Psalmist: "O Lord, our Lord, how majestic is thy name in all the earth!" (Ps 8:9). Hence, people of all times have used the name of God and everything related to him with reverence and love. This honor has been extended to sacred places and holy objects used in worship.

Blasphemy is particularly grievous when directed against the Most Holy Virgin Mary.

This respect is a living reality and changes over time, yet Christians should find ways to make the name of God heard more frequently, and should always do it reverently. Believers must show signs of faith that will contribute to giving Christian testimony in a society that renounces religious signs. But, on the contrary, one should avoid certain secular expressions that mention God or things related to him and the saints without proper reverence.

> Oaths which misuse God's name, though without the intention of blasphemy, show lack of respect for the Lord. (CCC 2148)

8. BLASPHEMY AGAINST GOD, THE VIRGIN MARY, AND THE SAINTS

Blasphemy is speaking contemptuously of God or his perfections. It may also be contempt directed toward the saints, and is particularly grievous when directed against the Most Holy Virgin Mary. St. Thomas Aquinas states:

> Even as God is praised in his saints, insofar as praise is given to the works that God does in his saints, so does blasphemy against the saints, redound, as a consequence, against God.[7]

The Tradition of the Church has underlined the gravity of blasphemy and classifies it as an intrinsically evil act.

Improper use of the name of God leaves room for a wide variety of abuses. Blasphemy was punished severely in the Old Testament. Leviticus narrates that a son of an Egyptian and an Israelite "blasphemed the Name" (Lv 24:11). When the boy was brought to Moses, God passed his sentence:

> "Bring out of the camp him who cursed; and let all who heard him lay their hands upon his head, and let all the congregation stone him. And say to the people of Israel, Whoever curses his God shall bear his sin. He who blasphemes the name of the Lord shall be put to death; all the congregation shall stone him; the sojourner as well as the native, when he blasphemes the Name, shall be put to death." (Lv 24:14-16)

With this act, God tries to root out this grave sin, which was quite common in neighboring towns (cf. 2 Mc 8:4; 9:28; Ez 35:12-15).

In the New Testament, the awareness of the serious nature of this sin continues. So, for example, the Jews try to stone Jesus to death by accusing him

The Jews try to stone Jesus to death by accusing him of blasphemy.

of blasphemy, since "we stone you for no good work but for blasphemy; because you, being a man, make yourself God" (Jn 10:33).

St. Paul considers himself a blasphemer when he hunted down Christians (cf. 1 Tm 1:13). Later, the Apostle laments that "the name of God is blasphemed among the Gentiles because of you" (Rom 2:24). In the New Testament, the seriousness of blasphemy is shown by the fact that it appears in lists of sins that merit condemnation (cf. 2 Tm 3:2; Col 3:8).

The *Catechism* shows the diverse forms that blasphemy may take:

> *Blasphemy* is directly opposed to the second commandment. It consists in uttering against God—inwardly or outwardly—words of hatred, reproach, or defiance; in speaking ill of God; in failing in respect toward him in one's speech; in misusing God's name. St. James condemns those "who blaspheme that honorable name [of Jesus] by which you are called" (Jas 2:7). The prohibition of blasphemy extends to language against Christ's Church, the saints, and sacred things. It is also blasphemous to make use of God's name to cover up criminal practices, to reduce peoples to servitude, to torture persons or put them to death. The misuse of God's name to commit a crime can provoke others to repudiate religion. (CCC 2148)

Besides blasphemous words and gestures, there are also blasphemous attitudes: those that mock God and ridicule any manifestation of Christian signs. Some anti-religious attitudes remind us of what some authors call *diabolic blasphemies.*

St. Thomas Aquinas argues that blasphemy may be even more serious than murder.

> If we compare the objects of murder and blasphemy, it is clear that blasphemy, which is a sin committed directly against God, is graver than murder, which is a sin against one's neighbor. On the other hand, if we compare them in respect of the harm wrought by them, murder is the graver sin, for murder does more harm to one's neighbor, than blasphemy does to God.
>
> Since, however, the gravity of a sin depends on the intention of the evil will, rather than on the effect of the deed...it follows that, as the blasphemer intends to do harm to God's honor, absolutely speaking, he sins more grievously than the murderer. Nevertheless murder takes precedence, as to punishment, among sins committed against our neighbor.[8]

Until recently, almost all governments imposed severe punishments on those who blasphemed in public, but there is now almost universal acceptance of blasphemy, as seen in the treatment of God on some television programs and movies.

If blasphemy has become a habit, the best immediate defense is quickly making an act of devotion—contrition, reparation, or adoration. Ultimately this vice will be overcome by the grace of the Holy Spirit bringing about a continual sense of recollection. These graces are poured out most abundantly in daily meditation, Mass, and regular Confession.

CONCLUSION

Since God is great, his name should be respected. Therefore, any use of God's name must be in the context of awe and respect. For this reason, many people have adopted the custom of making acts of reparation when they hear his name abused by saying some prayers to make up for the offense committed.

Any use of God's name must be in the context of awe and respect.

In a similar way, the use of his name—when taking an oath or making a vow—is so serious that it places the person in the presence of God in a special manner. Under no circumstances may a false oath be sworn, for this is an evil in all cases.

The best rule for respecting God's name is to use it only to give him honor, or when law requires it.

VOCABULARY

ASSERTORY OATH
A type of oath in which God is called upon as a witness to the truth of what is being said, as when a person takes an oath in court.

BLASPHEMY
Words or insulting gestures against God, the Virgin Mary, the saints, or the Church.

OATH
The calling of God as a witness to the truth of what is being said.

PERJURY
To make a promise without any intention of completing it, or to lie under oath.

PROMISSORY OATH
A type of oath in which God is called upon as a witness to something that will be done in the future, as when a public official solemnly swears to fulfill the duties of his office.

SACRILEGE
The violation of sacred persons, places, things.

VAIN
Empty, worthless, hollow; having no genuine substance, value, or importance.

VOW
A promise made freely and deliberately to God concerning something that is better than its opposite.

SUPPLEMENTARY READINGS

1. In many circumstances, the Christian is called to make *promises* to God. Baptism and Confirmation, Matrimony and Holy Orders always entail promises. Out of personal devotion, the Christian may also promise to God this action, that prayer, this alms-giving, that pilgrimage, and so forth. Fidelity to promises made to God is a sign of the respect owed to the divine majesty and of love for a faithful God.

"A *vow* is a deliberate and free promise made to God concerning a possible and better good which must be fulfilled by reason of the virtue of religion." [CIC, 1191 § 1] A vow is an act of *devotion* in which the Christian dedicates himself to God or promises him some good work. By fulfilling his vows he renders to God what has been promised and consecrated to Him. The *Acts of the Apostles* shows us St. Paul was concerned to fulfill the vows he had made (cf. Acts 18:18; 21:23-24).

— CCC 2101-2102

2. ... [A]s you have now made the vow, as you have now bound yourself, you are not free to do anything else. Before you incurred the obligation of the vow, you were free to choose the less perfect way, although such liberty deserves no credit when what is not owed is paid, to one's own gain. But, now that your promise binds you before God, I do not invite you to great perfection, I warn you to avoid a great sin. If you do not keep what you have vowed, you will not be the same as you would have been if you had not made the vow. For, in that case, you will have been less perfect, not worse; whereas now—which God forbid!—you will be as much worse off if you break your word to God as you will be more blessed if you keep it. So then, do not regret having made the vow; rather, rejoice that you are no longer free to do what you might have done to your own great harm. Go forward boldly, then, and turn your words into deeds; he who inspired your vow will help you. Happy the necessity which forces us to better things!

— St. Augustine, *Letters*, 127, 8

"...he who inspired your vow will help you."

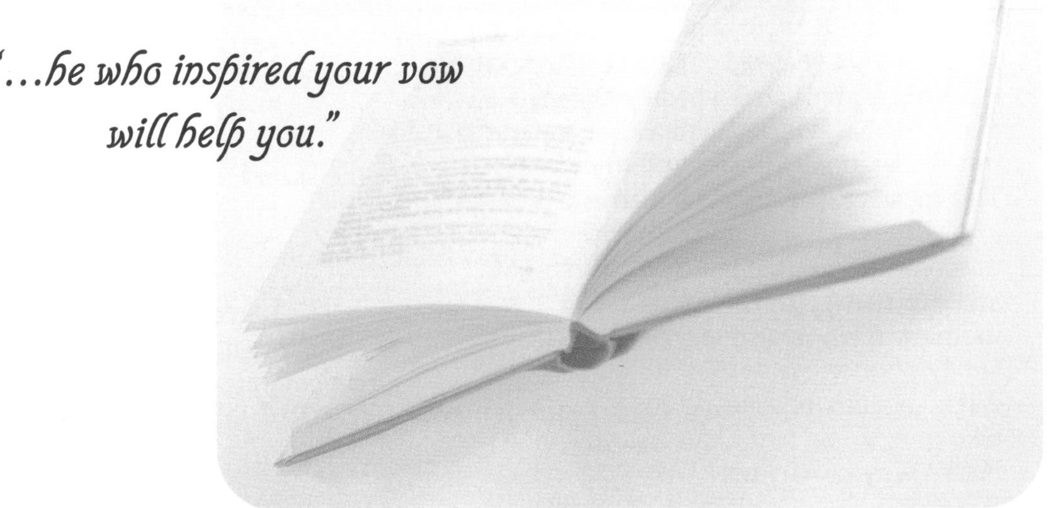

QUESTIONS

1. What does it mean to "confess the faith without giving way to fear"?

2. How does an assertory oath differ from a promissory oath?

3. Does God swear oaths? Why would someone swear an oath?

4. As a practical application of the virtue of religion, the second commandment has what three requirements?

5. Under what three conditions may an oath be refused?

6. List and briefly explain the three conditions when an oath may be legitimately sworn.

7. What is perjury?

8. List and briefly explain the additional conditions for a promissory oath.

9. Why would someone take a vow?

10. What is the difference between a vow and a simple promise?

11. List the six conditions for making a vow.

12. What is a dispensation from a vow?

13. Why would someone blaspheme?

14. Why is blasphemy intrinsically evil?

15. What has historically been the punishment for public blasphemy? Do you think this was appropriate?

PRACTICAL EXERCISES

1. In the following cases, to what degree do the oaths or vows taken oblige, and why?

a. Mark's sister Carrie recently married Allen, her boyfriend of four years. Things appeared to have been going well until Mark accidentally discovered one day that Allen had concealed from his sister the fact that he had been previously married and is the father of a six-year-old child. The situation is further complicated when Mark learns that Allen has not obtained a legal divorce or a declaration of nullity from the Church. This means that his sister's marriage is invalid. When Mark confronted Allen about this information, Allen denied the charges, and a terrible argument ensued. The next morning, Allen was gone. Mark feels that his family's honor has been destroyed by Allen's actions, and has personally vowed to take revenge on him. Does this vow bind Mark? Why or why not?

b. Laura and her sister Theresa have not spoken to one another for seven years as a result of a fight over some antiques that their grandmother left behind when she died. Because he was angry with Laura at the time of her argument with Theresa, their father supported Theresa and gave all of the property to her, an action he later deeply regretted. Although he apologized to Laura and asked Theresa to share the property with her sister, Theresa refused to do so, resulting in the rift between the sisters. Their father recently decided to rewrite his will, and Laura demanded that he swear to name her as his sole heir, leaving her sister out of his will. Because he still feels guilty about what occurred before, her father has done so, but his conscience is bothering him. Must he do what he swore to do?

PRACTICAL EXERCISES CONTINUED

c. Peter promised to give his friend Sara a ring that he won in a contest and she liked very much. Although he believed the ring to be of little value, he later discovered that it is actually worth quite a lot of money. Now he doesn't want to give Sara the ring. Must he?

d. Because he had been only an average student for the first three years of high school, David had found it difficult to be accepted to the extremely competitive premedical program at the college he had chosen at the beginning of his senior year. His family was poor and could not afford to send him to the school, and it wasn't very likely that he was going to get a scholarship because of his past academic performance. But David had thought and prayed about it, and he wanted to be a doctor. He worked hard during his senior year, and had succeeded in earning straight A's both semesters. In addition, he had gone to a local community college for one year, where he had also earned straight A's. The entire time that he was working on his lately developed dream of attending medical school, he had prayed to God to help him and to grant him the favor of becoming a doctor. At one point, after careful consideration, he had even vowed that if God would help him gain admittance to medical school, he would devote his first two years as a doctor to serving as a missionary doctor with a lay volunteer program in a poor country in Asia or Africa. Now that he has graduated at the top of his class from medical school, David has been offered a position at one of the most prestigious research hospitals in the US. He remembers the vow that he made, but this is a chance that he may not get again for a long time. What should he do?

2. Read the following Scripture passages about the punishment that befalls blasphemers:

- 1 Kgs 21:13-16
- 2 Kgs 19:4-6
- Tb 1:18

Why do you think that God punished so severely those who blasphemed his name among the People of Israel?

3. The *Catechism* explains the importance of the imposition on the baptized of the name "Christian":

In Baptism, the Lord's name sanctifies man, and the Christian receives his name in the Church. This can be the name of a saint, that is, of a disciple who has lived a life of exemplary fidelity to the Lord. The patron saint provides a model of charity; we are assured of his intercession. The "baptismal name" can also express a Christian mystery or Christian virtue. (CCC 2156)

Reflect on this text, and justify the reasons the Church gives for reserving the name "Christian" for the baptized.

FROM THE CATECHISM

2142 The second commandment *prescribes respect for the Lord's name.* Like the first commandment, it belongs to the virtue of religion and more particularly it governs our use of speech in sacred matters.

2147 *Promises* made to others in God's name engage the divine honor, fidelity, truthfulness, and authority. They must be respected in justice. To be unfaithful to them is to misuse God's name and in some way to make God out to be a liar (cf. 1 Jn 1:10).

2162 The second commandment forbids every improper use of God's name. Blasphemy is the use of the name of God, of Jesus Christ, of the Virgin Mary, and of the saints in an offensive way.

2163 False oaths call on God to be witness to a lie. Perjury is a grave offense against the Lord who is always faithful to his promises.

ENDNOTES

1. Leo J. Trese, *The Faith Explained,* 235-236.
2. CIC, 1199.
3. Cf. Ibid., 1199.
4. Ibid., 1191.
5. Ibid., 1194.
6. Cf. Ibid., 1196-1197.
7. St. Thomas Aquinas, *Summa Theologiae,* II-II, q. 13, a. 1 ad 2.
8. St. Thomas Aquinas, *Summa Theologiae,* II-II, q. 13, a. 3, ad 1.

Chapter 12

The Third Commandment: Remember To Keep Holy The Sabbath Day

The Lord's Day—as Sunday was called from Apostolic times—has always been accorded special attention in the history of the Church because of its close connection with the very core of the Christian mystery. In fact, in the weekly reckoning of time Sunday recalls the day of Christ's Resurrection. It is Easter which returns week by week, celebrating Christ's victory over sin and death, the fulfilment in him of the first creation and the dawn of "the new creation" (cf. 2 Cor 5:17). It is the day which recalls in grateful adoration the world's first day and looks forward in active hope to "the last day," when Christ will come in glory (cf. Acts 1:11; 1 Thes 4:13-17) and all things will be made new (cf. Rv 21:5).

The Resurrection of Jesus is the fundamental event upon which Christian faith rests (cf. 1 Cor 15:14). It is an astonishing reality, fully grasped in the light of faith, yet historically attested to by those who were privileged to see the Risen Lord. It is a wondrous event which is not only absolutely unique in human history, but which lies *at the very heart of the mystery of time.* In fact, "all time belongs to [Christ] and all the ages," as the evocative liturgy of the Easter Vigil recalls in preparing the Paschal Candle. Therefore, in commemorating the day of Christ's Resurrection not just once a year but every Sunday, the Church seeks to indicate to every generation the true fulcrum of history, to which the mystery of the world's origin and its final destiny leads.[1]

"Dies Domini" stresses the significance of the Christian Sabbath. Let us ask the following questions:

- What obligations does faithful observance of the third commandment place on Christians in modern society?
- How should Christians resolve the conflicts that sometimes arise between the demands of this commandment and other obligations?

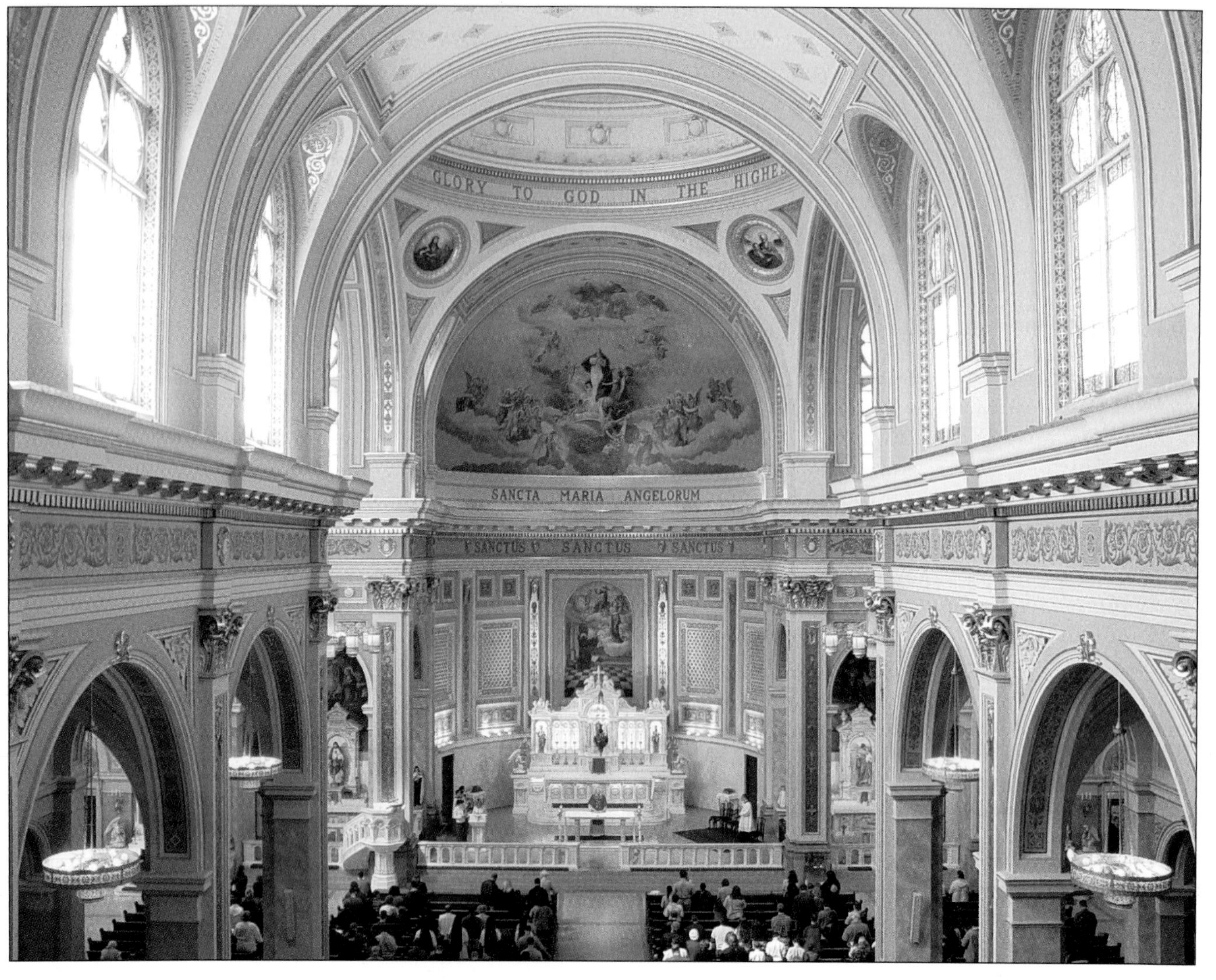

In the weekly reckoning of time, Sunday recalls the day of Christ's Resurrection.

INTRODUCTION

On the universal calendar, Sunday has always constituted an obligatory reference point for all social activities. Some non-Christian religions have their own day for worship: Saturday for Jews, Friday for Muslims. But in Western culture, Sunday is the day of rest and—for believers—worship.

In the Old Testament, the Father himself outlined the norms that people should follow to worship him. A very detailed law was established that included the institution of a priesthood, construction of temples, principal feasts, practices of worship, and above all, the celebration of the Sabbath.

The Sabbath day, which had an enormous importance throughout the religious experience of Israel, became the Christian Sunday. The redeeming death of Jesus Christ, his Resurrection on the first day of the week, and the descent of the Holy Spirit on Pentecost were decisive for the faith of the apostles, who were witnesses. From the start of the Church, the apostles were worshipping on Sunday (cf. Acts 20:7). The day of Christian worship was officially transferred to Sunday by the emperor Constantine.

By worshipping on Sunday, we celebrate the completion of the first creation, the new creation in Christ, and the Resurrection of Jesus, which occurred on a Sunday.

"*Remember the sabbath day, to keep it holy. Six days you shall labor, and do all your work; but the seventh day is a sabbath to the Lord your God.*"

1. THE IMPORTANCE OF THE SABBATH IN THE OLD TESTAMENT

From the very first page of the Bible, one can see the importance of the *seventh day.* Furthermore, it is widely believed that the narration of creation happening in seven days is done to highlight the importance of the seventh day and the obligation to dedicate this day to divine worship. In this way, the sacred writer certainly underlines the power of God in his creative action, but, above all, he wants to highlight the fact that God's power should be recognized by all men and women through worship:

> Thus the heavens and the earth were finished, and all the host of them. And on the seventh day God finished his work which he had done, and he rested on the seventh day from all his work which he had done. So God blessed the seventh day and hallowed it, because on it God rested from all his work which he had done in creation. (Gn 2:1-3)

Later, when the Father had made the Israelites his people, he made laws concerning the observance of the Sabbath:

> "Remember the sabbath day, to keep it holy. Six days you shall labor, and do all your work; but the seventh day is a sabbath to the Lord your God; in it you shall not do any work, you, or your son, or your daughter, your manservant, or your maidservant, or your cattle, or the sojourner who is within your gates; for in six days the Lord made heaven and earth, the sea, and all that is in them, and rested the seventh day; therefore the Lord blessed the Sabbath day and hallowed it." (Ex 20: 8-11)

In this passage, we see rest as primary, and divine worship as secondary. But soon after, Scripture gave the Sabbath a double end: It was also a day consecrated to God. Leviticus prescribed:

> "Six days shall work be done; but on the seventh day is a sabbath of solemn rest, a holy convocation; you shall do no work; it is a sabbath to the Lord in all your dwellings." (Lv 23: 3)

According to the Pentateuch, the bread of proposition would be renewed on Saturday (cf. Lv 24: 8) and sacrifices were to be celebrated:

> "This shall be yours of the most holy things, reserved from the fire; every offering of theirs, every cereal offering of theirs and every sin offering of theirs and every guilt offering of theirs, which they render to me, shall be most holy to you and to your sons. In a most holy place shall you eat of it; every male may eat of it; it is holy to you." (Nm 18: 9-10)

From the beginning, the Sabbath included rest and the obligation of sacrifices.

Consequently, from the beginning, the Sabbath included rest and the obligation of sacrifices. Both requirements showed the recognition of the power of God over his entire creation and over all people.

The sacrificial rites, together with the tasks that were forbidden, gradually became regulated. In this way, for example, it was forbidden to cook food (cf. Ex 16:23), light a fire (cf. Ex 35:3), collect firewood (cf. Nm 15:32-36), carry heavy objects on your shoulders (cf. Jer 17:21-22), or travel and do business (cf. Is 58:13) on the Sabbath. Slowly, the Pharisees created a casuistic (and at times ridiculous) morality that was strongly denounced and condemned by Jesus Christ.[2]

The Gospels retell the arguments between Jesus and the religious authorities of Israel in relation to the observance of the Sabbath. Jesus declared that the care of the sick comes before the Sabbath (cf. Lk 13:10-16; 14:1-5; Jn 5:9-10). Jesus proclaimed the true meaning of the Sabbath with these words: "The sabbath was made for man, not man for the sabbath" (Mk 2:27).

St. Ignatius, second bishop of Antioch; disciple of the Apostle John; martyred in the Roman Coliseum, c. 107. In his letter to the Church of Smyrna, written on the journey to Rome to face death by lions, the phrase *"the Catholic Church"* appears for the first time in Christian literature. He writes, "Wheresoever the bishop appears, there let the people be, even as wheresoever Christ is, there is the Catholic Church."

2. THE LORD'S DAY IN THE NEW TESTAMENT

The Resurrection of the Lord on the first day of the week introduced notable changes in the practice of divine worship, but this did not come about immediately. In fact, we know that the first Christians practiced the Jewish form of worship and the Christian liturgy simultaneously. The women delayed their visit to the sepulcher to fulfill the sabbatical precept (cf. Mt 28:1; Mk 15:42). Peter and John likewise went up to the temple at the customary hour of prayer, and they celebrated the Eucharist (cf. Acts 2:46). In addition, they already talked about the "Lord's Day" (cf. Rv 1:10).

Likewise, on "the first day of the week," they "gathered together to break bread" (Acts 20:7). On that day, the Church in Corinth also celebrated the "breaking of the bread" (cf. 1 Cor 11:17-34). And on that same day, they took up a collection for the poor (cf. 1 Cor 16:2).

At the beginning of the second century, St. Ignatius, bishop of Antioch, tried to lay the foundations for officially transferring the Lord's Day from Saturday to Sunday:

> If then they who walked in ancient customs came to a new hope, no longer living for the Sabbath, but for the Lord's Day, on which also our life sprang up through him and his death—though some deny him—and by this mystery we received faith, and for this reason also we suffer, that we may be found disciples of Jesus Christ our only teacher.[3]

The change of day also brought about a variation of name: The "Sabbath" was substituted by the "first day of the week" (Acts 20:7), or the "day of the sun" (St. Justin), and more generally, "the Lord's Day."

3. THE CHRISTIAN SUNDAY

In the second century, the Eucharist was celebrated on Sundays. The *Didache* (an anonymous first-century text) and the *First Apologia* (written by St. Justin) relate the details of the celebration of Christian worship on the day of the Lord. These two writings even transmit some of the ceremonies that accompanied this celebration to us.

But these celebrations were private. Sunday lacked a public character until A.D. 321, one year after Emperor Constantine recognized the Christian religion. At the same time, servile works were forbidden. On July 3 of that same year, the Emperor forbade other public activities (such as judicial action) and, gradually, all of the liberal professions began to rest on that day. In this era, rest and Eucharistic worship went together. For that reason, those acts that impeded attendance to the Eucharist were forbidden. Two councils of Orleans (in A.D. 511 and 538) engraved this on the conscience of the faithful so that they attended the Eucharist and made laws concerning the works that were not permitted on Sunday.

Together with Sundays, the custom of celebrating some solemnities (such as Christmas and other feasts that were used to "baptize" some pagan celebrations) was very quickly introduced. Also, the commemorative days of the martyrdom of saints were made solemnities. In this way, the Christian calendar was gradually formed.

Sunday stands out above all feasts because it commemorates the death and Resurrection of Jesus Christ.

Sunday stands out above all feasts because it commemorates the death and Resurrection of Jesus Christ, just as Vatican II reminds us:

> By a tradition handed down from the apostles, which took its origin from the very day of Christ's resurrection, the Church celebrates the paschal mystery every seventh day, which day is appropriately called the Lord's Day or Sunday. For on this day Christ's faithful are bound to come together into one place. They should listen to the word of God and take part in the Eucharist, thus calling to mind the passion, resurrection and glory of the Lord Jesus, giving thanks to God who "has begotten them again, through the resurrection of Christ from the dead, unto a living hope" (1 Pt 1:3). The Lord's Day is the original feast day, and it should be proposed to the faithful and taught to them so that it may become in fact a day of joy and of freedom from work. Other celebrations, unless they be truly of greatest importance, shall not have precedence over Sunday, which is the foundation and kernel of the whole liturgical year.[4]

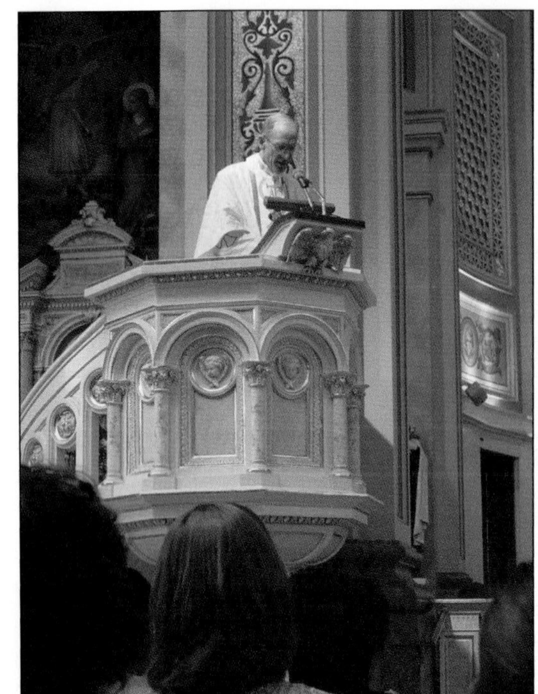

Sunday is the day on which we celebrate the heart of the redemptive mission carried out by Jesus Christ.

4. THE OBLIGATION OF ATTENDING HOLY MASS ON SUNDAYS AND HOLY DAYS OF OBLIGATION

The obligation of Catholics to take part in the Sunday Eucharistic celebration has two origins:

- The obligation of giving worship to God one day during the week, particularly on the Lord's Day.
- The importance of the Eucharist, which actualizes and testifies to the death and Resurrection of Jesus Christ, and renews the sacrifice of Christ.

Sunday is the day on which we celebrate the heart of the redemptive mission carried out by Jesus Christ. For this reason, it occupies the center of the Faith, or—as the Second Vatican Council teaches—the Eucharist is "the summit toward which the activity of the Church is directed; it is also the fount from which all her power flows."[5]

Pope Paul VI, in *Credo of the People of God*, teaches:

> We believe that the Mass, celebrated by the priest representing the person of Christ by virtue of the power received through the Sacrament of Orders, and offered by him in the name of Christ and the members of His Mystical Body, is the sacrifice of Calvary rendered sacramentally present on our altars. We believe that as the bread and wine consecrated by the Lord at the Last Supper were changed into His body and His blood which were to be offered for us on the cross, likewise the bread and wine consecrated by the priest are changed into the body and blood of Christ enthroned gloriously in heaven....[6]

Therefore, given the real importance that the celebration of the Eucharist has for the Church, as well as for the life of the baptized, the Church asks the faithful to actively participate in its weekly celebration, since this is the way a Christian fulfills his obligation to worship the Father, Son, and Holy Spirit.

The *Code of Canon Law* declares the importance of Sunday in Christian life and, secondly, proclaims the obligation of attending Sunday Mass:

> Sunday, on which by apostolic tradition the paschal mystery is celebrated, is to be observed in the universal Church as the primary holy day of obligation.[7]

The following canon declares the obligation to participate in the Holy Mass and to abstain from servile work:

> On Sundays and other holy days of obligation, the faithful are obliged to participate in the Mass. They are also to abstain from such work or business that would inhibit the worship to be given to God, the joy proper to the Lord's Day, or the due relaxation of mind and body.[8]

Holy days of obligation, on the other hand, are days on which the Church commemorates important saints and events in her history, or one of the important mysteries of the faith. Many of these feasts developed in response to particular historical circumstances, and have since been retained by the Church because of their importance for reminding the faithful of certain truths that the Church proclaims. An example is the Immaculate Conception, which was instituted to celebrate the fact that Mary was conceived free from all stain of original sin (cf. CCC 491).

Canon law lists ten days as holy days of obligation for the universal Church: *Christmas, Epiphany, the Body and Blood of Christ, the Ascension, Mary, Mother of God, the Immaculate Conception, the Assumption, St. Joseph, Sts. Peter and Paul* and *All Saints Day.* However, not every one is a holy day of obligation in every country. The *Code of Canon Law* permits the bishops' conferences of individual nations, with the prior approval of the Holy See, to suppress certain holy days or to transfer their observance to a Sunday.[9] In the United States, there are *six* solemnities that are holy days of obligation:

- Mary, the Mother of God (January 1)
- The Ascension of Jesus (40 days after Easter)
- The Assumption of Mary (August 15)
- The Feast of All Saints (November 1)
- The Immaculate Conception (December 8)
- Christmas Day (December 25)

Catholics are required to participate in the Eucharist on Sundays and holy days of obligation in order to be filled with the grace of the Holy Spirit.

The bishops of the United States have transferred the solemnities of *the Epiphany* and *the Body and Blood of Christ* to the Sundays that follow these feasts on the calendar, and have suppressed the solemnities of *St. Joseph* and *Sts. Peter and Paul* as holy days of obligation in the U.S. calendar. In most U.S. dioceses, *the Ascension of Jesus* has also been transferred to the following Sunday (the 7th Sunday of Easter).

5. FULFILLMENT OF THE PRECEPT OF ATTENDING MASS

Fulfilling the precept to attend Mass is clearly a grave obligation; whoever does not fulfill this precept commits a grave sin, except in situations where there is a serious reason to miss Mass, or in cases where it is impossible to be present at its celebration.

This same teaching is restated in the *Catechism:*

> **For this reason the faithful are obliged to participate in the Eucharist on days of obligation, unless excused for a serious reason (for example, illness, the care of infants) or dispensed by their own pastor (cf. CIC, 1245). Those who deliberately fail in this obligation commit a grave sin. (CCC 2181)**

It is clear that the worship of God also included rest on the Sabbath day.

Catholics are required to participate in the Eucharist on Sundays and holy days of obligation in order to be filled with the grace of the Holy Spirit. The Sunday requirement can be fulfilled by attending Mass on Saturday afternoon or evening (in some dioceses this may include a wedding Mass or funeral Mass). Similarly, one may attend Mass on the evening before a holy day of obligation instead of the holy day itself.[10]

Since attending the Eucharist on Saturday evening is a universal norm, one may opt for it whenever desired. But he ought to assure that the meaning of the day of the Lord, proper to Sunday, is not lost. For this reason, if the obligation is fulfilled on a Saturday, one should keep in mind that there is still the obligation to observe the rules regarding work on Sunday.

The fulfillment of the Sunday precept requires *participation* in the Mass. Some fall into the error of relating to the Eucharist in a minimal way by arriving late or leaving early. The Father who gave us his only Son should be treated in a better fashion.

A circumstance that excuses someone from attending the Sunday Eucharist is qualified in the law of the Church with the adjective "serious." Consequently, any cause for not attending Mass that is not serious is not a justified motive. The *Catechism* mentions illness and the care of infants as "serious reasons."[11] In other situations, the individual Catholic should consult a priest.

Finally, the obligation to attend the celebration of the Eucharist is limited to Saturday afternoons and evenings, Sundays, and holy days of obligation or vigils of these holy days. One cannot fulfill the precept on any other day of the week.

6. THE OBLIGATION TO REST

From the first paragraph of the Book of Genesis (cf. Gn 2:2-3) and laws that govern the conduct required of the people of Israel (cf. Ex 20:8-11; Dt 5:12-15), it is clear that the worship of God also included rest on the Sabbath day. There is a two-fold reason for this:

1. Rest facilitates the worship of God by eliminating the obstacles that one's professional occupation might pose.
2. The need for rest is a requirement of the human condition. No one is a machine. Rest replaces lost energies and makes time for other activities that cultivate the human spirit.

In our day, in which work occupies a special place in social life and working schedules are irregular, it is not always possible to distinguish what works are forbidden on Sundays and holy days of obligation.

7. ACTIVITY PERMITTED ON SUNDAY

Not all activity inhibits the worship of God or the rest that human beings need; therefore, there are some types of activity that are permitted on Sundays and holy days of obligation. In trying to decide whether or not a particular activity violates the sacred character of Sunday, some general guidelines are helpful. Work should not be undertaken on Sundays and holy days of obligation if it:

- impedes participation in the Eucharistic worship,
- inhibits the festive happiness of Sunday, or
- makes bodily or mental rest impossible.

Rest replaces lost energies and makes time for other activities that cultivate the human spirit.

Father Thomas Dubay makes the following distinctions between work and leisure:

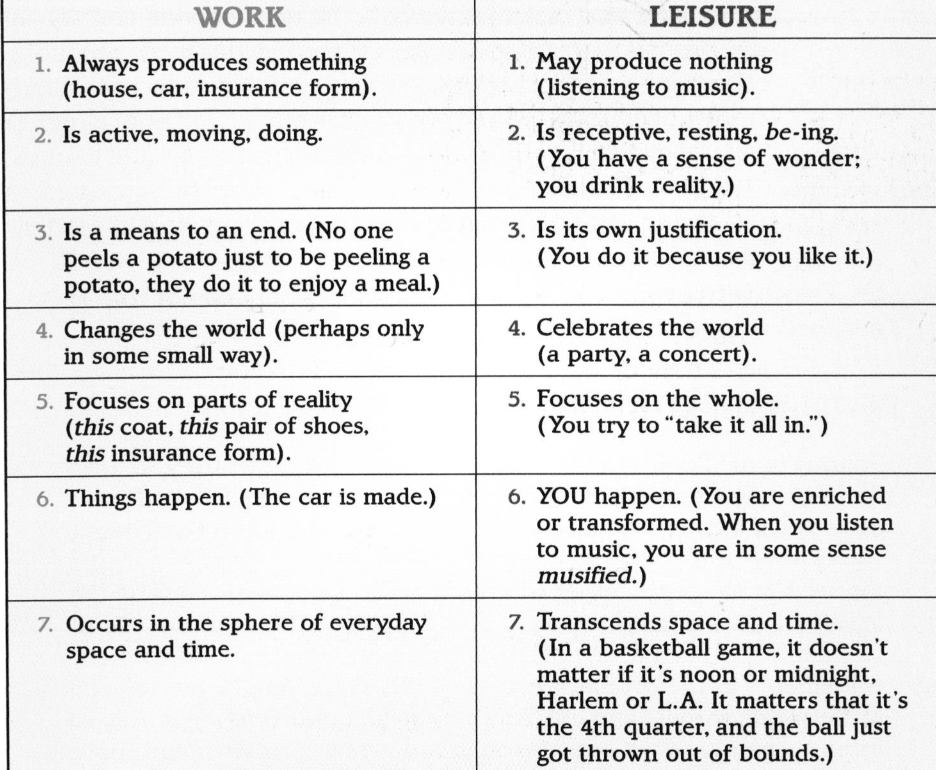

WORK	LEISURE
1. **Always produces something (house, car, insurance form).**	1. **May produce nothing (listening to music).**
2. **Is active, moving, doing.**	2. **Is receptive, resting, *be*-ing. (You have a sense of wonder; you drink reality.)**
3. **Is a means to an end. (No one peels a potato just to be peeling a potato, they do it to enjoy a meal.)**	3. **Is its own justification. (You do it because you like it.)**
4. **Changes the world (perhaps only in some small way).**	4. **Celebrates the world (a party, a concert).**
5. **Focuses on parts of reality (*this* coat, *this* pair of shoes, *this* insurance form).**	5. **Focuses on the whole. (You try to "take it all in.")**
6. **Things happen. (The car is made.)**	6. **YOU happen. (You are enriched or transformed. When you listen to music, you are in some sense *musified.*)**
7. **Occurs in the sphere of everyday space and time.**	7. **Transcends space and time. (In a basketball game, it doesn't matter if it's noon or midnight, Harlem or L.A. It matters that it's the 4th quarter, and the ball just got thrown out of bounds.)**

Consequently, work—including regular employment—that does not permit Mass attendance on Sundays or holy days of obligation should be avoided. Also, work that could be bothersome and could be an obstacle to living the festive character of Sunday is forbidden.

Likewise, work that may tire or fatigue an individual—or is arduous in itself or because it turns out to be such—is also forbidden. In this way, for an intellectual, it may be restful to do some manual work like gardening. On the other hand, a manual worker may rest by studying or engaging in other intellectual tasks.

> Sanctifying Sundays and holy days requires a common effort. Every Christian should avoid making unnecessary demands on others that would hinder them from observing the Lord's Day. Traditional activities (sport, restaurants, etc.), and social necessities (public services, etc.), require some people to work on Sundays, but everyone should still take care to set aside sufficient time for leisure...In spite of economic constraints, public authorities should ensure citizens a time intended for rest and divine worship. Employers have a similar obligation toward their employees. (CCC 2187)

It is necessary to recover the festive dimension of Sunday as a day of prayer and good works. Christians should proclaim happiness in the face of the serious problems of our times. In short, Sunday should be returned to the true Christian Easter celebration.

In the case of a task that needs to be finished, one can secure permission to be excused from the obligation to rest. In such situations, however, it is necessary to keep in mind the serious obligation of avoiding scandal (any word or deed that, either by commission or omission, is evil or has the appearance of evil and provides an occasion of sin to another). Canon law indicates:

> [A] parish priest, in individual cases, for a just reason and in accordance with the prescriptions of the diocesan Bishop, can give a dispensation from the obligation of observing a holy day or day of penance, or commute the obligation into some other pious works.[12]

The relaxed gathering of parents and children can be an opportunity not only to listen to one another but also to share a few formative and more reflective moments.

8. RE-CHRISTIANIZATION OF SUNDAY

> Sharing in the Eucharist is the heart of Sunday, but the duty to keep Sunday holy cannot be reduced to this. In fact, the Lord's Day is lived well if it is marked from beginning to end by grateful and active remembrance of God's saving work. This commits each of Christ's disciples to shape the other moments of the day—those outside the liturgical context: family life, social relationships, moments of relaxation—in such a way that the peace and joy of the Risen Lord will emerge in the ordinary events of life. For example, the relaxed gathering of parents and children can be an opportunity not only to listen to one another but also to share a few formative and more reflective moments. Even in lay life, when possible, why not make provision for special times of prayer—especially the solemn celebration of Vespers, for example—or moments of catechesis, which on the eve of Sunday or on Sunday afternoon might prepare for or complete the gift of the Eucharist in people's hearts?[13]

Modern times have placed a serious burden on many families through the requirement to work, which has led to Sunday being observed as just another day. Christians have a serious responsibility to return Sunday to the Lord by celebrating together as family, and by celebrating the Easter event. All Christians should recommit themselves to return the Lord's Day to family activities.

CONCLUSION

A Christian has a serious obligation to take part in the Eucharistic celebration on Sundays and holy days of obligation and thereby be filled with the grace of the Holy Spirit, and ought to abstain from works that impede proper rest. Obviously, the precept of attending Mass is more serious, but the obligation to refrain from unnecessary work also binds in conscience. Furthermore, not fulfilling the Sunday obligation has certain implications in regard to the whole Christian community because of the potential for scandal.

When a Catholic stops going to Sunday Mass, he loses all the gifts of the Holy Spirit.

Breaking the Sunday precept, besides being a grave sin, puts a certain distance between us and God, diminishes the sense of adoration that accompanies faith, and reduces one's sense of belonging to the Church. The worship that we give the Father, Son, and Holy Spirit on a determined day and in an official and specific way corresponds to a principle that is written on our conscience:

> The celebration of Sunday observes the moral commandment inscribed by nature in the human heart to render to God an outward, visible, public, and regular worship "as a sign of his universal beneficence to all" (St. Thomas Aquinas, *Summa Theologiae*, II-II, q. 122, a. 4). Sunday worship fulfills the moral command of the Old Covenant, taking up its rhythm and spirit in the weekly celebration of the Creator and Redeemer of his people. (CCC 2176)

One cannot avoid this moral duty and go on unaffected. When a Catholic stops going to Sunday Mass, he loses all the gifts of the Holy Spirit: his conscience soon becomes deadened, leading to a deterioration in attitudes and conduct.

VOCABULARY

DIDACHE
An early Christian work (c. A.D. 60) with an unknown author summarizing morality framed as a choice between the path of life and the path of death, liturgical practice (including two simple Eucharistic prayers), and disciplinary norms.

DIOCESE
A division of the Catholic Church, usually comprised of all the Catholics living within a particular geographic territory.

HOLY DAYS OF OBLIGATION
Feast days of such importance that participation in Mass is required.

LEISURE
To enjoy and enrich oneself by taking in beauty for its own sake; celebrating the world.

MASS or EUCHARIST
The memorial of the death and Resurrection of the Lord in which the sacrifice of the cross is renewed and the People of God are united (cf. CIC, 897). The richness of the Mass is also seen in the different names given to it (cf. CCC 1328-1332).

PARISH
A definite community of Catholics within a diocese, established by the bishop and entrusted to the care of a pastor.

SABBATH
The seventh day of the Jewish week, set aside for rest and the worship of God. For Christians, Sunday fulfills the Sabbath requirement in commemoration of Christ's Resurrection.

WORK
To actively exert oneself (mentally or physically) by operating upon a part of creation in order to do or make something.

SUPPLEMENTARY READINGS

1. At the Eucharist, offer the Eucharistic prayer in this way. Begin with the chalice: "We give thanks to thee, our Father, for the holy Vine of thy servant David, which thou hast made known to us through thy servant Jesus." *"Glory be to thee, world without end."*

Then over the particles of bread: "We give thanks to thee, our Father, for the life and knowledge thou hast made known to us through thy servant Jesus." *"Glory be to thee, world without end."*

"As this broken bread, once dispersed over the hills, was brought together and became one loaf, so may thy Church be brought from the ends of the earth into thy kingdom."

Assemble on the Lord's Day, and break bread and offer the Eucharist; but first make confession of your faults, so that your sacrifice may be a pure one.

— *Didache*, 9 and 14

2. And on the day called Sunday, all who live in cities or in the country gather together to one place, and the memoirs of the apostles or the writings of the prophets are read, as long as time permits; then, when the reader has ceased, the president verbally instructs, and exhorts to the imitations of these good things. Then we all rise together and pray, and, as we before said, when our prayer is ended, bread and wine and water are brought, and the president in like manner offers prayers and thanksgiving, according to his ability, and the people assent, saying *Amen*.

— St. Justin, *The First Apology*, Chapter 67

3. In respecting religious liberty and the common good of all, Christians should seek recognition of Sundays and the Church's holy days as legal holidays. They have to give everyone a public example of prayer, respect, and joy and defend their traditions as a precious contribution to the spiritual life of society. If a country's legislation or other reasons require work on Sunday, the day should nevertheless be lived as the day of our deliverance which lets us share in this "festal gathering," this "assembly of the firstborn who are enrolled in heaven" (cf. Heb 12, 22-23).

— CCC 2188

4. There are nowadays many opportunities favorable to the development of a universal culture, thanks especially to the boom in book publication and new techniques of cultural and social communications. Shorter working hours are becoming the general rule everywhere and provide greater opportunities for large numbers of people. May this leisure time be properly employed to refresh the spirit and strengthen the health of mind and body—by means of voluntary activity and study; of tourism to broaden the mind and enrich man with understanding of others; by means of physical exercise and sport, which help to create harmony of feeling even on the level of the community as well as fostering friendly relations between men of all classes, countries, and races. Christians, therefore, should cooperate in the cultural framework and collective activity characteristic of our times, to humanize them and imbue them with a Christian spirit.

— *GS*, 61

QUESTIONS

1. What do we celebrate by worshipping on Sunday?

2. Who gave the Jews their guidelines in the Old Testament?

3. What was included in this law?

4. What two Sabbath requirements demonstrated that Jews accepted the dominion of God?

5. What effect did the Resurrection have on Saturday as a day of worship?

6. Where does the virtue of religion reach its highest fulfillment?

7. What is the importance of the creation narration of seven days?

8. List the two Sabbath requirements that were present from the beginning.

9. What is the true meaning of the Sabbath?

10. When was Sunday made the official day of worship?

11. Name the two origins of the Sunday obligations.

12. Why do we say Sunday is the heart of the redemptive mission?

13. In what terms does *Sacrosanctum concilium* refer to the Eucharist?

14. Why does the Church celebrate holy days?

15. List the six holy days of obligation.

16. What are the effects of breaking the Sunday precept?

17. Explain clearly and in detail the causes that excuse the obligation to attend Sunday Mass.

18. What is the twofold reason for rest on the Sabbath?

19. List the three conditions that indicate when Sunday work is forbidden.

PRACTICAL EXERCISES

1. Compare how Exodus 20: 8-11 and Deuteronomy 5: 12-15 express the Mosaic requirement of fulfilling the Sabbath. How extensive was the prohibition against working on the Sabbath? What do you think was the responsibility of the head of the household in view of the fact that God forbade even servants, slaves, and beasts of burden from working on the Sabbath?

2. Sunday Mass has the character of a community experience that strengthens the life of faith. Formulate a response to these common objections:

- "I don't want to go to Mass every Sunday because I don't get anything out of it."
- "I think that a person can pray just as well at home as in Church."

3. Discuss and explain the problems that surround the requirement for Sunday rest. What can be done on Sundays and what ought to be avoided? In your opinion, does modern culture facilitate or inhibit the Christian observance of Sundays? Provide examples to support your statements.

4. Make a list of activities that families can do on Sunday that would facilitate a return to the festive character of Sunday.

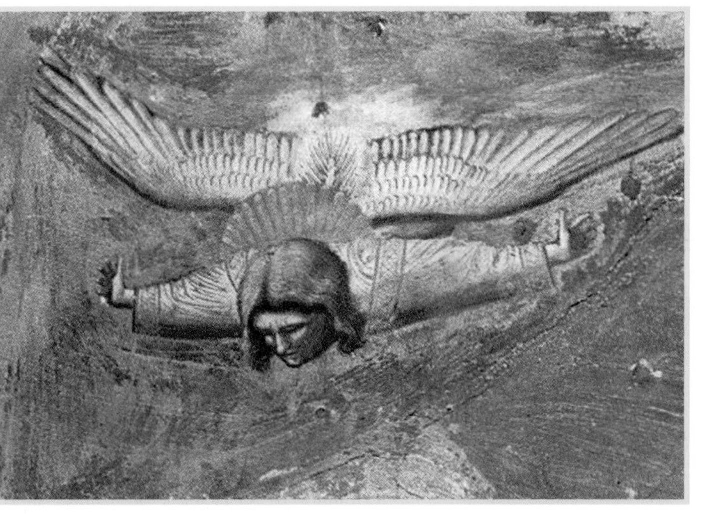

FROM THE CATECHISM

2189 "Observe the sabbath day, to keep it holy" (Dt 5:12). "The seventh day is a sabbath of solemn rest, holy to the Lord" (Ex 31:15).

2192 "Sunday...is to be observed as the foremost holy day of obligation in the universal Church" (CIC, 1246). "On Sundays and other holy days of obligation the faithful are bound to participate in the Mass" (CIC, 1247).

2193 "On Sundays and other holy days of obligation the faithful are bound...to abstain from those labors and business concerns which impede the worship to be rendered to God, the joy which is proper to the Lord's Day, or the proper relaxation of mind and body" (CIC, 1247).

2194 The institution of Sunday helps all "to be allowed sufficient rest and leisure to cultivate their familial, cultural, social, and religious lives" (*GS*, 67).

2195 Every Christian should avoid making unnecessary demands on others that would hinder them from observing the Lord's Day.

ENDNOTES

1. *DD*, 1, 2.
2. Cf. CCC, 2168-2173.
3. St. Ignatius of Antioch, *Letter to the Magnesians*, IX, 1.
4. *SC*, 106.
5. Ibid., 10.
6. Pope Paul VI, *Credo of the People of God*, 24.
7. CIC, 1246.
8. Ibid., 1247.
9. Cf. Ibid., 1246.
10. Cf. CIC, 1248.
11. Cf. CCC, 2181.
12. CIC, 1245.
13. *DD*, 52.

Chapter 13

The Fourth Commandment:
Honor Your Father And Mother

Jack, a 15-year-old, arrived home one night with his eyes blurry and his balance obviously affected. It was clear that he had been drinking. His family had never seen him like this before and was very concerned. Jack's older brother, Mike, was as worried as his mother. Mike knew what the problem was. He had been a bad example, and Jack was simply imitating him. Mike knew he had not given a specific bad example in drinking to excess, but he suspected he had undermined the authority of his parents by his actions and attitudes.

Mike had returned home after finishing college at the beginning of the summer. He had come with an attitude that he didn't have to obey as he had to before he went to college. But because he was living at home, his parents laid down the rules of the house. Mike's parents wanted him to come home at a certain time, not smoke in the house, and do chores around the house. Mike had grown accustomed to living with his roommates at college where he didn't have to do chores, and where he could come and go as he pleased. So Mike stayed out late many nights and, at times, smoked in the house around Jack and his other brothers and sisters. Mike's parents warned him that he was giving a bad example to the rest of the family. They had begun to notice that Jack especially had begun to disregard their authority by neglecting his homework and chores around the house.

The night Jack came home drunk, it hit Mike like a bad dream. He had been an influence for the worse in his disregard for his parents' rules. He realized that even as an adult he had to abide by the rules established by his parents in their home, and, more importantly, that his example as the eldest could influence his brothers and sisters who were still dependent on their parents' guidance and direction.

This story brings up issues of family relationships.
Let us ask these questions:

- How does the fourth commandment protect the integrity of familial relationships?
- What are some of the specific obligations that are enjoined upon parents and children by this commandment?
- What obligations does the fourth commandment entail for human relations outside the family?

Love creates good and gives it to others.

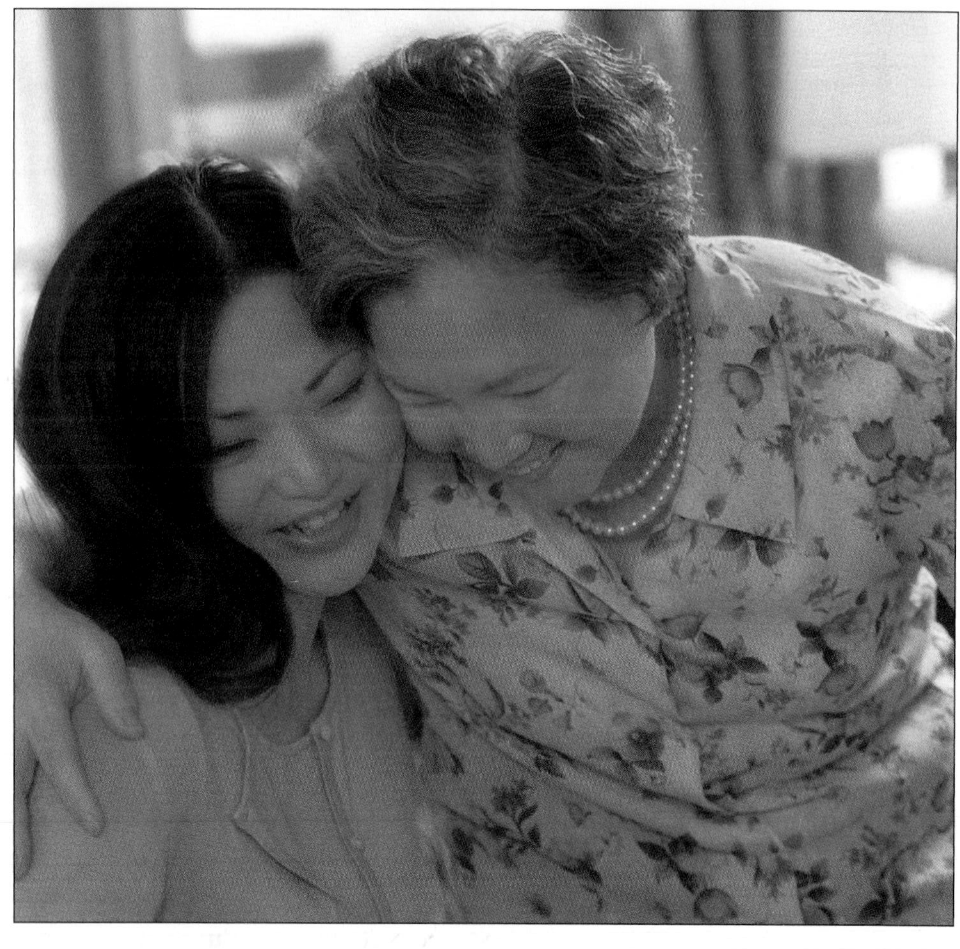

This commandment requires honor, affection, and gratitude toward elders and ancestors.

INTRODUCTION

Since God intended that life begin in a family, this chapter studies the fourth commandment, which regulates the moral links in family life. This includes the relationship between husbands and wives, parents and children, and children and their brothers and sisters. This commandment also includes the study of moral duties (derived from family life) toward grandparents and other relatives, as well as other relationships—such as those between students and teachers, and between citizens and governments.

1. LOVE: THE FOUNDATION OF THE FAMILY

Love is true when it creates the good of persons and communities; it creates good and gives it to others. Only one who is able to be demanding with himself in the name of love can give love to others. Love is demanding. It makes demands in all human situations. It is even more demanding in the case of those who are open to the Gospel. Is this not what Christ proclaims in "his" commandment?

> Nowadays, people need to rediscover this demanding love, for it is truly the firm foundation of the family, a foundation able to "endure

> all things".... At work within it is the power and strength of God himself who "is love." At work, also, within it is the power and strength of Christ, the Redeemer of mankind and the Savior of the world.[1]

Good moral conduct between parents and children (and vice versa) and among brothers and sisters is absolutely required.

Among the many commitments contained in love for one's neighbor, love between spouses is primary, followed by parent-child relationships. The most elemental biology ties members of the same family together in such a way that good moral conduct between parents and children (and vice versa) and among brothers and sisters is absolutely required.

Christian morality is the morality of charity. This *supernatural love* begins and grows in family life through the working of the Holy Spirit, and is reflected in the most intimate bonds of matrimony. The love between a husband and wife gives origin to children, and also joins brothers and sisters together. Therefore, ethically condemnable conduct in the bosom of a family is often called *unnatural* and even *monstrous.* In effect, it is "inhumane," for example, for a father to abandon his children, or for a child to hate his parents and not to attend to their needs.

All of these relationships are understood in the fourth commandment. The *Catechism of the Catholic Church* says:

> The fourth commandment is addressed expressly to children in their relationship to their father and mother, because this relationship is the most universal. It likewise concerns the ties of kinship between members of the extended family. It requires honor, affection, and gratitude toward elders and ancestors. Finally, it extends to the duties of pupils to teachers, employees to employers, subordinates to leaders, citizens to their country, and to those who administer or govern it.
>
> This commandment includes and presupposes the duties of parents, instructors, teachers, leaders, magistrates, those who govern, all who exercise authority over others or over a community of persons. (CCC 2199)

The relationships within the family bring an affinity of feelings, affections and interests, arising above all from the members' respect for one another. The family is a privileged community called to achieve a "sharing of thought and common deliberation as well as eager cooperation as parents in the children's upbringing."[2]

The family is a privileged community.

2. BIBLICAL FACTS ABOUT THE FOURTH COMMANDMENT

There are several places in the Old Testament where the fourth commandment is repeated. Two of these formulas are presented in the Books of Exodus and Deuteronomy:

> Honor your father and your mother, that your days may be long in the land which the Lord your God gives you. (Ex 20:12)
>
> Honor your father and your mother, as the Lord your God commanded you; that your days may be prolonged, and that it may go well with you, in the land which the Lord your God gives you. (Dt 5:16)

The words of Deuteronomy shed a new light by making happiness conditional upon the observance of this precept. New additions to these ethical minimums appeared with other teachings of the Old Testament. In this way, Leviticus insists:

> Every one of you shall revere his mother and his father, and you shall keep my sabbaths: I am the Lord your God. (Lv 19:3)

In addition, the Book of Proverbs offers this insight of love and obedience to one's parents:

> My son, keep your father's commandment, and forsake not your mother's teaching. Bind them upon your heart always; tie them about your neck. When you walk, they will lead you; when you lie down, they will watch over you; and when you awake, they will talk with you. (Prv 6:20-22)

The Book of Sirach also makes the following consideration:

> With all your heart honor your father, and do not forget the birth pangs of your mother. Remember that through your parents you were born; and what can you give back to them that equals their gift to you? (Sir 7:27-28)

This book, which contains religious moral doctrine concerning human behavior, also offers this profound reflection:

"Whoever honors his father will be gladdened by his own children, and when he prays he will be heard."

> Listen to me, your father, O children; and act accordingly, that you may be kept in safety. For the Lord honored the father above the children, and he confirmed the right of the mother over her sons. Whoever honors his father atones for sins, and whoever glorifies his mother is like one who lays up treasure. Whoever honors his father will be gladdened by his own children, and when he prays he will be heard. Whoever glorifies his father will have long life, and whoever obeys the Lord will refresh his mother; he will serve his parents as his masters. Honor your father by work and deed, that a blessing from him may come upon you. For a father's blessing strengthens the houses of the children, but a mother's curse uproots their foundations.

> Do not glorify yourself by dishonoring your father, for your father's dishonor is no glory to you. For a man's glory comes from honoring his father, and it is a disgrace for children not to respect their mother. O son, help your father in his old age, and do not grieve him as long as he lives; even if he is lacking in understanding, show forbearance; in all your strength do not despise him. For kindness to a father will not be forgotten, and against your sins it will be

> **credited to you; in the day of your affliction it will be remembered in your favor; as frost in fair weather, your sins will melt away. Whoever forsakes his father is like a blasphemer, and whoever angers his mother is cursed by the Lord. (Sir 3:1-16)**

It is necessary for both husband and wife to recognize that each is gifted by God to make complementary contributions to the marriage.

3. RELATIONSHIP BETWEEN SPOUSES

Among other precepts that regulate the relationship between husbands and wives, St. Paul teaches us a doctrine that has become classical for raising the relations between a wife and her husband to a very high ethical level:

> **Wives, be subject to your husbands, as to the Lord. For the husband is the head of the wife as Christ is the head of the church, his body, and is himself its Savior....Husbands, love your wives, as Christ loved the church and gave himself up for her, that he might sanctify her...that she might be holy and without blemish. (Eph 5:22-23, 25-27)**

There are many profound commentaries about this text, but we will limit ourselves to the following notes:

- The customs of the time regarding the role of women must be taken into account. It is never legitimate to take a part of Scripture out of the context in which it was written.
- In the ordinary course of family life, a woman often defers to her husband in the matter of decision-making. On the other hand, a husband is expected to consider the opinion and advice of his wife in his decisions. It is not a matter of one partner having all the correct answers. Rather, it is a matter of both partners working together to arrive at the correct answers.
- St. Paul's entire teaching depends upon his parallel between man and woman and the union of Christ and the Church. Not only is matrimony in general described in this comparison, but also a woman with respect to her husband.
- For St. Paul, there is a special identification between the Church and Jesus. The Church is the "Mystical Body" of Jesus Christ. That is, the Church is the "mysterious" body. Paul deduces this identity of Christ and the Church from his first meeting with the Lord. When he was going to Damascus to persecute the Church, Christ told him: "I am Jesus, whom you are persecuting" (Acts 9:5). Jesus directly identified himself with the Church.

- According to this analogy, the relation of man and woman has a mysterious character similar to Christ's relation with his Church. In keeping with the customs of the times, St. Paul discusses the authority of a husband (cf. Col 3:18-19; 1 Pt 3:1-7). Furthermore, he should love her "as Christ loves the church," for matrimony unites a man and a woman in such way that they "become one flesh" (Gn 2:24). With the understanding that the nature of authority is to serve, he adds that a husband should love his wife like his own body, because "no one ever hates his own flesh" (Eph 5:29). It is necessary for both husband and wife to recognize that each is gifted by God to make complementary contributions to the marriage.

- In this context, husband and wife should love each other mutually. The husband should love his wife "as himself," and vice versa.
- We should note that this passage, when talking about "loving," always uses the Greek term *agapan*, that is, "to appreciate" or, even better, "to have a great esteem for." This same term is used to talk about the "love" *(agape)* of God for mankind. As a result of grace, the natural love of husband and wife is raised to supernatural love. Marriage is not a so-called "fifty-fifty proposition." Both husband and wife are called upon to make whatever sacrifices are necessary to preserve and nurture their union.

The family, born of the Sacrament of Matrimony, should be a privileged place for love between the spouses, in equality of dignity and differences of functions. In that climate of love, children should be born and grow, and they must, in turn, contribute to that climate of love in everyday family life. The level of esteem in which the parents hold each other will be instructive for the children in regards to their own married lives.

4. PARENTS' RELATIONS WITH THEIR CHILDREN

The Apostle also gives advice to parents with respect to the education of their children: "Fathers, do not provoke your children to anger, but bring them up in the discipline and instruction of the Lord" (Eph 6:4).

Children have the serious obligation to accept their parents' instruction and to follow it in return.

In this mandate, the love of parents for their children is presupposed, and another three items of interest are added: that parents educate their children with discipline, that they not be excessively rigorous, and that they form them in the teachings of Jesus Christ.

That parents should correct their children is common sense and a law of nature. Children are born with immense potential for good and evil. For this reason, parents should guide them in good moral behavior. The Letter to the Hebrews proposes a comparison between a correction that the Father makes to his children and that which parents carry out with theirs:

> And have you forgotten the exhortation which addresses you as sons?
>
> "My son, do not regard lightly the discipline of the Lord, nor lose courage when you are punished by him. For the Lord disciplines him whom he loves, and chastises every son whom he receives."
>
> It is for discipline that you have to endure. God is treating you as sons; for what son is there whom his father does not discipline? If you are left without discipline, in which all have participated, then you are illegitimate children and not sons.
>
> Besides this, we have had earthly fathers to discipline us and we respected them. Shall we not much more be subject to the Father

> of spirits and live? For they disciplined us for a short time at their pleasure, but he disciplines us for our good, that we may share his holiness. For the moment all discipline seems painful rather than pleasant; later it yields the peaceful fruit of righteousness to those who have been trained by it. (Heb 12:5-11)

A child should be taught simple prayers to be said at bedtime with the parent participating.

Parents have the grave obligation to provide for the physical and spiritual needs as well as the education of their children. Children have the serious obligation to accept their parents' instruction and to follow it in return. This responsibility to follow parental instruction is more compelling today because of the present culture, which encourages children to reject the direction of their parents. Unfortunately, many parents are swayed by the culture, and have slowly begun to abandon this serious obligation.

In the area of education, Catholic parents have the duty to educate their children in the faith. This is a task that parents cannot ignore, even when they defer to other people or an institution to complement their children's education, for example, school and catechism class.[3]

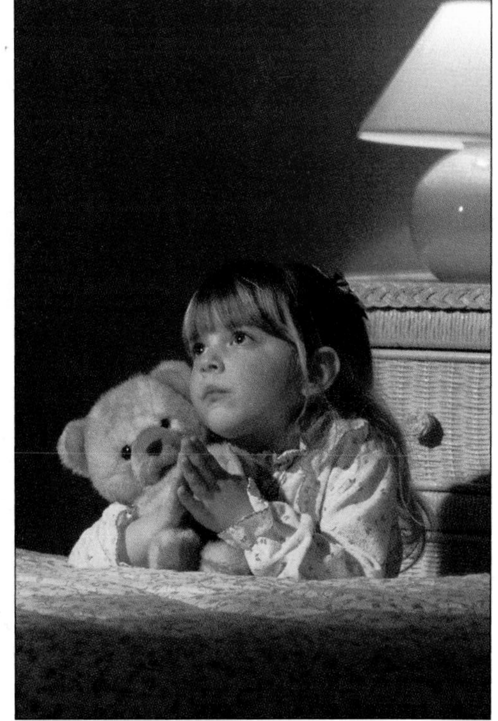

Beyond regular reception of the sacraments, the child should be taught simple prayers to be said at bedtime with the parent participating. As the child grows, the child should be instructed in the *Catechism* in a minimal way. Children's *Lives of the Saints* books should be employed as well. Many resources are available today to aid parents in the fulfillment of this task. Although both parents must attend to this especially grave obligation, studies have shown that fathers play an especially important part in forming their children's religious habits. Parents must remember there is a direct connection between their personal religious practice and that of their children. Instructing children in the faith does not mean, however, that parents choose the manner in which their children will lead their lives of faith in the future. On the contrary, parents must respect and encourage the vocational choices of their children to religious life, the married state, or single virginity.

The obligation of parents to correct their children is at least as serious as that of providing for their children's intellectual education. All too often, we see parents who think they are providing the "best education" for their children when, in reality, they place much less importance on their religious and moral upbringing than on their intellectual training.

5. CHILDREN'S RELATIONS WITH THEIR PARENTS

Besides honoring their parents, children are also expected to obey them. The Apostle adds a Christian motive for obedience: It is desired by Christ. St. Paul writes to the Colossians: "Children, obey your parents in everything, for this pleases the Lord" (Col 3:20). The *Catechism* states:

> Respect for parents *(filial piety)* derives from *gratitude* toward those who, by the gift of life, their love and their work, have brought their

> children into the world and enabled them to grow in stature, wisdom, and grace....
>
> As long as a child lives at home with his parents, the child should obey his parents in all that they ask of him when it is for his good or that of the family...Children should also obey the reasonable directions of their teachers and all to whom their parents have entrusted them. But if a child is convinced in conscience that it would be morally wrong to obey a particular order, he must not do so. (CCC 2215, 2217)

The family should live in such a way that its members care and take responsibility for the young, old, sick, handicapped, and poor.

The same thing is repeated in Paul's Letter to the Ephesians, explaining a passage from the Old Testament, but complementing it with these words:

> Children, obey your parents in the Lord, for this is right. "Honor your father and mother" (this is the first commandment with a promise), "that it may be well with you and that you may live long on the earth." (Eph 6:1-3)

Parents are called to conduct themselves so as to be worthy of honor.

You parents, the divine precept seems to say, should act in such a way that your life will merit the honor (and the love) of your children. Do not let the divine command that you be honored fall into a moral vacuum! Ultimately, then, we are speaking of mutual honor.

> The commandment "honor your father and your mother" indirectly tells parents: Honor your sons and daughters. They deserve this because they are alive, because they are who they are, and this is true from the first moment of conception.
>
> The fourth commandment then, by expressing the intimate bonds uniting the family, highlights the basis of its inner unity.[4]

It is good to keep in mind that when a parent does not act in an honorable way, his position as parent requires respect nonetheless. Children need to be reminded that they have an obligation to support their parents with prayer.

6. RELATIONS WITH OTHER MEMBERS OF THE FAMILY

The ties of blood do not end with parent-children relationships. They also extend to the extended family: grandparents, uncles, aunts, and cousins.

The structure of the family in modern society has changed noticeably in recent years. In previous centuries, Western society was largely agricultural. It was frequent to see family clans that sheltered two or three generations. In the early industrial era, the family home served grandparents and single aunts and uncles. Today, the immediate family usually lives alone.

The family should live in such a way that its members care and take responsibility for the young, old, sick, handicapped, and poor. There are some families who are at times incapable of providing this assistance. Only then does this responsibility devolve onto other persons, other families, and—in a subsidiary way—society to provide for their needs.

7. OBLIGATIONS OF CIVIL AUTHORITY

Given the social character of the human person, social life is essential. As a result, just as particular moral obligations arise in family life, ethical obligations and rights also arise in social life. Just as parents have obligations to their children, the civil authority must meet certain moral demands with society and with each citizen.

a. CITIZENS' OBLIGATIONS TO GOVERNMENT

According to Biblical teachings, authority comes from the Father, so legitimate authority should always be obeyed. Regarding this subject, we should note that the Apostle Paul's teachings are very demanding, and he was speaking about the authorities of the Roman Empire, who kept slaves and persecuted Christians:

> Let every person be subject to the governing authorities. For there is no authority except from God, and those that exist have been instituted by God. Therefore he who resists the authorities resists what God has appointed, and those who resist will incur judgment. For rulers are not a terror to good conduct, but to bad. Would you have no fear of him who is in authority? Then do what is good, and you will receive his approval, for he is God's servant for your good. But if you do wrong, be afraid, for he does not bear the sword in vain; he is the servant of God to execute his wrath on the wrongdoer. Therefore one must be subject, not only to avoid God's wrath but also for the sake of conscience. For the same reason you also pay taxes, for the authorities are ministers of God, attending to this very thing. Pay all of them their dues, taxes to whom taxes are due, revenue to whom revenue is due, respect to whom respect is due, honor to whom honor is due. (Rom 13:1-7)

St. Paul's teachings inspired early Christian doctrine concerning citizens' obligations toward legitimately established authority.

The richness of this testimony inspired early Christian doctrine concerning citizens' obligations toward legitimately established authority. The following affirmations are included in this doctrine:

- Authority, as the power of direction of the community, comes from God. That is, the natural necessity of exercising authority in society—and *not the particular form of exercising it*—is derived from God.
- Since authority has a divine origin, the Christian has the obligation in conscience of obeying whoever lawfully exercises it.
- Authority may never require one to act immorally.
- If one does not obey legitimate authorities, one may be justly punished by them.

Citizens have the obligation to work with civil authority to build up a society based on justice, truth, solidarity, and freedom.

- Taxes should be imposed by legitimate authority for good reason with due proportion. If the law is just, it obliges in conscience. Where there is a question of justice, the matter should be discussed with one's confessor.
- Respect is due to those who govern.

Simply stated, citizens have the obligation to work with civil authority to build up a society based on justice, truth, solidarity, and freedom.

All of these principles, though not mentioned by name, are included in the following passage from St. Peter, written in the era in which Christians lived under the disastrous reign of a cruel and tyrannical emperor, Nero:

> Be subject for the Lord's sake to every human institution, whether it be to the emperor as supreme, or to governors as sent by him to punish those who do wrong and to praise those who do right. For it is God's will that by doing right you should put to silence the ignorance of foolish men. Live as free men, yet without using your freedom as a pretext for evil; but live as servants of God. Honor all men. Love the brotherhood. Fear God. Honor the emperor. (1 Pt 2:13-17)

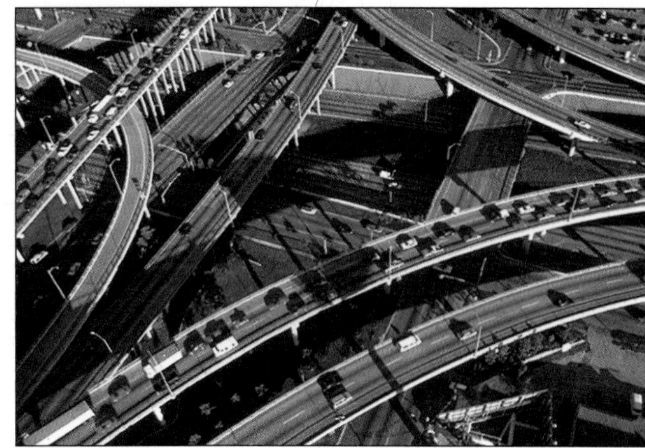

But moral theology, confronted with arbitrary and even tyrannical authorities, determined that a Christian can oppose and, in certain circumstances, overthrow illegitimate governments and unjust laws:

> The citizen is obliged in conscience not to follow the directives of civil authorities when they are contrary to the demands of the moral order, to the fundamental rights of persons or the teachings of the Gospel. *Refusing obedience* to civil authorities, when their demands are contrary to those of an upright conscience, finds its justification in the distinction between serving God and serving the political community. "Render therefore to Caesar the things that are Caesar's, and to God the things that are God's" (Mt 22:21). "We must obey God rather than men" (Acts 5:29). (CCC 2242)

Authority is necessary for the common good of all in society.

6. GOVERNMENTS' OBLIGATIONS TO CITIZENS

From the mentioned biblical texts, one can deduce that authority is a service to the common good of society and also a help to each one of its citizens. The nature of civil authority itself is not power, but rather service: the authority has *power* precisely because it must serve the community.

Public authority is obliged to respect the fundamental rights of the human person, as well as to guarantee the conditions that make the exercise of these rights possible. In effect, because human nature requires us to live in a society, authority is necessary for the common good of all in society.

The principle that guides the relations in society is the *principle of subsidiarity.* It states that the lower authority must not be interfered with by the higher authority without necessity. For example, the state must not intervene in the role of the parents to raise their children unless there is a necessity.

The fundamental reality that limits the exercise of authority is the dignity of the human person. Therefore, laws, institutions, and the state itself are justified to the degree that they facilitate dignified lives for their citizens. If the objective of the state is to obtain true common good, then it will pursue only morally acceptable means to help its citizens reach and live according to their dignity. The best forms of government are those whose laws make it possible for all people to seek their eternal destiny as God desires.

The success of all societies is based on the success of the family.

CONCLUSION

The success of all societies is based on the success of the family. As each organ of the body is crucial to the functioning of the whole body, so does the health of particular families contribute to the functioning of the body of society. It is necessary that all members of society make a concerted effort to promote the well being of the family. In this way, the well being of society is promoted. The *Catechism* offers the following summary:

> The fourth commandment *illuminates other relationships in society.* In our brothers and sisters we see the children of our parents; in our cousins, the descendants of our ancestors; in our fellow citizens, the children of our country; in the baptized, the children of our mother the Church; in every human person, a son or daughter of the One who wants to be called "our Father." In this way our relationships with our neighbors are recognized as personal in character. The neighbor is not a "unit" in the human collective; he is "someone" who by his known origins deserves particular attention and respect.
>
> Human communities are *made up of persons.* Governing them well is not limited to guaranteeing rights and fulfilling duties such as honoring contracts. Right relations between employers and employees, between those who govern and citizens, presuppose a natural good will in keeping with the dignity of human persons concerned for justice and fraternity. (CCC 2212-2213)

"In our brothers and sisters we see the children of our parents..."

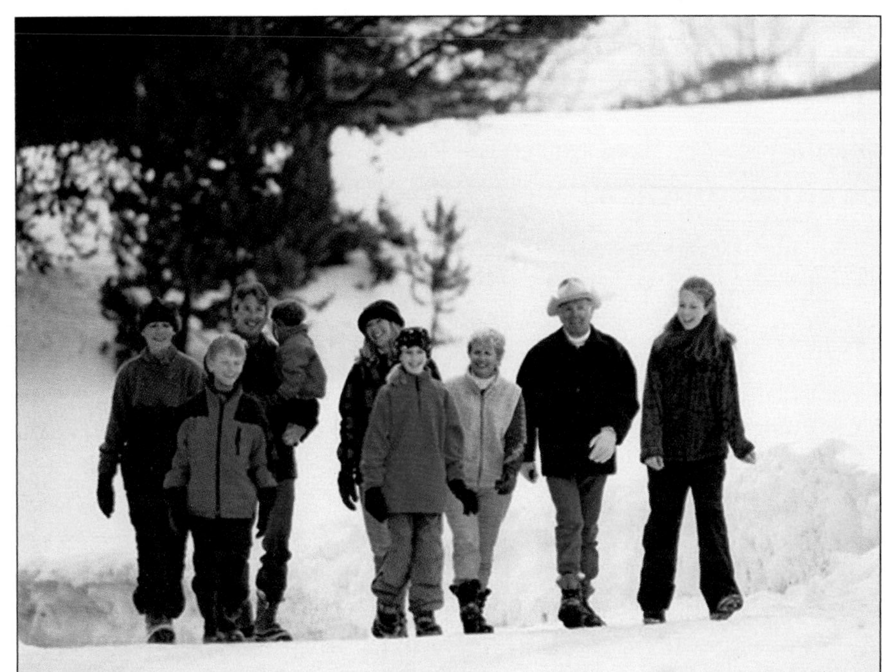

As taught by Jesus in the parable of the Good Steward (cf. Lk 12:42-48) and reaffirmed in St. Paul's Letter to the Romans (cf. Rom 13:1-5), the exercise of human authority is always a sharing in the authority of the Father, Son, and Holy Spirit. It is therefore necessary that this power be exercised with care, for God will call all to account for its use or misuse.

VOCABULARY

AGAPE
A word derived from the Greek term *agapan* (to have great esteem for); it is used in the New Testament to describe both the relationship that exists between Christ and his Church, and the relationship that ought to exist between a husband and wife.

CIVIL AUTHORITY
The characteristic of government and those who represent it by which they are able to dictate laws or oblige the fulfillment of them.

FAMILY
A group of persons united by bonds of kinship. In the strict sense of the word, it is the community of a man and woman and any children born from their marriage.

MANDATE
Command given by a superior.

POLITICS
The art of governing and conserving order and ethically correct customs.

PRINCIPLE OF SUBSIDIARITY
The principle that guides the relations in society. It states that the lower authority must not be interfered with by the higher authority without necessity.

STATE
The political body of a nation; director of the common good.

SOCIETY
A natural or contracted association of individual persons who collaborate in common works and objectives.

UNJUST LAW
A kind of violence in which rulers enact measures contrary to the moral order. These "laws" are not binding on the conscience and should be opposed.

SUPPLEMENTARY READINGS

1. In our days the State has come to be a formidable machine which works in a marvelous fashion, wonderfully efficient by reason of the quantity and precision of its means. Once it is set up in the midst of society, it is enough to touch a button for its enormous levers to start working and exercise their overwhelming power on any portion whatever of the social framework.

The contemporary State is the easiest seen and best-known product of civilization. And it is an interesting revelation when one takes note of the attitude that mass-man adopts before it.... Suppose that in the public life of a country some difficulty, conflict, or problem presents itself, the mass-man will tend to demand that the State intervene immediately and undertake a solution directly with its immense and unassailable resources.

This is the gravest danger that today threatens civilization: State intervention; the absorption of all spontaneous social effort by the State, that is to say, of spontaneous historical action, which in the long run sustains, nourishes, and impels human destinies. When the mass suffers any ill-fortune or simply feels some strong appetite, its great temptation is that permanent, sure possibility of obtaining everything—without effort, struggle, doubt, or risk—merely by touching a button and setting the mighty machine in motion....

The result of this tendency will be fatal. Spontaneous social action will be broken up over and over again by State intervention; no new seed will be able to fructify. Society will have to live *for* the State, man *for* the governmental machine. And as, after all, it is only a machine whose existence and maintenance depend on the vital supports around it, the State, after sucking out the very marrow of society, will be left bloodless, a skeleton, dead with that rusty death of machinery, more gruesome than the death of a living organism.

— José Ortega y Gasset, *The Revolt of the Masses*, pp. 119-121

"This is the gravest danger that today threatens civilization: State intervention..."

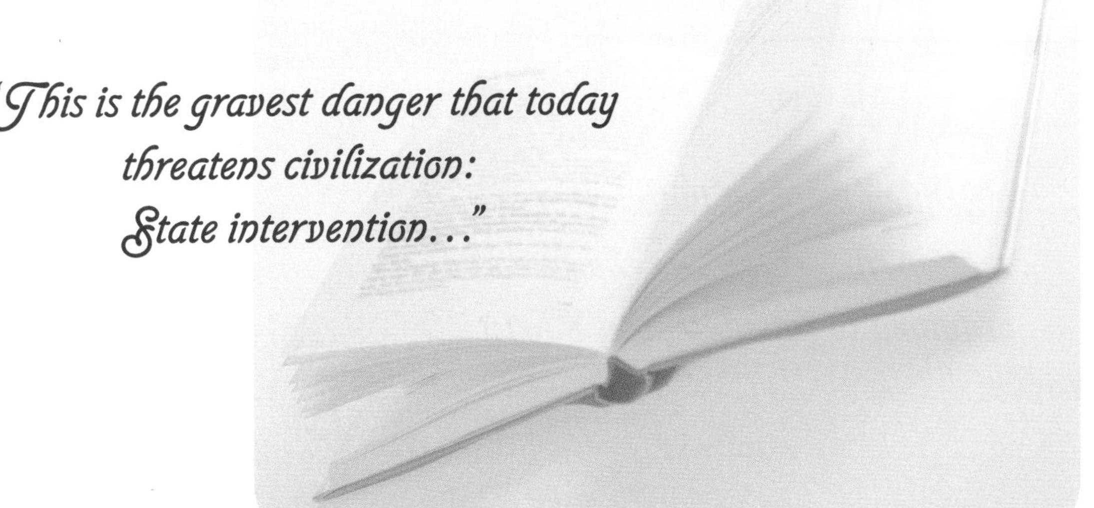

SUPPLEMENTARY READINGS CONTINUED

2. In matrimony and in the family a complex of interpersonal relationships is set up—married life, fatherhood, motherhood, filiation and fraternity—through which each human person is introduced into the "human family" and into the "family of God" which is the Church.

Christian marriage and the Christian family build up the Church: for in the family the human person is not only brought into being and progressively introduced by means of education into the human community, but by means of the rebirth of Baptism and education in the faith the child is introduced into God's family, which is the Church.

The human family, disunited by sin, is reconstituted in its unity by the redemptive power of the death and resurrection of Christ. Christian marriage, by participating in the salvific efficacy of this event, constitutes the natural setting in which the human person is introduced into the great family of the Church.

The commandment to grow and multiply, given to man and woman in the beginning, in this way reaches its whole truth and full realization. The Church thus finds in the family, born from the sacrament, the cradle and the setting in which she can enter the human generations, and where these in turn can enter the Church. (*FC*, 15)

"The Family finds in the plan of God, the Creator and Redeemer, not only its *identity*, what it *is*, but also its *mission*, what it can and should *do*." (*FC*, 17)

"The family, which is founded and given life by love, is a community of persons... Its first task is to live with fidelity the reality of communion in a constant effort to develop an authentic community of persons. The inner principle of that task, its permanent power and its final goal is love: without love the family is not a community of persons and, in the same way, *without love the family cannot live, grow and perfect itself as a community of persons*. What I wrote in the encyclical *Redemptor hominis* applies primarily to and especially within the family as such: 'Man cannot live without love. He remains a being that is incomprehensible to himself, his life is senseless, if love is not revealed to him, if he does not encounter love, if he does not experience and make it his own, if he does not participate intimately in it.'" (*FC*, 18; cf. also *RH*, 10)

"The church is deeply convinced that only by the acceptance of the Gospel are the hopes that man legitimately places in marriage and the family capable of being fulfilled. Willed by God in the very act of creation, marriage and the family are ordained to fulfillment in Christ and have need of his graces in order to be healed from the wounds of sin and restored to their 'beginning,' that is, to full understanding and the full realization of God's plan." (*FC*, 3)

"Willed by God in the very act of creation, marriage and the family are ordained to fulfillment in Christ..."

QUESTIONS

1. What do the last seven commandments cover?

2. Why does the Church insist that love is the foundation of the family?

3. What is Christian morality?

4. What is the key to loving properly?

5. In relationships between persons, what love relationship is primary?

6. What three obligations are owed to elders and ancestors in the family?

7. What reward does the Old Testament promise for those who honor their parents?

8. How should a husband love his wife?

9. What does the phrase "equality of persons and differences of functions" say about the marital relationship?

10. What does "revering your parents" mean?

11. List the five obligations parents have toward their children.

12. List the four obligations children have toward their parents.

13. What does true family responsibility require?

14. Why should legitimate authority always be obeyed?

15. What is the meaning of the sentence "All authority comes from God"?

16. List obligations citizens owe to public authority.

17. When may a person refuse to obey civil authority?

18. What obligations does the public authority owe its citizens?

PRACTICAL EXERCISES

1. Marriage presents the opportunity for the children to observe interactions between the parents. Write an essay describing some ideas regarding marriage you have learned by observing your parents.

2. Discuss some of the material benefits possessed by families in modern Western civilization and the positive and negative effects you think they have on family life. Do you think family life in less fortunate countries is generally better, or do you think that things are generally the same everywhere? Support your answer with specific examples.

3. Comment on each of the following situations, evaluating each person's attitude, actions, or decisions in light of the fourth commandment:

- Susan says that she should be allowed to live according to her own rules at home, since she is 18 years old.
- Peter's father arrives at home drunk on a regular basis, and starts screaming at family members. Peter plans to throw his father out of the house on the next occasion.
- Danny doesn't want to tell his parents that his brother has been hanging out with kids who are known to sell drugs at school because he doesn't want to be a squealer.

4. Imagine that you are a parent with four children. Discuss steps that can be taken to avoid or reduce sibling disagreements.

FROM THE CATECHISM

1918 "There is no authority except from God, and those authorities that exist have been instituted by God" (Rom 13:1).

1923 Political authority must be exercised within the limits of the moral order and must guarantee the conditions for the exercise of freedom.

2234 God's fourth commandment also enjoins us to honor all who for our good have received authority in society from God. It clarifies the duties of those who exercise authority as well as those who benefit from it.

2247 "Honor your father and your mother" (Dt 5:16; Mk 7:10).

2248 According to the fourth commandment, God has willed that, after him, we should honor our parents and those whom he has vested with authority for our good.

2251 Children owe their parents respect, gratitude, just obedience, and assistance. Filial respect fosters harmony in all of family life.

2252 Parents have the first responsibility for the education of their children in the faith, prayer, and all the virtues. They have the duty to provide as far as possible for the physical and spiritual needs of their children.

2256 Citizens are obliged in conscience not to follow the directives of civil authorities when they are contrary to the demands of the moral order. "We must obey God rather than men" (Acts 5:29).

ENDNOTES

1. Pope John Paul II, *Letter to Families,* 14 (1994).
2. *GS,* 52 § 1.
3. Cf. CCC, 1656-1657; 2223-2229.
4. Pope John Paul II, *Letter to Families,* 15 (1994).

Chapter 14

The Fifth Commandment: You Shall Not Kill

Now Abel was a keeper of sheep, and Cain a tiller of the ground. In the course of time Cain brought to the Lord an offering of the fruit of the ground, and Abel brought of the firstlings of his flock and of their fat portions. And the Lord had regard for Abel and his offering, but for Cain and his offering he had no regard. So Cain was very angry, and his countenance fell. The Lord said to Cain, "Why are you angry, and why has your countenance fallen? If you do well, will you not be accepted? And if you do not do well, sin is crouching at the door; its desire is for you, but you must master it."

Cain said to Abel his brother, "Let us go out to the field." And when they were in the field, Cain rose up against his brother Abel, and killed him. Then the Lord said to Cain, "Where is Abel your brother?" He said, "I do not know; am I my brother's keeper?" And the Lord said, "What have you done? The voice of your brother's blood is crying to me from the ground. And now you are cursed from the ground, which has opened its mouth to receive your brother's blood from your hand. When you till the ground, it shall no longer yield to you its strength; you shall be a fugitive and a wanderer on the earth." Cain said to the Lord, "My punishment is greater than I can bear. Behold, thou hast driven me this day away from the ground; and from thy face I shall be hidden; and I shall be a fugitive and a wanderer on the earth, and whoever finds me will slay me." Then the Lord said to him, "Not so! If anyone slays Cain, vengeance shall be taken on him sevenfold." And the Lord put a mark on Cain, lest any who came upon him should kill him. Then Cain went away from the presence of the Lord, and dwelt in the land of Nod, east of Eden. (Gn 4: 2-16)

The story of Cain and Abel is one of the most dramatic and instructive in Scripture. Along with the Decalogue, it forms the biblical foundation for the Church's absolute insistence on the inviolability and sacredness of innocent human life.

In light of this story, we may ask ourselves the following questions:

- Does God's revelation forbid all killing, or only some types of killing?
- What is the meaning of human suffering?
- Can the desire to prevent suffering ever justify taking someone's life?
- In light of the biblical prohibition against murder, can war ever be truly justifiable?
- Why does the Church teach that a person's stewardship over his own life does not include the right to end it?

Every human life, from the moment of conception until death, is sacred.

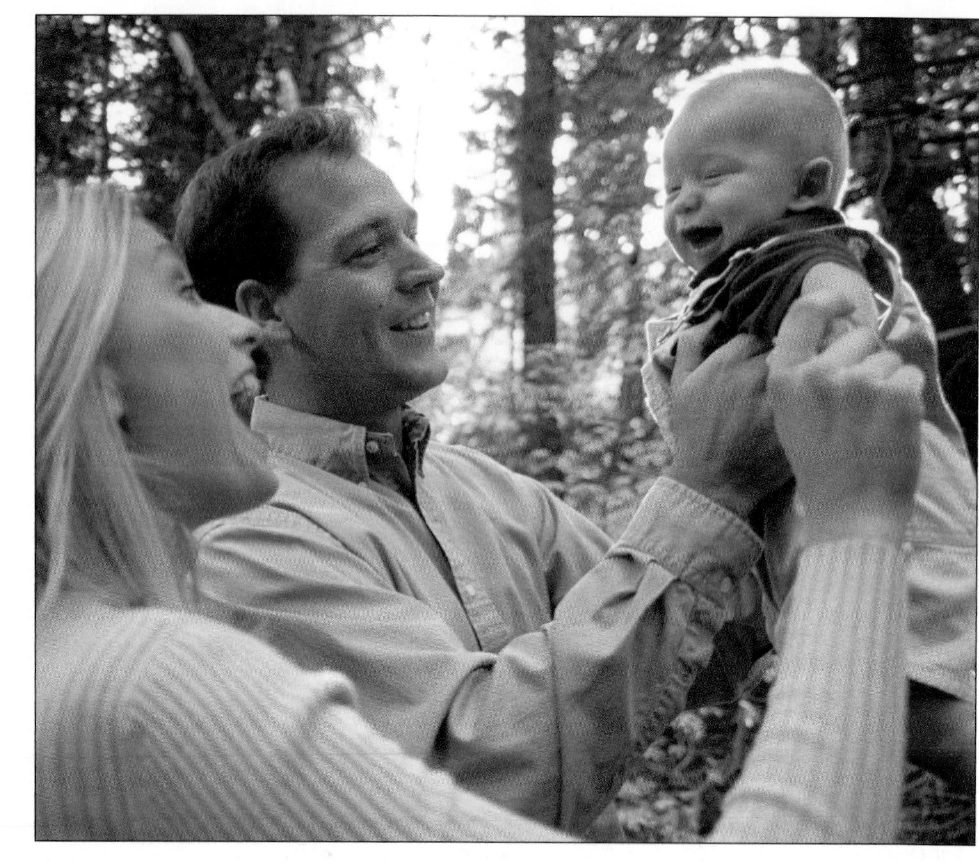

The human person can find the fullness of his being only in union with the Father, Son, and Holy Spirit.

INTRODUCTION

Life here is a preparation for life in the hereafter. The Father did not give human beings absolute dominion over their lives, but rather gives them the duty of guarding their own lives and the lives of those around them.

> Every human life, from the moment of conception until death, is sacred because the human person has been willed for its own sake in the image and likeness of the living and holy God. (CCC 2319)

This is how it is expressed in Deuteronomy: "'See now that I, even I, am he, and there is no god beside me; I kill and I make alive; I wound and I heal; and there is none that can deliver out of my hand'" (Dt 32:39).

> God proclaims that he is absolute Lord of the life of man, who is formed in his image and likeness (cf. Gn 1:26-28). Human life is thus given a sacred and inviolable character, which reflects the inviolability of the Creator himself. Precisely for this reason God will severely judge every violation of the commandment "you shall not kill," the commandment which is at the basis of all life together in society. He is the *goel*, the defender of the innocent (cf. Gn 4:9-15; Is 41:14; Jer 50:34; Ps 19:14). God thus shows that he does not delight in the death of the living (cf. Wis 1:13). Only Satan can delight therein: for through his envy death entered the world (cf. Wis 2:24). He who is "a murderer from the beginning," is also "a liar and the father of lies" (Jn 8:44). By deceiving man he leads him to projects of sin and death, making them appear as goals and fruits of life.[1]

This teaching supposes a specifically Christian understanding of God as all-powerful and all-loving Father. Human life has its origin in him and is dependent on him. Therefore, atheist and agnostic ideologies—and even some religions—will not accept some of Christianity's moral teachings about the value and meaning of life. Many philosophies view human beings as dependent only on themselves—the absolute masters of their own lives and destinies. But Christianity, in regarding the complete fulfillment of human life, rejects *autonomy* (dependence on one's self), and *heteronomy* (dependence on someone else), and only accepts *theonomy* (dependence on God). Such dependence is precisely the glory and salvation of humanity: The human person can find the fullness of his being only in union with the Father, Son, and Holy Spirit.

"This is my commandment, that you love one another as I have loved you."
— Jn 15:12

1. RESPECT FOR HUMAN LIFE

Christ demands that one should be reconciled with his enemies before talking with God.

The Catholic doctrine concerning the value of life is based on the fifth commandment: "You shall not kill." Killing an innocent person is a grave sin contrary to the natural law, the dignity of the person, and the holiness of the Creator. The Father commands everyone to respect his own life and the lives of others. This commandment deals with protecting the most fundamental human right: the right to existence itself. For that reason, God reminds humanity in the Old Testament that he is the only owner of life and that, when creating the human person, he gave him the personal right to defend it, for defense against an unjust aggressor is a grave obligation for the common good. No one can deny this right, and therefore to attempt to take one's own life or that of another is especially serious.

This commandment was completed and brought to perfection by Jesus Christ. In the Sermon on the Mount, he enriched it with these words:

> **"You have heard that it was said to the men of old, 'You shall not kill; and whoever kills shall be liable to judgment.' But I say to you that every one who is angry with his brother shall be liable to judgment; whoever insults his brother shall be liable to the council, and whoever says, 'You fool!' shall be liable to the hell of fire. So if you are offering your gift at the altar, and there remember that your brother has something against you, leave your gift there before the altar and go; first be reconciled to your brother, and then come and offer your gift." (Mt 5:21-24)**

In these words, Jesus introduces two new elements to the fifth commandment:

- He commands that not only should one respect the life of another, but also that one must value the dignity of every person in such a way that any offense that violates a person's dignity is condemned.
- He specifies that no one can direct himself to God when he holds his neighbors to be enemies. Christ demands

"The greatest personal possession of the natural order is life itself..."

that one should be reconciled with his enemies before talking with God. This shows the importance of love for one's neighbors, which is included in the generic and negative formula of "not killing."

But the "novelty" of the fifth commandment, as reinterpreted by Jesus Christ, is enriched with the proclamation of the commandment of love. In this way, the precept of not killing is converted into the new commandment of Jesus Christ: "This is my commandment, that you love one another as I have loved you" (Jn 15:12). The commandment of charity enriches the formulation of the fifth commandment of the Mosaic law.

2. CONSERVATION OF EXISTING LIFE

The greatest personal possession of the natural order is life itself, since it is the necessary condition for the enjoyment of all other blessings, even those that are spiritual. To deprive someone of life is to inflict upon him the greatest harm of the natural order...a sin that is obviously all the more serious because it is completely and totally irreparable. When someone is murdered, he stays murdered; a murderer cannot restore life.[2]

Only God is the absolute owner of human life, and one must try to live his life to the best of his abilities. For this reason, one is seriously obliged to take care of life as a good steward whose life is on loan from God.

a. THE DUTY TO CONSERVE ONE'S OWN LIFE

To protect one's own life, each person is permitted to defend himself when under attack, even if the consequence is the unintended death of an unjust aggressor. Self-defense permits only the force necessary to repel an unjust attacker.

If a person is not the owner of his own life, he certainly cannot dispose of the life of others.

Legitimate self-defense is morally acceptable.[3] However, no one can end one's own life; therefore, suicide and self-mutilation are forbidden.[4] Furthermore, because of the unique value of each human life, one has the serious duty of taking care of one's health. The use of illegal drugs and the excessive use of alcohol are therefore immoral.[5]

b. RESPECT FOR THE LIFE OF OTHERS

If a person is not the owner of his own life, he certainly cannot dispose of the life of others. Taking the life of an innocent person—murder or homicide—is a serious offense against God and the moral order.[6] Kidnapping, torture, and terrorism are also forbidden.[7]

c. ABORTION AND THE RIGHTS OF THE UNBORN

Abortion causes the death of a child before he can survive outside the mother's womb. It can be *spontaneous* or *induced*, depending on whether it occurs naturally or is brought about through human intervention.

One can distinguish three classes of induced abortion: *eugenic abortion* (done because of a malformation of the fetus), *therapeutic abortion* (as in cases of rape), and *psychological* or *psychosocial abortion* (done for psychological, economic, or social reasons). All induced abortion is gravely sinful.

The Magisterium of the Church has consistently proclaimed the gravely sinful nature of abortion throughout its history. The Fathers of the Church condemned it to combat the frequent practice in the Greco-Roman world. This condemnation is found in the *Didache*, a first-century Church text (ca. A.D. 80) that told Christians: "You shall not procure abortion. You shall not destroy a newborn child."

The Magisterium of the Church has consistently proclaimed the gravely sinful nature of abortion throughout its history.

This condemnation was repeated in Vatican Council II, and Paul VI and John Paul II reiterated this condemnation.

> Some people try to justify abortion by claiming that the result of conception, at least up to a certain number of days, cannot yet be considered a personal human life. But in fact, "from the time that the ovum is fertilized, a life is begun which is neither that of the father nor the mother; it is rather the life of a new human being with his own growth. It would never be made human if it were not human already. This has always been clear, and…modern genetic science offers clear confirmation. It has demonstrated that from the first instant there is established the program of what this living being will be: a person, this individual person with his characteristic aspects already well determined. Right from fertilization the adventure of a human life begins, and each of its capacities requires time—a rather lengthy time to find its place and to be in a position to act. (cf. Congregation for the Doctrine of the Faith, *Declaration on Procured Abortion*, 12, 13.) Even if the presence of a spiritual soul cannot be ascertained by empirical data, the results themselves of scientific research on the human embryo provide "a valuable indication for discerning by the use of reason a personal presence at the moment of the first appearance of a human life: how could a human individual not be a human person?"[8]
>
> Furthermore, what is at stake is so important that, from the standpoint of moral obligation, the mere probability that a human person is involved would suffice to justify an absolutely clear prohibition of any intervention aimed at killing a human embryo. Precisely for this reason, over and above all scientific debates and those philosophical affirmations to which the Magisterium has not expressly committed itself, the church has always taught and continues to teach that the result of human procreation, from the first moment of its existence, must be guaranteed that unconditional respect which is morally due to the human being in his or her totality and unity as body and spirit.[9]

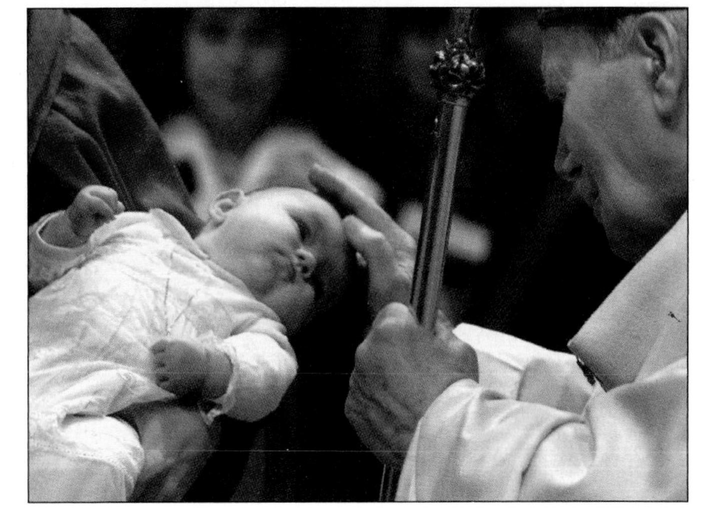

"I declare that direct abortion, that is, abortion willed as an end or as a means, always constitutes a grave moral disorder..."

— John Paul II

One who knows that abortion is condemned and performs it anyway is automatically excommunicated.

Pope John Paul II stated clearly the gravity of the sin of abortion in the following words:

> **Therefore, by the authority which Christ conferred upon Peter and his Successors, in communion with the bishops—who on various occasions have condemned abortion and who in the aforementioned consultation, albeit dispersed throughout the world, have shown unanimous agreement concerning this doctrine—*I declare that direct abortion, that is, abortion willed as an end or as a means, always constitutes a grave moral disorder,* since it is the deliberate killing of an innocent human being. This doctrine is based upon the natural law and upon the written Word of God, is transmitted by the church's tradition and taught by the ordinary and universal magisterium.[10]**

Such condemnation becomes even more serious with the punishment of excommunication (exclusion of a baptized person from participation in the ritual and sacramental life of the Church), which the *Code of Canon Law* imposes.[11] One who knows that abortion is condemned and performs it anyway is automatically excommunicated from the Church. If a person does not know that this sin is cause for excommunication, he is not excommunicated. All those who cooperate in the abortion are also subject to excommunication:

> **Formal cooperation in an abortion constitutes a grave offense. (CCC 2272)**

d. THE ERROR OF A PRO-CHOICE CATHOLIC (i.e., "FOR A FREE CHOICE")

Pro-choicers refuse to acknowledge that there is a human being in the womb.

Some Catholics defend what they call a "pro-choice position." According to them, a woman has the freedom to *choose* to abort her baby under a supposed "right to privacy," and they claim this right cannot be superseded. Abortion then is not considered as a life-death issue but as a rights-choice issue. They eliminate the unpleasant and potentially painful notion of the principal pro-life argument that abortion is murder. They refuse to acknowledge that there is a human being in the womb. Since the pro-choicers deny personhood to the unborn, they view abortion as something akin to the removal of a tumor.

Other Catholics, while maintaining that they are personally opposed to the practice of abortion, believe that it is morally wrong for them (or the Church as a social institution) to attempt to prohibit its practice. They insist that it would be wrong for them to allow their personal religious convictions to influence their political decisions.

John Paul rejected these pro-choice positions:

> **[W]e have what appear to be two diametrically opposed tendencies. On the one hand, individuals claim for themselves in the moral sphere the most complete freedom of choice and demand that the state should not adopt or impose any ethical position but limit itself**

> to guaranteeing maximum space for the freedom of each individual, with the sole limitation of not infringing on the freedom and rights of any other citizen. On the other hand, it is held that, in the exercise of public and professional duties, respect for other people's freedom of choice requires that each one should set aside his or her own convictions in order to satisfy every demand of the citizens which is recognized and guaranteed by law; in carrying out one's duties, the only moral criterion should be what is laid down by the law itself. Individual responsibility is thus turned over to the civil law, with a renouncing of personal conscience, at least in the public sphere.
>
> At the basis of all these tendencies lies the ethical relativism which characterizes much of present-day culture. There are those who consider such relativism an essential condition of democracy, inasmuch as it alone is held to guarantee tolerance, mutual respect between people and acceptance of the decisions of the majority, whereas moral norms considered to be objective and binding are held to lead to authoritarianism and intolerance.[12]

The approach decried by Pope John Paul II is based on the denial of absolute truth (cf. Chapter 7).

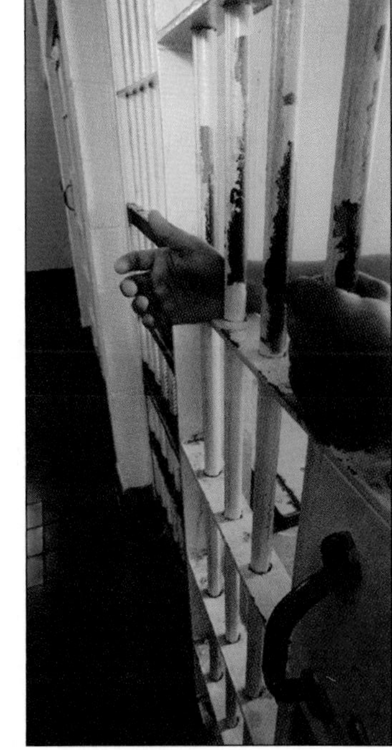

"If…non-lethal means are sufficient to defend and protect people's safety from the aggressor, authority will limit itself to such means…"

e. CAPITAL PUNISHMENT

Evangelium vitae formally confirmed the Church's resistance to the use of the death penalty. The encyclical did not declare that capital punishment in itself is unacceptable. However, it is seen as an extreme measure that should not be done except "in cases of absolute necessity." This would be the case when it is impossible to defend society without putting the prisoner to death, the Pope explained. But these cases, he noted, "are very rare if not practically nonexistent."[13]

The *Catechism of the Catholic Church* was amended to take into account the pope's words. Point 2267 now includes the teaching of *Evangelium vitae* and explains that while the Church does not absolutely exclude the death penalty, non-lethal means are preferred when they are sufficient to defend public safety.

> Assuming that the guilty party's identity and responsibility have been fully determined, the traditional teaching of the Church does not exclude recourse to the death penalty, if this is the only possible way of effectively defending human lives against the unjust aggressor.
>
> If, however, non-lethal means are sufficient to defend and protect people's safety from the aggressor, authority will limit itself to such means, as these are more in keeping with the concrete conditions of the common good and more in conformity with the dignity of the human person.
>
> Today, in fact, as a consequence of the possibilities which the state has for effectively preventing crime, by rendering one who has committed an offense incapable of doing harm—without definitively taking away from him the possibility of redeeming himself—the cases in which the execution of the offender is an absolute necessity "are very rare, if not practically non-existent"[14] (CCC 2267).

One of the causes of atheism in our times has been the enigma of pain.

The Church still teaches that the state has a right to impose capital punishment on people convicted of very serious crimes, however, "the classical tradition held that the State should not exercise this right when the evil effects outweigh the good effects."[15]

3. THE PROBLEM OF PAIN AND SUFFERING

The subject of pain and suffering has been one of the great questions of human life throughout history. Philosophical systems as well as religions have always asked: Why do we feel pain? What is the origin of suffering? Why do honorable, innocent human beings suffer?

These questions are even more disturbing if one takes into account that no one is free from suffering, that pain is widespread and common, and that suffering is often profound and severe. It is also possible to exaggerate the apparent senselessness of pain if one applies such adjectives as "useless" or "unjust" to pain, particularly the pain of innocent people.

One of the causes of atheism in our times has been the enigma of pain. This is the reason that those who do not believe in God often lift a shout of desperation up against him. Vatican II, when talking about the numerous causes of atheism in our time, teaches: "Not infrequently atheism is born from a violent protest against the evil in the world."[16]

> Suffering is certainly part of the mystery of man. Perhaps suffering is not wrapped up as much as man is by this mystery, which is an especially impenetrable one. The Second Vatican Council expressed this truth that "...only in the mystery of the Incarnate Word does the mystery of man take on light. In fact..., Christ, the final Adam, by the revelation of the mystery of the Father and His love, *fully reveals man to himself* and makes his supreme calling clear" (*GS*, 22). If these words refer to everything that concerns the mystery of man, then they certainly refer in a very special way *to human suffering.* Precisely at this point the "revealing of man to himself and making his supreme vocation clear" is particularly *indispensable.* It also happens—as experience proves—that this can be particularly *dramatic.* But when it is completely accomplished and becomes the light of human life, it is particularly *blessed.* "Through Christ and in Christ, the riddles of sorrow and death grow meaningful."...[17]
>
> The mystery of the Redemption of the world is in an amazing way *rooted in suffering,* and this suffering in turn finds in the mystery of the Redemption its supreme and surest point of reference.[18]

"Through Christ and in Christ, the riddles of sorrow and death grow meaningful."

Christians are called to join their sufferings to the suffering of Jesus Christ, who died on the cross for the sins of the world. In this way, human suffering assumes a meaning and purpose that transcends our ordinary understanding; it can become an offering to the Father in reparation for sin.

4. THE MEANING OF DEATH

For the Christian death is not the end, but rather a beginning.

St. Paul tells us, "But then what return did you get from the things of which you are now ashamed? The end of those things is death" (Rom 6:21), and "sin, working death in me through what is good, in order that sin might be shown to be sin, and through the commandment might become sinful beyond measure" (Rom 7:13), since "this perishable nature must put on the imperishable, and this mortal nature must put on immortality" (1 Cor 15:53). For the Christian, however, death is not the end, but rather a beginning.

In relation to death, the most urgent ethical problem is euthanasia. The word *euthanasia* comes from the Greek *eu* (good) and *thanatos* (death), so it means a good or sweet death.

> By euthanasia is understood as action or an omission which of itself or by intention causes death, in order that all suffering may in this way be eliminated. Euthanasia's terms of reference, therefore, are to be found in the intention of the will and in the methods used.[19]

While the Church does condemn euthanasia, it also recognizes the right to end unnecessary medical treatment in particular circumstances:

> Euthanasia must be distinguished from the decision to forgo so-called "aggressive medical treatment," in other words, medical procedures which no longer correspond to the real situation of the patient either because they are by now disproportionate to any expected results or because they impose an excessive burden on the patient and his family. In such situations, when death is clearly imminent and inevitable, one can in conscience "refuse forms of treatment that would only secure a precarious and burdensome prolongation of life, so long as the normal care due to the sick person in similar cases is not interrupted" (IOE, 4). To forgo extraordinary or disproportionate means is not the equivalent of suicide or euthanasia; it rather expresses acceptance of the human condition in the face of death....
>
> Taking into account these distinctions, in harmony with the magisterium of my predecessors and in communion with the bishops of the Catholic Church, *I confirm that euthanasia is a grave violation of the law of God,* since it is the deliberate and morally unacceptable killing of a human person. This doctrine is based upon the natural law and upon the written word of God, is transmitted by the church's tradition and taught by the ordinary and universal magisterium.[20]

"I confirm that euthanasia is a grave violation of the law of God..."

— *EV*, 65.

From the foregoing, the following conclusions may be drawn:

- To take directly the life of a sick person is murder.
- It is permissible to allow the imminent death of a person.
- Extraordinary means to maintain life are never required.
- In all cases, ordinary means (food, hydration, medicine, care of body) of sustaining life are always required.

The Christian should lead a life that gives good example to others.

Psychological disorders and illnesses can be dealt with and treated through psychotherapy. Drugs may be administered only for ethically legitimate reasons. The right of the patient to be informed as well as his right to refuse therapy must be considered when taking into account the ability of the patient to make these decisions.

This moral doctrine is reasonable because it recognizes the right to life, which is inherent to every human being.

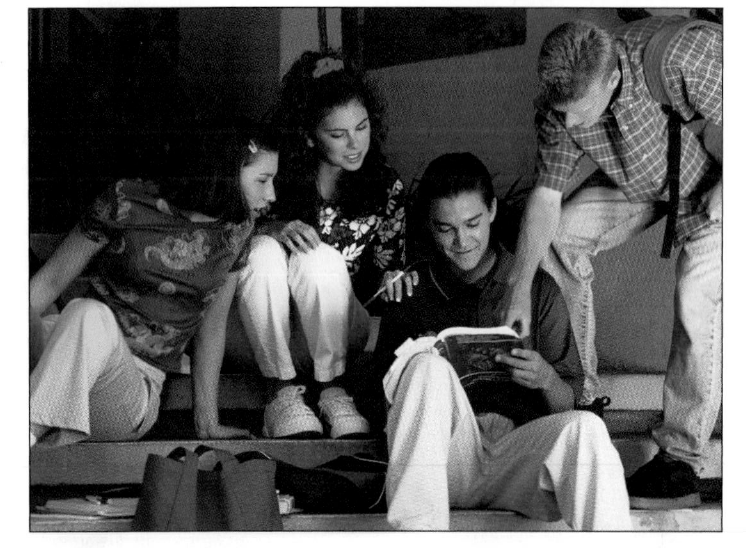

5. RESPECT FOR THE SOULS OF OTHERS: AVOIDING SCANDAL

The Christian should lead a life that gives good example to others. Time and time again in the Gospels, Jesus reminds his followers that they will be judged by the fruits produced by their conduct (cf. Mt 7:16-20), that they must be prepared to forgive one another if they wish to receive the Father's forgiveness (cf. Mt 6:14-15), and that others will know that they are his followers by the love they show toward one another (cf. Jn 13:34-35).

In equally forceful terms, however, Jesus also warns his followers about the opposing sin of scandal:

> "[W]hoever causes one of these little ones who believe in me to sin, it would be better for him to have a great millstone fastened round his neck and to be drowned in the depth of the sea.
>
> "Woe to the world for temptations to sin! For it is necessary that temptations come, but woe to the man by whom the temptation comes!" (Mt 18:6-7)

When a person does evil, he becomes the source of his neighbor's temptation.

Scandal is an attitude or behavior that leads another to do evil. When a person does evil, he becomes the source of his neighbor's temptation. Not only does the person damage his own virtue and integrity, but may even draw someone into sin and cause a break in his relationship with Jesus through mortal sin. The sin of scandal is grave when it leads others to mortal sin by deed or omission.[21] Those in authority have a particular responsibility to avoid scandal.

> Scandal takes on a particular gravity by reason of the authority of those who cause it or the weakness of those who are scandalized... Scandal is grave when given by those who by nature or office are obliged to teach and educate others. (CCC 2285)

Scandal can be provoked by laws (e.g., abortion), institutions (slavery), fashion (immodest dress), entertainment (some TV shows, movies, and popular music), parties, or opinions (racism).

6. JUST WAR

War, with all its horrors, is never desirable. Nonetheless, "insofar as men are sinners, the threat of war hangs over them and will so continue until the coming of Christ."[22] Everything reasonable must be done to avoid the evils and injustices of war. The Church insists that the moral law and universal principles must be honored during armed conflict to avoid crimes that could be committed in fighting the war.

The strict conditions for legitimate defense by military force require rigorous consideration.

The Church has established criteria to determine if a particular armed conflict is just:

> The strict conditions for *legitimate defense by military force* require rigorous consideration. The gravity of such a decision makes it subject to rigorous conditions of moral legitimacy. At one and the same time:
>
> - the damage inflicted by the aggressor on the nation or community of nations must be lasting, grave, and certain;
> - all other means of putting an end to it must have been shown to be impractical or ineffective;
> - there must be serious prospects of success;
> - the use of arms must not produce evils and disorders graver than the evil to be eliminated. The power of modern means of destruction weighs very heavily in evaluating this condition.
>
> These are the traditional elements enumerated in what is called the "just war" doctrine.
>
> The evaluation of these conditions for moral legitimacy belongs to the prudential judgment of those who have responsibility for the common good. (CCC 2309)

Along with the Church's teaching on just war, there is also its insistence on the respect that is due to every human person, even when nations may find themselves in conflict with one another. It is unfortunate that hostilities between nations often bring violence and suffering to the innocent and poor in the nations involved.

In such situations, everything possible must be done to insure that the innocent are protected as far as possible. Just as the Church condemns the targeting of civilian populations by military forces, so it also condemns *kidnapping, hostage taking,* and *terrorism* as gravely sinful and contrary to the moral law.[23] These means can never be used because they involve violence directed against innocent persons.

> Thus the message of the Gospel, which epitomizes the highest ideals and aspirations of mankind, shines anew in our times when it proclaims that the advocates of peace are blessed "for they shall be called sons of God" (Mt 5:9).

The human body is a wonderful instance of the Father's majestic creation.

It should not be degraded or disfigured by mutilation or abuse.

> Accordingly, the Council proposes to outline the true and noble nature of peace, to condemn the savagery of war, and earnestly to exhort Christians to cooperate with all in securing a peace based on justice and charity and in promoting the means necessary to attain it, under the help of Christ, author of peace.[24]

7. RESPECT FOR THE BODY: MUTILATION AND ORGAN TRANSPLANTS

The human body is a wonderful instance of the Father's majestic creation. As such, it should not be degraded or disfigured by mutilation or abuse. Any type of mutilation or disfigurement of the body is contrary to the moral law. As St. Paul pointed out, "Do you not know that your body is a temple of the Holy Spirit within you, which you have from God? You are not your own" (1 Cor 6:19).

At certain times, however, it may be necessary to remove an organ or limb to save the life of a seriously ill person. Such action is morally permissible.

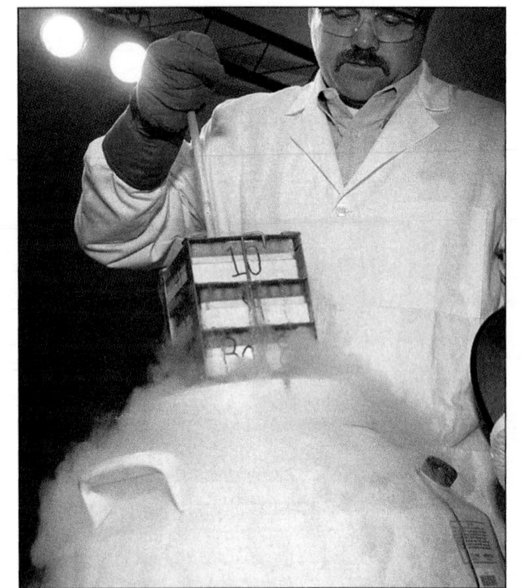

In recent years, organ transplants have been performed with increasing frequency. Organ transplants are permitted when both the donor and the recipient (or those who speak for them) give informed consent, the physical and psychological dangers and risks are proportionate to the good sought, and a qualified surgical team and required equipment are present.

It is morally impermissible to bring about the disabling mutilation or death of a human being by removing an organ, even in order to delay the death of another person.[25] "The brain and gonads may not be transplanted because they ensure the personal and procreative identity respectively."[26]

8. CLONING

Recent breakthroughs in scientific technology have added yet another dimension to the continuing debate over the dignity of human life. The announcement in early 1997 of the successful cloning of a sheep by genetic scientists in Scotland has raised new moral and ethical concerns for the Church. As many as ten years before the successful completion of a cloning experiment, however, the Church—aware of the direction in which scientific research was proceeding—had condemned the procedure on human beings in the document *Donum vitae.*

Human cloning is gravely sinful and contrary to the moral law.

Human cloning is gravely sinful and contrary to the moral law because it opposes the dignity of both the conjugal union between husband and wife and human procreation. Cloning, like artificial insemination, *in vitro* fertilization, and the use of frozen embryos, is a technology that aims at producing human beings selected according to gender or other predetermined quality. It reduces human beings to objects that can be manufactured and manipulated according to whim, rather than unique and irreplaceable creations of God, each possessing his or her own integrity and identity.

9. ILLICIT DRUG USE, SMOKING, AND THE ABUSE OF ALCOHOL

The use of illicit drugs and the abuse of alcohol are forbidden because, in addition to damaging the body, they reduce a person to the levels of an animal by impairing his ability to think clearly. The human soul distinguishes us from the other animals, and to directly inhibit its faculties assaults the dignity of the human person.[27]

The temptation to "play God" is very strong, particularly when human science discovers techniques to manipulate nature.

10. STERILIZATION

Sterilization is alteration of the reproductive organs, depriving a person of his or her procreative capability. We have no authority to destroy our procreative faculties. Christian morality declares voluntary sterilization seeking contraceptive ends to be ethically condemnable.

One should distinguish between *direct* and *indirect sterilization.*

- *Direct sterilization* is intended to destroy procreative capability. Direct sterilization is a sin against the fifth commandment, because it is not only mutilation of the body, but is also an attack on the integrity of the person. Practices such as tying the fallopian tubes or a vasectomy are examples of direct sterilization.
- *Indirect sterilization* is a secondary result of a different medical procedure or as a result of an accident. The Magisterium has accepted indirect sterilization as morally licit *only under necessary medical conditions,* as, for example, in the case of a woman whose ovaries must be removed because of ovarian cancer. The operation is performed for a legitimate medical reason—the prevention of cancer.

The temptation to "play God" is very strong, particularly when human science discovers techniques to manipulate nature, but experience shows that, in the long run, the lack of respect for nature has demonstrably resulted in the most serious moral disorders. The Christian should exercise faith and trust in God. We will discover by experience that both divine and natural law are sure lights that guide human existence in the face of evil.

Anyone guilty of a grave sin against the Fifth Commandment should talk to a priest.

CONCLUSION

Life on earth is preparation for life in the hereafter. In the Father's plan, the human being is a steward over his soul and body, so the Father who gave both has requirements for the right use of both. This naturally includes requirements regarding relations with the souls and bodies of others. Since God gives responsibility for the origin of new life to man, there is an obligation to treat the sources of life as God wishes. His wishes are found in the authentic teaching of the Church, which he has left as a guide for our moral choices. In sum, we have an obligation to develop ourselves in body and soul while respecting the rights of others in all of these matters. Anyone guilty of a grave sin against the fifth commandment should talk to a priest and receive the Sacrament of Reconciliation before receiving Communion.

VOCABULARY

ABORTION
Procuring the expulsion or destruction of a child at any time after conception and prior to birth.

ASSISTED SUICIDE
Any action or omission of an action that assists another person in bringing about his or her own death.

AUTONOMY
The belief that one is entirely independent and is responsible only to himself for his actions and the direction of his life.

BIOETHICS
Derived from the Greek words *bios* (life) and *ethos* (ethics), it is the science that studies the morality of the problems related to life, from conception until death.

CLONING
The technique of producing a genetically identical duplicate of an organism by replacing the nucleus of an unfertilized ovum with the nucleus of a body cell from the organism. This process is not moral in the case of humans.

EUTHANASIA
An action or omission of an action that, by itself or by intention, causes a person's death in order to eliminate suffering.

EUGENICS
The application of biological laws of heredity with the goal of perfecting the human species.

EXCOMMUNICATION
Exclusion of a baptized person from participation in the ritual and sacramental life of the Church.

EXTRAORDINARY MEANS
Treatments that exceed the common degree of medical treatment. Extraordinary means are never required to prolong one's life.

HETERONOMY
The belief that one is entirely dependent on others for happiness and meaning in his life.

JUST WAR
The principle that war may be legitimately waged, under certain specific conditions, for the protection of a nation's rights.

MURDER
The intentional killing of an innocent person.

MUTILATION
The disfigurement of the human body.

SCANDAL
An attitude or behavior that leads another to do evil.

STERILIZATION
The destruction of human procreative powers.

SUICIDE
To voluntarily take one's own life.

THEONOMY
The belief that one depends upon God for the meaning, direction and purpose of his life.

SUPPLEMENTARY READINGS

1. I swear by Apollo, the Physician, the Aesculapius and health and all-heal and all the gods and goddesses that, according to my ability and judgment, I will keep this oath and stipulation:

To reckon him who taught me this art equally dear to me as my parents, to share my substance with him and relieve his necessities if required: to regard his offspring as on the same footing with my own brothers, and to teach them this art if they should wish to learn it, without fee or stipulation, and that by precept, lecture, and every other mode of instruction, I will impart a knowledge of the art to my own sons and to those of my teachers, and to disciples bound by a stipulation and oath, according to the law of medicine, but to none others.

I will follow that method of treatment that, according to my ability and judgment, I consider to the benefit of my patients, and abstain from whatever is deleterious and mischievous. I will give no deadly medicine to anyone if asked, nor suggest any such counsel; furthermore, I will not give to a woman an instrument to produce abortion.

With purity and holiness I will pass my life and practice my art. I will not cut a person who is suffering with a stone, but will leave this to be done by practitioners of this work. Into whatever houses I enter, I will go into them for the benefit of the sick and will abstain from every voluntary act of mischief and corruption; and further from the seduction of females or males, bond or free.

Whatever, in connection with my professional practice, or not in connection with it, I may see or hear in the lives of men that ought not to be spoken abroad, I will not divulge, as reckoning that all such should be kept secret.

While I continue to keep this oath unviolated, may it be granted to me to enjoy life and the practice of the art, respected by all men at all times, but should I trespass and violate this oath, may the reverse be my lot.

— Hippocrates, *The Hippocratic Oath*

"With purity and holiness I will pass my life and practice my art."

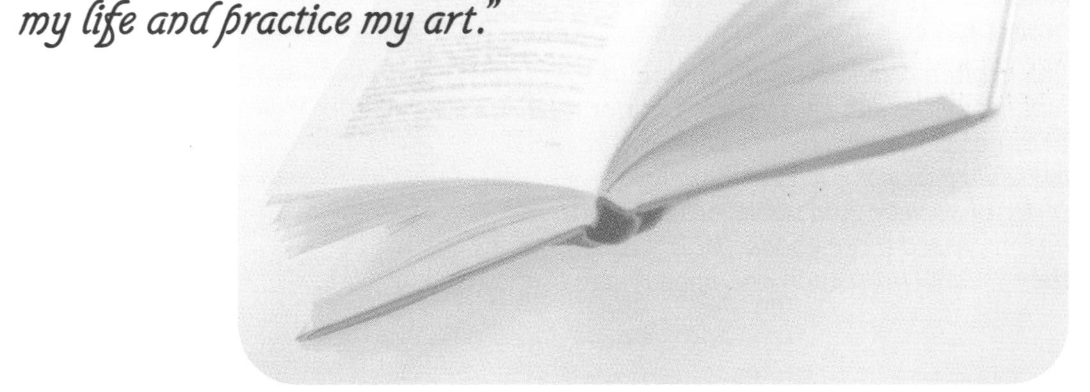

SUPPLEMENTARY READINGS CONTINUED

2. Joseph Cardinal Bernardin was the Archbishop of Chicago, Illinois, from 1982 to 1996. In 1995, he was diagnosed with cancer. Thought to have been cured through treatment, he was diagnosed as suffering from pancreatic cancer early in 1996. Informed that summer that his cancer was terminal, Cardinal Bernardin chose to discontinue treatment for his illness in August 1996. Shortly before his death on November 18, 1996, Cardinal Bernardin wrote the following letter to the Justices of the U.S. Supreme Court, who were preparing to meet to hear arguments in a case favoring the *"right"* of terminally ill patients to commit suicide with the assistance of their doctors.

Dear Honorable Justices:

I am at the end of my earthly life. There is much that I have contemplated these last few months of my illness, but as one who is dying I have especially come to appreciate the gift of life. I know from my own experience that patients often face difficult and deeply personal decisions about their care. However, I also know that even a person who decides to forgo treatment does not necessarily choose death. Rather, he chooses life without the burden of disproportionate medical intervention.

In this case, the Court faces one of the most important issues of our times. Physician-assisted suicide is a decidedly public matter. It is not simply a decision made between patient and physician. Because life affects every person, it is of primary public concern.

I have often remarked that I admire the writings of the late Father John Courtney Murray, who argued that an issue was related to public policy if it affects the public order of society. And public order, in turn, encompassed three goods: public peace, the essential protection of human rights, and commonly accepted standards of moral behavior in the community.

Our legal and ethical tradition has held consistently that suicide, assisted suicide, and euthanasia are wrong because they involve a direct attack on innocent human life. And it is a matter of public policy because it involves a violation of a fundamental human good.

There can be no such thing as a "right to assisted suicide" because there can be no legal and moral order which tolerates the killing of innocent human life, even if the agent of death is self-administered. Creating a new "right" to assisted suicide will endanger society and send a false signal that a less than "perfect" life is not worth living.

Physician-assisted suicide also directly affects the physician-patient relationship and, through that, the wider role of physicians in our society. As has been noted by others, it introduces a deep ambiguity into the very definition of medical care, if care comes to involve killing. Beyond the physician, a move to assisted suicide and, perhaps beyond that, to euthanasia creates social ambiguity about the law. In civilized society, the law exists to protect life. When it begins to legitimate the taking of life as a policy, one has a right to ask what lies ahead for our life together as a society.

In order to protect patients from abuse, and to protect society from a dangerous erosion in its commitment to preserving human life, I urge the Court not to create any right to assisted suicide.

With cordial wishes, I am
Sincerely yours,
Joseph Cardinal Bernardin,
Archbishop of Chicago
November 7, 1996

SUPPLEMENTARY READINGS CONTINUED

3. Man suffers in different ways, ways not always considered by medicine, even in its most advanced specializations. Suffering is something which is *still wider* than sickness, more complex and at the same time still more deeply rooted in humanity itself. A certain idea of this problem comes to us from the distinction between physical suffering and moral suffering. This distinction is based upon the double dimension of the human being and indicates the bodily and spiritual element as the immediate or direct subject of suffering. Insofar as the words "suffering" and "pain" can, up to a certain degree, be used as synonyms, *physical suffering* is present when "the body is hurting" in some way, whereas *moral suffering* is "pain of the soul."

— *SD*, 5

4. But I am not so discouraged by what has happened to me that I complain now of the attacks of wicked men against virtue; the reason for my surprise is that they have accomplished what they set out to do. The desire to do evil may be due to human weakness; but for the wicked to overcome the innocent in the sight of God—that is monstrous. I cannot blame that friend of yours who said, "If there is a God, why is there evil? And if there is no God, how can there be good?"

— Boethius, *Consolation of Philosophy*, Bk 1, Prose 4

5. All human beings, from their mothers' womb, belong to God who searches them and knows them, who forms them and knits them together with his own hands, who gazes on them when they are tiny shapeless embryos and already sees in them the adults of tomorrow whose days are numbered and whose vocation is even now written in the "book of life"...

— *EV*, 61; cf. also Ps 139, 1; 13-16

6. The political debate about abortion has produced much muddled thinking about the possibilities of conscientious dissent from the Church's teaching on the dignity of all human life. It is all too common for Catholic politicians to say they are "personally" opposed to abortion but will nevertheless vote to permit it, and even fund it, out of respect for the consciences of those who hold different views. This "respect" for another's conscience should never require abandoning one's own. Conscientious opposition to abortion, rooted in an understanding of the sanctity of human life, may not be sacrificed to the mistaken consciences of those who would unjustly take the life of an unborn baby.

— Bishop John J. Myers, *Pastoral Statement*, July 1990)

7. Techniques of fertilization *in vitro* can open the way to other forms of biological and genetic manipulation of human embryos, such as attempts or plans for fertilization between human and animal gametes and the gestation of human embryos in the uterus of animals, or the hypothesis or project of constructing artificial uteruses for the human embryo.

These procedures are contrary to the human dignity proper to the embryo, and at the same time they are contrary to the right of every person to be conceived and to be born within marriage and from marriage. Also, attempts or hypotheses for obtaining a human being without any connection with sexuality through "twin fission," cloning or parthenogenesis are to be considered contrary to the moral law, since they are in opposition to the dignity of both human procreation and of the conjugal union.

— DoV, 1.6

ADVANCED CONCEPTS

TERMINAL ILLNESS

1. APPROPRIATE MEDICAL TREATMENT

According to the *Charter for Health Care Workers*, the issue of the terminally ill and their care is complex, and requires that a careful balance be maintained between the issue and principles involved in the discussion. These issues include:

- The question of appropriate types of medical treatment,
- The Christian understanding of the nature and value of human suffering,
- The obligation of the Christian to alleviate the sufferings of others, and
- The morality of discontinuing, refusing, or withholding medical treatment in the case of terminally ill patients.

The principle...of appropriate medical treatment in the remedies can be specified and applied:

- In the absence of other remedies, it is lawful to have recourse, with the consent of the patient, to the means made available by the most advanced medicine, even if they are still at an experimental stage and not without some element of risk.
- It is lawful to interrupt the application of such means when the results disappoint the hopes placed in them," because there is no longer due proportion between "the investment of instruments and personnel" and "the foreseeable results" or because "the techniques used subject the patient to suffering and discomfort greater than the benefits to be had."
- It is always lawful to be satisfied with the normal means offered by medicine. No one can be obliged, therefore, to have recourse to a type of remedy which, although already in use, is still not without dangers or is too onerous." This refusal "is not the equivalent of suicide." Rather it might signify "either simple acceptance of the human condition, or the wish to avoid putting into effect a remedy disproportionate to the results that can be hoped for, or the desire not to place too great a burden on the family or on society."[28]

2. DISCONTINUING MEDICAL TREATMENT

The right to life is specified in the terminally ill person as "a right to die in total serenity, with human and Christian dignity." This cannot be interpreted as the power to kill oneself or to give this power to others, but to experience dying in a human and Christian way and not flee from it "at any cost." This right is being explicitly expressed by people today in order to safeguard themselves at the point of death against "the use of techniques that run the risk of becoming abusive."

Contemporary medicine, in fact, has at its disposal methods which artificially delay death, without any real benefit to the patient. It is merely keeping one alive or prolonging life for a time, at the cost of further, severe suffering. This is the so-called "therapeutic tyranny," which consists "in the use of methods which are particularly exhausting and painful for the patient, condemning him in fact to an artificially prolonged agony."

This is contrary to the dignity of the dying person and to the moral obligation of accepting death and allowing it at last to take its course. "Death is an inevitable fact of human life"; it cannot be uselessly delayed, fleeing from it by every means.

Aware that he is "neither the lord of life, nor the conqueror of death," the health care worker, in evaluating means, "should make appropriate choices, that is, relate to the patient and be guided by his real condition."

ADVANCED CONCEPTS CONTINUED

Here he will apply the principle—already stated—of *"appropriate medical treatment,"* which can be specified thus: "When inevitable death is imminent, despite the means used, it is lawful in conscience to decide to refuse treatment that would only secure a precarious and painful prolongation of life, but without interrupting the normal treatment due to the patient in similar cases. Hence the doctor need have no concern; it is not as if he had failed to assist the person in danger."

The administration of food and liquids, even artificially, is part of the normal treatment always due to the patient when this is not burdensome for him: their undue suspension could be real and properly so-called euthanasia.

Discontinuing medical procedures that are burdensome, dangerous, extraordinary, or disproportionate to the expected outcome can be legitimate; it is the refusal of "over-zealous" treatment. Here one does not will to cause death; one's inability to impede it is merely accepted. The decisions should be made by the patient if he is competent and able or, if not, by those legally entitled to act for the patient, whose reasonable will and legitimate interests must always be respected. (CCC 2278)

Only a patient has the right to refuse life-saving medical procedures if they are extraordinary means. If the patient is not capable, then it is the next of kin who relates only what he or she knows the wishes of the patient to be. Physicians do not make this decision. They are responsible for providing the best medical treatment for their patients.

3. THE CHRISTIAN MEANING OF SUFFERING

In the messianic program of Christ, which is at the same time the program *of the kingdom of God,* suffering is present in the world in order to release love, in order to give birth to works of love towards neighbor, in order to transform the whole of human civilization into a "civilization of love." In this love the salvific meaning of suffering is completely accomplished and reaches its definitive dimension. Christ's words about the Final Judgment enable us to understand this in all the simplicity and clarity of the Gospel.

These words about love, about actions of love, acts linked with human suffering, enable us once more to discover, at the basis of all *human sufferings, the same redemptive suffering of Christ.* Christ said: "You did it to me." He himself is the one who in each individual experiences love; he himself is the one who receives help, when this is given to every suffering person without exception. He himself is present in this suffering person, since his salvific suffering has been opened once and for all to every human suffering. And all those who suffer have been called once and for all to become sharers "in Christ's sufferings," just as all have been called to "complete" with their own suffering "what is lacking in Christ's afflictions." At one and the same time Christ has taught us *to do good by our suffering and to do good to those who suffer.* In this double aspect he has completely revealed the meaning of suffering.

This is the meaning of suffering, which is truly supernatural and at the same time human. It is *supernatural* because it is rooted in the divine mystery of the Redemption of the world, and it is likewise deeply *human* because in it the person discovers himself, his own humanity, his own dignity, his own mission.[29]

ADVANCED CONCEPTS CONTINUED

4. MORE ON THE CHRISTIAN MEANING OF SUFFERING

For the Christian, pain has a lofty penitential and salvific meaning. "It is, in fact, a sharing in Christ's Passion and a union with the redeeming sacrifice which he offered in obedience to the Father's will." Therefore, one must not be surprised if some Christians prefer to moderate their use of painkillers, in order to accept voluntarily at least part of their sufferings and thus associate themselves in a conscious way with the sufferings of Christ.

Acceptance of pain, motivated and supported by Christian ideals, must not lead to the conclusion that all suffering and all pain must be accepted, and that there should be no effort to alleviate them. On the contrary this is a way of humanizing pain. Christian charity itself requires of health care workers the alleviation of physical suffering.

In the long run pain is an obstacle to the attainment of higher goods and interests. It can produce harmful effects for the psychophysical integrity of the person. When suffering is too intense, it can diminish or impede the control of the spirit. Therefore it is legitimate, and beyond certain limits of endurance, it is also a duty for the health care worker to prevent, alleviate and eliminate pain. It is morally correct and right that the researcher should try "to bring pain under human control."

Anesthetics like painkillers, by directly acting on the more aggressive and disturbing effects of pain, gives the person more control, so that suffering becomes a more human experience.[30]

QUESTIONS

1. Why is human life sacred?

2. On what is the Catholic doctrine on the value of life based?

3. What two new elements did Jesus introduce to the fifth commandment?

4. What "novelty" did Jesus add to the fifth commandment?

5. What three duties bind all people regarding human life?

6. When is self-defense legitimate?

7. What is the difference between spontaneous and procured abortion?

8. Where and when is the earliest Catholic condemnation of abortion found?

9. Where is the most recent condemnation found?

10. Explain excommunication with regard to abortion.

11. What is the error of the "pro-choice" position?

12. How are Christians called to deal with suffering?

13. Contrast extraordinary and ordinary means to preserve life.

14. List the four conclusions that apply to care of the sick.

15. List the conditions for a just war.

16. Why are kidnapping, hostage taking, and terrorism gravely sinful?

17. Under what conditions may one be a recipient of an organ transplant?

18. Why is there a prohibition against transplanting the brain and gonads?

19. Why is cloning a sin?

20. Give three reasons that illicit drug use is forbidden.

21. What is the difference between direct and indirect sterilization?

22. Why is physician-assisted suicide immoral?

PRACTICAL EXERCISES

1. Karen is 16 years old and has been dating Jim for three months. Because she has been taught by her parents to practice her faith, she knows that her parents would be very upset to discover that she has involved herself in a sexual relationship with him. Things are complicated further when she finds out that she is pregnant. Now, Karen is afraid and thinks that she wants to have an abortion so that her parents won't find out that she is pregnant. When her friend Tiffany objects, Karen tries to rationalize her decision by saying, "It's all right because this doctor I saw on TV said that it's not truly human for the first three months, anyway." Imagine that you are Tiffany. What arguments could you offer, drawing upon what you have learned in this chapter, to persuade Karen that having an abortion would be a terrible mistake?

2. Dan has been selling marijuana at school. When confronted by his friend Marco, he justifies his actions by arguing that marijuana is no more addictive than alcohol. Whether or not this is true, why is Dan's argument in defense of his actions irrelevant? Why is it still immoral for Dan to use and sell marijuana?

3. What are some of the moral problems arising out of drug use and the abuse of alcohol?

4. Summarize what the *Catechism* says about the death penalty (2266-2267). In light of the teaching contained in the *Catechism*, can the death penalty ever be legitimately used in the United States? Why or why not?

5. Bearing in mind what this chapter explains about mutilation, what do you think of practices such as tattooing and body piercing? Are these forms of mutilation, and therefore immoral? Why or why not?

6. Because Christians are obliged to preserve the lives of others, to protect their dignity and to do no harm, do you believe that there can ever be a good reason for an individual to fight with another person (i.e., in the case of a young man whose sister's reputation has been damaged by a lie)? Why or why not? Provide specific examples to support your argument.

FROM THE CATECHISM

2307 The fifth commandment forbids the intentional destruction of human life. Because of the evils and injustices that accompany all war, the Church insistently urges everyone to prayer and to action so that the divine Goodness may free us from the ancient bondage of war (cf. *GS*, 81 § 4).

2318 "In [God's] hand is the life of every living thing and the breath of all mankind" (Jb 12:10).

2320 The murder of a human being is gravely contrary to the dignity of the person and the holiness of the Creator.

2321 The prohibition of murder does not abrogate the right to render an unjust aggressor unable to inflict harm. Legitimate defense is a grave duty for whoever is responsible for the lives of others or the common good.

2322 From its conception, the child has the right to life. Direct abortion, that is, abortion willed as an end or as a means, is a "criminal" practice (*GS*, 27), gravely contrary to the moral law. The Church imposes the canonical penalty of excommunication for this crime against human life.

2324 Intentional euthanasia, whatever its forms or motives, is murder. It is gravely contrary to the dignity of the human person and to the respect due to the living God, his Creator.

2325 Suicide is seriously contrary to justice, hope, and charity. It is forbidden by the fifth commandment.

2326 Scandal is a grave offense when by deed or omission it deliberately leads others to sin gravely.

2327 Because of the evils and injustices that all war brings with it, we must do everything reasonably possible to avoid it. The Church prays: "From famine, pestilence, and war, O Lord, deliver us."

2330 "Blessed are the peacemakers, for they shall be called sons of God" (Mt 5:9).

ENDNOTES

1. *EV*, 53.
2. Richard Butler, O.P. *Responding to God*, 219.
3. Cf. CCC, 2263-2267.
4. Cf. Ibid., 2259-2262; 2297-2298.
5. Cf. Ibid., 2288-2291.
6. Cf. Ibid., 2268-2269.
7. Cf. Ibid., 2297-2298.
8. DoV, 1, 1.
9. *EV*, 60.
10. Ibid., 62.
11. Cf. CIC, 1398.
12. EV, 69-70.
13. Ibid., 56.
14. Ibid., 56.
15. Avery Cardinal Dulles, "Catholicism and Capital Punishment." *First Things*, April 2001.
16. *GS*, 19.
17. Ibid., 22.
18. *SD*, 31.
19. IOE, 14.
20. *EV*, 65.
21. Cf. CCC, 2284.
22. *GS*, 78.
23. Cf. CCC, 2297-2298.
24. *GS*, 77.
25. Cf. CCC, 2292-2296.
26. CHCW, 88.
27. Cf. Ibid., 94-99.
28. Ibid., 65.
29. *SD*, 30-31.
30. CHCW, 69-70.

Chapter 15

The Sixth And Ninth Commandments:

You Shall Not Commit Adultery. You Shall Not Covet Your Neighbor's Wife.

Now when Jesus had finished these sayings, he went away from Galilee and entered the region of Judea beyond the Jordan; and large crowds followed him, and he healed them there.

And Pharisees came up to him and tested him by asking, "Is it lawful to divorce one's wife for any cause?" He answered, "Have you not read that he who made them from the beginning made them male and female, and said, 'For this reason a man shall leave his father and mother and be joined to his wife, and the two shall become one'? So they are no longer two but one. What therefore God has joined together, let no man put asunder." They said to him, "Why then did Moses command one to give a certificate of divorce, and to put her away?" He said to them, "For your hardness of heart Moses allowed you to divorce your wives, but from the beginning it was not so. And I say to you: whoever divorces his wife, except for unchastity, and marries another, commits adultery; and he who marries a divorced woman commits adultery." (Mt 19:1-9)

In this passage of Scripture, Jesus strongly defends the dignity of marriage as created by the Father. Many people in Western societies today have begun to question the value or even the necessity of marriage.

In light of this, it is helpful to consider the following questions:

- What is the nature and purpose of marriage?
- Why do Christians view marriage as more than a social or legal contract?
- In what way does marriage provide for the good of children?
- Why does any use of our human sexuality outside marriage tend toward the loss of our personal dignity?
- How does the virtue of chastity protect both personal dignity and the integrity of marriage?
- What are some trends in modern society that tend to undermine marriage?

Marriage is a fundamental and natural part of human life.

"Be fruitful and multiply..."

INTRODUCTION

Marriage is a fundamental and natural part of human life. There are only a few reasons—usually very elevated ones—for voluntarily and freely renouncing marriage, such as needing to give attention to one's existing family or giving oneself to God in religious life, the priesthood, or the apostolate of the faithful.

Regarding marriage, God created man and woman with natural sexual differences. One's gender describes not only the constitution of one's body, but also one's very identity: Sexuality affects us at the most elementary level of personhood. To insure the continuation of the race, the Father has created man and woman with a strong attraction to each other that must be understood and respected if serious sin is to be avoided.

1. MAN AND WOMAN CREATED IN A STATE OF MARRIAGE

At the very beginning of the Bible, man and woman appear united as husband and wife. Genesis contains two complementary narratives of the appearance of the human couple:

a. THE FIRST CREATION STORY

The first chapter describes the simultaneous creation of man and woman in these words:

> Then God said, "Let us make man in our image, after our likeness; and let them have dominion over the fish of the sea, and over the

> birds of the air, and over the cattle, and over all the earth, and over every creeping thing that creeps upon the earth." So God created man in his own image, in the image of God he created him; male and female he created them. And God blessed them, and God said to them, "Be fruitful and multiply, and fill the earth and subdue it; and have dominion over the fish of the sea and over the birds of the air and over every living thing that moves upon the earth." (Gn 1: 26-28)

This unity is so intimate that, in biblical language, it will form "one flesh."

6. THE SECOND CREATION STORY

The second chapter gives us a complementary story. The biblical writer relates the following words from the mouth of God:

> "Then the Lord God said, 'It is not good that the man should be alone; I will make him a helper fit for him.'" (Gn 2: 18) The narration shows the equality of man and woman through the creation of woman from the very body of man:
>
> [A]nd the rib which the Lord God had taken from the man he made into a woman and brought her to the man. Then the man said,
>
> "This at last is bone of my bones and flesh of my flesh; she shall be called Woman, because she was taken out of Man."
>
> Therefore a man leaves his father and his mother and cleaves to his wife, and they become one flesh. And the man and his wife were both naked, and were not ashamed. (Gn 2: 22-25)

If we consider these two narrations in parallel, we can deduce the following truths:

- Man and woman are equal in dignity: God created both in his own image and likeness.
- Man and woman are destined to form a new social unit. For that reason, man and woman will leave their fathers and mothers to become a new family.
- This unity is so intimate that, in biblical language, it will form "one flesh": Husband and wife will become "two in one."
- The man-woman relationship, united in marriage, has a procreative end. God directed his blessing precisely to this end.

According to the Bible and the natural law, the origin of a new human life should take place within marriage.

2. THE PROCREATION OF HUMAN LIFE IN THE FAMILY

According to the Bible and the natural law, the origin of a new human life should take place within marriage. For this reason, one is forbidden to seek the works of the flesh outside of marriage. From the first pages of the Bible, we can see that the Father creates man and woman united in marriage with the end of procreation (cf. Gn 1: 28).

This intention of God for marriage is so fundamental that all cultures have condemned procreation outside of matrimony. This same teaching is in the New Testament, with the condemnation of fornication and adultery (cf. Mt 15: 19; Mk 7: 21).

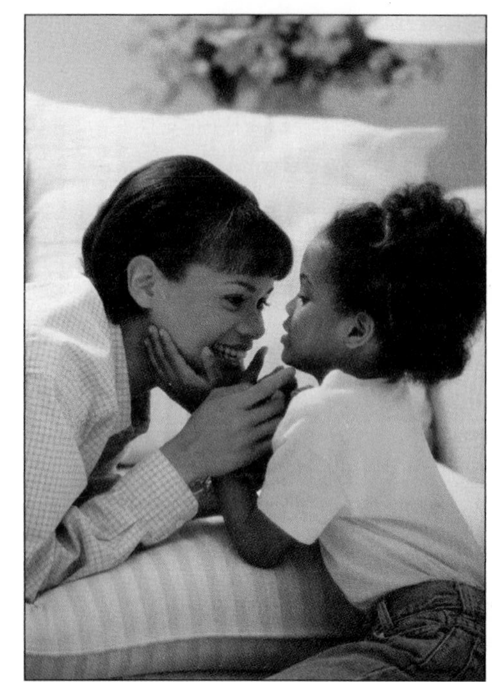

Every person has the right to be born of a known man and a known woman, whom he can call father and mother, and to carry out his normal existence in a home. This should be emphasized because a child is born a helpless creature and needs the assistance of his parents for quite a long time. A child has both a material and a spiritual need for the continuous and prolonged attention of his parents.

The family is the foundation of society. Nonetheless, a new life begun outside of matrimony should be protected and should share the same rights as a baby born inside marriage, since the child is not responsible for the illegitimacy and even less for the sin of his parents.

3. PURPOSES OF MARRIAGE

a. GOOD OF THE SPOUSES

The sexual union of a husband and wife in marriage is noble and honorable. The performance of this act fosters their complete self-giving and deepens their love for one another. This union is a most unique gift, for the gift can be received in its proper sense only as a result of its first being given to the other in marriage. It is both a sign and a cause of the perfect union with one another to which the Holy Spirit calls them.

A child has both a material and a spiritual need for the continuous and prolonged attention of his parents.

b. PROCREATION

The structure of conjugal love is a participation in a great mystery that, taken as a whole, results directly in the procreation of new life. When a couple participates in the procreation of new life, they are cooperating with God in the creation of their children. This is fundamentally different from simple reproduction.

> Marriage and married love are by nature ordered to the procreation and education of children. Indeed children are the supreme gift of marriage and greatly contribute to the good of the parents themselves. God himself said: "It is not good that man should be alone" (Gn 2: 18), and "from the beginning (he) made them male and female" (Mt 19: 4); wishing to associate them in a special way with his own creative work, God blessed man and woman with the words: "Be fruitful and multiply" (Gn 1: 28). Without intending to underestimate the other ends of marriage, it must be said that true married love and the whole structure of family life which results from it is directed to disposing the spouses to cooperate valiantly with the love of the Creator and Saviour, who through them will increase and enrich his family from day to day.[1]

Children are always a source of joy when they are born out of the parents' love for one another. The Church, following the testimony of Sacred Scripture, has traditionally viewed large families as a sign of God's blessing and the generosity of the parents.[2]

4. JOYS OF MARRIAGE

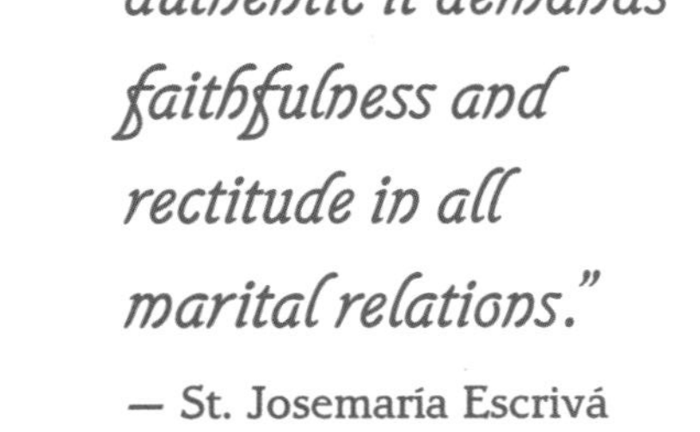

"When love is authentic it demands faithfulness and rectitude in all marital relations."

— St. Josemaría Escrivá

The marital act, when done as God wills, gives glory to God, and is needed to achieve the perfect union between spouses. Far from believing sex to be tainted or somehow dirty, as some erroneously think, the Church upholds its dignity.

> The love of the spouses requires, of its very nature, the unity and indissolubility of the spouses' community of persons, which embraces their entire life: "so they are no longer two, but one flesh."[3] They "are called to grow continually in their communion through day-to-day fidelity to their marriage promise of total mutual self-giving."[4] This human communion is confirmed, purified, and completed by communion in Jesus Christ, given through the sacrament of Matrimony. It is deepened by lives of the common faith and by the Eucharist received together. (CCC 1644)

Sexual intercourse, by which the intimate and chaste union of the spouses takes place, is noble and honorable; the performance of these acts, by the grace of the Sacrament of Matrimony, fosters the self-giving they signify and enriches the spouses in joy and gratitude.

The Creator himself established that spouses should experience pleasure and enjoyment of the body and spirit in the marital act. Therefore, the spouses do nothing evil in seeking this pleasure and enjoyment as long as the natural purpose of the act is honored. Whether or not a conception results from their conjugal union, the spouses accept what the Creator has intended for them.

As Saint Josemaría Escrivá wrote:

> When love is authentic it demands faithfulness and rectitude in all marital relations. St. Thomas Aquinas comments that God has joined to the exercise of the different functions of human life a pleasure or satisfaction, which is, therefore, something good. But if man, inverting the proper order of things, seeks satisfaction as an aim in itself, in contempt of the good to which it is joined and which is its aim, he perverts its true nature and converts it into a sin, or an occasion of sin.[5]

5. PROPERTIES OF MARRIAGE

From this teaching, one can deduce that matrimony is characterized by two essential properties: exclusivity and indissolubility.

a. EXCLUSIVITY

Since marriage involves a total self-giving from each spouse, it follows that this gift cannot be shared with a third party, in which case it would be incomplete. One cannot give oneself totally to more than one person in the same way.

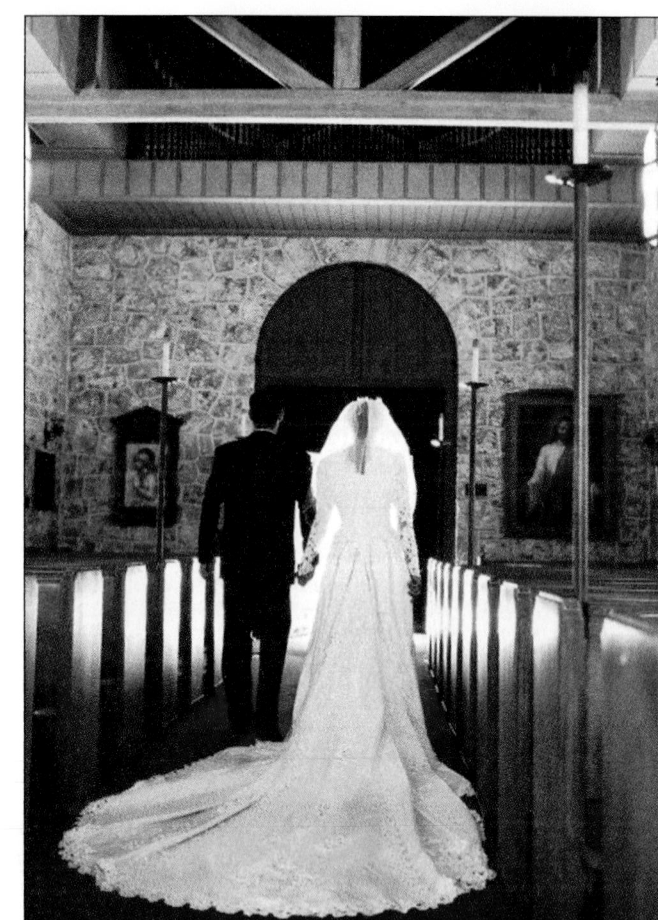

Consequently, polygamy, in its two forms—polygany (having many wives) and polyandry (having many husbands)—violates the nature of matrimony. It is interesting to note that when a society recognizes the dignity of women as being equal to that of men, polygamy disappears in that society.

6. INDISSOLUBILITY

It is evident that marriage demands stability, unlike occasional unions between men and women. But natural morality and Christian revelation strongly state that this stability is permanent; the unit created through the matrimonial bond cannot be divided. We can adduce two arguments: First, if one gives oneself totally to one's spouse, that totality is not complete if it is not lifelong. Second, matrimony unites two people, but not only in isolated acts. Thus, this personal giving of oneself demands lifelong permanency, for it is impossible to give oneself totally to two different persons at the same time.

If we take a deeper look at these arguments, we discover that they are conclusive. They are not derived from only the Christian faith, but rather from the very essence of the matrimonial union of man and woman.

A ratified and consummated sacramental marriage between a baptized man and a baptized woman is indissoluble by any human power.

A Christian also believes that a ratified and consummated sacramental marriage between a baptized man and a baptized woman is indissoluble by any human power or by a cause other than death. Jesus, when asked about divorce, categorically stated the indissolubility of matrimony (cf. Mk 10:2-9).

Jesus states that no human will, neither civil nor ecclesiastical—including the will of the two spouses—has the power to break the link borne of the spouses' self-giving in marriage. It is not accurate to say that the Church does not *grant* divorces (since it is not within its power to do so). Rather, the Church does not *recognize* divorces (since it is impossible to break the sacramental union of a man and woman).

Those who remarry after a civil divorce from a lawful marriage in which the first spouse is still alive are still members of the Church, but may not receive the Eucharist. Any children born of this arrangement should be educated in the faith. However, when no sacramental bond exists, a marriage may be *dissolved* when:

- it is a natural—not sacramental—bond of a legitimate and consummated marriage of non-baptized parties, such as a marriage between two Muslims. This is known as the Pauline Privilege (cf. 1 Cor 7:12-15). The previous marriage is not dissolved by the Church but by a second marriage of either party. The Church merely judges that the necessary conditions for the second marriage are present;[6]

- it is a natural—not sacramental—bond of a legitimate and consummated marriage between a baptized party and a non-baptized party. This is known as the Petrine Privilege. The pope himself, exercising his authority as the Vicar of Christ, makes the decision to dissolve such a non-sacramental marriage in order that a new marital bond—preferably a sacramental one—may be entered;
- it is a non-consummated marriage between baptized persons or between a baptized party and a non-baptized party. Such a marriage can be dissolved only for a just cause, at the request of both parties or one of the parties if the other party is unwilling. A decision of this nature can be made only at the discretion of the Roman Pontiff.[7]

Human sexuality contains psychological components, and is subject to the intellect and will.

In some exceptional cases, the Church may also dissolve a *ratified*, though not *consummated*, marriage among Christians by a papal decision.

6. ANNULMENT

There are obstacles that can prevent two people from contracting a *valid* marriage, such as a lack of full, free, and voluntary consent, an existing prior marriage, or a deficiency in the form (for instance, two Catholics married before a judge). In such circumstances, the Church, after careful investigation by an ecclesiastical court, may issue a *declaration of annulment*. This is a declaration that no true marriage existed from the beginning.

Strictly speaking, therefore, the term *annulment* is incorrect, since the Church cannot nullify a valid marriage. The Church can determine that what was thought to be a valid marriage in fact never was because of some impediment that was not discovered at the time the wedding vows were exchanged.

7. THE DIFFERENT DIMENSIONS OF HUMAN SEXUALITY

The reality of marriage and family makes human sexuality very important. One should distinguish some of the diverse and complementary aspects of human sexuality.

a. HUMAN AFFECTION

Sexuality is not merely an instinct in humans as it is in animals, which is manifested in their very defined cycles. Human sexuality contains psychological components, and is subject to the intellect and will. This is why a person can control and direct it.

For this reason, the proper exercise of sexuality should include affection between the husband and wife. The sexual exercise is considered a personal and loving "meeting" between husband and wife. This joining in love profoundly differs from fleeting sexual relations, in which one looks to satisfy his instincts for temporal pleasure.

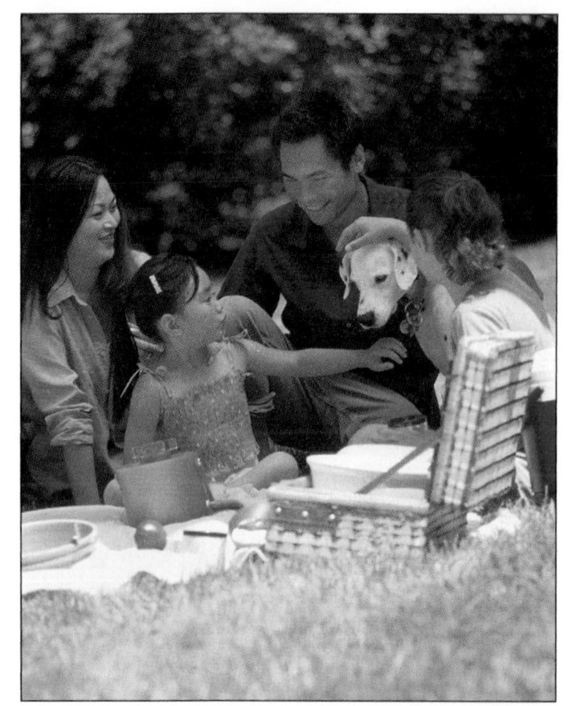

b. PHYSICAL MANIFESTATION

Sexuality obviously manifests itself in the male and female genitalia. Furthermore, sexual intercourse is an important part and normative expression of human sexuality. From the complementariness of male and female genitalia, it is apparent that the exercise of sexuality is meant to be between a man and a woman. Through this unique union of the persons, the bodies and spirits of the couple are drawn closer together. This is one of the principal reasons that there cannot be a marriage between persons of the same gender.

c. PLEASURE

Sexual pleasure is total when sensual joy goes together with the love, affection, and sacrifice that cultivate this joining of the spouses. For this reason, if love is lacking or if one seeks only to satisfy his passions without regard to his spouse, the exercise of sexuality could lead to a separation between the spouses, as it loses its dignity and becomes nothing more than selfishness.

d. PROCREATION

By the Creator's wise design, a natural use of sex includes the harmonious integration of four dimensions: human affection, physical manifestation, pleasure, and procreation.

Procreation synthesizes the three prior dimensions. The human race is required to reproduce itself, and this requirement is manifested in the complementariness of the human genitalia. Human affection, in order to be total and true, must be open to procreation, which adds to the pleasure experienced by the spouses. For these reasons, couples who put up obstacles to conception sin gravely.

Still, marriage and sexual activity carried out within marriage are not exclusively for having children. As the Second Vatican Council teaches:

> **But marriage is not merely for the procreation of children: its nature as an indissoluble compact between two people and the good of the children demand that the mutual love of the partners be properly shown, that it should grow and mature. Even in cases where despite the intense desire of the spouses there are no children, marriage still retains its character of being a whole manner and communion of life and preserves its value and indissolubility.[8]**

It is important to note that marriage gives the couple a right to the procreative act, but it does not give the right to have children. This would require God to make all marriages fertile.

By the Creator's wise design, a natural and human use of sex includes the harmonious integration of these four dimensions involved in human sexuality. If any of these four dimensions are lacking, the use of sex may lead to dissatisfaction, perversity, promiscuity, immorality, and an inversion of the true meaning of love.

8. CATHOLIC DOCTRINE REGARDING SEXUALITY

Christian morality maintains that a person needs to ask the Holy Spirit to help him control his sexual instincts.

Catholic doctrine on human sexuality is in accord with the physiological and psychological nature of the human being. Christian morality respects human nature and takes it as its starting point. In this sense, we should summarize Catholic doctrine with these three basic affirmations:

a. POSITIVE VALUE OF SEXUALITY

Christian morality begins from this fundamental affirmation: Man and woman are destined by God for procreation. The Father created and desires the profound and positive meaning of sexuality. Catholic morality deduces the value of sexuality from biblical passages that tell us about the relationship between God and his people in terms of betrothed love: Jesus is the bridegroom, madly in love with his people—the Church—who are in turn his bride.

For this reason, the Church has always condemned movements that doubted the value of sex. In recent years, when faced with devaluation of sexuality and the resultant proliferation of sexual sins, the Congregation for the Doctrine of the Faith published the declaration *Persona humanae*, which reaffirms the positive meaning of human sexuality.

b. HUMAN CONTROL OF SEXUALITY

Christian morality maintains that a person needs to ask the Holy Spirit to help him control his sexual instincts. If one is to be master of all his energies—physical strength, will, emotions—he must control his sexual instinct. The force of passion is so strong and so instinctive that if a person does not control it, he will be controlled by it.

Therefore, it is important that one be educated in sexuality with the objective of self-control. Education is indispensable for all ages: in puberty, when the sexual instinct awakens; in adolescence, when the desire for closer and more intimate relations begins; and in adulthood, when one has more freedom to use one's sexuality for good or evil. Self-control must be exercised even within marriage, not following blind instincts in conjugal relations, but rather controlling them rationally and with honest love. The *Catechism of the Catholic Church* devotes a large section to encouraging everyone in the "struggle against concupiscence of the flesh."[9]

Self-control education is indispensable for all ages.

c. UPRIGHT USE OF SEXUALITY

As has been stated, the end of sexuality is not exclusively for pleasure, but also for procreation in marriage. For this reason, Catholic morality teaches that the only permissible use of sexuality takes place within marriage. Consequently, extra-marital, pre-marital, homosexual, and solitary sexual acts are forbidden by Christian morality and constitute grave sins. These sins are best prevented through relying on the graces given by the Holy Spirit in daily prayer and frequent reception of the Sacraments.

The virtue that protects chastity is modesty.

9. CHASTITY AS A VIRTUE: PURITY OF BODY AND HEART

Christ is the model for us in relation to chastity, and every baptized person is called to live in his or her particular state of life in a chaste manner. Chastity is the moral virtue that moves a person to moderate the use of the sexual faculties out of love for God and a desire to please him by avoiding anything that would harm the dignity of other people. As such, chastity is another expression of the virtue of temperance. To be chaste, one must integrate the sexual function within the whole person with the help of the Holy Spirit. This self-mastery can be accomplished only by cooperating with the Holy Spirit in training the will to develop the virtue of chastity and avoid temptations that easily lead to unchaste actions.

Without a genuine desire to love God and neighbor and the grace of the Holy Spirit, living chastely is nearly impossible. Furthermore, chastity is also an expression of love for God and neighbor. By chastity, a person shows that he desires to submit his will to the natural purpose for human sexuality, and that he loves his neighbor by avoiding any kind of relationship that treats another person as an object or means to satisfy his own selfish desires.

However, simply abstaining from sexual activity does not mean that a person is living a chaste life. It is important here to remember Jesus' teaching that the hidden thoughts and desires of the human heart are equally sinful as our actions, for it is from these sinful desires that sinful actions are born (cf. Mt 5:27-30; 15:16-20). The person who abstains from illicit sexual activity may be practicing the virtue of *continence*, but it cannot be said that he is living a truly chaste life if he still willfully desires those activities.

The history of Christianity is filled with examples of men and women like St. Maria Goretti who have lived chaste lives, and this fact is sufficient to prove that purity of body and heart is indeed possible. There is an even greater need today for heroism and self-sacrifice in a world where many have given themselves totally to pleasure. Young people especially need role models who are not afraid to be pure, and demonstrate that purity is possible.

The practice of modesty leads to patience, decency, and discretion in one's social relations.

Much of the difficulty arises from the fact that few young people plan to live a life of purity. To be successful in living a chaste life, the correct means must be utilized. These include:

- regular reception of the Sacraments of the Eucharist and Reconciliation,
- complete honesty in confession,
- a prayerful relationship with Jesus and Mary,
- having friends who think and act with purity,
- avoiding occasions and situations in which temptations may arise,
- having pure intentions at all times, and
- keeping the eyes, mind, and moods under control.

Acquiring or preserving the virtue of chastity is not easy, but if a person truly wants to live a pure life, then he must be willing to take the necessary steps and make the sacrifices required to possess this great virtue.

Modesty regulates external behavior, recreation, and the use of clothing.

The virtue that protects chastity is modesty. Modesty regulates external behavior, recreation, and the use of clothing. The practice of modesty leads to patience, decency, and discretion in one's social relations. A Christian has a serious moral obligation to not lead others into sin through conversation or the way he or she dresses. Men and women are obliged to talk and dress according to good taste and self-respect. Clothing exists to cover and protect the body, and must not be used intentionally as a device to lead others to sinful thoughts and activities. Clothing that is considered fashionable may not always be moral. *The Christian is called to be counter-cultural when the culture is counter to Christ.*

10. SINS AGAINST CHASTITY: OLD TESTAMENT TEACHINGS

The goal of sexual life and the satisfaction that comes with it are reached only when the four dimensions of human sexuality are fulfilled. Outside of these aspects, one finds himself en route to evil and sin. Prohibitions against unchastity are not only formulated by Catholic moral theology, but are also found in the Bible and Sacred Tradition. The following is a list of the sins that are condemned in the Old Testament:

- Adultery is sexual relations between a married person and someone other than that person's spouse. Exodus clearly formulates this principle: "You shall not commit adultery" (Ex 20: 14).
- Fornication (or pre-marital sex) is forbidden in an extremely rigorous manner. Besides the moral prohibition, a fine was also included (cf. Dt 22: 20-21, 28-29; Sir 41: 17-34).
- Onanism (the withdrawal of the male member before ejaculation) is condemned in the Old Testament because Onan's intent was contraceptive; he refused to provide offspring for his sister-in-law in his deceased brother's place, as was required by the custom of the time (cf. Gn 38: 4-10).
- Prostitution is prohibited because it uses a person for sexual pleasure.
- Bestiality (sex with an animal) is a vice punished with death (cf. Lv 20: 15-16; Ex 22: 19).
- Incest (sexual activity among relatives) is prohibited (cf. Lv 20:11-12, 17).
- Homosexuality is forbidden, as it is contrary to the nature of man and of the sex act itself (cf. Gn 19:4-10).

The Christian is called to be "counter-cultural" when the culture is counter to Christ.

"For this is the will of God,... that each one of you know how to control his own body in holiness and honor..."

11. SINS AGAINST CHASTITY: NEW TESTAMENT TEACHINGS

In light of the corruption of the pagan world, the apostles warned Christians about letting themselves be contaminated by the evil pagan customs. The Church clearly taught converts to live purity and abandon the vices that they had practiced before.

St. Paul had this to say about the vices of the Romans:

> **Therefore God gave them up in the lusts of their hearts to impurity, to the dishonoring of their bodies among themselves, because they exchanged the truth about God for a lie and worshiped and served the creature rather than the Creator, who is blessed forever! Amen.**
>
> **For this reason God gave them up to dishonorable passions. Their women exchanged natural relations for unnatural, and the men likewise gave up natural relations with women and were consumed with passion for one another, men committing shameless acts with men and receiving in their own persons the due penalty for their error.**
>
> **And since they did not see fit to acknowledge God, God gave them up to a base mind and to improper conduct. (Rom 1: 24-28)**

In other writings, St. Paul warns against every kind of sin of impurity:

> **For this is the will of God, your sanctification: that you abstain from immorality; that each one of you know how to control his own body in holiness and honor, not in the passion of lust like heathen who do not know God; that no man transgress, and wrong his brother in this matter, because the Lord is an avenger in all these things, as we solemnly forewarned you. For God has not called us for uncleanness, but in holiness. (1 Thes 4: 3-7)**

St. Justin Martyr; martyred in Rome, c. 165; also known as Justin the Philosopher

Pagan philosopher who converted at age 30 by reading the Scriptures and witnessing the heroism and faith of martyrs. Used his philosophical skills to debate with pagans and explain the faith. Opened a school of public debate in Rome.

All of the sins against chastity can be found in the writings of St. Paul (cf. 1 Cor 6: 9-11, 15-20; Gal 5: 19-24).

In the same way, Jesus condemns sins of desire: "[E]very one who looks at a woman lustfully has already committed adultery with her in his heart" (Mt 5: 28). This reinforces the Old Testament prohibition of covetousness, and contains a strong pedagogical force, due to the influence that thoughts, will, and emotions have in the area of purity.[10]

12. SINS AGAINST CHASTITY: DOCTRINE OF SACRED TRADITION

Following these biblical teachings, Christian tradition reminded converts that, in conformity with their new life, they should guide their sexual conduct in accord with the ethical norms established in the New Testament. At the beginning of the second century, in a letter addressed to Emperor Antoninus Pius, St. Justin highlights the difference between Christians and pagans in living human sexuality:

> For our Master, not only are they sinners who contract a double marriage..., but also they who look at a woman with desire, since for him they should refuse not only to commit the act of adultery, but also to wish to commit it, just as the wish to be before God is evident not only in works, but also in desires. And among us there are many men and women who having become disciples of Christ as children, remain incorrupt for sixty or seventy years, and I am amazed at the power of this demonstration to all races of man. And this countless crowd of those who have converted after a dissolute life.[11]

13. SINS AGAINST CHASTITY: THE TEACHING OF THE MAGISTERIUM

The Magisterium of the Church—confirming the teaching of the Old Testament, the New Testament and Sacred Tradition—has also urged these same teachings throughout history. Some examples of people whom the *Catechism* names as violating the sixth and ninth commandments are:

- spouses who break their promise of fidelity for life, and do not freely and responsibly accept children by impeding conception with artificial means;
- married persons who have sexual relations outside of marriage and unmarried persons who have pre-marital sexual relations;
- those who have more than one spouse (polygamy);
- those who seek sexual pleasure with another member of the same sex;
- those who seek sexual pleasure with themselves in masturbation;
- those who seek unnatural sexual pleasure through oral or anal sex;
- those who entertain themselves with impure thoughts or desires (covetousness);
- those who induce impure thoughts and desires through magazines, pornographic movies, conversations, etc.[12]

All of the sins against chastity can be found in the writings of St. Paul.

Numerous Church documents attest to the consistent teaching of the Church in regard to matters of chastity. A brief sample of some of these documents may be found in the Supplementary Readings section at the end of this chapter.

14. CHASTITY IN MARRIAGE: RESPONSIBLE PARENTHOOD AND NATURAL FAMILY PLANNING

Life itself is sacred, and because of this very fact, sexual intercourse, unlike other physical actions, is itself also sacred. By it, couples share God's creative power and fatherhood. Every married couple must be aware of their mission to *responsible parenthood*, which requires them to conform their sexual activity to the creative intention of God.[13]

Nevertheless, *responsible parenthood* is not incompatible with recourse to *natural family planning* (NFP). NFP is the practice of engaging or abstaining from intercourse based on the woman's natural cycles of fertility and infertility. NFP is available for those who, for serious reasons, need to postpone a new birth. It requires from the spouses both knowledge and respect of the biological laws that apply to the human person, as well as self-denial in living chastity.

The Magisterium has often repeated the principle that, according to God's design, the unitive and procreative ends of the conjugal act are inseparable. NFP respects and preserves these ends while providing a licit means to postpone conception. The lawful use of NFP involves the use of the temperature method, the ovulation method, or the sympto-thermo method. They may be used under the following conditions:

- Each and every conjugal act must be open to the transmission of life.
- The judgment to use NFP should be made with an upright conscience—a conscience informed by the teachings of the Church.
- The individual couple determines the number of children they wish to have, but they must have serious reasons for using NFP.
- There should be no occasion of sin for either of the spouses, like serious danger of infidelity due to long periods of abstinence.
- Any act for sexual pleasure that by its nature is not directed or destined for the procreating and uniting aspects of married love (like oral sex or self or mutual masturbation) is a grave sin. These acts must not take the place of sexual intercourse.

Each and every conjugal act must be open to the transmission of life.

NFP permits the married couple to plan the number of children they wish to have, while allowing God the option to send additional children if, in his wise providence, he deems otherwise.

15. CONTRACEPTION AND THE DESTRUCTION OF MARRIAGE

Contraception—action against conception—has as its goal the prevention of the transmission of life. It is an abuse of the reproductive faculties, and it violates one of the purposes of marriage. It is a direct refusal or saying "no" to God's plan for one's life and vocation to bring forth new life. Since the Father knows everyone intimately, he alone truly knows the number of children a couple can raise. Contraception is an act that says to God, "I do not trust you in this matter; I will decide for myself."

> **God, who is love and life, has inscribed in man and woman the vocation to share in a special way in his mystery of personal communion and in his work as Creator and Father. For this reason marriage possesses specific goods and values in its union and in procreation which cannot be likened to those existing in lower forms**

> of life. Such values and meanings are of the personal order and determine from the moral point of view the meaning and limits of artificial interventions on procreation and on the origin of human life. These interventions are not to be rejected on the grounds that they are artificial. As such, they bear witness to the possibilities of the art of medicine. But they must be given a moral evaluation in reference to the dignity of the human person, who is called to realize his vocation from God to the gift of love and the gift of life.[14]

To impede the sources of life is intrinsically evil and a violation of the natural law.

Artificial birth control can never conform to Church teaching, even in extreme cases. To impede the sources of life is intrinsically evil and a violation of the natural law, as well as a misuse of the gifts that God has granted to mankind. The use of contraception indicates that a person is moved by fear or selfishness rather than love.

Ironically, spouses who contracept experience less intimacy in the midst of more frequent sexual acts. Love is no longer authentic. It non-verbally communicates: "I accept the part of you that brings pleasure, but not the part that brings forth new life." The innate language of the marital act that expresses the total self-giving of husband and wife is overlaid, through contraception, by an objectively contradictory language, namely that of not giving oneself totally to the other. This leads not only to a positive refusal to be open to life, but also to a betrayal of the inner truth of conjugal love, which ought to be a gift of one's self in personal totality.

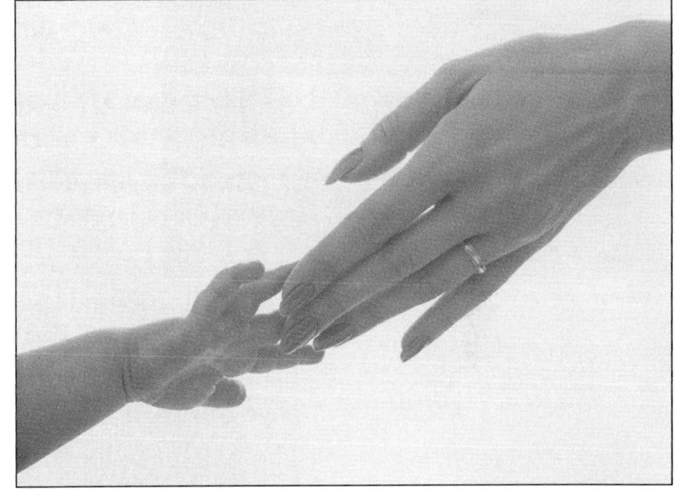

The Catholic Church prohibits the use of artificial birth control, such as the pill, withdrawal, condoms, or the use of an intrauterine device. These can never be used licitly, for they are intrinsically evil. Conversely, when there is chastity in the love of married persons, their marital life is authentic.

While some forms of artificial birth control have contraception as their goal, the actual result is often abortion. Others, such as the IUD, the pill, or the morning-after (abortifacient) pills (e.g. RU-486) are always abortifacients, for they destroy the new life—the already fertilized egg. These abortifacient methods of "contraception" are especially immoral, because, as life begins at conception, they cause the death of a new human life.

16. ASSISTED FERTILIZATION AND ARTIFICIAL INSEMINATION

Today, advances in medicine and biology allow the conception of a human being by a means other than sexual intercourse. These techniques are called artificial insemination or *artificial fertilization.*

Moral judgments concerning these new problems are not found in revelation, because these methods were unknown then. The teachings of the Magisterium help us to make the correct judgments.

Not all that is technically possible is ethically good.

It is clear that the intentions that may lead to the use of artificial fertilization can be noble. Think, for example, about the objective of correcting some disease, or fulfilling the wishes of parents who cannot have children. But the ends do not justify the means, so moral judgment must be directed toward the permissibility of the means used. Catholic ethical doctrine distinguishes four distinct situations:

a. ASSISTED FERTILIZATION

In this case, the sexual act does not result in fertilization because of natural causes, so medical techniques are used to help obtain the desired effect. In a case in which the conjugal act cannot be carried out, or the union of the sperm and the egg is somehow impossible, a doctor can use means to assist the conjugal act, as long as the procedure occurs in conjunction with it, either to facilitate its performance or to enable it to achieve its objective. The liceitness of this assisted fertilization has always been accepted by the Magisterium.[15]

b. HOMOLOGOUS ARTIFICIAL INSEMINATION

This is the name for fertilization outside the conjugal act, but with the sperm of a woman's own husband. This can be done in two ways: inside the body of the woman or in a laboratory. The first kind is called *in vivo* and the second is called *in vitro.*

In vivo fertilization is frequently accomplished by using a needle to place the sperm into the uterus of the woman. Catholic moral doctrine considers it illicit for two reasons. First, the usual means of obtaining sperm from the man—masturbation—is immoral. Secondly, the Magisterium has often repeated the principle that according to God's design, the unitive and procreative ends of the conjugal act are inseparable. This doctrine surprises many Catholics, especially when artificial insemination is the only way to have a child. If medical science makes it possible, why is it considered illicit?

According to God's design, the unitive and procreative ends of the conjugal act are inseparable.

The answer is founded on the general principle: Not all that is technically possible is ethically good. For example, the use of nuclear weapons on civilian targets, while technically possible, is clearly immoral.

> **Artificial insemination as a substitute for the conjugal act is prohibited by reason of the voluntarily achieved dissociation of the two meanings of the conjugal act. Masturbation, through which the sperm is normally obtained, is another sign of this dissociation: even when it is done for the purpose of procreation, the act remains deprived of its unitive meaning.[16]**

In vitro fertilization is carried out outside the mother's body. Several eggs are fertilized in a laboratory and placed inside the womb of the woman. In many cases, the procedure fails and has to be repeated; this is done without consideration for the loss of life involved. The Church judges these techniques to be morally evil because they deny the unitive and procreative ends of the conjugal act. In addition, the fertilized embryo—an unborn child—is often killed or frozen for future use, which clearly offends the dignity of that child, because it is murder in the first case, and in the second, the child is treated as a piece of property.

The Ninth Commandment forbids sinful carnal desires in relation to another person.

c. HETEROLOGOUS ARTIFICIAL INSEMINATION

In this situation, an egg is fertilized with the sperm of someone other than a woman's own husband. There are multiple forms, which could be *in vivo* or *in vitro,* with semen from a known or unknown man. As for the mother, it could be the wife herself, or a "surrogate mother," as in the case of a so-called "rented uterus."

Catholic morality's negative judgment on this issue coincides with many pieces of civil legislation that prohibit it. Besides involving masturbation—which in itself is intrinsically evil—this practice degrades the dignity of the conjugal act and the natural purposes of the human reproductive organs. Furthermore, it deprives the child of the opportunity to be born to a loving mother and father who brought him into life by their mutual self-giving.

The last reason for the disapproval of the Church is respect for the human person, specifically in the natural faculty of transmitting life. For this reason, the Magisterium often calls upon doctors to serve people and their dignity:

> The humanization of medicine, which is insisted upon today by everyone, requires respect for the integral dignity of the human person first of all in the act and at the moment in which the spouses transmit life to a new person.[17]

17. "YOU SHALL NOT COVET YOUR NEIGHBOR'S WIFE."

> St. John distinguishes three kinds of covetousness or concupiscence: lust of the flesh, lust of the eyes, and pride of life (cf. 1 Jn 2:16). In the Catholic catechetical tradition, the ninth commandment forbids carnal concupiscence; the tenth forbids coveting another's goods. (CCC 2514)

To covet is to sinfully desire. In effect, the ninth commandment forbids sinful carnal desires in relation to another person.

Married persons are entitled not only to the actions proper to marriage, but also to enjoy the thoughts that arise directly out of those actions. In other words, a married couple has a right to enjoy considerations of their most intimate actions.

Single persons enjoy no such right, for they are not married. In the tradition of the Catholic Church, single persons who look upon another as a sexual object are guilty of lust, as are married persons who look upon someone other than their spouses in a lustful way.

Not only are spiritual sacrifices and prayer a part of a Christian marriage, but so are sacrifices of time and pleasures.

Jesus said, "every one who looks at a woman lustfully has already committed adultery with her in his heart" (Mt 5:28). This warning applies equally to men and women. One result of original sin is the struggle between flesh and spirit that is part of one's spiritual battle:

> The heart is the seat of moral personality: "Out of the heart come evil thoughts, murder, adultery, fornication..." (Mt 15:19). The struggle against carnal covetousness entails purifying the heart and practicing temperance. (CCC 2517)

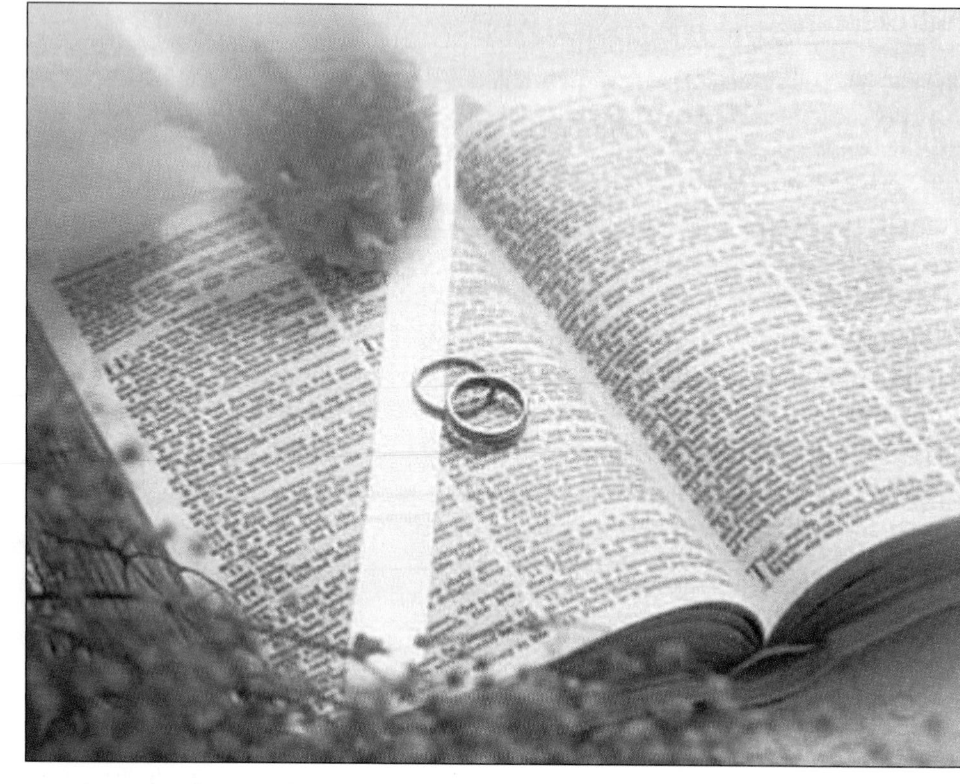

CONCLUSION

When all of the major elements of marriage are present, Christian matrimony is a "great mystery" (Eph 5:32). An important part of this sacrament is the witnessing accomplished by those who conform their marriages to the natural law and the teaching of the Church. And, valuing the sacrament, the spouses will happily accept children and live the moral and ascetical demands of responsible parenthood.

Asceticism (self-discipline and sacrifice) in marriage means living a life in which everything that does not contribute to the salvation of each member of the family is sacrificed. In short, not only are spiritual sacrifices and prayer a part of a Christian marriage, but so are sacrifices of time and pleasures for the good of the family. The greatest sacrifice in marriage is the sacrifice of both individual's will for the common good of the marriage.

VOCABULARY

ADULTERY
A carnal act between a married person and someone to whom he or she is not married.

CHASTITY
The virtue that consists in moderating the sexual appetite according to one's state in life.

CONCUBINAGE
Cohabitation, or "living together," between unmarried persons. Often called "trial marriage."

CONTINENCE
Abstaining from any type of sexual act, as well as from those activities that excite the passions and incline a person to the sexual act.

DECLARATION OF NULLITY
The finding of an ecclesiastical court that a valid marriage never existed from the beginning.

DIVORCE
The authority given to a civil magistrate to separate spouses joined in civil matrimony.

EROTICISM
Exaggeration of the passion for sex and sexual pleasure.

HEDONISM
The philosophy that considers pleasure as the supreme end of life.

INDISSOLUBILITY
A quality of matrimony that the marital union can be broken only by the death of one of the spouses.

LUST
An inordinate desire for sexual pleasure.

MASTURBATION
The deliberate stimulation of the genital organs in order to derive sexual pleasure.

MATRIMONY
The bond between a man and a woman joined in a conjugal union for life. This bond is ordered—through its very nature—to the good of the spouses and the procreation and education of children. This alliance was elevated by Christ to the dignity of a sacrament (cf. CIC, 1055).

MODESTY
The virtue that regulates dress, conversation, and conduct in relation to the individual and society according to faith and right reason.

POLYGAMY
A man's being married to two or more wives (polygyny), or a woman's being married to two or more husbands (polyandry).

PORNOGRAPHY
Any written, visual, or audible material that excites the sexual appetite.

SEXUALITY
The group of anatomical and physiological conditions that characterize many organic beings, and through which they are either male or female. In human beings, psychological conditions are also included in sexuality.

UNITY
The quality derived from the essence of the marital contract itself that demands that marriage be carried out between one man and one woman.

SUPPLEMENTARY READINGS

1. Dear friends in Christ: As you know, you are about to enter into a union which is most sacred and most serious, a union which was established by God himself. By it, he gave to us a share in the greatest work of creation, the work of the continuation of the human race. And in this way he sanctified human love and enabled man and woman to help each other live as children of God, by sharing a common life under his fatherly care.

Because God himself is thus its author, marriage is of its very nature a holy institution, requiring of those who enter into it a complete and unreserved giving of self. But Christ our Lord added to the holiness of marriage an even deeper meaning and a higher beauty. He referred to the love of marriage to describe his own love for his Church, that is, for the people of God whom he redeemed by his own blood. And so he gave to Christians a new vision of what married life ought to be, a life of self-sacrificing love like his own. It is for this reason that his apostle, St. Paul, clearly states that marriage is now and for all time to be considered a great mystery, intimately bound up with the supernatural union of Christ and the Church, which union is also to be its pattern.

This union then is most serious, because it will bind you together for life in a relationship so close and so intimate that it will profoundly influence your whole future. That future, with its hopes and disappointments, its successes and its failures, its pleasures and its pains, its joys and its sorrows, is hidden from your eyes. You know that these elements are mingled in every life and are to be expected in your own. And so, not knowing what is before you, you take each other for better or for worse, for richer or for poorer, in sickness and in health, until death.

Truly, then, these words are most serious. It is a beautiful tribute to your undoubted faith in each other, that, recognizing their full import, you are nevertheless so willing and ready to pronounce them. And because these words involve such solemn obligations, it is most fitting that you rest the security of your wedded life upon the great principle of self-sacrifice. And so you begin your married life by the voluntary and complete surrender of your individual lives in the interest of that deeper and wider life which you are to have in common. Henceforth you belong entirely to each other; you will be one in mind, one in heart, and one in affections. And whatever sacrifices you may hereafter be required to make to preserve this common life, always make them generously. Sacrifice is usually difficult and irksome. Only love can make it easy; and perfect love can make it a joy. We are willing to give in proportion as we love. And when love is perfect, the sacrifice is complete. God so loved the world that he gave his only begotten Son, and the Son so loved us that he gave himself for our salvation. "Greater love than this no one has, that one lay down his life for his friends."

No greater blessing can come to your married life than pure conjugal love, loyal and true to the end. May, then, this love with which you join your hands and hearts today, never fail, but grow deeper and stronger as the years go on. And if true love and the unselfish spirit of perfect sacrifice guide your every action, you can expect the greatest measure of earthly happiness that may be allotted to man in this vale of tears. The rest is in the hands of God. [Nor will God be wanting to your needs; he will pledge you the lifelong support of his graces in the holy sacrament which you are now going to receive].

— Liturgikon, *Rite of Marriage*

SUPPLEMENTARY READINGS CONTINUED

2. According to contemporary scientific research, the human person is so profoundly affected by sexuality that it must be considered as one of the factors which give to each individual's life the principal traits that distinguish it. In fact it is from sex that the human person receives the characteristics which, on the biological, psychological and spiritual levels, make that person a man or a woman, and thereby largely condition his or her progress towards maturity and insertion into society. Hence sexual matters, as is obvious to everyone, today constitute a theme frequently and openly dealt with in books, reviews, magazines and other means of social communication.

— PH, 1

3. All is common among us—except our wives. At that point we dissolve our partnership, which is the one place where the rest of men make it effective. Not only do they use the wives of their friends, but also most patiently yield their own to their friends. They follow (I take it) the example of those who went before them, the wisest of men—Greek Socrates and Roman Cato, who shared with their friends the wives they had taken in marriage, to bear children in other families too. And I don't know whether the wives objected; for why would they care about a chastity, which their husbands gave away so easily? O model of Attic wisdom! O pattern of Roman dignity! The philosopher, a panderer, and the censor, too!

— Tertullian, *Apologia*, XXXIX, 11-13

4. Experience teaches us that love must find its safeguard in the stability of marriage, if sexual intercourse is truly to respond to the requirements of its own finality and to those of human dignity. These requirements call for a conjugal contract sanctioned and guaranteed by society—a contract which establishes a state of life of capital importance both for the exclusive union of the man and the woman and for the good of their family and of the human community. Most often, in fact, premarital relations exclude the possibility of children. What is represented to be conjugal love is not able, as it absolutely should be, to develop into paternal and maternal love. Or, if it does happen to do so, this will be to the detriment of the children, who will be deprived of the stable environment in which they ought to develop in order to find in it the way and the means of their insertion into society as a whole.

The consent given by people who wish to be united in marriage must therefore be manifested externally and in a manner which makes it valid in the eyes of society.

— PH, 7

SUPPLEMENTARY READINGS CONTINUED

5. In the pastoral field, homosexuals must certainly be treated with understanding and sustained in the hope of overcoming their personal difficulties and their inability to fit into society. Their culpability will be judged with prudence. But no pastoral method can be employed which would give moral justification to these acts on the grounds that they would be consonant with the condition of such people. For according to the objective moral order, homosexual relations are acts which lack an essential and indispensable finality. In Sacred Scripture they are condemned as a serious depravity and even presented as the sad consequence of rejecting God. This judgment of Scripture does not of course permit us to conclude that all those who suffer from this anomaly are personally responsible for it, but it does attest to the fact that homosexual acts are intrinsically disordered and can in no case be approved of.

— PH, 8

6. Whatever the force of certain arguments of a biological and philosophical nature, which have sometimes been used by theologians, in fact both the Magisterium of the Church—in the course of a constant tradition—and the moral sense of the faithful have declared without hesitation that masturbation is an intrinsically and seriously disordered act. The main reason is that, whatever the motive for acting this way, the deliberate use of the sexual faculty outside normal conjugal relations essentially contradicts the finality of the faculty. For it lacks the sexual relationship called for by the moral order, namely the relationship which realizes "the full sense of mutual self-giving and human procreation in the context of true love." [*GS*, 51] All deliberate exercise of sexuality must be reserved to this regular relationship. Even if it cannot be proved that Scripture condemns this sin by name, the tradition of the Church has rightly understood it to be condemned in the New Testament when the latter speaks of "impurity," "unchasteness" and other vices contrary to chastity and continence.

— PH, 9

7. For a Christian, marriage is not just a social institution, much less a mere remedy for human weakness. It is a real supernatural calling. A great sacrament, in Christ and in the Church, says St. Paul. At the same time, it is a permanent contract between a man and a woman. Whether we like it or not, the sacrament of matrimony, instituted by Christ, cannot be dissolved. It is a permanent contract that sanctifies in cooperation with Jesus Christ. He fills the souls of husband and wife and invites them to follow him. He transforms their whole married life into an occasion for God's presence on earth.

— Saint Josemaría Escrivá,
Christ Is Passing By, 23

"He fills the souls of husband and wife and invites them to follow him."

SUPPLEMENTARY READINGS CONTINUED

8. [C]onjugal love requires in husband and wife an awareness of their mission of "responsible parenthood," which today is rightly much insisted upon, and which also must be exactly understood. Consequently it is to be considered under aspects which are legitimate and connected with one another.

In relation to the biological processes, responsible parenthood means the knowledge and respect of their functions; human intellect discovers in the power of giving life biological laws which are part of the human person.

In relation to the tendencies of instinct or passion, responsible parenthood means that necessary dominion which reason and will must exercise over them.

In relation to physical, economic, psychological and social conditions, responsible parenthood is exercised, either by the deliberate and generous decision to raise a large family, or by the decision, made for grave motives and with due respect for the moral law, to avoid for the time being, or even for an indeterminate period, a new birth.

Responsible parenthood also and above all implies a more profound relationship to the objective moral order established by God, of which a right conscience is the faithful interpreter. The responsible exercise of parenthood implies, therefore, that husband and wife recognize fully their own duties towards God, towards themselves, towards the family and towards society, in a correct hierarchy of values.

In the task of transmitting life, therefore, they are not free to proceed completely at will, as if they could determine in a wholly autonomous way the honest path to follow; but they must conform their activity to the creative intention of God, expressed in the very nature of marriage and of its acts, and manifested by the constant teaching of the Church.

— *HV*, 10

9. The Church has always been mindful of the relation between spirit and flesh; this has shown up in her definitions of the double nature of Christ, as well as in her care for what may seem to have nothing to do with religion—such as contraception. The Church is all of a piece. Her prohibition against the frustration of the marriage act has its true center perhaps in the doctrine of the resurrection of the body. This again is a *spiritual* doctrine, and beyond our comprehension. The Church doesn't say what this body will look like, but the doctrine proclaims the value of what is least about us, our flesh. We are told that it will be transfigured in Christ, that what is human will flower when it is united with the Spirit.

The Catholic can't think of birth control in relation to expediency but in relation to the nature of man under God. He has to find another solution to the problem.

— *Flannery O'Connor Collected Works*, "Letter to Cecil Dawkins," 23 December 1959, p. 1117

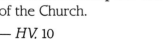

ADVANCED CONCEPTS

1. PRE-MARITAL SEX

There is a time and a place for everything. For sex, the time and place is within marriage, which gives grace to the spouses to love each other in Christian charity.

Only within marriage does human sexuality achieve its full sense and perfection as a vehicle for a love that is mutual, exclusive, permanent, and total self-giving between a man and a woman. *Sex cannot be a manifestation of love if it violates God's plan.*

When a society permits sexual behavior to be torn from its moorings in human love and marriage, when it treats sex as a mechanism for personal pleasure, it encourages a destructive mentality and diminishes the value of personal commitment, and human life itself.

The purposes of sex are procreation and the conjugal union between husband and wife. There is an inseparable connection between the unifying and the procreative significance of the marriage act that human beings may not break on their own initiative.

At the same time, the marital act unites husband and wife in the closest intimacy, and makes them capable of generating new life together. This union fosters the mutual self-giving of the spouses: by means of the reciprocal gift that is proper and exclusive to them, husband and wife tend toward that communion of their beings whereby they help each other toward personal perfection in order to collaborate with the Father in the begetting and rearing of new life.

The Church teaches that these two aspects of marital intercourse—the strengthening of interpersonal unity between spouses and the procreation of new life—are two inseparable goods. For this reason, separation of sex from marriage is one of the great contemporary sins. Sex without marriage goes against the plan that the Father had from the beginning.

Sexuality—by which man and woman give themselves to one another through the acts that are proper and exclusive to spouses—is not simply biological, but concerns the innermost being of the human person. It is achieved in a truly human way only if it is an integral part of the love by which a man and a woman commit themselves totally to each other until death. The total *physical* self-giving is a lie if it is not the sign and fruit of a total *personal* self-giving, in which the whole person (including the temporal dimension) is present: If the person were to withhold something, he or she would not be giving totally.

Sex outside the bonds of marriage involves selfishness, which is contrary to the plan of God. It treats sex not as the giving of oneself exclusively and forever to another, but rather as a satisfaction of a momentary urge or need, no more significant or important than the urge or need itself. The sexual act between husband and wife, on the other hand, when done in accordance with the plan of the Father, is both sacred and holy. Used correctly, sex becomes a joyful affirmation of true love between husband and wife.

When there is impurity, love is stifled, blinded, and questioned. Impurity is a mere self-centered pursuit of pleasure without commitment or responsibility. Through concupiscence, a person tends to treat another human being as his own possession. Signs of affection between unmarried persons are right and good when they are in keeping with the demands of modesty and are true signs of pure love. They must not be actions that arouse passions.

ADVANCED CONCEPTS CONTINUED

2. MORE ON CONTRACEPTION

Considering God as the ultimate cause of all things, we should keep in mind that there is a creative act of God at the origin of every human person. No one comes into existence by chance; he or she is always the object of God's creative love. From this fundamental truth of faith, it follows that the procreative capacity, inscribed in human sexuality, is, in its deepest truth, a cooperation with the Father's creative power. And it also follows that man and woman are neither the arbiters of this capacity nor its masters. The biological phenomenon of human reproduction, wherein the human person finds his or her beginning, also has its end in the emergence of a new person, unique and unrepeatable, made in the image and likeness of God.

The use of contraception deprives the marital act of its sacred nature, saying "no" to the transmission and to the value of life. Furthermore, once the primary purpose of sexual relations is excluded, there is little to distinguish it from other sexual perversions (pre-marital sex, masturbation) which seek as their primary end sensual satisfaction without openness to life.

In the conjugal act, husband and wife are called to confirm in a responsible way the mutual gift of self that they have made to each other in the marriage covenant. The logic of the total gift of self to the other involves a potential openness to procreation: in this way the marriage is called to even greater fulfillment as a family. Certainly, the mutual gift of husband and wife does not have the begetting of children as its only end, but is in itself a mutual communion of love and of life. The intimate truth of this gift must always be safeguarded. The person can never be considered a means to an end; above all never a means of "pleasure." The person is—and must be nothing other than—the end of every act. Only then does the action correspond to the true dignity of the person.

No one comes into existence by chance; he or she is always the object of God's creative love.

QUESTIONS

1. Where is the ultimate meaning of marriage found?
2. In what state did God create man and woman?
3. What four truths can be deduced from the creation story?
4. What are the two purposes of marriage?
5. What are the two essential properties of marriage?
6. Explain the ways in which married love is fruitful.
7. What is an annulment?
8. List the different dimensions of human sexuality.
9. List the three points of Catholic doctrine in regard to sexuality.
10. List the aids to purity.
11. List the sins against the sixth and ninth commandments condemned by the Old Testament.
12. How are these condemnations reflected in the New Testament?
13. List the sins against chastity forbidden by the Magisterium.
14. Why is contraception wrong?
15. What is assisted fertilization?
16. Why is artificial insemination wrong? Is it ever morally permissible?
17. What is an abortifacient?
18. What harm is caused by sex outside of marriage? Why is even oral sex considered wrong?
19. What does the ninth commandment forbid?
20. What does asceticism in marriage mean?

PRACTICAL EXERCISES

1. Comment on the following text defining matrimony contained in the *Code of Canon Law:*

The marriage covenant, by which a man and a woman establish between themselves a partnership of their whole life, and which of its own very nature is ordered to the well-being of the spouses and to the procreation and upbringing of children, has, between the baptised, been raised by Christ the Lord to the dignity of a sacrament.[18]

2. Analyze Supplementary Reading 8 and outline the principle characteristics of "responsible parenthood," according to the encyclical *Humanae vitae.*

3. Explain why the following statements and ideas are seriously erroneous:

- "For me, premarital sex is not a sin because I love my boyfriend and we are planning to get married someday."
- "My wife and I don't intend to have any children. The world is overpopulated already, and it would be irresponsible to bring more children into such a situation."
- "Masturbation isn't wrong because it is normal and doesn't hurt anyone."
- "If a person is not happy with his or her marriage, then he or she should get a divorce. It's stupid to stay with someone when you're unhappy."
- "Calling those sex talk numbers is okay because they are just harmless fantasies, and I am not involved in any sexual activity."

PRACTICAL EXERCISES CONTINUED

4. Kimberly is engaged to Marcus and thinks they should discuss the number of children they will have. Whenever she brings up the subject, he says he doesn't want to think about children yet, and that they can decide after they are married. Should Kimberly be concerned about his attitude? Explain. Do you think that this is a good approach to marriage in general? Why or why not?

5. Katie has been dating Matt for six months. She feels that their kissing has gone too far but is afraid to say anything out of fear of losing him. At the same time, she is afraid that he will soon try to go farther than simply kissing, although she hopes that this won't happen. She has confided all this to you, and you can see that she is very uncertain about what to do. Do you see any danger signs in this relationship? What do you think are the chances that Matt will try to go too far? What would you advise her to do next?

6. Imagine that you and your boyfriend/girlfriend are double-dating with the following couples. How would you react to the following situations, and what would you say to the people involved?

- You are at your senior prom with José and Marisa. José suggested they get a hotel room for the night and told Marisa, "Don't worry; there are two double beds in the room. You can sleep in one; I'll sleep in the other."
- You and your boyfriend/girlfriend have gone to a party at a friend's house with Gino and Anne. Upon arrival, you discover that there is a lot of alcohol making its way around the party. You overhear Gino saying to Anne, "You can drink as much as you like; you're safe with me."

7. Javier and Melanie are young newlyweds, married for just over two years. They already have two children and have decided that they do not want to have any more. Since he is skeptical of other methods of contraception, Javier thinks that they should seek sterilization as a solution. Melanie objects, saying that this would be a sin. She proposes that they simply use natural family planning to prevent pregnancy, arguing that because it is a natural method and is approved by the Church, they would not be committing a sin. There are three problems with both Javier's and Melanie's dispositions and their reasoning according to Catholic moral teaching. What are they?

8. Tania and David have been married for just over five years. They love each other very much, but they have never been able to have children. They started fighting regularly over a year ago. After a year filled with petty arguments and a great deal of stress, Tania is thinking that maybe it is time to call it quits. When she raises the subject with her sister Emily, Emily suggests that Tania should seek an annulment and not just a divorce. Emily tells Tania that an annulment is a sort of "Catholic divorce" and that she had better get one if she ever wants to get married in the Church again. Is Emily's description of an annulment correct? What is a declaration of nullity, and is there any evidence given that would support Tania's seeking one? What advice would you give Tania regarding her marital problems?

FROM THE CATECHISM

1659 St. Paul said: "Husbands, love your wives, as Christ loved the Church....This is a great mystery, and I mean in reference to Christ and the Church" (Eph 5: 25, 32).

2394 Christ is the model of chastity. Every baptized person is called to lead a chaste life, each according to his particular state of life.

2397 The covenant which spouses have freely entered into entails faithful love. It imposes on them the obligation to keep their marriage indissoluble.

2399 The regulation of births represents one of the aspects of responsible fatherhood and motherhood. Legitimate intentions on the part of the spouses do not justify recourse to morally unacceptable means (for example, direct sterilization or contraception).

2400 Adultery, divorce, polygamy, and free union are grave offenses against the dignity of marriage.

2528 "Everyone who looks at a woman lustfully has already committed adultery with her in his heart" (Mt 5: 28).

2529 The ninth commandment warns against lust or carnal concupiscence.

ENDNOTES

1. *GS*, 50.
2. Cf. CCC, 1652.
3. Mt 19: 6; cf. Gn 2: 24.
4. *FC*, 19.
5. St. Josemaría Escrivá, *Christ is Passing By*, 25.
6. Cf. CIC, 1143.
7. Cf. Ibid., 1142.
8. *GS*, 50.
9. CCC, 2520; cf. 2521-2527.
10. Cf. Ibid., 2514-2519; 2531-2533.
11. St. Justin, 1 *Apologia* XV, 5-7.
12. Cf. CCC, 2351-2359.
13. Cf. *HV*, 11.
14. DoV, 3.
15. Cf. Pius XII, *Discourse to the Fourth International Congress of Physicians*, September 29, 1949.
16. DoV, II, 6.
17. Ibid., II, 7.
18. CIC, 1055.

Chapter 16

The Seventh And Tenth Commandments:

You Shall Not Steal.
You Shall Not Covet Your Neighbor's Goods.

God destined the earth and all it contains for all men and all peoples so that all created things would be shared fairly by all mankind under the guidance of justice tempered by charity. No matter what the structures of property are in different peoples, according to various and changing circumstances and adapted to their lawful institutions, we must never lose sight of this universal destination of earthly goods. In his use of things man should regard the external goods he legitimately owns not merely as exclusive to himself but common to others also, in the sense that they can benefit others as well as himself...

Private property or some form of ownership of external goods assures a person a highly necessary sphere for the exercise of his personal and family autonomy and ought to be considered as an extension of human freedom.[1]

Catholic teaching has always maintained the right of individuals to own private property. Yet because original sin distorts our perceptions, we should ask ourselves the following questions:

- What is the relationship of humans to the material goods of this world?
- How does one maintain a balance between private ownership of goods and the demands of Christian charity?

Passages of Genesis indicate the intimate relationship that the Father establishes between humans and exterior reality.

INTRODUCTION

Catholic social teaching, from Leo XIII through Benedict XVI, has been a cry for justice in the economic and moral wilderness of modern society. The Church has spoken time after time the truth that economic systems must serve the common good. Social progress is possible only on the basis of sound moral principles.

Both the human person and the family have priority over the state, with the latter existing to serve the former, not vice versa. While individual and private initiatives should be encouraged as the best way of producing wealth, morality must supersede pure competition in decisions concerning the distribution of goods. The Church has a right to make judgments regarding social and economic matters when it is a question of fundamental rights or the salvation of souls. The achievement of the common good in this life is directly related to the quest for eternal life.

Property must always be used in accordance with what best serves the common good. Wages paid to a breadwinner should be sufficient for the support of a family, so that people have the opportunity to dedicate themselves wholly to the rearing and education of their children. Human beings have a fundamental right to form and act through their own private associations (labor unions, for example) unobstructed by the power of the state. The resources of human labor must be recognized and protected as more valuable and more important than capital or material resources. Social actions should be carried out at the appropriate level—in other words, where possible, the individual should act on behalf of himself or others, through his work, his family, the local community, and so on. The *principle of subsidiarity* states that the function of lower levels of society should not be usurped by higher levels except when necessary.

In this chapter, we will explain the moral principles concerning human rights and duties, and the injustices that keep us from achieving peace and social justice.

The purpose of the world's material resources is to serve humanity.

1. BIBLICAL DOCTRINE CONCERNING HUMAN RELATIONS TO MATERIAL THINGS

According to the Bible, God created the world with its multitude of things and variety of animals. And he gave everything to man, so that he may be lord over it. Human dominion over creation is described in this way in Genesis:

> **Then God said, "Let us make man in our image, after our likeness; and let them have dominion over the fish of the sea, and over the birds of the air, and over the cattle, and over all the earth, and over every creeping thing that creeps upon the earth." (Gn 1: 26)**

Immediately following this, God explains the purpose of created things: They are destined for the use and service of humanity:

> **And God said, "Behold, I have given you every plant yielding seed which is upon the face of all the earth, and every tree with seed in its fruit; you shall have them for food." (Gn 1: 29)**

With figurative language, Genesis narrates the superiority and dominion of humans over all creation:

> **So out of the ground the Lord God formed every beast of the field and every bird of the air, and brought them to the man to see what he would call them; and whatever the man called every living creature, that was its name. The man gave names to all cattle, and to the birds of the air, and to every beast of the field. (Gn 2: 19-20)**

2. UNIVERSAL DESTINY OF CREATED GOODS

The passages of Genesis indicate the intimate relationship that the Father establishes between humans and exterior reality. These texts contain at least five truths:

- Human superiority over the rest of creation is indicated by the fact that man "gave them their names."
- The purpose of the world's material resources is to serve humanity.
- People can be served by all things, but our dominion is not absolute: We can use them, but must also protect and develop them.
- Created goods are destined for all people and not only for some of them.

- Our dominion over creation cannot be separated from moral obligations in regards to the use of goods. This concern extends to future generations.

The *Catechism of the Catholic Church* formulates this biblical teaching in the following terms:

> In the beginning God entrusted the earth and its resources to the common stewardship of mankind to take care of them, master them by labor, and enjoy their fruits (cf. Gn 1: 26-29). The goods of creation are destined for the whole human race. (CCC 2402)

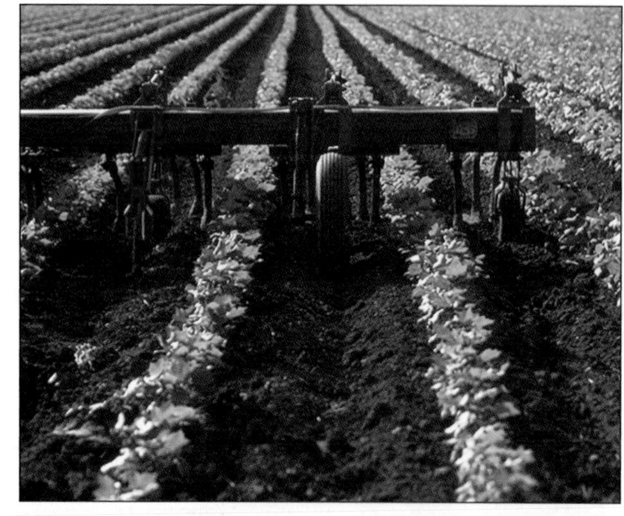

3. THE RIGHT TO PROPERTY

In emphasizing that the goods of this world are intended for the assistance of all, the Bible also indicates that every person must have access to the basics of food, clothing and shelter necessary for living a human life. By the "right to private property" each person has the right to possess things as one's own. This right is founded on human nature itself:

- As rational beings, we are able to plan our future. For this reason, we need the security that the possession of some things offers us. To deny someone the right to possess is to present him with insecurity, which is what contradicts the desire to assure his life's future.
- Man is a free being. Freedom demands that we possess basic necessities as our own. If we did not, we would not have the minimum necessary to enable us to work out our salvation.
- Family life would be notably difficult if the family did not possess things to satisfy the innumerable and unforeseen needs that must be met.
- A person is not property. Since the Father has made us free, every social system that could enslave people by whatever means is to be condemned.
- Finally, work needs to be equitably compensated. For that reason, one has the right and duty to claim the fruit of his work as his own.

Our dominion over creation cannot be separated from moral obligations in regards to the use of goods.

This teaching is mentioned in the *Catechism of the Catholic Church:*

> However, the earth is divided up among men to assure the security of their lives, endangered by poverty and threatened by violence. The appropriation of property is legitimate for guaranteeing the freedom and dignity of persons and for helping each of them to meet his basic needs and the needs of those in his charge. It should allow for a natural solidarity to develop between men. (CCC 2402)

4. THE UNIVERSAL DESTINY OF GOODS AND THE RIGHT TO PRIVATE PROPERTY

Catholic morality, while affirming the natural right to private property, has always taught that possessions are nevertheless created by God to help every person. This condition of property is called the social function of property, and is a part of the common good. The seventh commandment requires that the use of earthly goods and the fruits of people's labor must always be joined to justice and charity, for the human being is the author, center, and goal of all economic life.

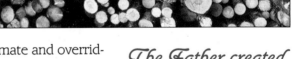

The Seventh Commandment requires that the use of earthly goods and the fruits of people's labor must always be joined to justice and charity.

One must then ask which of these two principles (that is, the particular right to own property or the social function of private property) is the more important.

To promote the correct attitude in regard to property, the Church teaches the concept of stewardship. In Jesus' time, the person who was in charge of his master's goods was called a steward. He managed the property but did not own it, and he could be held accountable for his use of the goods. The Church uses the term *stewardship* to remind people that the Father did not give him an absolute right to use goods as he sees fit, for we are responsible for their use.

Catholic moral doctrine teaches that the natural right to private property is subordinate to the social function of property in such a way that, when there is a dispute between private property and its social function, the social principle prevails over the private because the Father created goods for the use of all people. Thus, when only some possess many goods and make it impossible for the majority of people to live in dignity, the Father's plan is not fulfilled:

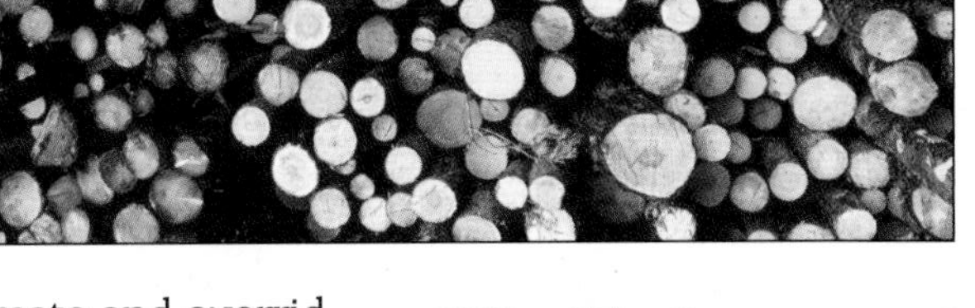

> The *universal destination of goods* remains primordial, even if the promotion of the common good requires respect for the right to private property and its exercise. (CCC 2403)

In addition, the state can intervene so that private property not only does not oppose the common good, but also has a positive repercussion for the good of society. In the same way, the state can claim some goods of special interest for the public. For instance, the state can use the right of *eminent domain*, the principle that states that a government can claim private property—with appropriate payment to the owner—because of a legitimate and overriding public concern (i.e., a farmer's land is needed for an interstate highway).

The Father created goods for the use of all people.

5. THE SOCIAL DOCTRINE OF THE CHURCH

Moral theology has always studied the right use of goods, defending the possession of them and condemning their abuse. But with the start of industrialization, serious social problems appeared as a result of poor working conditions.

To address these problems, a new moral science was begun called the social doctrine of the Church—that is, the moral teaching of the Church on social problems brought about by an industrial society with new ways of life and the appearance of wage-earning masses.

The encyclical *Rerum novarum* is normally considered the first piece of this new teaching. The latest addition is John Paul II's encyclical *Centesimus*

Catholic morality underlines the ethical rights and duties necessary for the international solidarity of different peoples and cultures.

annus. The teaching of the Church regarding social life, economics, and politics of all peoples continues to be the object of attention for moral theology.

The social doctrine of the Church covers work and its just wages, private property and its social function, the right to belong to associations and labor unions, the defense of justice and the morality of strikes, and the social function of economics and political life. In short, everything related to the common good and to justice in social life.[2]

The Church reminds us that true development concerns the whole of creation. The Father wishes all to participate in the goods of creation in accordance with justice and the help of charity, so they can respond to their vocations as God desires.

6. THE DUTY OF CHRISTIANS TO PARTICIPATE IN PUBLIC LIFE

The fact that we live in community with others—and Jesus Christ's universal redemption—oblige Christians to take an active part in social life.

Christian moral conduct is not concerned only with purely individual acts. It also requires participation and collaboration in public activity so that the different dimensions of social life (for instance, politics, economics, law) are fulfilled and that they follow the ethical demands contained in the Gospel.

Frequently, people—including Christians—recognize their sins resulting from individual and interpersonal actions, but ignore the relation of their acts to society. This individualistic ethics has been rejected by the Second Vatican Council:

> The pace of change is so far-reaching and rapid nowadays that no one can allow himself to close his eyes to the course of events or indifferently ignore them and wallow in the luxury of a merely individualistic morality. The best way to fulfil one's obligations of justice and love is to contribute to the common good according to one's means and the needs of others, even to the point of fostering and helping public and private organizations devoted to bettering the conditions of life.[3]

The mission of Christians is to convey the spirit of the Gospel in public life. In civic life, the Christian is equipped to make choices that demonstrate clear moral thinking.

7. INTERNATIONAL SOLIDARITY

The rapidity of communication and the economic relations that exist among peoples cause the problems of one nation or continent to affect the rest of the world. For this reason, Catholic morality underlines the ethical rights and duties necessary for the international solidarity of different peoples and cultures.

> It is above all a question of interdependence, sensed as a system determining relationships in the contemporary world, in its economic, cultural, political and religious elements, and accepted as a moral category. When interdependence becomes recognized in this way, the correlative response as a moral and social attitude, as a "virtue," is solidarity. This then is not a feeling of vague compassion or shallow distress at the misfortunes of so many people, both near and far. On the contrary, it is a firm and persevering determination to commit oneself to the common good; that is to say to the good of all and of each individual, because we are all really responsible for all. This determination is based on the solid conviction that what is hindering full development is that desire for profit and that thirst for power already mentioned.[4]

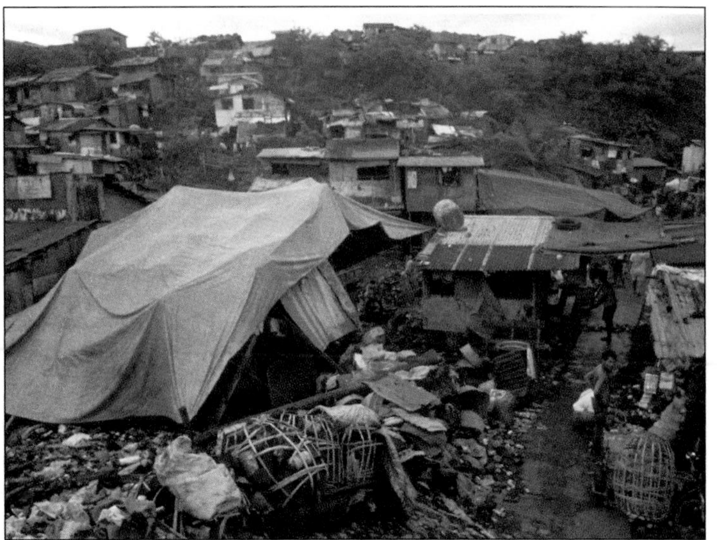

Those who have greater wealth and goods should contribute out of their excess of wealth to programs that will reduce the excessive social and economic inequalities that are often sinful in nature.

The *Catechism of the Catholic Church* devotes an entire section to "solidarity among the nations." It is not surprising that it analyzes the causes of unjust inequalities among diverse peoples and notes the reasons for living solidarity among different nations:

> *Rich nations* have a grave moral responsibility toward those which are unable to ensure the means of their development by themselves or have been prevented from doing so by tragic historical events. It is a duty in solidarity and charity; it is also an obligation in justice if the prosperity of the rich nations has come from resources that have not been paid for fairly. (CCC 2439)

Rich nations have a grave moral responsibility toward those which are unable to ensure the means of their development by themselves.

8. RESPECT FOR NATURE: ECOLOGY

Ecology is derived from the Greek *oikos* (which means "hearth" or "patrimony") and *logos* (meaning "law" or "treaty"). In the etymological sense, ecology is a treaty with nature, which should be considered as the "house" of all. Ecology, then, deals with protecting the residence in which human life is developed.

If one must respect another's goods, one must also respect nature and animals. This is a consequence of the universal destiny of goods for the use of people. This teaching is of such importance that it has been incorporated into the catechesis of the Catholic Faith:

> The seventh commandment enjoins respect for the integrity of creation. Animals, like plants and inanimate beings, are by nature destined for the common good of past, present, and future humanity (cf. Gn 1:28-31). Use of the mineral, vegetable, and animal

> resources of the universe cannot be divorced from respect for moral imperatives. Man's dominion over inanimate and other living beings granted by the Creator is not absolute; it is limited by concern for the quality of life of his neighbor, including generations to come; it requires a religious respect for the integrity of creation (cf. CA, 37-38). (CCC 2415)

Since the *environment* is the world common to all people, it should be respected. Nevertheless, some ecological interpretations are exaggerated, since they forget a basic principle: Mineral as well as plant and animal resources are at the service of humanity. For this reason, people can make use of them, but may not abuse them. Consequently, one cannot use things at his own caprice, destroying nature or mistreating animals. The dominion to which the Bible refers is not a despotic dominion, because the human being is not an absolute lord over nature, but an administrator of it.

9. "DO NOT STEAL": RESPECT FOR PRIVATE PROPERTY

Theft is the taking of another's goods against his reasonable wishes. For example, to do unjust damage to property, spray-paint property, remove street signs, refuse to pay just wages, cheat others through pricing, or charge excessive interest are all forms of stealing. One may also break the seventh commandment by not paying back what is owed, spending more of someone else's money than is necessary, not doing honest work, or failing to fulfill a business contract.

The dominion to which the Bible refers is not a despotic dominion.

The human being is not an absolute lord over nature.

Robbery, which is taking property by force, adds additional malice to stealing. Damage to goods may involve either private or state property, and all who effectively cooperate in doing damage are obliged to make restitution. The complexity of social life nowadays offers different ways of unjustly appropriating the goods of another. The *Catechism of the Catholic Church* proposes the following cases, which are more frequent in today's social life:

> The following are also morally illicit: speculation in which one contrives to manipulate the price of goods artificially in order to gain an advantage to the detriment of others; corruption in which one influences the judgment of those who must make decisions according to law; appropriation and use for private purposes of the common goods of an enterprise; work poorly done; tax evasion; forgery of checks and invoices; excessive expenses and waste. Willfully damaging private or public property is contrary to the moral law and requires reparation. (CCC 2409)

Likewise, one "steals" from society when one neglects to contribute equally to the common good by not paying just taxes.

> There is no theft if consent can be presumed or if refusal is contrary to reason and the universal destination of goods. This is the case in obvious and urgent necessity when the only way to provide for immediate, essential needs (food, shelter, clothing...) is to put at one's disposal and use the property of others (cf. *GS*, 69 § 1). (CCC 2408)

Greed.
Avarice.
Envy.

The cure for these sins is to love poverty of spirit.

10. "YOU SHALL NOT COVET."

The tenth commandment forbids coveting—the sinful desire for the goods of others. Our natural appetite leads us to desire things that are good in themselves, but an excessive desire leads to sin. This commandment forbids greed, avarice, and envy.

Greed is the desire for earthly goods without limit. "Conspicuous consumption" is the cultural term applied to this phenomenon. It means buying things solely to look rich and powerful in the eyes of one's neighbors.

Avarice is a passionate desire for riches that leads one to use money to control others. The avaricious person becomes hardhearted, unjust, and deceitful. Ebenezer Scrooge is the enduring model of the avaricious person.

Envy is unhappiness at the sight of another's good fortune. Besides being sinful in itself, it leads directly to the sinful desire to acquire them by whatever means are available.

Avarice is the sinful desire for wealth, while envy is the sinful desire for the goods of one's neighbor. They are capital sins that easily lead to personal destruction through the great harm that is done to self and others.

The cure for these sins is to love poverty of spirit. This virtue leads one to accept the goods of this life as on loan from God in the expectation that one will have to give an account before the Father at the conclusion of life. Those who by grace have fixed their love on God possess goods without their goods possessing them, and will not be distracted by the wealth of this life.

11. RESTITUTION

The word *restitution* refers to the obligation to return things to the state in which they were before theft, damage, or robbery. Restitution must be made for all sins against justice. There is an obligation to make restitution for anything stolen as well as for any damage done to property. In difficult cases, the best thing to do is to consult a priest in confession.

CONCLUSION

The Church has always defended human dignity when it is not sufficiently recognized in the complexity of social life, economics, and politics.

The seventh and tenth commandments involve many complex obligations that arise from one's right to own property and his relations with his neighbor and the whole of society. The best solution to these problems is to refer to the Church's continuing instruction on the ownership of property and the obligation to see it in light of the universal destiny of goods.

The social doctrine of the Church is a moral teaching, not a detailed technical response to problems in social life and politics. It is up to citizens, society, and the state to find practical and specific solutions. The Church offers only the principles.

The reason that the Church proposes these teachings on human life is twofold: the human person's dignity and his social nature. The Church has always defended human dignity when it is not sufficiently recognized in the complexity of social life, economics, and politics. Whenever the dignity of the human person is at risk, the Church emphasizes the scriptural basis for acknowledging human dignity. Everyone was created in the image and likeness of God, requiring that his or her dignity be respected.

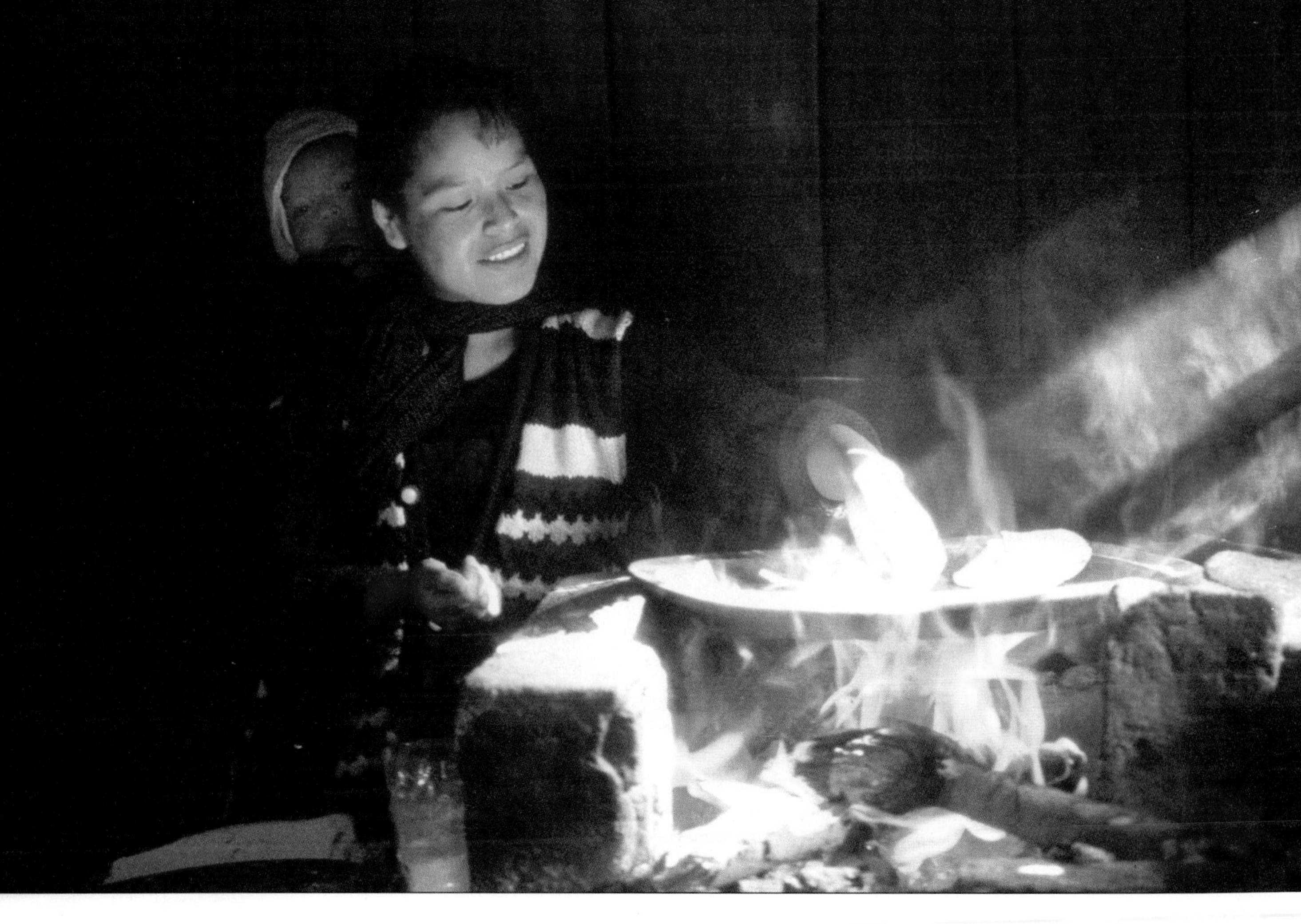

VOCABULARY

AVARICE
A passionate desire for riches that leads one to use money to control others.

ECOLOGY
The science that deals with protecting the residence in which human life is developed.

EMINENT DOMAIN
The principle that states that a government can claim private property, with appropriate payment to the owner, because of a legitimate and overriding public concern.

JUSTICE
The constant determination to give every person his due.

PRINCIPLE OF SOLIDARITY
The duty of cooperating and harmonizing all of the rights of the individual and the demands that are derived from the sociability of man. It represents the entire effort—a joint effort—to reach the good of the individual and of society.

PRINCIPLE OF SUBSIDIARITY
"[A] community of a higher order should not interfere in the internal life of a community of a lower order, depriving the latter of its functions, but rather should support it in case of need and help to coordinate its activity with the activities of the rest of society, always with a view to the common good" (CCC 1883). With this principle, the Church opposes all forms of collectivism or nationalism.

PRINCIPLE OF THE COMMON GOOD
The primacy of the common good over individual interests. The term "common good" is applied to the effort to achieve a social good that makes possible the full development of one's own perfection.

PRIVATE PROPERTY
The right of a person to possess things as his own.

RESTITUTION
Reparation of an injustice committed, since, if the damage is not repaired, a permanent state of injustice is produced.

SOCIAL JUSTICE
The justice that characterizes and regulates relations among individuals or among diverse groups and social classes in all areas of social interaction.

THEFT
Taking the goods of another against his reasonable will. When theft is carried out with violence, it is called *robbery.*

SUPPLEMENTARY READINGS

1. In *Rerum novarum*, Leo XIII strongly affirmed the natural character of the right to private property, using various arguments against the socialism of his time. This right, which is fundamental for the autonomy and development of the person, has always been defended by the Church up to our own day. At the same time, the Church teaches that the possession of material goods is not an absolute right, and that its limits are inscribed in its very nature as a human right.

While the Pope proclaimed the right to private ownership, he affirmed with equal clarity that the "use" of goods, while marked by freedom, is subordinated to their original common destination as created goods, as well as to the will of Jesus Christ as expressed in the Gospel.

— *CA*, 30

2. In the light of today's "new things," we have reread *the relationship between individual or private property and the universal destination of material wealth.* One fulfills oneself by using one's intelligence and freedom. In so doing a person utilizes the things of this world as objects and instruments and makes them his own. The foundation of the right to private initiative and ownership is to be found in this activity. By means of his work a person commits himself, not only for his own sake but also *for others* and *with others.* Each person collaborates in the work of others and for their good. One works in order to provide for the needs of one's family, one's community, one's nation, and ultimately all humanity.

— *CA*, 43

3. It is well known how strong were the words used by the Fathers of the Church to describe the proper attitude of persons who possess anything towards persons in need. To quote Saint Ambrose: "You are not making a gift of your possessions to the poor person. You are handing over to him what is his. For what has been given in common for the use of all, you have arrogated to yourself. The world is given to all, and not only to the rich." [*De Nabuthe*, c. 12, n. 53; (P.L. 14, 747). Cf. J.-R. Palanque, *Saint Ambroise et l'Empire romain*, Paris: de Boccard, 1933, pp. 336 f.] That is, private property does not constitute for anyone an absolute and unconditioned right. No one is justified in keeping for his exclusive use what he does not need, when others lack necessities. In a word, "according to the traditional doctrine as found in the Fathers of the Church and the great theologians, the right to property must never be exercised to the detriment of the common good." If there should arise a conflict "between acquired private rights and primary community exigencies," it is the responsibility of public authorities "to look for a solution, with the active participation of individuals and social groups." [Letter to the 82nd Session of the French Social Weeks (Brest 1965), in "L'homme et la revolution urbaine," Lyons: Chronique sociale 1965, pp. 8 and 9. Cf. *L'Osservatore Romano*, July 10, 1965, *Documentation catholique* t. 62, Paris, 1965, col 1365].

— *PP*, 23

"One works in order to provide for the needs of one's family, one's community, one's nation, and ultimately all humanity."

SUPPLEMENTARY READINGS CONTINUED

4. God entrusted animals to the stewardship of those whom he created in his own image (cf. Gn 2:19-20; 9:1-4). Hence it is legitimate to use animals for food and clothing. They may be domesticated to help man in his work and leisure. Medical and scientific experimentation on animals is a morally acceptable practice if it remains within reasonable limits and contributes to caring for or saving human lives.

— CCC 2417

5. The permanent validity of the Catholic Church's social teaching admits of no doubt. This teaching rests on one basic principle: individual human beings are the foundation, the cause and the end of every social institution. That is necessarily so, for men are by nature social beings. This fact must be recognized, as also the fact that they are raised in the plan of Providence to an order of reality which is above nature.

On this basic principle, which guarantees the sacred dignity of the individual, the Church constructs her social teaching. She has formulated, particularly over the past hundred years, and through the efforts of a very well informed body of priests and laymen, a social doctrine which points out with clarity the sure way to social reconstruction. The principles she gives are of universal application, for they take human nature into account, and the varying conditions in which man's life is lived. They also take into account the principal characteristics of contemporary society, and are thus acceptable to all.

— *MM*, 218-220

6. In order to achieve their task directed to the Christian animation of the temporal order, in the sense of serving persons and society, the lay faithful *are never to relinquish their participation in "public life,"* that is, in the many different economic, social, legislative, administrative and cultural areas which are intended to promote organically and institutionally the *common good.* The Synod Fathers have repeatedly affirmed that every person has a right and duty to participate in public life, albeit in a diversity and complementarity of forms, levels, tasks and responsibilities. Charges of careerism, idolatry of power, egoism and corruption that are oftentimes directed at persons in government, parliaments, the ruling classes, or political parties, as well as the common opinion that participating in politics is an absolute moral danger, does not in the least justify either skepticism or an absence on the part of Christians in public life.

— *CL*, 42

SUPPLEMENTARY READINGS CONTINUED

7. In the political sphere, it must be noted that truthfulness in the relations between those governing and those governed, openness in the relations between those governing and those governed, openness in public administration, impartiality in the service of the body politic, respect for the rights of political adversaries, safeguarding the rights of the accused against summary trials and convictions, the just and honest use of public funds, the rejection of equivocal or illicit means in order to gain, preserve or increase power at any cost—all these are principles which are primarily rooted in, and in fact derive their singular urgency from, the transcendent value of the person and the objective moral demands of the functioning of States. When these principles are not observed, the very basis of political coexistence is weakened and the life of society itself is gradually jeopardized, threatened and doomed to decay (cf. Ps. 14:3-4; Rv 18:2-3, 9-24). Today, when many countries have seen the fall of ideologies which bound politics to a totalitarian conception of the world—Marxism being the foremost of these—there is no less grave a danger that the fundamental rights of the human person will be denied and that the religious yearnings which arise in the heart of every human being will be absorbed once again into politics. This is *the risk of an alliance between democracy and ethical relativism*, which would remove any sure moral reference point from political and social life, and on a deeper level make the acknowledgment of truth impossible. Indeed, "if there is no ultimate truth to guide and direct political activity, then ideas and convictions can easily be manipulated for reasons of power. As history demonstrates, a democracy without values easily turns into open or thinly disguised totalitarianism."

— *VS*, 101

"...if there is no ultimate truth to guide and direct political activity, then ideas and convictions can easily be manipulated for reasons of power."

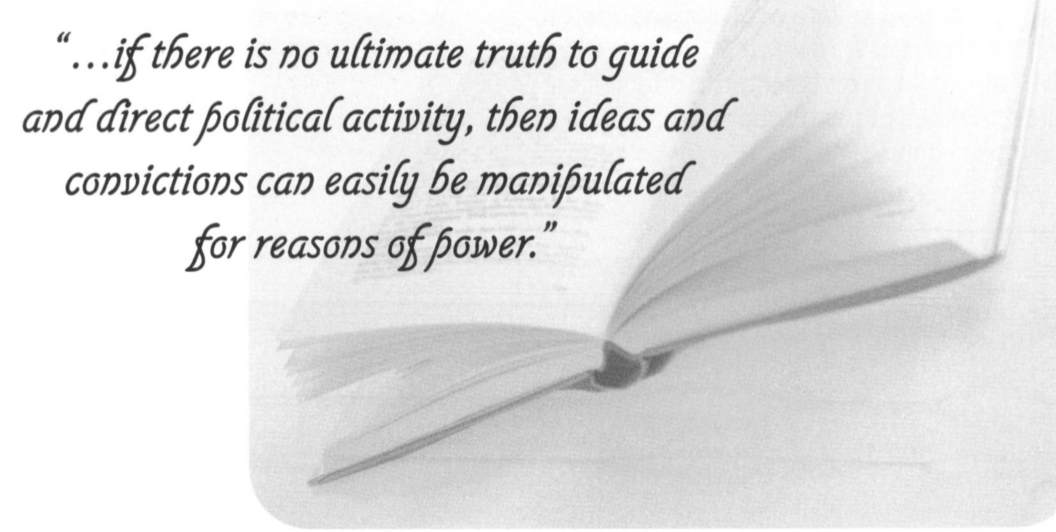

ADVANCED CONCEPTS

SOCIAL JUSTICE AND WORKING FOR THE COMMON GOOD

The moral virtue of justice is the constant and permanent determination to give to everyone what is his due. Justice in the dealings of individual persons among themselves is called *commutative justice.* That which exists between the community and an individual is called *distributive justice.* That between the subject and the community is called *legal justice.*

Social justice leads to the formulation of juridical and social norms that the common good demands for individuals. Social justice also means giving to all classes and groups their rights. When government laws are directed to the benefit of only one group, or a few, but not all the citizens of that society, then social justice is violated.

A good Catholic must also be a good citizen of his country, and must work for the common good. He must therefore exercise his civic duties and practice civic virtues. A good citizen loves his country, is sincerely interested in its welfare, and respects and obeys its lawful authority.

With regard to the seventh commandment of the Decalogue, a good citizen has to value the things that are of common use (the *res publica*). He has to have a constant concern for the common good and the welfare of others.

The following text of Pope Pius XI in *Quadragesimo Anno* equates the "requirements of the common good" to the "rules of social justice":

Since the present system of economy is founded chiefly upon ownership and labor, the principles of right reason, that is, of Christian social philosophy, must be kept in mind regarding ownership and labor and their association together, and must be put into actual practice.

So as to avoid the reefs of individualism and collectivism, the twofold character, that is, individual and social, both of capital and of work or labor must be given due and rightful weight. Relations of one to the other must be made to conform to the laws of strictest justice—commutative justice, as it is called—with the support, however, of Christian charity.

Free competition, kept within definite and due limits, and still more, economic dictatorship, must be effectively brought under public authority in these matters which pertain to the latter's function. The public institutions themselves of nations, moreover, ought to make all human society conform to the needs of the common good; that is, to the norm of social justice.

QUESTIONS

1. Why is the Church concerned with property rights?

2. What is the universal destiny for which God created all the goods of this world?

3. For what does the Church use the term *stewardship*?

4. What does it mean to say that human beings have a "common stewardship" over the goods of the earth?

5. What are the principal subjects covered by the Church's social doctrine?

6. Why are Christians obliged to take an active part in social life?

7. What is the mission of the Christian in public life?

8. What obligation does mankind have in regards to the goods of creation found in nature?

9. What is the purpose of the state?

10. What is necessary for social progress?

11. Why do you think the Church promotes the principle of subsidiarity?

12. What is the biblical doctrine regarding mankind and the things of the world?

13. List four truths deduced from the universal destiny of goods.

14. List four reasons that justify private property.

15. Why is private property subordinate to the social function of property?

16. Why is our dominion over nature not absolute?

PRACTICAL EXERCISES

1. Discuss the practical consequences for the social and political order that can be drawn from the following texts:

Christian tradition has never upheld this right [of ownership or property] as absolute and untouchable. On the contrary, it has always understood this right within the broader context of the right common to all to use the goods of the whole of creation: the right to private property is subordinated to the right to common use, to the fact that goods are meant for everyone.[5]

The ownership of any property makes its holder a steward of Providence, with the task of making it fruitful and communicating its benefits to others, first of all his family. (CCC 2404)

2. Evaluate the morality of the individuals in the following cases in light of the seventh and the tenth commandments:

- George's parents went out of town for the weekend and left the car keys home, so that George could use their car for necessary errands. George took the car one evening to go out with his friends, which his parents would almost certainly not have allowed. While they were out, he permitted his friend Katie to drive the car as well. Did he do anything wrong?
- Perry found a credit card and charged some sports equipment before destroying the card. Later, his conscience started to bother him, and he realized that he must make restitution. How do you think he should go about it?

3. Look for and comment on some passages of the New Testament that praise the spirit of poverty and condemn the anxiety for riches.

4. Resolve the following case: Margaret, Theresa, and Ann went to California on the train. In the station, Margaret found a wallet with $1,000 in it, but there was no identification in the wallet. They decided to distribute the money among themselves. They considered this an extraordinary piece of luck, and proceeded to spend the money. Some days later, Ann told her mother about the incident, and her mother said she should not have spent the money. Ann told Theresa and Margaret about what her mother said and they started to worry. Should they have spent the money? If your answer is no, then what do you think they should do now?

FROM THE CATECHISM

2450 "You shall not steal" (Ex 20:15; Dt 5:19). "Neither thieves, nor the greedy…, nor robbers will inherit the kingdom of God" (1 Cor 6:10).

2451 The seventh commandment enjoins the practice of justice and charity in the administration of earthly goods and the fruits of men's labor.

2453 The seventh commandment forbids theft. Theft is the usurpation of another's goods against the reasonable will of the owner.

2457 Animals are entrusted to man's stewardship; he must show them kindness. They may be used to serve the just satisfaction of man's needs.

2552 The tenth commandment forbids avarice arising from a passion for riches and their attendant power.

2556 Detachment from riches is necessary for entering the Kingdom of heaven. "Blessed are the poor in spirit."

2557 "I want to see God" expresses the true desire of man. Thirst for God is quenched by the water of eternal life (cf. Jn 4:14).

ENDNOTES

1. *GS*, 69, 71.
2. Cf. *VS*, 99-100.
3. *GS*, 30.
4. *SRS*, 38.
5. *LE*, 14.

Chapter 17

The Eighth Commandment:
You Shall Not Bear False Witness Against Your Neighbor.

Now Peter was sitting outside in the courtyard. And a maid came up to him, and said, "You also were with Jesus the Galilean." But he denied it before them all, saying, "I do not know what you mean." And when he went out to the porch, another maid saw him, and she said to the bystanders, "This man was with Jesus of Nazareth." And again he denied it with an oath, "I do not know the man." After a little while the bystanders came up and said to Peter, "Certainly you are also one of them, for your accent betrays you." Then he began to invoke a curse on himself and to swear, "I do not know the man." And immediately the cock crowed. And Peter remembered the saying of Jesus, "Before the cock crows, you will deny me three times." And he went out and wept bitterly. (Mt 26: 69-75)

Dishonesty and falsehood are traits that no one appreciates in others. Beyond the personally offensive nature of such traits, however, a deeper issue exists.

Consider the following:

- Is there a relationship between personal freedom and truthfulness?
- What are the consequences of dishonesty for individuals and society as a whole?
- Do Christians have particular obligations that surpass those of other people in regard to the truth?

"You shall not bear false witness against your neighbor."

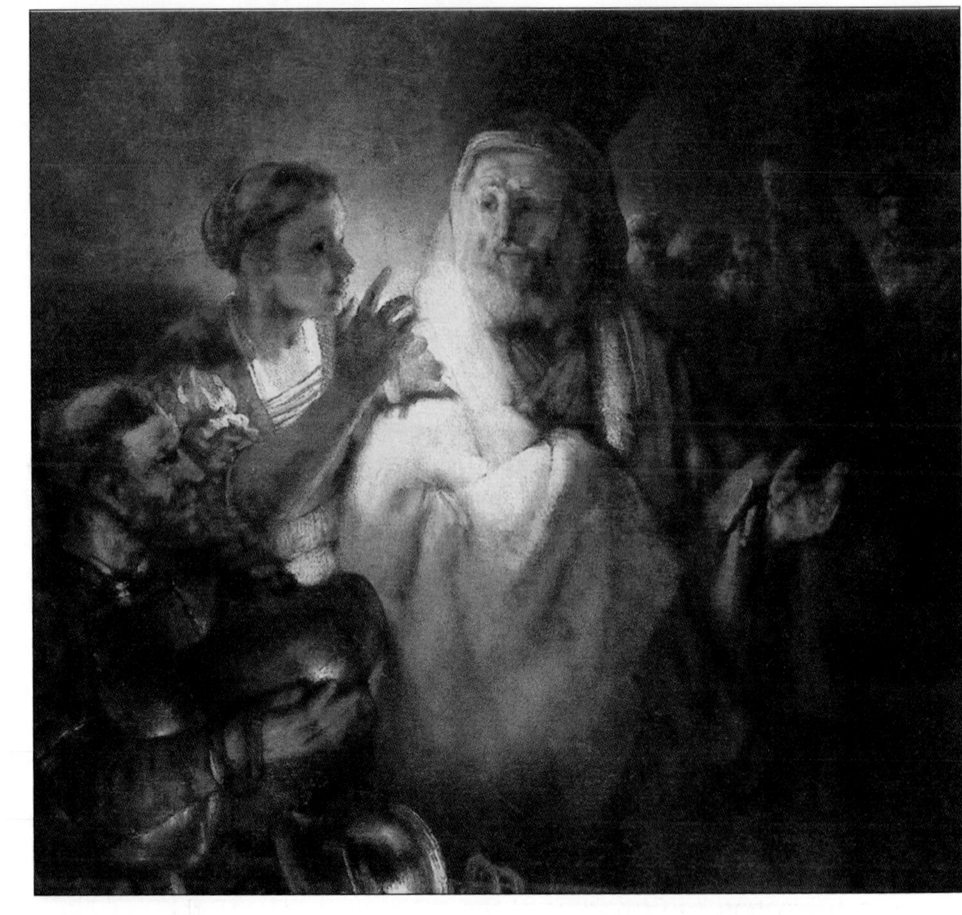

Any culture that pursues knowledge of the truth is characterized by a primacy of reason.

INTRODUCTION

Truthfulness is the bond that binds men together and makes life in society possible.

> **Truth or truthfulness is the virtue which consists in showing oneself true in deeds and truthful in words, and guarding against duplicity, dissimulation, and hypocrisy. (CCC 2505)**

Ever since Greek philosophy claimed that reason distinguished the human being from all other creatures (man is a "rational animal"), the history of Europe has been characterized by a great enterprise to seek the truth about reality. First, Greek and Roman and later all Western philosophy was marked by a desire to know what things are. Not only philosophy, but also technological progress was transmitted by the Greeks to the countries of Europe and America. As heirs to the emphasis on reason and the love of truth, Europe and America have dedicated themselves to knowledge of the laws that govern matter and life.

Rational knowledge, with Roman law and the monotheism of Israel, is the heart of the common legacy that the ancients passed down to Europe first, and through Europe to the rest of the world.

Any culture that pursues knowledge of the truth is characterized by a primacy of reason. Since man—as a rational being seeking to know what things are—desires to know and understand the truth about God, humanity, and the other realities surrounding him, we can see that there is placed within him an inclination toward his proper end.

The Eighth Commandment points out an ethical minimum.

1. TRUTH IN THE OLD TESTAMENT

The wording of the eighth commandment is almost the same in Exodus and Deuteronomy, the two books that contain the Decalogue: "You shall not bear false witness against your neighbor" (Ex 20: 16; cf. Dt 5: 20).

This commandment should be understood in light of the seven previous ones. God establishes a minimum of moral demands in the Decalogue, which is why they are formulated negatively and only the most generic sins are condemned. In this way, besides polytheism and other things related to divine worship (first through third commandments), God forbids disobedience to one's parents (fourth commandment), taking innocent life (fifth), adultery (sixth), robbery (seventh), and in the eighth, Yahweh condemns a lack of respect for the truth.

Evidently, the formulation of the eighth commandment is as generic as the rest of the Decalogue. It only points out an ethical minimum: protecting the dignity of the person, since social life would be impossible if truth is not respected as the foundation of social communication.

This natural attitude of the human person toward the truth is also characteristic of the message of the Bible. In fact, revelation is the manifestation by God to us of the truth about himself, the meaning of human existence, and the value and end of all creation. God reveals himself precisely in order to manifest the saving truth to humanity. In the Old Testament, Yahweh testifies that he tells the truth. God's revelation to Moses is accompanied by extraordinary signs—miracles—that illustrate the truth of what God has revealed (cf. Ex 4: 1-17).

God's revelation to Moses is accompanied by extraordinary signs—miracles—that illustrate the truth of what God has revealed.

In the Book of Numbers, Balach repeats the teaching of Yahweh, who testifies to his truthfulness in everything he does and says: "God is not man, that he should lie, or a son of man, that he should repent. Has he said, and will he not do it? Or has he spoken, and will he not fulfil it?" (Nm 23: 19).

The Book of Proverbs exults in the truthfulness of Yahweh and honors those who seek knowledge and the love of truth. When one acts in this way, he is on his way to reaching true wisdom:

> **Hear, for I will speak noble things, and from my lips will come what is right; for my mouth will utter truth; wickedness is an abomination to my lips. All the words of my mouth are righteous; there is nothing twisted or crooked in them. They are all straight to him who understands and right to those who find knowledge. Take my instruction instead of silver, and knowledge rather than choice gold; for wisdom is better than jewels, and all that you may desire cannot compare with her. I, wisdom, dwell in prudence, and I find knowledge and discretion. (Prv 8: 6-12)**

The Psalms poetically narrate the history of Israel and express the sentiments of the people. They worship the Father whose "word is firmly fixed in the heavens. Thy faithfulness endures to all generations; thou hast established the earth, and it stands fast" (Ps 119:89-90).

2. TRUTH IN THE NEW TESTAMENT

Truth is the correlation between the idea in the mind and exterior reality. In order to present the truth with precision, force, and love, it is necessary to go back to the definition of the human being as a rational animal. Since we distinguish ourselves from animals through our thought, our natural vocation is the desire to know the truth, profess it, defend it, and communicate it. Therefore, our relations with one another must be founded on truth, not lies.

But the teaching of Jesus Christ highlights the importance of honesty. The subject of truth is one of the characteristics of the Gospel of St. John. For example, when speaking of the person of Jesus, he states that "the Word became flesh and dwelt among us, full of grace and truth" (Jn 1:14). Jesus speaks of himself: "I am the way, the truth, and the life" (Jn 14:6), and he declares before Pilate that he has come "to bear witness to the truth. Every one who is of the truth hears my voice" (Jn 18:37). For those who follow him and those who believe in him, "the Spirit of truth" (Jn 14:17) will always accompany them. It is not surprising that Jesus' prayer for his disciples is precisely that the Father "[s]anctify them in the truth; thy word is truth" (Jn 17:17). For this reason, he asked "that they also may be consecrated in truth" (Jn 17:19).

Jesus declares before Pilate that he has come "to bear witness to the truth. Every one who is of the truth hears my voice."

— Jn 18:37

Finally, the action of the Holy Spirit on the apostles is that of a guide leading them "into all the truth" (Jn 16:13). Consequently, to grow in faith is to grow in truth. Later, tradition identifies revelation with truth. So to persevere in faith is to stay with the truth.

As in the rest of the commandments, the eighth is also enriched by the New Testament, Sacred Tradition, and the Magisterium. The richness of the eighth commandment is understood in Catholic morality as a precept of love and defense of the truth, not only regarding the good name of a person, but in all aspects of human life:

> **The eighth commandment forbids misrepresenting the truth in our relations with others. This moral prescription flows from the vocation of the holy people to bear witness to their God who is the truth and wills the truth. Offenses against the truth express by word or deed a refusal to commit oneself to moral uprightness: they are fundamental infidelities to God and, in this sense, they undermine the foundations of the covenant. (CCC 2464)**

3. TRUTH AND FREEDOM: "THE TRUTH WILL SET YOU FREE."

In conversations with the Jews, Jesus declared: "If you continue in my word, you are truly my disciples, and you will know the truth, and the truth will make you free" (Jn 8:31-32). These words of Jesus contain two clear points.

First, Jesus gives a preview of what he will say on another occasion: that he is "the truth" (Jn 14:6). Moreover, he tells us that the truth consists in following and accepting his doctrine. Consequently, a disciple of Christ is on the way to reaching the fullness of truth through the help of the Holy Spirit. This does not mean that a Christian has more knowledge of scientific truths, but rather that he will possess the truth about life, moral principles and, in general, the meaning of human existence.

If one really wishes to be free, he should profess love for the truth and seek it under the guidance of the Holy Spirit and the Magisterium.

Secondly, the way to reach true freedom is through the knowledge of truth. Ignorance, error, mistakes, or falsehoods inhibit human freedom. If one really wishes to be free, he should profess love for the truth and seek it under the guidance of the Holy Spirit and the Magisterium. This doctrine is explained at great length in the encyclical *Veritatis splendor.*

Consequently, all humans are obliged to seek the truth. It is not worthy of the human person to live contrary to the truth. One must develop his intelligence with the objective of being capable of discovering the truth in everything, from everyday life to the events that make up human existence.

This search for the truth is even more obligatory regarding the truth about God as Father, Son, and Holy Spirit. This belief is contained in the "principle of religious freedom" formulated in the Second Vatican Council:

> **It is in accordance with their dignity that all men, because they are persons, that is, beings endowed with reason and free will and therefore bearing personal responsibility, are both impelled by their nature and also bound by a moral obligation to seek the truth, especially religious truth. They are also bound to adhere to the truth, once they come to know it and direct their whole lives in accordance with the demands of truth. But men cannot satisfy this obligation in a way that is in keeping with their own nature unless they enjoy both psychological freedom and immunity from external coercion.**[1]

In this way, truth, freedom, and the absence of coercion are joined together.

4. SPREADING THE TRUTH

The principle that "good is diffusive" is fulfilled in the truth because truth is also a good. Consequently, it is not enough to merely speak truth, but it also must be *discussed and propagated.* Truth should be affirmed in all circumstances, especially in the following:

Christians should talk about the teachings of revelation and the doctrine of the Magisterium concerning the many problems of life.

- *The spreading of Christian truth.* Christians should talk about the teachings of revelation and the doctrine of the Magisterium concerning the many problems of life.
- *The communication of the truth in social life.* For example, information about drug trafficking, terrorism, or social fraud ought to be communicated to the legitimate authority.
- *Revelation of a secret* if doing so obtains a social good proportional to the serious duty of keeping a secret. The exception to this guideline regards professional secrets. The duty to maintain a professional secret, except in cases of serious danger, must never be neglected.

The case of the news media presents a special problem. Their purpose is to inform society about people and events on a daily basis. Often, when divulging the truth, they violate people's privacy. Being a public figure does reduce the boundaries of private life, but the privacy of public figures nevertheless should be respected.

> **Everyone should observe an appropriate reserve concerning persons' private lives. Those in charge of communications should maintain a fair balance between the requirements of the common good and respect for individual rights. Interference by the media in the private lives of persons engaged in political or public activity is to be condemned to the extent that it infringes upon their privacy and freedom. (CCC 2492)**

The individual must always possess a critical attitude toward the media, in such a way that he avoids falling into error and losing the meaning and love of truth. Recognizing the importance of the media, the Magisterium not only values its use, but also emphasizes the ethical dimension of the professions involved in this field.

5. TO TELL THE TRUTH: HONESTY VERSUS DISHONESTY

Love for the truth should bring all people, and especially Christians, to tell the truth and avoid falsehood. Jesus expressed this with this aphorism: "Let what you say be simply 'Yes' or 'No'; anything more than this comes from evil" (Mt 5:37; cf. Jas 5:12). Lies come from the devil, the author and father of all lies:

> **You are of your father the devil, and your will is to do your father's desires. He was a murderer from the beginning, and has nothing to do with the truth, because there is no truth in him. When he lies, he speaks according to his own nature, for he is a liar and the father of lies. But, because I tell the truth, you do not believe me. (Jn 8:44-45)**

To lie is to speak against the truth in order to induce a person entitled to it into error. According to this definition, telling a lie requires the following conditions:

- Speaking against the truth, that is, to say the contrary of what is thought or known.
- The intention of leading the listener into error.

A person lies only when saying something false to someone who has the right to know the truth. For this reason, silence is permitted when the other person does not have the right to know.

Since to lie is to say the contrary of what one thinks, lying is an evil in itself—it is evil by its very nature. Besides, it also brings a series of evils with it. For example:

a. A LIE CAUSES DAMAGE TO THE ONE WHO TELLS IT.

When a person lies, he betrays himself in thought and word. Furthermore, a lie connotes a weakness in one's personality if he lies because he lacks the fortitude to tell the truth and the responsibility to assume the consequences of professing the truth, whatever the cost.

b. IT PRODUCES VICE IN HUMAN RELATIONS.

When a person lies to his neighbor, he induces him into error and sows doubt and suspicion in social relations.

When a person lies to his neighbor, he induces him into error and sows doubt and suspicion in social relations.

c. IT DAMAGES SOCIETY.

Social and political life are directed toward solving the true problems in everyday life. Thus, the deceits of politicians are the cause of serious harm.

The *Catechism* enumerates these evils in the following terms:

> **Since it violates the virtue of truthfulness, a lie does real violence to another. It affects his ability to know, which is a condition of every judgment and decision. It contains the seed of discord and all consequent evils. Lying is destructive of society; it undermines trust among men and tears apart the fabric of social relationships. (CCC 2486)**

6. THE GRAVITY OF A LIE

A lie is an evil in itself; it is always a sin. But it will be more or less serious in conformity with the following criteria, which are cited in the *Catechism:*

> **The *gravity of a lie* is measured against the nature of the truth it deforms, the circumstances, the intentions of the one who lies, and the harm suffered by its victims. (CCC 2484)**

To judge the gravity of a lie, one should take these four fundamental criteria into account:

a. THE MATERIAL RELATED TO THE LIE

The object of a lie determines its gravity: A lie is a venial sin if the matter is less serious, or grave if the matter is serious. For example, calumny, when a serious defect is attributed to a person, would be a grave sin.

b. THE INTENTION

Lying can be more grave if the one who lies tries to cause serious damage, whether by deception or by distorting reality.

c. THE CIRCUMSTANCES THAT MOTIVATE THE LIE

A lie may cause serious evil depending on the circumstances. Such could be the case of a lie that unfavorably influences a person's professional life.

d. THE EFFECTS OF A LIE

Sometimes a lie may cause serious evils, such as a lie concerning an important issue that causes social disturbances.

Even if the lie is not serious, it should be carefully refrained from, because all dishonesty injures the trustworthiness of the person. Dishonesty goes against human dignity—dignity demands that a person be truthful. In extreme cases, Christians should rely on the grace of the Holy Spirit to enable them to be capable of being honest and reward that honesty in Heaven.

7. SINS AGAINST ANOTHER'S REPUTATION

a. CALUMNY

Calumny is a lie told about someone accusing him of something of which he is not guilty. Calumny is what is directly forbidden in the Old Testament: "You shall not bear false witness against your neighbor" (Ex 20:16; cf. Dt 5:20).

Everyone has the right to fame and honor. *Fame* is the positive or negative opinion that is commonly held about another person. *Honor* is the testimony of the excellence of a person's character. Attacking a person's fame or honor is called *disparagement* or *slander*. When one disparages or slanders, he takes away someone's fame. For this reason, to defame or dishonor is to wound a person in himself and damage his dignity. Calumny makes society wrongly judge a worthy person as undignified. Consequently, calumny is a sin against charity and justice.

Detraction is telling a harmful truth about someone to an individual who has no right to know.

b. DETRACTION

Detraction is telling a harmful truth about someone to an individual who has no right to know. It is allowed to reveal the faults of another only in situations when an evil could befall another person or grave harm could come to society if the faults were not revealed.

c. RASH JUDGMENT

This sin is the interior or exterior judgment made about the reputation of a person, without sufficient reason, with which one attributes a moral defect to his neighbor.

8. THE DUTY TO MAKE REPARATION

Since lying causes harm, one has the obligation to make restitution for it. Great harm always happens in the case of calumny. When calumny is committed, it is not sufficient to repent, or even to ask for forgiveness; one must make up for the harm committed. A lie is not only a sin against truth and charity, but also against justice. And justice, by its very nature, demands reparation.

If the injury requires it, reparation should be carried out publicly. In other cases, it can be accomplished privately. Reparation may include restitution by means of economic compensation. This reparation—and in some cases, restitution—obliges in conscience. This means that there is no forgiveness of sins if one does not have the intention of making reparation.

This means that there is no forgiveness of sins if one does not have the intention of making reparation.

The *Catechism of the Catholic Church* says:

> **Every offense committed against justice and truth entails the *duty of reparation*, even if its author has been forgiven. When it is impossible publicly to make reparation for a wrong, it must be made secretly. If someone who has suffered harm cannot be directly compensated, he must be given moral satisfaction in the name of charity. This duty of reparation also concerns offenses against another's reputation. This reparation, moral and sometimes material, must be evaluated in terms of the extent of the damage inflicted. It obliges in conscience. (CCC 2487)**

9. SECRETS

We are obliged to keep a secret when the good of our neighbor demands it.

We are obliged to keep a secret when the good of our neighbor demands it, we have promised to keep it, or our profession or office requires it.

We may reveal a secret—even after making a promise not to—when it is necessary to correct a wrong or avoid a great harm to the common good. For the correction of faults, it is allowed to tell these secrets to parents or superiors who may not know them. For example, in a community or boarding school—where, by rule, the faults of the residents should be revealed to the superior—it is a serious obligation to reveal grievous disorders that may easily corrupt the innocent.

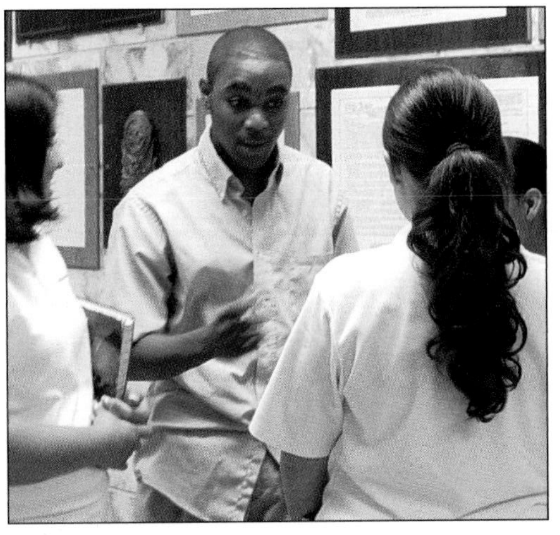

Professional secrets are most seriously binding. Even the common good of society is not sufficient reason for a physician, lawyer, or priest, for instance, to reveal a secret impediment to marriage that he may happen to know in the exercise of his office.

The most binding of all secrets is that of Confession. Under the pain of sacrilege and excommunication for himself, a priest may not reveal for any cause or reason anything that he learns in Confession, even at the cost of his own life. This is called the "Seal of Confession."

CONCLUSION

In order for society to function properly, the keystone of social interaction must be the truth. There can be no social relations if people cannot trust one another. All people have an obligation to speak the truth themselves, and to speak out in defense of the truth. The truth is the glue that not only binds society together, but also binds us to our Savior Jesus Christ who called himself "the Truth."

VOCABULARY

CALUMNY
False accusation, done maliciously to cause damage.

DETRACTION
Revealing the hidden faults of another person to someone who has no right to know about them, thus damaging or destroying his good reputation.

FALSEHOOD
A lack of correspondence between what one thinks and what one says.

HONOR
Respect or good reputation that is acquired through the practice of virtue or heroic acts. The quality that brings people to be guided by the most elevated moral norms.

OBJECTIVE TRUTH
Reality that exists outside of a person's intellect, and that is independent of his acknowledgment of its existence.

REALISM
The theory of knowledge that justly values the role of reason and reality of objects in themselves, outside of the mind.

REPUTATION
The good or bad opinion commonly held about another person.

REPARATION
Making amend for a wrong done or for an offense, especially for sin, which is an offense against God.

RESTITUTION
The return of what has been unjustly taken from another.

SLANDER
Destroying the honor or fame of another by accusing him of something of which he is not guilty.

SUBJECTIVISM
The theory of knowledge that exaggerates the function of reason, placing it above the objectivity of what is known.

TOLERANCE
Respect for other people, though we may disagree with their ideas.

TRUTH
The correlation between the idea in one's mind and external reality.

VERACITY
Truthfulness; the disposition of a person to tell the truth.

SUPPLEMENTARY READINGS

1. "Do you not know," I said, "that the true lie, if such an expression may be allowed, is hatred of gods and men?"

"What do you mean?" he said.

"I mean that no one is willingly deceived in that which is the truest and highest part of himself, or about the truest and highest matters; there, above all, he is most afraid of a lie having possession of him."

"Still," he said, "I do not comprehend you."

"The reason is," I replied, "that you attribute some profound meaning to my words; but I am only saying that deception, or being deceived or uninformed about the highest realities in the highest part of themselves, which is the soul, and in that part of them to have and to hold the lie, is what mankind least likes—that, I say, is what they utterly detest."

"There is nothing more hateful to them."

"And, as I was just now remarking, this ignorance in the soul of him who is deceived may be called the true lie; for the lie in words is only a kind of imitation and shadowy image of a previous affliction of the soul, not pure unadulterated falsehood. Am I not right?"

"Perfectly right."

"The true lie is hated not only by the gods, but also by men?"

"Yes."

— Plato, *The Republic*, Bk. 2

2. *Professional secrets*—for example, those of political office holders, soldiers, physicians, and lawyers—or confidential information given under the seal of secrecy must be kept, save in exceptional cases where keeping the secret is bound to cause very grave harm to the one who confided it, to the one who received it or to a third party, and where the very grave harm can be avoided only by divulging the truth. Even if not confided under the seal of secrecy, private information prejudicial to another is not to be divulged without a grave and proportionate reason.

— CCC 2491

"...no one is willingly deceived in that which is the truest and highest part of himself,..."

SUPPLEMENTARY READINGS CONTINUED

3. It is essential that all those involved should form a correct conscience on the use of the media, especially with regard to certain issues which are particularly controversial today.

The first of these issues is information, or the search for news and its publication. Because of the progress of modern society and the increasing interdependence of its members on one another, it is obvious that information is very useful and, for the most part, essential. If news or facts and happenings are communicated publicly and without delay, every individual will have permanent access to sufficient information and thus will be enabled to contribute effectively to the common good. Further, all of them will more easily be able to contribute in unison to the prosperity and the progress of society as a whole.

There exists therefore in human society a right to information on the subjects that are of concern to men either as individuals or as members of society, according to each man's circumstances. The proper exercise of this right demands that the content of the communication be true and—within the limit set by justice and charity—complete. Further, it should be communicated honestly and properly. This means that in the gathering and in the publication of news the moral law and the legitimate rights and dignity of man should be upheld. All knowledge is not profitable, but on the other hand "love builds" (1 Cor 8:1).

— *IM*, 5

4. Those who receive the means of social communication—readers, viewers, audiences—do so of their own free choice. Special obligations rest on them in consequence. A properly motivated selectivity would be wholly in favor of whatever excels in virtue, culture and art. Likewise, it would avoid whatever might be a cause or occasion of spiritual harm to the recipients or might be a source of danger to others through bad example; it would avoid whatever might hinder the communications of the good and facilitate the communication of what is evil. This last usually occurs when financial help is given to those who exploit the media solely for profit.

If they are to obey the moral law, those who use the media ought to keep themselves informed in good time about assessments arrived at by the authorities with competence in this sphere and to conform to them as a right conscience would dictate. They should take appropriate steps to direct and form their consciences so that they may more readily resist less wholesome influences and profit more fully from the good.

— *IM*, 9

5. The lie supposes such contempt, that when the greatness of God is affirmed, the grace of the deity is reduced, and the lowest things, elevated as the truth, are praised as noble.

— Leonardo da Vinci

"...in the gathering and in the publication of news the moral law and the legitimate rights and dignity of man should be upheld."

ADVANCED CONCEPTS

1. THE VALUE OF HUMAN REASON AND THE MEANING OF TRUTH

There has occasionally been a certain exaggeration of the value of reason in past times. The European rationalism of the eighteenth and nineteenth centuries was an overestimation of reason, and finally led to *idealism,* which stresses the importance of what we conceive things to be, rather than what things truly are. Rationalism represents a decay in rational knowledge because it exposes itself to the caprice of humans by only accepting what people are capable of knowing, which leaves Christian revelation outside the realm of rationalist thought, but not refuted by it.

On the other hand, it is frequently said that modern culture has gone to the other extreme. That is, modern culture distrusts reason and no longer professes a love for the truth. Hence, it is very urgent that the importance of reason and the love of truth be reacquired. In all times and in all cultures, the Christian must echo Christ's promise that *"the truth will make you free"* (Jn 8:32).

2. FREEDOM AND TRUTH

"Jesus then said to the Jews who had believed in him, 'If you continue in my word, you are truly my disciples, and you will know the truth, and the truth will make you free'" (Jn 8:31-32). Christ proposes here that knowing and living the truth is the way to an authentic freedom.

A comparison between the Church's teaching and today's social and cultural situation immediately makes clear the urgent need for the Church herself to develop an intense pastoral effort precisely with regard to this fundamental question.

Human persons must seek the truth and strive to live in that truth since freedom is bound to the truth. "If there is no transcendent truth, in obedience to which a person achieves his full identity, then there is no sure principle for guaranteeing just relations between people."[2]

It is therefore urgently necessary for the future of society and the development of a sound democracy to rediscover those essential and innate human and moral values which flow from the very truth of the human being and express and safeguard the dignity of the person: values which no individual, no majority, and no state can ever create, modify or destroy, but must only acknowledge, respect and promote.

Consequently, there is a need to recover the basic elements of a vision of the relationship between civil law and moral law, which are put forward by the church, but which are also part of the patrimony of the great juridical traditions of humanity.[3]

The Church encourages political leaders to make decisions that will lead to the establishment of the moral values that come from the objective truth. Otherwise, *ethical relativism* will undermine the foundation of freedom. *Centesimus annus* teaches that "if there is no ultimate truth to guide and direct political activity, then ideas and convictions can easily be manipulated for reasons of power."[4]

QUESTIONS

1. What two emphases set Western philosophy apart from all others?

2. What common legacy did the ancients pass on to Europe and the world?

3. Why do we say that the commandments are generic?

4. What is revelation, according to the chapter?

5. What is the foundation of human relations?

6. What is the action of the Holy Spirit on the apostles?

7. What two points are made in Jesus' statement that "the truth will make you free"?

8. What points were made in the statement regarding the "principle of human freedom"?

9. Under what circumstances should truth be affirmed?

10. List the damages of lying.

11. List the circumstances that determine the gravity of a lie.

12. What points does the *Catechism* make regarding reparation?

13. When are we obliged to keep a secret?

14. When may we reveal a secret?

15. What is the "Seal of Confession"?

PRACTICAL EXERCISES

1. Based upon your understanding of the principles contained in this chapter, resolve the following questions:

- Terence's friend is dating a girl who had an abortion five years earlier. Terence knows they are talking about getting married. May he tell his friend that the girl had an abortion?
- Maria and her friend Anita had a terrible argument. As a result, Maria told another person at the law firm where she and Anita work that, while they were in college, Anita had cheated on an important final exam, using information she had obtained illicitly. (The story is untrue, because although Anita did have the opportunity to find out what was going to be on the exam before the test, she never followed through. Her conscience would not permit her to do it.) As a result, Anita's reputation at the firm has been severely damaged. One of the senior partners at the firm has even said that she is concerned about Anita having access to confidential documents, because she is afraid that she will misuse the information. What is the specific nature of the sin of which Maria is guilty? What sort of restitution do you think Maria needs to make to Anita for the damage that has been done to her reputation? How do you think she can do this?

2. Do you know of any instances in which the media has distorted or misrepresented the truth in their reporting of the news? What obligations does the media have with regard to the truth?

FROM THE CATECHISM

2504 "You shall not bear false witness against your neighbor" (Ex 20:16). Christ's disciples have "put on the new man, created after the likeness of God in true righteousness and holiness" (Eph 4:24).

2507 Respect for the reputation and honor of persons forbids all detraction and calumny in word or attitude.

2508 Lying consists in saying what is false with the intention of deceiving one's neighbor.

2509 An offense committed against the truth requires reparation.

ENDNOTES

1. *DH*, 2.
2. *CA*, 44.
3. *EV*, 71.
4. *CA*, 46.

Art and Photo Credits

Cover
Christ Icon: Corbis Royalty Free image

Introduction
iii Corbis Royalty Free Image
iv *Madonna and Child*, Simone Martini; Pinacoteca Nazionale, Siena; Web Gallery of Art
x Christ Icon: www.SaintIgnatiusChurch.org

Part 1
1 *Christ*, El Greco; National Gallery, Prague; Web Gallery of Art

Chapter 1
2 *Christ Giving His Blessing*, Hans Memling; Norton Simon Museum, Pasadena; Web Gallery of Art
3 *Holy Trinity*, Hendrick van Balen; Sint-Jacobskerk, Antwerp; Web Gallery of Art
4 Corbis Royalty Free Image
5 *Christ in the House of Simon*, Dieric the Elder Bouts; Staatliche Museen, Berlin; Web Gallery of Art
6 *Assumption of the Virgin* (detail), Titian; Santa Maria Gloriosa dei Frari, Venice; Web Gallery of Art
7 Andrean High School, Gary, Indiana; Julie Koenig, photographer
8 *Gesu Buon Pastore*, Missale Romanum
9 Mother Teresa: AP/Wide World Photos
10 Midwest Theological Forum; Luke Mata, photographer
11 Willows Academy, Des Plaines, Illinois; Julie Koenig, photographer
12 Digital Vision Royalty Free Image
13 Midwest Theological Forum; Luke Mata, photographer
14 *The Ecstasy of St. Cecilia*, Bernardo Cavallino; Museo Nazionale di Capodimonte, Naples; Web Gallery of Art
15 Digital Vision Royalty Free Image
16 *Jesus Giving Blessing*, from Latin prayerbook; Museum Facsimiles, Pittsfield, Massachusetts
17 Willows Academy, Des Plaines, Illinois; Julie Koenig, photographer
18 Midwest Theological Forum; Luke Mata, photographer

Chapter 2
23 *Christ the Redeemer*, Andrea Del Sarto; SS. Annunziata, Florence; Web Gallery of Art
24 *Jesus Teaching*, Cristo Pantocrator, P. Sofronov, 20th century
25 Corbis Royalty Free Image
26 Comstock Royalty Free Image
27 *Baptism of St. Augustine*, Benozzo Gozzoli; Apsidal Chapel, Sant'Agostino, San Gimignano; Web Gallery of Art
28 *Appearance on the Mountain in Galilee*, Duccio; Museo dell'Opera del Duomo, Siena
29 Willows Academy, Des Plaines, Illinois; Julie Koenig, photographer
30 Midwest Theological Forum; Luke Mata, photographer
31 *St. Paul Preaching in Athens*, Raphael; Victoria and Albert Museum, London; Web Gallery of Art
32 Pope John Paul II; AP/Wide World Photos
33 Rubberball Royalty Free Image
34 St. Peter's, Midwest Theological Forum Archives
36 Digital Vision Royalty Free Image
41 *Christ Blessing the Children*, Nicolaes Maes; National Gallery, London; Web Gallery of Art
43 *The Good Samaritan*, Julius Schnorr Von Carolsfeld; Dover Publications
44 *Christ in the Sepulchre with Two Angels*, Andrea Del Castagno; Sant'Apollonia, Florence

Chapter 3
45 *The Tribute Money*, Titian; Gemäldegalerie, Dresden; Web Gallery of Art
46 *Jesus Washing Peter's Feet*, Ford Madox Brown; Tate Museum, London; ArtMagick
47 *Aristotle with a Bust of Homer*, Rembrandt; Metropolitan Museum of Art, New York; Web Gallery of Art
48 *The Temptation of Christ* (detail), Botticelli; Cappella Sistina, Vatican; Web Gallery of Art
49 Andrean High School, Gary, Indiana; Julie Koenig, photographer
50 Andrean High School, Gary, Indiana; Julie Koenig, photographer
51 Stockbyte Royalty Free Image
52 Midwest Theological Forum; Wojtek Dubis, photographer
53 Midwest Theological Forum; Luke Mata, photographer
54 Comstock Royalty Free Image
55 Comstock Royalty Free Image
59 *Jesus Is Anointed in Bethany*, Julius Schnorr Von Carolsfeld; Dover Publications

Art and Photo Credits

Chapter 4

61 *The Capture of Christ* (detail), Cimabue; Upper Church, San Francesco, Assisi
62 Urb. Lat. 2 304v; Vatican Library
63 Midwest Theological Forum; Luke Mata, photographer
64 Rubberball Royalty Free Image
65 Comstock Royalty Free Image
66 Willows Academy, Des Plaines, Illinois; Julie Koenig, photographer
67 Digital Vision Royalty free Image
68 *Jerome;* Midwest Theological Forum Archives
69 Willows Academy, Des Plaines, Illinois; Julie Koenig, photographer
70 *Apostle St. Matthew,* El Greco; Museo del Greco, Toledo; Web Gallery of Art
71 Andrean High School, Gary, Indiana; Julie Koenig, photographer
72 Rubberball Royalty Free Image
75 *Christ the Redeemer,* Ukrainian Icon, 16th century; National Museum of L'viv, Ukraine
77 *Madonna and Child with Two Angels,* Francesco Martini; Lowe Gallery, Coral Gables, Florida; Web Gallery of Art

Chapter 5

79 *Ecce Homo,* Guido Reni; Pinacoteca Nazionale, Bologna; Web Gallery of Art
80 *The Slaughter of the Innocents,* Pieter the Elder Bruegel; Kunsthistorisches Museum, Vienna; Web Gallery of Art
81 Galaxies NGC2207 and IC2163, Hubble Space Telescope; NASA and The Hubble Heritage Team
82 *Vitruvian Man,* Leonardo Da Vinci; Gallerie dell'Accademia, Venice; Web Gallery of Art
83 Comstock Royalty Free Image
84 *Christ Surrounded by Musician Angels,* Hans Memling; Koninklijk Museum voor Schone Kunsten, Antwerp; Web Gallery of Art
85 *La Trinita,* Messale Koulenbourg, Prima Meta Del Secolo XV, Seminario Maggiore, Bressanone
86 *Triumph of St. Thomas Aquinas,* Francesco Traini; Santa Caterina, Pisa
87 Martin Luther King; AP/Wide World Photos
88 Comstock Royalty Free Image
95 *The Sermon on the Mount,* Julius Schnorr Von Carolsfeld; Dover Publications
96 *Angel of the Annunciation,* The Ghent Altarpiece (detail), Jan Van Eyck; Cathedral of St. Bavo, Ghent; Web Gallery of Art

Chapter 6

97 *Christ at the Column* (detail), Antonello Da Messina; Musée du Louvre; Web Gallery of Art
98 Rubberball Royalty Free Image
99 Midwest Theological Forum; Luke Mata, photographer
100 *Expulsion of the Moneychangers from the Temple,* Giotto; Cappella Scrovegni, Padua; Web Gallery of Art
101 Andrean High School, Gary, Indiana; Julie Koenig, photographer
102 *Kiss of Judas,* Giotto; Cappella Scrovegni, Padua; Web Gallery of Art
103 Photo courtesy of Mt. St. Joseph, Lake Zurich, Illinois
104 *Virgin and the Man of Sorrow* (detail), Simon Marmion; Groeninge Museum, Bruges; Web Gallery of Art
105 *The Four Holy Men* (Mark and Paul), Albrecht Dürer; Alte Pinakothek, Munich; Web Gallery of Art
106 Photo courtesy of Mt. St. Joseph, Lake Zurich, Illinois
107 Comstock Royalty Free Image

Chapter 7

115 *Baptism of Christ,* Piero Della Francesca; National Gallery, London; Web Gallery of Art
116 *The Merciful Christ* (detail), Juan Montáñez; Cathedral, Seville; Web Gallery of Art
117 Earth (Apollo 17), NASA; Jupiter Productions Royalty Free Image
118 Famine; AP/Wide World Photos
119 Digital Vision Royalty Free Image
120 *Pope Pius XII,* Midwest Theological Forum Archives
121 Corbis Royalty Free Image
122 Midwest Theological Forum; Luke Mata, photographer
123 Corbis Royalty Free Image
124 *Man of Sorrows,* Hans Memling; Palazzo Bianco, Genoa; Web Gallery of Art
125 Corbis Royalty Free Image
126 *Christ and the Adulteress,* Lucas the Elder Cranach; Museum of Fine Arts, Budapest; Web Gallery of Art
127 *Ascension of Christ,* Garofalo; Galleria Nazionale d'Arte Antica, Rome; Web Gallery of Art
128 *Crucifix with the Stories of the Passion,* Unknown Italian Master; Galleria degli Uffizi, Florence; Web Gallery of Art
129 *Advent and Triumph of Christ* (detail), Hans Memling; Alte Pinakothek, Munich; Web Gallery of Art

Art and Photo Credits

Part 2

137 *Christ*, Rembrandt; Staatliche Musen, Berlin; Web Gallery of Art

Chapter 8

138 *Christ Enthroned* (detail), Bartolomeo Vivarini; Museo di Bassano, Grappa; Web Gallery of Art
139 *Moses and the Tables of Law*, Piero Di Cosimo; Cappella Sistina, Vatican; Web Gallery of Art
140 Comstock Royalty Free Image
141 St. Paul of the Cross Church, Park Ridge, Illinois; Julie Koenig, photographer
142 Andrean High Schoolary, Indiana; Julie Koenig, photographer
143 St. Mary of the Angels Church, Chicago, Illinois; Julie Koenig, photographer
144 *Sermon on the Mount*, Piero Di Cosimo; Cappella Sistina, Vatican; Web Gallery of Art
145 Corel Royalty Free Image
146 Corbis Royalty Free Image
147 Sts. Peter and Paul Church, Naperville, Illinois; Julie Koenig, photographer

Chapter 9

151 *Christ*, El Greco; Museo del Greco, Toledo; Web Gallery of Art
152 *The Handing-Over of the Keys*, Raphael; Victoria and Albert Museum, London; Web Gallery of Art
153 Midwest Theological Forum; Wojtek Dubis, photographer
154 Digital Vision Royalty Free Image
155 Media Rights Royalty Free Image
156 Midwest Theological Forum; Luke Mata, photographer
157 *Christ and the Woman Taken in Adultery*, Tintoretto; Galleria Nazionale d'Arte Antica, Rome; Web Gallery of Art
158 Media Rights Royalty Free Image
159 *St. Elizabeth Clothes the Poor*, Unknown German Master; Wallraf-Richartz Museum, Cologne; Web Gallery of Art
160 Corbis Royalty Free Image
161 Midtown, Chicago, Illinois; Julie Koenig, photographer
162 *Mary Magdalen Speaking to the Angels*, Giotto; Magdalen Chapel, Lower Church, San Francesco, Assisi
164 Angel (detail from *Flight into Egypt*), Giotto; Cappella Scrovegni, Padua; Web Gallery of Art
165 Angel (detail from *Presentation at the Temple*), Giotto; Cappella Scrovegni, Padua; Web Gallery of Art

Chapter 10

167 *Jesse*; St. Damiano's Sanctuary crucifix, Assisi, Friar Innocenzo da Palermo, (1637)
168 Midtown, Chicago, Illinois; Julie Koenig, photographer
169 *Crucifixion*, Simon Vouet; Chiesa del Gesù, Genoa; Web Gallery of Art
170 Andrean High School, Gary, Indiana; Julie Koenig, photographer
171 *Saint Catherine of Alexandria at Prayer*, Titian; Museum of Fine Arts, Boston; Web Gallery of Art
172 Willows Academy, Des Plaines, Illinois; Julie Koenig, photographer
173 Andrean High School, Gary, Indiana; Julie Koenig, photographer
174 Corbis Royalty Free Image
175 St. Mary of the Angels Church, Chicago, Illinois; Julie Koenig, photographer
176 Corbis Royalty Free Image
177 *Blessed Virgin Mary*; La Chapelle Notre Dame de la Medaille Miraculeuse; Yvon Meyer, photographer
178 Comstock Royalty Free Image
183 Comstock Royalty Free Image
187 *The Virgin and the Child with Angels*, Giovanni Baglione; Royal Collection, Windsor; Web Gallery of Art
188 *Virgin Enthroned with Angels*, Cimabue; Musée du Louvre, Paris; Web Gallery of Art

Chapter 11

189 *The Transfiguration* (detail), Raphael; Pinacoteca, Vatican; Web Gallery of Art
190 *The Coronation of the Virgin*, Fra Angelico; Convento di San Marco, Florence; Web Gallery of Art
191 Eyewire Royalty Free Image
192 *David and Uriah*, Rembrandt; The Hermitage, St. Petersburg; Web Gallery of Art
193 *Apostle St. Paul*, El Greco; Museo del Greco, Toledo; Web Gallery of Art
194 Julie Koenig, photographer
195 *The Rest on the Flight into Egypt*, Correggio; Uffizi, Florence; The Artchive
196 *Pilate's First Interrogation of Christ* (detail), Duccio; Museo dell'Opera del Duomo, Siena; Web Gallery of Art
197 Digital Stock Royalty Free Image
198 *Jesus Washes the Disciples' Feet*, Julius Schnorr Von Carolsfeld; Dover Publications
202 Angel (detail from *Lamentation*), Giotto; Cappella Scrovegni, Padua; Web Gallery of Art

Art and Photo Credits

Chapter 12

203 *The Resurrection of Christ,* Rubens; O.-L. Vrouwekathedraal, Antwerp; Web Gallery of Art
204 St. Mary of the Angels Church, Chicago, Illinois; Julie Koenig, photographer
205 St. Paul of the Cross Church, Park Ridge, Illinois; Julie Koenig, photographer
206 St. Ignatius Icon; www.catholic-forum.com
207 St. Mary of the Angels Church, Chicago, Illinois; Julie Koenig, photographer
208 St. Mary of the Angels Church, Chicago, Illinois; Julie Koenig, photographer
209 St. Mary of the Angels Church, Chicago, Illinois; Julie Koenig, photographer
210 Comstock Royalty Free Image
211 Rubberball Royalty Free Image
212 Rubberball Royalty Free Image
213 *The Last Supper;* Museo del Prado, Madrid; Oronoz, photographer.
214 Angel (detail from *Lamentation*), Giotto; Cappella Scrovegni, Padua; Web Gallery of Art
216 Angel (detail from *Lamentation*), Giotto; Cappella Scrovegni, Padua; Web Gallery of Art
217 Angel (detail from *Lamentation*), Giotto; Cappella Scrovegni, Padua; Web Gallery of Art

Chapter 13

219 *The Temptation of Christ* (detail), Juan De Flandes; National Gallery of Art, Washington; Web Gallery of Art
220 Digital Vision Royalty Free Image
221 Digital Vision Royalty Free Image
222 *Holy Family,* Claudio Coello; Museum of Fine Arts, Budapest; Web Gallery of Art
223 Comstock Royalty Free Image
224 Midtown, Chicago, Illinois; Julie Koenig, photographer
225 Comstock Royalty Free Image
226 Corbis Royalty Free Image
227 *St. Paul,* Masaccio; Museo Nazionale, Pisa; Web Gallery of Art
228 Media Rights Royalty Free Image
229 Photodisc Royalty Free Image
230 Angel (detail from *Lamentation*), Giotto; Cappella Scrovegni, Padua; Web Gallery of Art

Chapter 14

235 *Christ on the Cross,* El Greco; Musée du Louvre, Paris; Web Gallery of Art
236 Rubberball Royalty Free Image
237 Andrean High School, Gary, Indiana; Julie Koenig, photographer
238 Rubberball Royalty Free Image
239 Pope John Paul II; AP/Wide World Photos
240 Corbis Royalty Free Image
241 Corbis Royalty Free Image
242 *The Crowning with Thorns,* Caravaggio; Kunsthistorisches Museum, Vienna; Web Gallery of Art
243 Comstock Royalty Free Image
244 Corbis Royalty Free Image
245 Corel Royalty Free Image
246 Cloning; AP/Wide World Photos
247 Photospin Royalty Free Image
255 Angel (detail from *Lamentation*), Giotto; Cappella Scrovegni, Padua; Web Gallery of Art

Chapter 15

257 *Resurrection* (detail), Dieric the Elder Bouts; Norton Simon Museum of Art, Pasadena; Web Gallery of Art
258 Corbis Royalty Free Image
259 Comstock Royalty Free Image
260 Comstock Royalty Free Image
261 Comstock Royalty Free Image
262 Stockbyte Royalty Free Image
263 Comstock Royalty Free Image
264 Digital Vision Royalty Free Image
265 Corbis Royalty Free Image
266 Corbis Royalty Free Image
267 Corbis Royalty Free Image
268 St. Justin Martyr Icon; www.goarch.org
269 *St. Paul,* Franz Anton Maulbertsch; Hungarian National Gallery, Budapest; Web Gallery of Art
270 Rubberball Royalty Free Image
271 Comstock Royalty Free Image
272 Comstock Royalty Free Image
273 Digital Vision Royalty Free Image
274 Comstock Royalty Free Image

Art and Photo Credits

Chapter 16

285 *Doubting Thomas*, Guercino; Residenzgalerie, Salzburg; Web Gallery of Art
286 *The Creation of the Animals*, Raphael; Loggia, Palazzi Pontifici, Vatican; Web Gallery of Art
287 Media Rights Royalty Free Image
288 Media Rights Royalty Free Image
289 Flat Earth Royalty Free Image
290 Flat Earth Royalty Free Image
291 Flat Earth Royalty Free Image
292 Flat Earth Royalty Free Image
293 Midwest Theological Forum; Luke Mata, photographer
294 Midwest Theological Forum; Luke Mata, photographer
299 *Angel Annunciating*, Lorenzo Lotto; Church of Sts. Vincent and Alexander, Ponteranica; Web Gallery of Art
300 *The Angel Gabriel Sent by God*, Giotto; Cappella Scrovegni, Padua; Web Gallery of Art
301 *Madonna and Child with Angels*, Francesco Martini; Pinacoteca Nazionale, Siena; Web Gallery of Art

Chapter 17

303 *Man of Sorrows*, Hans Memling; Christian Museum, Esztergom; Web Gallery of Art
304 *Peter Denouncing Christ*, Rembrandt; Rijksmuseum, Amsterdam; Web Gallery of Art
305 *Moses and the Brazen Serpent*, Sébastien Bourdon; Museo del Prado, Madrid; Web Gallery of Art
306 *Christ Before Pilate Again*, Duccio; Museo dell'Opera del Duomo, Siena; Web Gallery of Art
307 Andrean High School, Gary, Indiana; Julie Koenig, photographer
308 Andrean High School, Gary, Indiana; Julie Koenig, photographer
309 Stockbyte Royalty Free Image
310 Corbis Royalty Free Image
311 Andrean High School, Gary, Indiana; Julie Koenig, photographer
313 Plato; *Wisdom of the West*, Crescent Books
317 *The Angel of the Annunciation*, Simone Martini; Koninklijk Museum voor Schone Kunsten, Antwerp; Web Gallery of Art

322 *Madonna and Child with Saints and an Angel* (detail), Lorenzo Lotto; Kunsthistorisches Museum, Vienna; Web Gallery of Art

Index